A Political History
of Journalism

In memory of Fred W. Friendly

A Political History of Journalism

Géraldine Muhlmann

Translated by Jean Birrell

polity

First published in French as *Une histoire politique du journalisme* © Presses Universitaires de France, Paris, 2004.

This English translation © Polity Press, 2008.

Polity Press
65 Bridge Street
Cambridge CB2 1UR, UK

Polity Press
350 Main Street
Malden, MA 02148, USA

ISBN-13: 978-07456-3573-6
ISBN-13: 978-07456-3574-3 (pb)

A catalogue record for this book is available from the British Library.

Typeset in 10.5 on 12 pt Plantin
by Servis Filmsetting Ltd, Manchester
Printed and bound in India by Replika Press PVT Ltd, Kundli

For further information on Polity, visit our website: *www.polity.co.uk*

Ouvrage publié avec le concours du Ministère français chargé de la culture – Centre National du Livre.

Published with the assistance of the French Ministry of Culture – National Centre for the Book.

This book is supported by the French Ministry for Foreign Affairs, as part of the Burgess programme headed for the French Embassy in London by the Institut Français du Royaume-Uni.

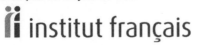

institut français

Contents

Acknowledgements

I would like to thank all those who have helped me in this work:

Miguel Abensour, who supervised my thesis and whose ideas on current debates in political philosophy continue to inspire me; such attentive supervisors are rare.

My dear Ruth Friendly, always welcoming, affectionate and generous with her encouragement. She helps to keep alive the memory of Fred W. Friendly, that great American journalist, who loved a critical spirit and encouraged it in those he loved. Ruth introduced me to Joe Wershba and his wife, and I thank them for their memories and their ready help.

The teachers in the Department of Journalism, New York University, where I studied for a year before embarking on the thesis that led, eventually, to this book, and where I have since found attentive listeners. To Susie Linfield I owe the discovery of several jewels of American journalism and many stimulating conversations, and to Brooke Kroeger a great saving of time thanks to her energetic and generous help. And in this English edition of my book, I would like to pay special tribute to Ellen Willis, who died last year, to whom I owe an affection for the spirit of the New Journalism, and who embodied so well a certain New York way of being curious about the world, about all worlds.

The journalists who shared their memories and their reflections with me, Marc Kravetz and Francis Déron, but also all those whose work I read but never met, and who have helped to make their profession a zone of freedom.

The institutions and libraries which allowed me to collect the most varied documents in record time. I think in particular of the attentive assistance of the staff of the Bibliothèque Marguerite Durand in Paris, whose efficiency is well known but still deserves special mention; the staff of the New York Public Library and the warm welcome I received at the Centre de Documentation of the Centre de Formation et de

Perfectionnement des Journalistes in Paris; as for the American Library in Paris, I thank it simply for existing.

Anne-Sophie Menasseyre, David Muhlmann, Vincent Valentin and my parents, for their affectionate support and their relentless questioning and reading; in full knowledge that those close to you are those for whom no words are adequate to express one's gratitude.

Introduction

Towards the middle of the nineteenth century, a number of technological advances in the Western democracies transformed journalism. The growth of railway transport facilitated the circulation of newspapers and assured them a far wider readership; the extension of the telegraphic communication network meant news could be gathered with greater frequency and from further afield. The newspaper ceased to be simply a forum for the expression of diverse opinions and became a source of news, ever more news, gathered by people who began to call themselves 'reporters'. The nascent press agencies increasingly established 'reporting' as the core of journalistic activity and, broadly speaking, journalism embarked on the path to its professionalization.

In the eloquent metaphor used by one media specialist to describe these changes, 'The press no longer gave voice, or less so. It relayed. The newspaper had been a voice. It became an echo.'[1] Unlike the 'voice', which comes from a particular place and is heard within a limited perimeter, the 'echo' comes from the immensity of the universe and reaches the most far-distant ears. In seeking to be an 'echo', therefore, the new journalism of the nineteenth century was setting out to interest a mass readership for the first time.

The mass circulation, cheap and popular press was effectively born in the decades before the mid-nineteenth century. The 'penny press' appeared in the United States in the 1830s. The *New York Sun*, founded in 1833, was a pioneer in the field, followed two years later by the *New York Herald*, which had a circulation of 40,000 at the end of fifteen months, and that rapidly reached 100,000. The 1830s saw a spectacular increase in the number of American newspapers and in the number of newspaper readers: in 1830 there were 650 weekly and 65 daily American papers, the latter with a circulation of around 1,200, that is, a global daily circulation of some 78,000; by 1840 there were 1,141 weeklies and 138 dailies, with an average circulation of 2,200 in the case of the latter, hence a global daily circulation of about 300,000.[2] Europe followed suit within a few decades: in France *Le Petit Journal*, which cost five centimes, was launched in 1863; *Le Petit Parisien* appeared in 1876, and *Le Matin* in 1883. In Great Britain, the 'halfpenny papers' were born in the 1880s, *The Evening News* in 1881, *The Star* in 1888.[3]

The experts see this popular press as having invented the modern concept of 'news'.[4] It was only in the 1880s, however, they argue, that the 'reporter' truly became the new face of American journalism. Here, the two major events were the takeover of the *New York World* by Joseph Pulitzer, in 1883, and the purchase by William Randolph Hearst of the *New York Journal*, which became its most immediate rival. These two great papers are, for reporters, a sort of holy of holies.

Europe was not to be outdone: here, too, at the turn of the nineteenth and twentieth centuries, the reporter was the emerging figure in the world of journalism.[5] The cult of 'facts' was beginning to rule supreme, and the journalist-reporter set to work, that is, to observe and to write, on behalf of an ever larger public. In all the Western democracies, the 1880s marked a sort of beginning of modern journalism.

This is also the period when there emerged those concerns about journalism that have dogged it ever since. The criticisms have varied in content, but they all, then as now, start from the same sombre diagnosis: journalism is responsible for a powerful trend to homogenize the public sphere of opinions and gazes, which is prejudicial to democratic life, itself dependent on the exchange of a variety of points of view.

This diagnosis has been for some critics an opportunity to vent their hatred of democracy. This was the case with Gustave Le Bon, who, in 1895, published *The Crowd: A Study of the Popular Mind*, in which he compared the new readers of newspapers to 'crowds'. For Le Bon, the 'crowd' was a gathering with essentially psychological characteristics; a readership could, therefore, though invisible, resemble a crowd, that is, be something he saw as hateful, incapable of subtlety, and paving the way for the degeneration of the French 'race'. For Le Bon, the press concentrated vices which were in practice inherent in democracy itself.

But there is also unease among thinkers who, in contrast, want a true democracy, plural and marked by multiple exchanges. Many of them point to the paradox of democracy, which, as it has developed, has led to the neutralization of conflicts, a 'reification' of discourses and gazes, and a 'closed society'. This is how the scholars of the Frankfurt School, for example, describe the new form of domination which characterizes contemporary society. In the 1940s Adorno and Horkheimer examined the new relationship to culture which had become dominant along with industrial society;[6] television, responsible for the destruction of critical thinking, was one of their chief targets.[7] For Marcuse, the media played a major role in this 'trend to integrate, which, for the most part, proceeded without open terror: democracy consolidated domination more firmly than absolutism; administered liberty and instinctive repression became constantly renewed sources of productivity'.[8] For Habermas, here heir to the first thinkers of the Frankfurt School, the advent of the mass circulation press marked the beginning of the corruption of Publicity, in the critical sense of the word (that is, of that virtuous exposition before the public to whom opinions are submitted so that they can be improved thanks to an exchange of opposing views) into a consummate 'Publicity', which dominates minds and standardizes judgements. The new media of the twentieth century, he believed, had only intensified this corruption, which dated back to the end of the nineteenth century.[9]

Current critics of television, though they sometimes proclaim the novelty of the problems posed by the omnipotence of television, offer analyses which are mostly little different in essentials from the concerns created by the press revolution at the end of the nineteenth century. According to Pierre Bourdieu, for example:

> Television's power of diffusion means that it poses a terrible problem for the print media and for culture generally. Next to it, the mass circulation press that sent so many shudders up educated spines . . . doesn't seem like much at all. By virtue of its reach and exceptional power, television produces effects which, though not without precedent, are completely original.[10]

The last sentence of this passage suggests that it is, after all, a difference of degree rather than of kind that differentiates the current problems posed by the triumph of television from the effects of the press revolution of the late nineteenth century. Increasing 'uniformity' remains central to Bourdieu's analysis,[11] which he, too, sees as a pernicious form of domination over individuals and, in particular, as a neutralization of the conflicts which permeate the social sphere. Media 'events' are thus designed not to 'offend anyone'; they 'must never bring up problems' or, if they do, 'only problems that don't pose problems', as when, in daily life, we talk about the rain and the fine weather in order to avoid any subject that might cause annoyance or lead to conflict.[12]

No one who has observed the development of modern journalism closely can deny that there exists within it a desire to *integrate* the community of its readers (potentially the entire political community): reporters unify their public behind them. This journalistic process of *unifying* can be traced in history, whether one studies how journalism speaks about, presents and understands itself, or only how it is practised, that is, its 'productions'. This *unifying* is probably the big idea of modern journalism.

Does this mean, however, that we have to keep automatically repeating what is said about it, that it kills democratic conflictuality and leads to a blandness of attitudes? Is it as simple as that? Should we not recognize that journalistic practices differ? Are there not many types of 'unifying' journalism, some of which, far from shunning whatever causes conflict, base their practice of the unifying process on a conflict they reveal and activate?

Also, if the conflicts that are revealed in the gaze of 'unifying' journalists are dismissed as too limited and too constrained, should we not ask whether the history of journalism contains other approaches? Should we not ask whether a journalism of 'resistance' has ever emerged in opposition to the dominant unifying journalism? Does there exist, and in what forms, a journalism that seeks to re-inject a more radical conflict into the democratic community, that seeks to make visible what we, united and clustered round our 'centre', do not see, or no longer see, that is, a journalism that *decentres*?

It is time to put platitudes aside and address these questions. This book, as will have become clear, has no interest in hasty judgements on the routine mediocrity of journalism. Since the criticism of journalism is generally directed at a certain journalistic 'modernity', let us dare to study this seriously: what can we learn from the history of journalism since the end of the nineteenth century? And since what lies at the heart of this criticism is a heavy sigh in the face of a hopelessly homogeneous gaze, one that smoothes over social reality and irons out its failings and its contradictions, let us examine the journalistic gaze seriously, beginning with the question of conflict: how can it present conflict, misunderstanding and confrontation? Is it really helpless to do this? Might it not be possible to distinguish journalisms that are primarily 'unifying', that reveal a conflict only as a test for the political community, enabling it ultimately to reconstitute itself and to reactivate within it the feeling of a 'we', and journalisms that are 'decentring', that seek to expose a conflict more serious, more threatening to the collective identity, and more disturbing for the 'we'? What are the advantages, the difficulties and the limitations of each of these approaches?

I have discussed elsewhere the philosophical foundations and issues of an approach to journalism on the basis of the problems posed by the presentation of conflict.[13] Here, I propose to apply this approach concretely, by a journey through the history of journalism: who are the 'unifiers' and who are the 'decentrers'? What do they each reveal about these processes they practise through their gaze? Current work on journalism too often lacks substance and historical depth. This book tries to lay down a few markers and to suggest 'figures' which I hope will help readers to think about journalism today. It is a sort of personal and political history of modern journalism – a portrait gallery, in order concretely to explore the political processes of *unifying* and *decentring*, which can operate in the journalist's gaze.

1

Unifying and Decentring in Modern Journalism

To appeal to the largest number: this has been, from the beginning, what modern journalism is all about. The desire to bring people together, to *unify*, is most visible in journalism's concern to give readers the 'truth' – that is, something that is acceptable to all, beyond differences of opinion. My study will show that the 'unifying' journalist often assumes the features of what I will call a *witness-ambassador*, key figure in the 'dominant' modern journalism. I will then ask what figures 'of resistance' can be opposed to the witness-ambassador, in fact, whether a journalism that *decentres* is possible.

1. Unifying journalisms: the triumph of the witness-ambassador

'Facts' acceptable to all

As many studies have shown,[1] it was the penny press and its modern conception of 'news' that gave rise to the journalistic concern for factual accuracy. The ideal of objectivity in modern journalism has its roots, therefore, in a press often despised by elites, who called it, to discredit it, the 'yellow press'. This requirement of the 'popular' press of the nineteenth century to provide true information, accurate and 'objective' facts, was closely linked to its concern to *unify*; it clung to the 'facts' so that it could bring together readers who might well have different opinions on a subject, and hence reach the common denominator of an increasingly large readership. The spectacular growth of this readership led, therefore, to 'the triumph of "news" over the editorial and of "facts" over opinion', and created 'the journalist's uneasy allegiance to objectivity'.[2]

Those involved in this 'revolution' often explicitly declared their desire to unite the public for whom they wrote. The *New York Sun* of Benjamin Day proclaimed in its heading: 'It Shines for All'. This 'shining' was clearly intended to bring this 'all' together, as Day suggested in an article of 28 June 1838:

> Since the *Sun* began to shine upon the citizens of New York, there has been a very great and decided change in the condition of the labouring classes and the mechanics. Now every individual, from the rich aristocrat who lolls in his carriage to the humble labourer who wields a broom in the streets, reads the *Sun*; nor can even a boy be found in New York City or the neighbouring country who will not know, in the course of the day, what is promulgated in the *Sun* in the morning. Already we perceive a change in the mass of the people. They think, talk, and act in concert. They understand their own interest, and feel that they have numbers and strength to pursue it with success.[3]

Similarly, James Gordon Bennett, founder of the *New York Herald*, emphasized that his paper was 'equally intended for the great masses of the community – the merchant, mechanic, working people – the private family as well as the public hotel – the journeyman and his employer – the clerk and his principal'.[4]

We see, furthermore, that the 'public' was often represented in this wide circulation press as an entity transcending partisan divisions, as a great *body*, united by this very demand for truth, and urging journalists to honour this demand. The metaphor of the body to evoke the public is clear in the writing of, for example, Bennett, who evokes 'the whole body of the people',[5] who understand only the language of 'common sense', far removed from partisan political allegiances: 'Our only guide', wrote Bennett,

> shall be good, sound, practical commonsense, applicable to the business and bosoms of men engaged in everyday life. We shall support no party, be the organ of no faction or coterie, and care nothing for any election, or any candidate from president down to a constable. We shall endeavor to record facts on every public and proper subject stripped of verbiage and coloring with comments when suitable, just, independent, fearless, and good-tempered. If the *Herald* wants the mere expansion which many journals possess, we shall try to make it up in industry, good taste, brevity, variety, point, piquancy and cheapness.[6]

Associated in this way with the natural requirement for 'common sense', the concern for factual truth was closely linked to the more general conviction of serving the public interest and what was right against partisan divides. Let us quote, in this connection, the words of Dan Schiller, a specialist in the field:

> The impartiality and independence claimed by the penny press successfully ushered in its stewardship of the pursuit of enlightened reason in the

public sphere. Although different penny journals had distinct identities, which were subject to change in various contexts, they shared what Bennett termed 'the great focus of intelligence, news, wit, business, independence, and true knowledge' (*Herald*, 31 March 1836). The preemptive claim staked by the cheap journals to the defence of natural rights and public good was . . . the enduring foundation upon which the structure of news objectivity was built.[7]

The reporters of the 1880s were simply continuing in the same vein as the penny press a few decades earlier. By providing only the 'facts', and by suppressing their personal opinions, they were supposed to be appealing to 'common sense', which enabled them to reach the largest possible public. The ultimate aim remained to *unify*; this explains the slogan 'ACCURACY, ACCURACY, ACCURACY!' chosen by Joseph Pulitzer to decorate his office wall, and, more generally, it explains the draconian rules imposed on reporters by their editors. Thus, one of the clauses in the code of the *Chicago Daily News*, whose managing editor was then Charles Dennis, ran: 'Put no editorial comments or debatable statements into news matter. Keep your personal likes and dislikes out of your copy.'[8] The frustrations provoked by these rules in many budding writers, required to efface their own unique voice in their writing, are well known. Lincoln Steffens, for example, said of his years on the *Evening Post*, 'Humor or any sign of personality in our reports was caught, rebuked, and, in time, suppressed. As a writer, I was permanently hurt by my years on the *Post*.'[9]

All this discipline was intended to enable the reporter to provide what American journalism still calls a 'story', that is, a narrative that could be received collectively, in fact 'de-singularized', and so of interest to the largest number. When the story turned out well, it could give the public, seen as a unified entity (a body), a true experience by proxy. In fact, it is in these very terms that the American sociologist Helen M. Hughes defines the function of the story: 'to make a word picture that will be a substitute to . . . readers for the experience of perceiving'.[10]

In the first half of the twentieth century, the sociologists of the Chicago School, to which Hughes belonged, and which produced pioneering studies of the historical development of the press in the United States, also developed a notion crucial to an understanding of this modern journalism: that of 'human interest'.[11] By this they meant that part of human curiosity that is common to the largest number, that is of *general* interest, and that is seen by the wide circulation press as its prime aim. To put the notion of human interest at the heart of the 'popular' journalism born at the end of the nineteenth century is simply to emphasize that its main concern, its founding act, was to *unify*.

This aim continues to show through whenever journalism insists, especially in discussions of an ethical nature, on its ideal of 'truth', whether the vocabulary is that of factual accuracy, objectivity, impartiality or fairness. In fact, beyond the apparent nuances, the aim seems to remain always the same: to emphasize that journalism addresses a public perceived as a unified entity, or at least as an entity that is capable of being unified, and that has a right to obtain what is its due, that is, a description which is not exclusively singular, but applies the criteria of common sense and so presents a *common* reality.

This aim is clear in the various professional codes which punctuate the history of American and European journalism. In, for example, the ethical code of the journalistic professional association Sigma Delta Chi of 1926, one of the first American codes to proclaim the duty of the journalist to 'serve the truth', and to use the words 'accuracy' and 'objectivity', it is clear that this imperative is part of the recognition of a 'public right'.[12] Professional and legal development in the twentieth century has been broadly in the direction of a conception of press freedom increasingly viewed from the standpoint of the 'consumer', that is, of a public represented as an entity with rights.[13] The Declaration of Bordeaux, adopted by European journalists in 1954 and amended in June 1986, states that 'respect for the truth and for the right of the public to truth is the first duty of the journalist'; the Munich Charter, adopted in 1971 by the Union of Journalists of the European Community, Switzerland and Austria, urged the profession 'to respect the truth whatever the consequences for itself [journalism], on the grounds of the public's right to know the truth'.[14]

The notion of objectivity – a notion more often formulated than explained – is part of the same logic. It was evoked, for example, in the encyclical of John XXIII of 1963, *Pacem et Terris*, where it is explicitly linked to the notion of the possibility of a common world view, shared by all; it is for the media, it follows, to provide this 'collective' view.[15] The notion of 'objective reality' was also emphasized by the UNESCO Declaration of 1983: 'People and individuals have the right to acquire an objective picture of reality by means of accurate and comprehensive information . . .'[16]

The notion of fairness, sometimes evoked as a way of distancing the speaker from the ideal of objectivity, belongs, nevertheless, to this same 'unifying' ambition. Hubert Beuve-Méry, founder and first editor of *Le Monde*, said he preferred fairness to an always inaccessible objectivity. While this notion is part of a very French tradition of circumspection,[17] it is not without its advocates in the United States. In 1989, when he drew up a new code of ethics for the *Washington Post*, Benjamin C. Bradlee claimed to be breaking new ground when he emphasized, in opposition to the notion of objectivity, which had led to interminable controversies, the more flexible and more concrete concept of fairness.[18] Nevertheless, if we look closely at the paragraph in this charter devoted to fairness, we see that the issues remain the same. In the first place, the epistemological difficulty is far from resolved: journalists are called on to make 'fair' choices in the gaze they direct at the world, in particular to know how to distinguish between 'secondary news' and 'significant facts'. One can imagine the epistemological debate seizing on this 'fairness' and miring it in a confusion not unlike that in which it customarily sinks the notion of 'objectivity'. Secondly, the socio-political aim of *unifying* remains the same: it is still a matter of producing a collectively acceptable gaze that conforms to the general norms of the 'public'. More than ever, the reference to a 'common sense' guiding the journalist's gaze seems clear, if implicit. 'Fairness includes recognition of what is relevant,' states this charter; it seems clear that the criteria of relevance, and journalistic choices in general, are actually those of the 'community'. The charter also declares that 'the *Washington Post* is intensely concerned with the national interest and with that of the community'. In essence, therefore, there is little difference between this 'new' requirement for 'fairness' and the old injunctions of nineteenth-century editors to their reporters to silence any personal voice in favour of an approach concerned only with 'facts'. The aim was still appropriately to incorporate the criteria of the widest public – criteria which defined what was a 'fact' and its 'relevance' in relation to other facts; that is, to make this public have an experience by proxy.

The requirement for 'true', 'objective' and 'fair' journalistic descriptions should still be seen, therefore, whichever adjective is employed, from a *unifying* perspective. This may explain the great epistemological poverty of the concrete rules current in the journalistic profession and supposed to respect this requirement for objectivity, a poverty emphasized by most researchers. The aim is not epistemological rigour in itself, but to apply the rules which the public regards as acceptable, and as defining 'objectivity' *in its eyes*. It means honouring a pact with the public, which allows journalists to aspire to a collectively acceptable approach; but it is a pact that does not necessarily have great epistemological coherence.

This point was made by Gaye Tuchman, in 1978, in an article on what she called the 'rituals of objectivity' in the journalistic profession.[19] These are 'rituals' in the sense that many practices are defined as marks of objectivity, but without clear epistemological coherence. The few epistemological principles which seem to emerge are hardly rigorously applied, and they are contradicted by other associated practices. Take the case of the much-quoted rule to the effect that every 'fact' must be empirically verified, or else must always be relativized by reference to the authenticating source. Tuchman shows that this practice is not invariable. Journalists still put their trust in 'sources' which have not been carefully checked; otherwise, how many articles would read like this? 'Robert Jones and his alleged wife, Fay Smith Jones, yesterday held what they described as a cocktail party in their supposed home, 187 Grant Street, City, purportedly in honour of a woman claiming to be Mrs John Smith, commonly thought to be the aunt of the woman of the self-described hostess.'[20] Always supposing that empirical verification is the way to establish factual veracity, it is clear that it cannot, short of going to absurd lengths, be rigorously applied in the case of every 'fact' included in the newspapers.

More generally, Tuchman shows that the notion of 'fact' is dependent on 'common sense': that is, on criteria defined by the community, and not on methods of verification more solidly based at the epistemological level. The choice of 'facts' depends, in reality, on what journalists themselves call 'news judgement'. This is particularly important, in the American journalistic tradition, in the writing of the 'lead', that is, the first sentence of the article, supposed to summarize the essence of the news and lay out what is most important in the story about to be told. But this judgement, if it is to be acceptable ('objective', 'fair' and so on), applies *common* criteria, with foundations that are more sociological than epistemological. Tuchman goes further: a material fact that is verifiable empirically may very well not be mentioned if it goes against common sense, just as, as we saw above, a fact which 'makes sense' will be mentioned as such even though its 'materiality' has not been empirically verified.

Other 'rituals' influence the requirement to give the reader *material facts* (that is, facts materially verified, or held to be verified). Often, rather than verify a fact 'A' stated by a person 'X', the journalist regards as a fact the statement 'X said A'.[21] Under the appearance of rigour, an obvious bias emerges, because if this statement is no more than a worthless opinion (A is untrue), it would be questionable to give it a place in the article. This amounts, in fact, to giving equal space to verified facts and simple mistaken opinions, themselves regarded, in this case, as facts. Tuchman observes that journalists often try to get round this difficulty, of which they are aware, by giving at least one other opinion ('Y said B'). But she is quick to point out that this addition does nothing to solve the problem, in reality: a new opinion is reported as a 'fact', when its content has no more been verified than that of the first. 'Inasmuch as "objectivity" may be defined as "intentness on objects external to the mind",' she writes, 'and "objective" as "belonging to the object of thought rather than the thinking subject" (both dictionary definitions), it would appear difficult to claim – as newspapermen do – that presenting conflicting possibilities fosters objectivity.'[22] Yet, questionable though it may be at the epistemological level, the juxtaposition of many points of view is certainly a ritual of objectivity in the journalistic profession.

In fact, this ritual corresponds to what a certain deontological tradition called 'fairness' – before Bradlee revived the use of this word for the *Washington Post*. Thus the Fairness Doctrine, set out in 1949 by the Federal Communications Commission, required 'a balanced point of view', which implies reference to at least two different opinions on a subject.[23] Admittedly, this text also mentioned the need for factual verification, that is, the need to investigate the content, or 'matter', of the opinions. But Tuchman shows how, in contemporary journalistic practice, the doctrine of fairness often frees itself from the rule of factual verification and itself becomes the ritual of objectivity, however weak at the epistemological level.

Other media specialists have also emphasized the aberrations brought about by the Fairness Doctrine. Journalists, says one:

> attempt to chain opinions to their opposites, hoping, it seems, that these beasts will annihilate each other, leaving what passes in journalistic thinking for the truth. The technique conveniently frees journalists from responsibility for looking beyond competing arguments to find the truth. Some events and issues, after all, are unbalanced, and the effort to balance them in itself adds a kind of bias. Moreover, since there rarely is sufficient room on this seesaw to seat the whole range of arguments issues inspire, usually no more than two or three widely held – i.e., mainstream – points of view per issue are deemed worthy of balanced consideration. The choice of where to place the fulcrum in this balance is necessarily a subjective decision.[24]

To quote opinions and give their source does not exonerate journalists from the choices they make in presenting them, and is hardly cause for self-congratulation on their part. For example, in the 1950s, the American press published lists of 'suspects' compiled by Senator Joseph McCarthy; the journalists may have believed that, by specifying the source of these lists ('he said'), they were not giving aid to McCarthy, but it is clear that, in practice, this precaution hardly clears them from blame because, by publishing these lists, the press gave McCarthyism a huge boost.[25]

Objectivity, therefore, is primarily a collection of rituals defined by a tacit pact between journalists and the public; this does not, of course, preclude the possibility of misunderstandings between them with regard to the precise nature of this pact, in particular, mistaken interpretations by journalists of public expectations. Some of these rituals may have a precise epistemological basis, such as, for example, the rule requiring empirical verification of the facts presented. As we have seen, however, they coexist with others with little epistemological basis, such as, for example, the rule that there should be a 'balanced point of view'. Even more absurd, some rituals actually consist of knowing how, in certain situations, to suspend others. For example, it is a common journalistic practice to oppose at least two points of view (the 'both sides' rule), but journalists also need to know when not to apply this rule, especially in the treatment of tragic events. As observed by Schudson, 'by unspoken understanding, there are not two sides to human tragedies'. It is only in theory that, if a climatic catastrophe were to destroy many wealthy residences, a reporter would ask the owners why they were so stupid as to build there in the first place.[26]

'Common sense', therefore, is far from producing a coherent set of principles. And journalism pays the price, even if it sometimes finds itself interpreting 'common' expectations improperly or erroneously. As a general rule, the contradictions between its different 'rituals of objectivity' only confirm that the essential act, at the heart of modern journalism, is that of unifying the largest possible public.

The truth is visible

Among the major rituals of journalism, which make it possible to present 'facts' acceptable to all, that is, not reducible to a single point of view, but objectified, we need to emphasize the use of the sense of *sight*. From the beginning, 'unifying' journalism seems to have relied on the *eye, as opposed to the voice*, as a means of objectification; to unify, to be collectively received as a group of facts, and not of singular opinions, the newspaper had to provide something to *see*, and had to cease (at last) to be content, like the newspapers of opinion, with *saying*.

The lexical field of seeing and light certainly found favour with the penny press, which routinely engaged in *exposure* – those reportages 'revealing' for all to see previously hidden facts. Even the definition of 'facts' seems closely linked to a visual dimension: a 'fact' is what is *visible* or can be made visible to all (as suggested by the *New York Sun*'s 'It Shines for All'), as opposed, that is, to what is simply *said*. The cult of the *seen* as generally acceptable proof, unlike rumour (voices), was a constant feature in the popular American journalism of the second half of the nineteenth century. For example, the reporting of Nellie Bly in 1887 for Pulitzer's *New York World*, which caused a huge stir at the time (and which we will examine more closely in chapter 3), was clearly based on the following line of argument: they (that is, singular voices) *tell of* terrible things happening in the Blackwell's Island psychiatric hospital for women (there had been editorials in several newspapers on these rumours in the preceding months); Nellie Bly, for her part, goes there to *see*.

The 'objectifying', and hence 'unifying', nature of the visual seems, therefore, to have been appreciated by journalists of the written word even before the invention of television. Not only did the photograph very quickly become a mainstay of the popular press, but it can be argued that the text itself attempted to appropriate this unifying power of the image. The precision of the visual notations required of reporters in the second half of the nineteenth century was the counterpart of the requirement to avoid any expression of their personal opinions. The eye against the voice: this opposition is clear, especially in the way the American press represented itself in the nineteenth century. A poem of 1845, for example, referred to the old partisan press as a *tongue* – a metaphor for idle chatter – and deplored its inability to distinguish the true from the false:

> What is the Press? 'Tis what the tongue
> Was to the world when Time was young,
> When, by tradition, Sire to son
> Conveyed what'er was known and done;
> But fact and fiction so were mix'd,
> That boundaries never could be fixed.[27]

This world of rumour was replaced, then, by the modern press, which preferred, as a way of representing itself, the visual metaphors of the mirror or of photography, in particular the daguerreotype. In fact an article of 1848 referred to Bennett's *Herald* as 'the daily daguerreotype of the heart and soul of the model republic'.[28]

Indeed, we may wonder to what extent the journalism of opinion itself, that journalism of before the Industrial Revolution, to which the contemporary editorial is heir, was conscious of its intrinsic weakness (as a journalism of the voice, it risked being seen as no more than a voice) and already freely employed techniques masking the 'suspect' voice under an 'innocent' gaze. It is, after all, an old stylistic device to offer a distanced description, with no explicit sign of the feelings of the author, as a way of giving maximum persuasive force to, for example, a denunciation. It was a procedure already dear to the Montesquieu of the *Lettres Persanes*. It was also appreciated by the partisan press, although typical of a journalism of the voice. Even before the advent of reporting, the political press realized the 'unifying' power of visual notations, the impact of description and the virtues of the 'innocent' eye, which get round the risk of 'singularization' that is inherent in any statement in which the author speaks.

This advantage conferred by visual notations, including in partisan texts, is confirmed, notably, by Marc Angenot's analysis of 'agonic' texts. Angenot distinguishes three types of agonic discourse. 'Polemic' is, in a sense, the default position, in which the two adversaries hold each other in equal esteem; polemic puts its own discourse on the same level as that of its opponent: 'The polemical discourse supposes, like the polemical essay, an underlying common ground between the interlocutors.'[29] In polemic, he goes on, 'the two discourses that confront each other are on an equal footing: polemicists flatter themselves that their discourse succeeds only thanks to this metaphysical extra, its intrinsic truth.'[30] 'Satire', on the other hand, spontaneously places itself in a position of superiority; it sets itself up as the truth, and it is unifying: 'The satirical is firmly established in the truth; it is its adversary who is without status.'[31] The satirist, Angenot says, 'has "people behind him"; laughter has the effect of bringing people together, whereas the adversary is kept at a distance'.[32] This position is characterized by an abundance of visual notations; satire describes and presents the adversary, or the world it criticizes, in order to discredit it in the eyes of all those gathered behind it: 'Everything lies in the detachment, the "outside view".'[33] The power of satire seems to reside in this very capacity to transmute the voice – which is singularizing – into a gaze – which is unifying. In short, satire does not denounce, it does not even discuss, it portrays, and it is in this distanced attitude that the superiority which characterizes it resides. The 'pamphlet', finally, locates itself at the opposite pole from satire; pamphleteers put themselves in a position of inferiority from the outset; their discourse, even action, habitually says that it is lost in advance, fruitless, singular, already forgotten. There is a morbid enjoyment of marginality and failure in the pamphleteering discourse, says Angenot. And it is a discourse which contains scarcely any description, even suffers from a visual deficit. The 'I see' which is sometimes expressed in the pamphlet discourse often conceals a confession of blindness, or if it expresses a singular lucidity, this is routinely presented as impossible to share. Pamphleteers spend little time on their 'visions', at best saying what effect they produce on them. In other words, pamphleteers remain in the register of the *voice*, expressing the despairing indignation produced in them by their own vision. The only thing the pamphlet likes to put on display is the image of its failure, hence the image, dear to the pamphleteering discourse, of the bottle in the ocean: 'This letter,' wrote Georges Bernanos, 'like its predecessor, is only a lost message tossed into a future I shall not know.'[34] Thus the images of the pamphleteering discourse are representations of the self more than portraits of the world. They derive from a certain morbid and unproductive narcissism, so characteristic of the pamphlet, implying that 'the evidence supporting the argument is impossible to convey'.[35] Here Angenot speaks of a 'logo-centric' discourse which, far from seeking to silence the voice which inspires it, speaks of it alone.[36] In this sense, the pamphlet is precisely the type of agonic discourse which, far from seeking reinforcement in the unifying description which satire uses to such good effect, itself wants only to be a voice and even takes pleasure in the weakness of its position. Furthermore, the image of the bottle in the ocean, far from representing the pamphlet as a *gaze*, is much more the metaphor of a voice which has little chance of being heard; a singular voice, then, in every sense of the word, and particularly in that which emphasizes its inability to unify.

This analysis of the agonic discourses also, therefore, emphasizes the strangely unifying nature of visual descriptions: the singular voice which begins to *describe* gives the impression of fading away before that which is obvious in the eyes of all. Unlike the pamphlet, that pure and weak voice, satire is the prime example of a discourse which pretends to disappear before the gaze and to refuse the explicit expression of opinion and which, in so doing, 'has people behind it'; it is the prime example, in fact, of a discourse which seeks to benefit from techniques concealing the very fact that it is (and is only) a discourse.

To pass from the singular voice to a more unifying gaze is surely to attempt to turn discourse, as far as possible, into narrative. Narrative, says the French critic Gérard Genette,[37] who also uses the word 'diegetic' in this connection, requires description. This complementarity of narration and description also explains why, having discussed their differences, Genette rejects a strict separation between these two forms of writing: there is always, he says, description in narration; narration, with its descriptive dimension, is thus of the nature of *story*, as distinct from that of *discourse*. 'In discourse', he writes, 'someone speaks, and their situation as they speak is the focus of the most important meanings; in the story, as Benveniste emphasizes, *no-one speaks*, in the sense that at no time do we need to ask ourselves, in order to appreciate the full meaning of the text, *who is speaking*, or *where*, or *when*, etc.'[38] Though Genette is strongly of the belief that no watertight frontier exists between discourse and narrative, he is equally convinced that story has its own rules and that 'telling' is consequently different from 'discoursing': 'Discourse can "tell" without ceasing to be discourse,' he says; 'the story cannot "discourse" without ceasing to be story.'[39] One may wonder if the specificity of the story does not lie precisely in the importance in it of the descriptive, in other words, in the fact that it uses a gaze as well as a voice.[40] In this way, the voice that tells, instead of simply discoursing, makes people listen in a way familiar to skilled polemicists, always careful to intersperse their indignant denunciations with stories, that is, with narrations that include, as we have seen, description. The more you tell and describe, the less you give the impression of discoursing.

This well-known technique of the journalism of opinion, this strange effacement of the voice in the 'diegetic' (in fact, the voice turns into a *narrative* voice), strategically so effective as a way of unifying, further suggests that we should not necessarily see the transition from the journalism of opinion to the journalism of reportage in the second half of the nineteenth century as a pure and simple rupture. The great journalists of opinion were in many ways already excellent reporters, or at least excellent narrators. Some individuals whose biography seems to indicate a journalistic conversion – from the 'traditional' journalism of opinion to reportage – perhaps only took to its logical conclusion a sensibility to the power of the 'diegetic', a sensibility already apparent in their more polemical writings. One thinks here of a figure like Séverine (who will be discussed more fully in chapter 2), whose articles of opinion and, in particular, texts of indignation were always exceptionally visual, descriptive and narrative.[41] Her 'reportage' of the trial of Dreyfus, published in *La Fronde* in 1899, should not, therefore, be seen as a break in her itinerary, but rather as an extension of a particularly heightened sensibility to the intrinsic weakness of *saying*, and the need to bolster her words by *seeing*. In this reportage, she expresses with great force her distaste for the 'rhetorical' journalists who do not go to see things from close up. She seems, therefore, to be breaking with the traditional polemical journalism in favour of a writing based on a lived, sensitive and notably visual testimony. Nevertheless, her way of practising the journalism of opinion she is now denouncing had already revealed this uneasy awareness of a certain weakness in voices which spoke without ever providing anything to see.

This cult of *seeing* was, of course, part of a 'ritual of objectivity' and was unrelated to an objectivity solidly based at the epistemological level. It was once again a pact with the public, which reflects the rising status of the sense of sight in social life during the nineteenth century – we should not forget that this was the century of the birth of photography and the cinema. For many specialists in the notion of objectivity, this trust in sight as an instrument of truth is also evidence that ideas about the nature of objectivity were still far from profound and relatively untroubled. The cult of 'facts' current in the journalism of the late nineteenth century derived, according to Michael Schudson, from a 'naive empiricism',[42] that is, from a deep confidence in the capacity of an 'I' – on condition it observed and did not simply discourse – to establish the 'facts' and so provide a sort of collectively acceptable experience, in which everyone could recognize themselves. This ran so deep that, according to Schudson, the question of objectivity did not exist as such in journalism; rather, it was as if settled in advance, defused by this 'naive empiricism' which, far from fearing subjectivity, put its faith in it.

It was only in the aftermath of the First World War, says Schudson, that the question of objectivity really began to exercise American journalism, in a context that was then one of a deep mistrust of subjectivity. The turning point was an article by Walter Lippmann and Charles Merz, published in 1920,[43] in which they condemned the coverage of the Soviet revolution and ensuing war by the reporters of the *New York Times*. They analysed in detail the way these journalists had looked at the revolution and accused them, in effect, of having seen only what they wanted to see. 'Observers' must in future offer guarantees; it was no longer enough to see, you had to see clearly. We should note, however, that the critique of Lippmann and Merz did not lead them totally to discredit the position of the witness, but rather to demand greater professionalism on the part of witnesses. Further, though he continued throughout his life to criticize those journalists whose 'gaze' seemed to him biased, Lippmann retained his faith in the possibility of a 'true' testimony.[44]

Whatever the relevance of the periodization adopted by Schudson, which concerns, we should remember, American journalism, it at least draws attention to a phenomenon that runs more generally through the history of the notion of objectivity. This history moves in the direction of an increasingly strong distrust of subjectivity. Just as Schudson believes that the notion of objectivity did not really emerge in journalism until a time when distrust of the 'I' (of the reporter-observer) had become deep-rooted, so, more generally, some specialists in the notion of objectivity believe that it only became fully formalized once it was historically grounded in a deep distrust of subjectivity. For Lorraine Daston, for example, the notion of objectivity became established at a time when, particularly in nineteenth-century science (seemingly here in advance of social practices such as journalism), it took this radical turn, that is, in the direction of 'aperspectival objectivity', implying a principled fear of subjectivity and the limitations it implies.[45] Objectivity then became, as it were, the ideal of a gaze which was no longer reduced to a perspective and which eliminated all trace of the observer.

Daston shows that the ideal had not yet been formulated in these terms in the eighteenth century. What Adam Smith, for example, valued most highly, at the epistemological, aesthetic and moral levels, was the model of the interchangeable observer, that is, a capacity for universal empathy, an ability to espouse, in turn, a myriad different points of view. From the end of the eighteenth century, however, the desire to be wholly 'disinterested' was increasingly formalized into an ideal which might be called total 'disconnectedness', under the influence of a growing distrust of subjectivity. Daston explains the consequence of this development for the expectations of a readership faced with supposedly 'objective' texts: a relationship based on trust in an author, in an 'I' (their presence unobjectionable as long as they were trustworthy, that is, potentially interchangeable, so that everyone could identify with them), was replaced by a distrust on principle, which took the form of constant demands for proof, for 'technical' signs guaranteeing that the observation was truly independent of any singular perspective.

It is certainly possible that journalism too, but a little later, was eventually infected by this mistrust of the simplicity of the 'I see' (the 'naive empiricism' of Schudson) and that one can only date its anxious quest for objectivity, strictly speaking, to this period. At the same time, we may wonder if the solutions it was able to bring to this quest really went beyond the position of 'I see', that is, the structure of the subject who observes and tells what he saw, the structure of the *witness*. Did it produce an 'aperspectival' gaze, without a subject to anchor it? This is far from certain, which may lead to the conclusion that journalism has not yet fully emerged from its nineteenth century.

The figure of the witness-ambassador

What exactly is meant, however, by a gaze that is 'aperspectival', wholly de-singularized, lacking perspective, disconnected and 'total'? Is this not a pure abstraction, the wholly theoretical aspiration for a sort of *non-place* or *nowhere*, a 'view from nowhere', to adopt the formula of the philosopher Thomas Nagel?[46]

It would be mistaken, however, to claim that this type of abstraction has not appealed to modern journalists. Writing in the 1970s, Edward Jay Epstein chose as the title of one of his books on American journalism *News from Nowhere: TV and the News*.[47] This raises a number of questions: has the appearance of the televisual media made feasible, for the first time, the journalistic ideal of a completely unanchored or 'total' gaze? Has aperspectival objectivity at last found a way of being achieved, thanks to a technique that eliminates all those subjective, singular traces which, in contrast, 'sully' the gaze of the journalists of the written word? And has a gaze at last emerged that is stripped of all voice, that cannot be reduced to a single *point of view* or discredited as simple *testimony*, that is, an inevitably subjective and singular perspective?

Has the technical image – the photograph, and even more film and video, since they can capture the passage of time – made it possible to transcend the limitations inherent in the position of the *witness*? In which case, can it not achieve the goal of total unification, because it will offer, at last, the vision of no one in particular, hence of everyone?[48] In the words of the famous American TV journalist Dan Rather, the camera has such power because it is an eye that never blinks.[49] And we should also remember that the logo of the American network CBS is an eye without a face to surround or anchor it. Photographic and film images really do seem to possess a novel power to objectify, supplanting the gaze of written reporting, heavy with voice, and which can never claim, a priori, to be other than testimony, with all the weaknesses inherent in it.

'Facts' established by means of a camera, concealed or not, have an undeniable demonstrative power. A few years ago a major scandal erupted as a result of a film shot, unknown to those involved, by a photographer at the English model agency 'Élite', which revealed racist behaviour on the part of the employers and their abuse of minor models. The scandal led to the resignation of the Élite directors, a sign of the power of the image, a proof which appears self-evident, without need to question the source from which it comes – in this case, the 'I' who had made the film, the journalist disguised as an agency photographer.[50] In the 1980s Günter Wallraff exposed the treatment of Turkish workers at the hands of many German industrialists by disguising himself as a Turk and getting himself hired. His first report took the form of a book,[51] but he himself then felt the need to make a film out of the pictures he had taken by means of a hidden camera.

Yet it is by no means certain that the TV image can supplant the figure of the journalist-witness. The reflections of Jacques Derrida, in his *Echographies of Television*, are illuminating here. Certainly, he observes, the televised image delivers, or gives the impression of delivering, an immediate and as if de-subjectified representation of reality, that is, a *proof*, as opposed to a *testimony*, which inevitably remains a first-person discourse, in which an 'I' speaks in their own name. The paradox, however, is that by transcending the subjective bias inherent in testimony, the possibility of an even greater level of manipulation is opened up. The possibilities of montage and special effects, especially thanks to digital imaging, implant serious doubts at the very heart of this instrument of *proof*. The proof may also be manipulation. 'The extremely refined instruments of archivization we now have are double-edged,' says Derrida:

> On the one hand, they can give us, more 'authentically' than ever, more faithfully, the reproduction of the 'present as it was'; but on the other hand, for this very reason, thanks to this same capability, they offer us more refined means of manipulating, cutting, recomposing, producing computer-generated images, etc. The synthetic presents us here, with a greater field and chance for authentification, and at the same time, with a greater threat to the authentification in question. This value of authenticity is both made possible by technics and threatened by it, indissociably.[52]

So, if the risk of deception is the dark side of the authenticating power of the image, and if the moment when the goal – a gaze purged of all voice – seems to be attained is also the moment when this access can be most put in doubt, testimony may well, in the end, be more reliable than the proof: 'This is why people will continue to prefer, even if only naively, supposedly living testimony to the archive: people like to believe that, when a witness comes into the stand and speaks in his name, he is himself! He speaks . . . Even if he lies, or even if he forgets, or even if his testimony is insufficient or finite, at least it can be truthful.'[53] Derrida discusses the example of the film, shot by an amateur, which showed the physical abuse inflicted on Rodney King by policemen in California. These images appeared in newspapers all over the world; they were established as a proof which seemed to supplant all the eyewitness accounts. It was certainly 'unifying':

> . . . this scene was filmed and shown to the entire nation. No one could look the other way, away from what had, as it were, been put right before his eyes, and even forced into his consciousness or on to his conscience, apparently without intervention, without mediator. And all of a sudden this became intolerable, the scene seemed unbearable, the collective or dele-gated responsibility proved to be too much.[54]

Yet Derrida approved of the legal requirement, which emerged at the time of the trial, that a proof, an exhibit, should not be confused with testimony: the young cameraman was called into the witness box to certify what *he himself* had seen:

> . . . the videographic recording may have served as an archive, perhaps even as an exhibit, perhaps as evidence, but it did not replace testimony. Proof or evidence – evidence! – of this fact is that the young man who shot the footage was asked to come himself and attest, swearing before the living persons who constituted the jury and who were legitimate as such, swear-ing that it was really he who held the camera, that he was present at the scene, that he saw what he shot, etc. There is therefore a heterogeneity of testimony to evidence and, consequently, to all technical recording. Technics will never produce a testimony.[55]

So although the televised image makes it possible to go beyond testi-mony, the 'de-subjectified' gaze which is the result carries the intrinsic risk of even greater subjective manipulation than before. The trusting 'unification' round the 'proof' can very quickly turn into suspicious dis-persal. This may help to explain the spectacular lurch to extremes observed in certain major crises of televisual journalism, for example, in France, following the Timisoara 'massacre' in Romania in 1989, a famous example of media manipulation through the photographic image. Proof by images was suddenly replaced by total distrust, which has been quick to resurface since, in the form of what is often called the 'Timisoara syndrome'. Above all, it raises the question of whether, in spite of its limitations, the key figure in integrating journalism does not remain that of the witness who says 'I see'.

The presence of the 'I' gives the gaze reliability, a face to which one can relate, an extreme visibility which claims to unify. And this is why the weakness of the witness can be turned into a great strength, as long as the witness is invested with legitimacy by the community which receives his testimony. Discussing the literature on the problems posed by judicial testimony, the sociologist Renaud Dulong emphasizes that 'there may be nothing more convincing than a human being who stands up, points a finger at the accused, and says: "That's him"'.[56] In this way, the 'I saw it', though it may sometimes be discredited from the outset, is also, in certain social contexts, truly all-powerful. A gaze, and the discourse in which it is deployed, can therefore be socially 'objectified' without the need for this constant battle against the element of subjectivity they contain, but rather by relying on it. There is then a type of objectification which has no connection with the ideal of aperspectival objectivity, and which is even its opposite: far from being considered odious, and an obstacle on the path to objectivity, the 'I' appears as the actual instrument of that objectification.

This is because a sort of tacit contract exists between this 'I' and the 'we' who recognize ourselves in that 'I'. The witness is no longer fragile and suspect, because his experience is perceived as what each of 'us' would have had in his place. His 'I' unifies a community, because it sees him, in the very singularity of his experience, as its ambassador. I will call this mode of objectification, or this unifying process, the figure of the *witness-ambassador*. For those who practise it, it means constantly reminding us, more or less implicitly, that they see *in all our names*, hence reminding us of the pact which binds them to 'us', enabling them to give 'us' a sort of experience by proxy. It is as if the 'I', singular though it may be, is at the same time 'collective'.

This figure of the *witness-ambassador* remains true, in a way, to return to the analyses of Daston, to the old model, dear to the eighteenth century, of the interchangeable observer, before the stricter demands constituted by the appearance of the ideal of aperspectival objectivity. Indeed, in spite of the crises of public confidence in journalists, and in spite of the demands for a more professional, that is, in particular, a more introspective gaze (is what I see all that there is to see, or am I being blinded by my own stereotypes?), we may question whether journalism has altogether broken away from this now ancient structure of the 'I see', which translates as: 'I make all of you see', or 'you are all unified behind me'. This is perhaps rather more fundamental to the history of journalism than the contemporary dreams of a purely technical and de-subjectified gaze, dreams which, as we have seen, may turn permanently into nightmares. Perhaps as a result of the intangible nature of this 'aperspectival objectivity', what remains triumphant in unifying journalism is rather the figure of the witness-ambassador, which emerged at the end of the nineteenth century: such journalists present themselves as simple witnesses, but witnesses legitimated by an entire community, as singular but mandated and justified observers. Thus, the gaze of the journalist says 'I' and 'we' at the same time.

This figure of the witness-ambassador was undoubtedly the favoured figure of the popular journalism of the second half of the nineteenth century. One sign of this is the repeated presence of the 'I' in the journalistic writing of that period, even though, as we have seen, it was then that the desire to offer only the 'facts', independently of the journalist's opinion, emerged. This is a paradox, in which the effacement of the subject in the name of 'factuality' was very far from involving the complete disappearance of the 'I'. The paradox was resolved by the 'naive empiricism' evoked by Schudson: the 'I' was not suspect as long as he let his feelings speak and did not allow opinions ('I think that . . .') to interfere with lived experience ('I see'). It is the belief in the possibility of separating these two orders, of feelings and of opinion, the eye that 'receives' and the voice that 'expresses', that underpinned this 'naive empiricism' – one might also speak of a sensualist positivism – and which justified trust in the reporter. Because the reporters do not discourse, but tell what they see, their 'I', anchored in their feelings, is not an impediment but potentially 'collective'. However, this 'sensualism', this confidence in the senses as an instrument of truth, seems, in this century of the birth of reporters, to be sustained by something quite different: that is, by the impression that these particular journalists represent us especially well, that they are perfect incarnations of the average Joe Public. If they are our ambassadors, it is not simply because they are *bodies*, ruled by their feelings, tied to their 'I see'; it is because they are so very much *us*. Indeed, this is why their bodies feel as ours do and why their eyes are potentially the eyes of all of us.

It was the first reporters themselves who kept reminding us of these 'certainties' and using them in their writing. In their very way of seeing, they needed to seal the pact which bound them to their public, so as to perpetuate the unifying power of their gaze. This is why the 'I' is omnipresent in the writing of nineteenth-century reporters; they are forever legitimating themselves, setting out their mandate as 'our' ambassador. This is particularly clear, for example, in the work of James

Gordon Bennett. Take this page which provided the *New York Herald* with its first popular success, in connection with a news item, the murder of a prostitute, Helen Jewett, by a young man called Robinson. Bennett, who had conducted the investigation for the *Herald*, constantly puts himself into his reporting:

> I knocked at the door. A Police Officer opened it, stealthily. I told him who I was. 'Mr B., you can enter,' said he with great politeness. The crowds rushed from behind seeking also an entrance.
> 'No more comes in', said the Police Officer.
> 'Why do you let that man in?', asked one of the crowd.
> 'He is an editor – he is on public duty'.[57]

As we see, the pact between the journalist and his public is constantly referred to, and the bringing together behind the reporter is shown literally ('The crowds rushed from behind'; the journalist is 'on public duty'). The 'I' can – even must – be omnipresent because it is, in a way, 'collective', full of 'us', and the embodiment of the public.

The paradox of this technique is that the integrating process operates not against the expression of an 'I', but through it. The description of the crime scene in the report just quoted is marked by Bennett's constant references to his own presence. The use of the first person singular is all-pervasive at a time when reporters, as we saw above, were asked not to express their personal opinions. In reality, if *opinions* were forbidden, *feelings* were, in contrast, essential. It was they that authenticated the collectively acceptable 'facts', and they were the paradoxical instrument of objectification, the mediation between 'I' and 'us'. This sensualist positivism is unrelated, therefore, to the ideal of aperspectival objectivity which abhors subjectivity. It retained, in a sense, a foot in the positivism of the nineteenth century (it claimed to address facts that had a validity beyond the singularity of the perspective within which they emerged) while giving it a particular coloration, which was a consequence of this penchant for sensory experience, and this confidence in the *feelings* as a way of getting at the 'facts'.

That this technique, dear to the reporting of the nineteenth century, should still be in favour is perhaps more surprising. Yet even television journalism seems often to resort to the figure of the witness-ambassador, relying much less than tends to be assumed on the impersonal, 'technical' character of the televisual image. The French TV programmes that cover major international events or practise 'investigative reporting' (such as 'Zone Interdite' (Forbidden Zones) or 'Envoyé spécial' (Special Correspondent)) revert to it with increasing frequency: after showing a 'story', they invite in to the television studio the reporter, that is, the voice that had spoken but not been seen during the 'news' section, the face that had been there, behind the camera. The presenter then asks the reporter to explain the circumstances in which he met the persons concerned, what he knows about what has happened to them since the date of the programme, and so on. The itinerary and the personal perspective of the observer, far from being erased, are deliberately displayed.

What these quality programmes seem to be trying to do by this practice is to compensate for certain characteristics of ordinary television journalism. Perhaps influenced by a belief in the importance of a 'view from nowhere', the latter tends to juggle with multiple, scattered gazes; it is quite common for the 'topics' presented on television to consist of pictures from a variety of sources, often drawn from image banks, and frequently edited, often by a succession of different people. This does not necessarily prevent the re-formulation, on each occasion, of an 'angle', as it is called in the profession, clearly structuring the journalistic approach, but it needs to be recognized that it tends to encourage a rather 'de-structured' visual 'product'. It seems to me significant, therefore, that some of the reporting that is called investigative tries, in contrast, to restore a presence (in fact, that of a narrator), that is, to show a face or an 'I' behind the 'technical' gaze; it is as if the televisual filming and editing needs to be rethought as the expression of an anchored gaze, a point of view, in fact, as a piece of writing. Such initiatives suggest, at all events, that we should reject the idea of a gulf separating the written and the televisual media; irrespective of the type of media, the question remains how best to gain the benefits of being anchored in an 'I', an eye-witness or a first-person narrator.

More than a century after the first reporters, much written reporting, too, continues to experiment with different forms of the figure of the witness-ambassador. The techniques have not, perhaps, changed all that much. The writing of the French journalist Edwy Plenel is a good example. In his appeal to fight the 'battle of secrecy',[58] and flush out the truth in the 'forbidden territories' of government,[59] Plenel even uses the word 'revelation' to describe the journalistic process. The concern for objectification could hardly be clearer, implying a desire to unify differently from the artificial way which suits the powers that be. He writes: 'To restore dissenting information against the fait accompli, the intractable liberty of the former against the sweet tyranny of the latter. To restore news which is meaningful against the communiqué which says nothing. The revelation which disturbs against the communication which is convenient.'[60] Here, it is 'our' gaze which is invoked against the words of a few. We are back with the 'It Shines for All' of the old *New York Sun*: that is, the combination of the themes of unifying and visibility. It is in the interest only of a few to leave the 'hidden' where it is, behind the scenes; to make people see is to be the ambassador of the 'we', who are many, against this small group.

As with the reporters of the nineteenth century, Plenel's writing is characterized by an omnipresent 'I'. The figure of the witness-ambassador, of the unifying 'I', permeates his style, for example in his book of 1992 on the Mitterand presidency, in which the use of such a figure is most obvious: frequent self-legitimation, the insistent reminder that the 'I' sees in all our names and reveals for all of us, in fact is a 'we'. Thus, in the passages in which Plenel emphasizes his fellow feeling with all those guardians of the truth forced into silence by the authorities, he speaks at length about himself and his own feelings in the face of the situations he describes. These effusions, which may at first sight seem like digressions, are actually an essential component of the text. By this means, Plenel, a man moved by injustice, a person *like us*, with the heart and the values of the 'citizen', presents himself as worthy to be our representative, worthy to be the witness in whom we put our trust. See, for example, how he justifies his attitude towards Bernard Jégat, a witness whose decision to speak out got him into serious difficulties:

> As a result, he held a grudge against me – and still does. On that October evening in 1985, I strongly advised him to go to the judge, the only effective protection. I even left him little choice: we now knew his story, we were going to publish it, and at the very most we might wait for his hearing before the magistrate. Purists will say that I overstepped the mark, crossed the white line that separates the spectator from the actor. They probably believe that an impenetrable barrier can be erected between the journalist and the citizen. If by any chance it exists, this disinterested journalism, bloodless and dispassionate, is an education in cynicism. One is entitled to prefer the 'right of follow-up' invoked in the 1920s by Albert Londres at the end of his investigations, harassing ministers and governments, calling on them to halt the injustices he had witnessed.[61]

Plenel pretends to be on the defensive, responding to those for whom the individual citizen should keep out of the journalistic gaze, but his response is actually a decisive and an 'offensive' moment in his book, appearing towards the beginning. Far from saying 'I am, in spite of everything, a journalist', he makes his personal attachment to certain values the very keystone of his journalistic legitimacy. You see, he seems to be saying, I share the generally accepted sense of what is right, hence I am the legitimate *witness*, the one who sees and speaks on behalf of us all; and he also seeks a typical journalistic model in the unifying figure of the witness-ambassador Albert Londres.[62]

In fact, this figure of the witness-ambassador makes it *essential to speak of oneself*, of one's body and one's passion; it is part of the technique, which is based on a labour of self-legitimation. This can take subtle forms: the journalist makes a pretence of having a singularly devious spirit – with the express intention of showing that this is the very thing he has not, rather that he is, in fact, absolutely 'straight', that he is like 'us' and not like 'them' (those in power). Take, for example, this brief observation in the part of his book that ends his account of various events: 'Only troublemakers, of which I am one, can still see this as a matter of cause and effect,'[63] an observation which means, of course, 'If I am a troublemaker, aren't we all?' He is not trying to eliminate the 'I', but rather to make it a constant presence, justified and legitimated by a tacit pact with the public. In the affair of the alleged Irish 'terrorists' of Vincennes, in 1982, the 'I' incarnates simple, united, generous human-ity, all of 'us', contemplating a Socialist government on the road to ruin: 'I might as well admit it,' wrote Plenel:

> *I do not think I succeeded in saving the left in this débâcle* which swept away Jean-Michel Beau, victim of the injustice of a Socialist government. The worst of injustices for a soldier: that inflicted on you by your weapon, your family, your brothers; that in which everything gets confused, loyalty and liberty, principles and duty; that in which everything falls to pieces. In the days that followed the confessions of Pierre Caudan, when the ground opened up under his feet, when Prouteau and Barril no longer answered his calls, Beau went into a depression. He came out of it by choosing to fight. *I have seen* this big, authoritarian man break down, contemplate the worst follies, fall into despair. *I have tried*, often, to rebuild his morale by suggesting to him that his misadventure was a blessing, that it had taught him more about life than twenty-six years of obedience and discipline. *I would probably have* made a good confessor.[64]

There is no embarrassment here in saying 'I', rather a happy insistence, because the 'I' is here collective, appointed as 'our' ambassador by the writing itself.

The 'I' need not always be so prominent, of course, for it to be present. The figure of the witness-ambassador can take many forms; all it needs is for the journalist to pose as representative of the public, as 'our' represen-tative. Interviewers in the media in general frequently resort to this tech-nique, seeking to convey the impression that they are posing *our* questions, and that it is this that gives them their legitimacy. The consequence is the familiar and symmetrical response of the interviewee in difficulty, who casts the journalist in the role of a 'biased', singular interrogator, who is not really representing the 'public' as he or she should. It is a characteristic of the figure of the witness-ambassador that he serve as the focus of the uni-fication, that is, the reporter himself or herself, the 'I'; but this can be done in many ways, which takes us back to the many ways there are of *unifying*.

This figure of the witness-ambassador points, therefore, to the need for a nuanced discussion of this process of unifying. It is not enough to reject, *en bloc* and with contempt, a method that is not, in fact, a single process, but takes many forms. It is mistaken, in particular, to see the journalistic process of unifying as implying a smoothing over of all the conflicts in this unified community. Witness-ambassadors, who set themselves up as the centre of the community and who, in so doing, define this centre, open a latent debate about 'our' identity. In many cases – including the most combative pages of modern journalism – this debate about identity involves *putting 'us' to the test*: the journalists, by their gaze, introduce something which questions 'our' identity and which sets off a conflict around this very identity; it is through the presentation of this conflict that they reaffirm the centre. The unification is achieved, therefore, both in and through a test.

It is this process of unifying in and through a test that I wish to discuss in this book. What sort of tests are the journalists who choose to be witness-ambassadors able to inflict on the community, simply by deploying their own gaze? And what sorts of conflict can take place within this process of bringing the public together?

These questions suggest that we should focus our attention on the best, or at least the most interesting, products of the journalistic process of *unifying*. But is this to rehabilitate this unifying journalism, the most common and dominant journalism, yet criticized on all sides? I would prefer to speak not of rehabilitation but of a desire to take it seriously, a desire at last to study with care the history of a journalism that is often misunderstood, a journalism in which even the dominant forms involve more complex processes than is generally believed, and a journalism that is vital for our modern democracies, one that combines the desire to *unify* with that to inject *conflict*.

2. Journalisms that decentre: acts of daring, difficulties and pitfalls

The dilemma of the decentring journalist

Unifying journalisms are not necessarily strangers to conflict, therefore; they often base themselves on it, and then construct the 'centre' of the community by means of a conflict shown through the gaze of the reporter. Nevertheless, we are entitled to remain sceptical about the nature of the conflicts which this journalistic process is capable of revealing and exposing. They are, by definition, conflicts which lead back to the centre and which, at the end of the day, make their readers feel the identity of a 'we'. Without despising this type of approach, one may wish to engage in a more radical resistance to all those gazes which, in the history of journalism, bind together and rebind the political community.

This brings us to the figure of the journalist who decentres. Decentring journalists seek to make the public which 'receives' their gaze feel something very different, something deeply disturbing to the 'we'; not just a bone of contention by means of which the community ultimately reconstructs itself, but an otherness liable to dissolve the 'we', something which says to it: you hardly exist as a constituted or a to-be-constituted 'we'; the 'we' that you are, or think you are, is undone.

In contrast to the unifying journalisms, which are the dominant journalisms and easy to identify in history, the decentring journalists are resistance fighters who have to be tracked down, often on frontiers: for example, that between journalism and literature. The 'decentring' is always, first, an attempt, an experiment. It lacks the triumphant aura of the unifiers. It takes shape gradually, opens up unexplored avenues and runs into difficulties. This is because it has a profoundly paradoxical dimension, which explains the failures it sometimes encounters, the risks of being blown off course by which it is constantly threatened, and the despair it often induces in those who attempt it.

To understand this paradoxical dimension, let me begin with an anecdote I was told by a journalist who was for a long time correspondent of *Le Monde* in China. When we met, in March 1999, this journalist, Francis Déron, made the following observation: 'What is fascinating about China is that you are faced with the radical other.' The job of the correspondent, he went on, writing for a French public, was to make them see this otherness, while respecting it as far as possible; confronted like this with the 'other', readers see their own cultural particularity, its relativity, and have their stereotypes challenged.

Described in this way, this journalistic method is very close to what I call 'decentring'. As we see, the relationship with the public is here very different from that characterizing the unifying figure of the witness-ambassador. The latter is as if mandated by the public: the witness-ambassador is 'our' representative. Here, in contrast, the journalists set themselves apart from 'us' from the outset, so that they can address us as 'you'. They say to their readers: what *I* see is precisely what *you* do not see and probably cannot easily see, so profoundly does it challenge your usual categories; it is because I exclude myself from you, and because I am not like you, that I see. Admittedly, I make you see something, so you can say 'we see something together', but this collective spectacle is intended to point out the limitations of your usual 'seeing'.

I sow confusion in your 'we', far from constituting or reconstituting it; I 'undo' you, and perhaps I am in this way going to change you.

This implies that the gaze offered to 'us' confronts us with a 'non-us', an 'other'; unlike the unifying journalisms for which the representation of an adversity makes it possible to unify and rebind 'us', this 'other' aims to destroy the 'us/non-us' frontier itself. Decentring journalists put themselves in a position of 'non-belonging' to 'us' in order to provoke a conflict which touches on the collective identity; they confront 'us' by means of an exteriority-otherness, and in this way undo us.

The decentring gaze is therefore a gaze which, as well as what it looks at, looks at *us*, and in a very different way from that of the simple appeal or putting to the test which characterize the unifying journalisms. In this case, the gaze interrogates to the point of inducing a crisis in the very person who looks through it; the public is as if overwhelmed by its own spectacle, because there is something in the spectacle which looks at *it*.

During our meeting, Déron described a scene which reveals all the difficulty – and perhaps, the impossibility – of this process of decentring. One day, when he was covering the conflicts on the frontier between Laos and Thailand, he questioned a Laotian survivor of a Thai camp. He was trying to get at his experience, his own singular view of the sufferings he had experienced. The Laotian described all the horrors he had endured. Déron then asked him the following question (perhaps a peculiarly Western question): 'What, in the end, was hardest for you?' To his amazement, the man replied: 'It was the fact that there were evil spirits in the camps.' Of all the tortures and privations he had endured, it was this idea of 'evil spirits', obscure to a Westerner, which the Laotian finally chose as the mark of absolute horror.

The Western 'decentring' journalist, determined to confront his readers with an otherness presented as such, is expected to report what is said to him. But can a remark like this make any sense to a Western reader? Is this not of a degree of remoteness that signals the end of all understanding? The otherness here seems so extreme as to be beyond any possible connection with such a reader. Quoted without comment, the words of the Laotian risk appearing so strange, so 'other', that they would, in the end, no longer decentre. But if the journalist translates them, or omits them, so as to expose sufferings more accessible to a Western public, is he really going to decentre this public? Will this translation or selection not amount, in fact, to taming the otherness to the point where it will, in a sense, be betrayed? It would then be a false otherness, a tamed and therefore denatured otherness that would 'decentre', and the decentring would be a shabby and dishonest decentring.

This anecdote, through which a journalist described the difficulties inherent in his trade as correspondent in a foreign – very foreign, by his own admission – country, neatly encapsulates the problem inherent in the journalistic process of decentring. Perhaps we should speak of a contradiction: there would seem to be a contradiction between the *aim* of the decentring process – to confront 'us' with an 'other' which describes and reveals us as a 'you' – and the *possibility* of achieving it – that the 'other' is not, in fact, wholly other, that is, that it remains, in the last analysis, connected to us. The decentring journalist has to make 'us' have the experience of something which breaks with us, but this can only happen if not every link with 'us' is cut.

Making us see otherness and connecting it to us

This paradox might be called the paradox of the rupture and the link. It is the cause of the trials and tribulations which, as we will see, haunt the journalisms of decentring: should they try to show a radical otherness, at the risk that it will no longer have any meaning for their readers, and that these readers will, ultimately, be little affected, not 'decentred' at all? Or should they, on the contrary, resign themselves to taming the otherness so as to make it have an effect, make it truly 'decentring'; can it really, however, in that case, be said to 'decentre', since, in a way, a tamed otherness means that a confrontation has been avoided with what is at the furthest possible point from the 'centre'?

How can decentring journalists overcome this difficulty, which is inherent in their method? This is the question that will guide our discussion. It is one that will, I believe, enable us to appreciate the most important issues in those movements which, in the history of journalism, have tried to resist the dominant journalism. The most significant of these is certainly the movement of the 1960s known as the New Journalism, in the United States. Another journalistic project which may be seen as an attempt at decentring is that of the French daily newspaper *Libération*, in the 1970s, a project which was also much more concerned to explain itself and which often referred to the 'New Journalism' in this context.

My question will make it possible to show the pitfalls encountered by these different journalistic movements. One example is that of the temptation for decentring journalists to pose as *travellers* within otherness: they navigate among 'other' points of view; they merge their gaze into this multiplicity of other points of view and re-create them for the 'us' they address ('look at these others . . .'). But if it is so easy, is this not, perhaps, a sign that they have failed to penetrate a real otherness? If 'communication' between 'them' and 'us' is so easy, if all that is needed is a travelling journalist to get access to 'them', is this not, perhaps, because 'they' are being falsely portrayed, domesticated by a gaze which is obsessed by the need to communicate?

This decentring journalist, a triumphant traveller within a misrepresented otherness, succumbs to what might be called the *temptation of ubiquity*. As we will see, the way in which Tom Wolfe defines the New Journalism project provides an excellent example of this temptation, particularly when he compares the 'New Journalist' to a chameleon, capable of navigating within the multiplicity of points of view and, by re-creating them, showing a generalized conflict. But it can be argued that this leads, in the end, to a rather bland representation of the sphere of points of view, revealing a difficulty in grasping the depth of the conflicts and the misunderstandings, the power of the 'incommunicable'.

Other temptations lie in wait for decentring journalists: for example, that of seeing themselves as the witness-ambassadors of the dominated, hence of creating a new 'we', against the 'we' of the dominant. This temptation to *unify the dominated* was felt in the early years of the French daily newspaper *Libération*.

In essence, and this is a point to which I will return, the risks inherent in the decentring method correspond to deviations into forms of . . . unifying. The temptation of ubiquity can lead to something close to unifying everybody, in a bland representation of the sphere of points of view; in the end, a 'we' re-forms, more inclusive than ever. The temptation to merge the dominated into a 'we', on the other hand, leads to the invention of a new community, unified in the gaze of the journalist, who then becomes the witness-ambassador of the dominated rather than the decentrer of the dominant.

Of course, put baldly like this, these risks seem rather abstract and intangible. But a closer examination of these key moments in decentring journalism will give substance to these initial claims and demonstrate the intrinsic difficulties of the attempt to decentre. In this case, also, as for the unifying journalisms, it will be useful to identify several different forms of this journalistic process, which will help us to grasp the issues and the pitfalls of decentring by means of concrete examples.

But the archetypal figure of the decentring journalist, in a way key point of reference for all who decentre, probably cannot emerge at the beginning of our discussion, because it can only be a synthesis of attempts made, of failed bold moves, and of trial and error. It is relatively easy to define, at the outset, the archetypal features of the unifying figure of the witness-ambassador, because this figure emerges so clearly in the history of journalism, even if we then have to describe its variant forms. As soon as we turn our attention to those who decentre, however, we have to uncover buried actions and hesitant and complex initiatives before reaching a position from which we can gradually define the archetypal figure who, far from overcoming these hesitations and difficulties, synthesizes and reflects them.

We cannot, therefore, study the decentring journalists in the same way as the unifying journalists. Nevertheless, it is this twofold approach, each with its own logic, that will structure my book. We will travel through the history of journalism, pausing to examine some particularly significant approaches that help us to understand the two journalistic approaches of unifying and decentring. My aim is to define universal figures in modern journalism, so enabling us to reflect concretely on the roles it is called on to play in our democratic societies.

2

An Archetype of the Witness-Ambassador: Séverine, Reporter at the Trial of Captain Dreyfus
(*La Fronde*, 6 August–15 September 1899)

Like many French anarchists, Séverine (1855–1929) was not among the early Dreyfusards. We should not be misled by precocious commitments such as that of Bernard Lazare with regard to the real level of support for the cause of Alfred Dreyfus in anarchist, anti-militarist and often Judaeo-phobic circles (the 'Jew' being classed with the 'bourgeois').[1] A contributor to the *Libre Parole* of the anti-Dreyfusist writer Édouard Drumont in the years 1894–6, Séverine for a long time showed little repugnance for the anti-Semitic press, or at least failed to give it serious attention.[2]

Yet she was touched by Dreyfus the man when she read a report in the *Petit Parisien* describing the convict's departure for the Île de Ré. 'Reaching with his sword over the head of a gendarme, an infantry officer of the line from the La Rochelle garrison struck Dreyfus with the pommel and inflicted a wound from which the blood flowed,' said the article. Shocked by this image of one man alone in the face of military violence, Séverine published an indignant article in *L'Éclair* on 25 January 1895. It elicited a warm response from the captain's wife, Lucie Dreyfus, but Séverine refused to meet her. 'Many people', she wrote in this article, 'even patriots who have regretted it was impossible to condemn Dreyfus to death, will be filled with sadness and disgust at the idea that an officer of the French army could so forget himself as not only to insult but to strike a prisoner.'[3]

Her commitment to the cause of Dreyfus continued to be coloured by this emotion. It was, in a sense, a commitment of 'sensibility', which was not inspired by any ideological position; it might even be said that it was *in spite of* her entrenched ideological prejudices that Séverine, once *touched*, finally saw Dreyfus as a victim, to whom, she said, the defenders of the people's cause against state violence could not remain indifferent.

This Dreyfusism brought Séverine closer to Émile Zola. Their relations had been cool in the years preceding Zola's involvement on behalf of Dreyfus. Though Jules Vallès and Séverine felt real admiration for Zola's work, he was frequently criticized in the 1880s in *Le Cri du Peuple*, the paper which had played a crucial role under the Commune and which Séverine had helped Vallès to revive in 1883. What *Le Cri du Peuple* denounced in the Zola of that period was a contempt for politics and a desire to keep literature separate from commitment; the paper came to Zola's defence when *Germinal* was banned, but Séverine did not miss the opportunity to observe, ironically, that politics had sent its regards to Zola . . . Then, in 1898, she was genuinely enthused by *J'Accuse*, not least because it meant that Zola had finally resolved to play the political role which she and her friends had long wanted for him.[4]

When her support for Dreyfus led to her articles being rejected by many publications to which she had once been a regular contributor, Séverine decided to join *La Fronde*, a daily paper written entirely by women, which had been founded in 1897 by the Dreyfusard Marguerite Durand. The first issue appeared on 10 December 1897, in the middle of the Dreyfus affair. In the weeks that followed, *La Fronde* reproduced in full Zola's *J'Accuse*, which meant that Marguerite Durand risked prosecution in the same way as Clemenceau, owner of *L'Aurore*.[5] Séverine covered Zola's trial, from 8 to 24 February 1898, for *La Fronde* and also for the Belgian paper *Le Petit Bleu*.[6] She declared herself in favour of the re-trial of Dreyfus, which was finally granted, and was then sent by *La Fronde* to Rennes, where this trial took place between 5 August and 8 September 1899.

Throughout the trial, Séverine produced a daily column under the heading '*Notes d'une Frondeuse*' ('Notes of a Troublemaker').[7] Another reporter from *La Fronde*, Jeanne Brémontier, was also present; Marcelle Tinayre and Marguerite Durand produced regular editorials. On some days, Séverine wrote a longer article which replaced her regular column: on Tuesday 8 August, for example, a portrait of Dreyfus was headed 'The Man'; on Saturday 12 August, an article intended to emphasize the hospitality of the people of Rennes had the title 'Good Homes'; on Wednesday 16 August, 'Chouannerie' (after the Breton royalist guerrilla wars of 1793–1815); on Monday 28 August, 'The Three Steps'; and on Tuesday 12 September, 'Res adjudicata'. Only once during this period (Monday 11 September) did the paper appear without a single line over Séverine's signature; perhaps she was taking a short rest after the verdict. In any case, she prepared a long article for Tuesday 12 September ('Res adjudicata'). She then resumed her chronicle until 15 September, describing the atmosphere in Rennes in the days following the conclusion of the trial.

I have chosen to concentrate on the group of Séverine's articles which appeared in *La Fronde* between 6 August and 15 September 1899, though I will occasionally refer to earlier texts, in particular her coverage of the trial of Zola the previous year. This small body of work constitutes, in a particularly concentrated form, a writing that is wholly emblematic of the figure of the witness-ambassador. In fact, in this string of articles written on the occasion of the trial of Dreyfus, Séverine skilfully condenses all the themes which this journalistic figure constantly exploits. She pushes them to their limits and provides the archetype.

We will see, in particular, how the witness-ambassador constructs herself by putting herself in the foreground. The 'I' is made the focus of a collective experience. It is presented as pure *body*, which feels the event and, through its feelings, gets at this event's essential truth. It is what we will call the 'radical sensualism' of Séverine, that is, her conception of the body as a completely reliable 'true' source, a centre of universality and not of confinement in purely singular experiences. She is constantly contrasting the journalism of *saying*, which touches nothing and remains singular and shallow talk, with the journalism of *seeing*, to which she lays claim and which grasps reality through the eyes and the whole body; in Séverine, *seeing* appears as one of the ways of *feeling* in general. For Séverine, the sole requirement that must be respected by reporters anxious to convey to their readers the truth of the event is to anchor their testimony in their *bodies*, so as to offer a truly sensitive gaze, as remote as possible from all abstract discourse. It is this that makes her a witness-ambassador, whose experience is universalized and hence acceptable to all of us who read her.

The labour of self-legitimation by the witness-ambassador is particularly well developed in the writing of Séverine. She is constantly making it known that she is more a *body* than a person, and that this makes her the ultimate witness, who achieves universality. She makes an asset, for example, of what had always been a handicap in her journalistic career, that is, her femininity, which is presented as a closeness to the body, an anchorage in sensibility, hence an advantage in getting at the 'facts'. But she is also at pains to remind her readers that she, more than anyone, is mandated by the people, precisely because they have recognized her as *the* body *par excellence*, hence their perfect ambassador. The figure of the witness-ambassador is pushed to the limit, to the point of coming close to incarnation: Séverine seems to say: *my body*, because it is absolutely body, a passive body, pure receptivity, seat of feelings not directed by a single will, *is the body of the people themselves*; where the people are not present 'in person', I can replace them and give them an experience by proxy, give them a body. This way of 'embodying the people' through her journalistic gaze is a near-perfect example of the act of unifying.

1. The truth of the senses

The 'witness' against the 'rhetoricians'

The great theme at the heart of the writing of Séverine is the opposition between the witness, the observer who *sees* the event and, through this closeness, feels it with their whole body, and the traditional journalist, who speaks about the event from a distance. In the writing of Séverine, testimony never appears as something fragile, giving rise to doubt, even distrust – does the witness see 'properly'? It is the supreme mode of access to the facts, acceptable to all. It is the words not rooted in the 'felt' which are discredited as shallow and singular, simple opinions which are unlikely to unify behind them.

The word 'rhetorician' crystallizes the reporter's contempt for journalists who travel rarely and discourse ceaselessly. What Séverine aims at, in contrast, is a journalism of sensitive testimony. One of the clearest formulations of this opposition is found in the article which followed the verdict. Séverine refuses to give in before the 'final judgement' and exclaims:

> Which one? That of 1894? Those of 1898, the Esterhazy trial, the Zola trial? Those of 1890, Court of Cassation or Council of War? Which of these are we being urged to respect?
>
> *I do not speak as a rhetorician; I speak as a witness.* I have never considered this mystery as a blank canvas for my thoughts or as an empty page to be embellished with fine phrases: *I have seen, I have listened; for two years I have employed all the inner strength of my being in observing, in listening and in reflecting, like an honest mirror, facts on which my will could have no effect.*[8]

The mirror, we should note, is necessarily 'honest'; trust in this body which feels, and which concentrates on its feelings, is total. And this is precisely what is lacking in the 'rhetoricians'. They, in contrast, are dismissed with the contemptuous judgement flung at them by Séverine at the time of Zola's trial: 'Facts? Few. Words? Many.'[9]

In opposing the rhetorician and the witness, Séverine is contrasting the active and constructed character of discourse with the passivity and simplicity of feelings. If witnesses are reliable, it is because they let themselves be caught up in the event, not seeking to control it by their will; to discourse on the subject of an event reflects a desire to exert control, as opposed to passive feeling. If this passivity of the feelings is the journalists' ideal, we should then note the paradoxical character of the effort that is expected of them, that is, to become all witness, wholly abandoning the posture of the rhetorician, in other words, to 'employ all the inner strength of their being' so as to produce this fruitful passivity, this capacity to *reflect*. This paradoxical theme – an effort to achieve passivity – appears in oxymoronic forms: thus, in her article of 4 September, Séverine notes the 'strength of the passive action' which emanates from the gaze when you go to the scene to observe events:

> Regret nothing, you who have come, you who savour the dreary ennui of the 'uprooted', far from familiar places and surroundings, from the daily round and your loved ones. Even apart from the goal of justice which brings us here, look around you – and understand the beauty, the power of passive action, of the influence which emanates from the principle without the will even being involved.[10]

And in an article of 1 September she also speaks of 'feeble powers': a few days before the verdict, to assure her readers of the sincerity of her conviction (the innocence of Dreyfus), she declares that she *feels* deeply, and almost in spite of herself, what she proclaims, and hence that her 'feeling' is not produced by some 'opinion', that it comes from the body and not from a garrulous brain. 'In my heart and soul, with all my feeble powers, with all the energy of my sincerity,' she writes, 'I believe Alfred Dreyfus is innocent!' The article in question had the title 'Gossipmongers!' and begins with a denunciation of all the scandalmongers who were spreading rumours about Dreyfus's guilt: 'all these prattlers, all these tittle-tattlers, all these cruelties, all these vulgarities, it makes one sick at heart!' We should note that it is the heart that is sickened, once again presenting a picture of passivity. So, in opposition to this obscene *saying*, based simply on opinions and dubious wishes, Séverine presents her *feeling*, a passive force imposing itself on the soul.[11]

   The lauding of the position of the witness, who is present and feels the situation in his or her flesh, instead of speaking about it from a distance, springs from the conviction that the witness accedes to a materiality that the 'rhetoricians' ignore or reject. Indeed, the very fact that they do not go to the scene, and so remain at a distance from the sole source of truth, feeling, is evidence that they have little desire, in reality, to correct the 'errors' likely to result from this remoteness – ah, the pernicious will . . . Thus, on 14 September, Séverine notes that the anti-Dreyfusards had not shown themselves 'particularly anxious to come here, to the very source, to seek precise and accurate facts'; 'I regret this,' she goes on, 'because no person of good faith, *having seen and having listened*, and being, therefore, in a position to monitor the accounts, the so-called record in the majority of the nationalist newspapers, would be other than amazed, and a little ashamed, to have given credence to such . . . imaginings!' The beginning of the article had appealed to these 'persons of good faith', ready to submit themselves to the test of their feelings:

'I would like all those who have been fooled and misled, who are still being misled and fooled, to be present in person at the debates of the Council of War; would like them *to see and touch*, like St Thomas, the truths that have been concealed from them or misreported.'[12]

In fact, physical presence is essential to guarantee a proper perception of the situation. This explains Séverine's anxiety – which she makes her readers share – in certain articles in which she refers to the events taking place in Paris and at which she cannot, consequently, be present, while Rennes seems to be relegated to a backdrop:

> We know nothing, we pace restlessly around, we chew our fingernails, in the terrible ignorance and impotence of being far away! What is happening there, in Paris?
>
> While here the judicial tragedy unfolds, in a nostalgic and perhaps deceptive peace, we suspect, we feel, we know that the real battle is being fought far away, beyond the closed horizon.
>
> *The meditative find consolation; but those who are alive and passionate have, since this morning, been wandering around like ghosts, in search of news, lamenting, longing to leave.* The telegraph and the telephone have been active, in official circles; but so much uncertainty still reigns![13]

This cult of *being present at the scene*, which has had such a profound influence on contemporary journalism (to be on the spot is to grasp the 'truth' of the event, that which is felt and is obvious to all, beyond the partisan divides which characterize interpretations), has as its corollary the anxiety of distance. Séverine seems never to be free of it; it is part of a more general anxiety that the 'real' things, which provide the key to a situation, take place where they cannot be witnessed, that is, in the spheres of a power hidden from view. 'Far from here we cannot know all that is going on behind the scenes,' she writes on 27 August, referring to the secret negotiations which might well determine the outcome of the trial she was attending:

> The secret discussions every afternoon to prepare the statements for next day (everyone has to make his report, play his role, corroborate, support, refute, after the morning's hearing); M. Cavaignac, lying in ambush in the Place de la Comédie, seat of resistance, centre of agitation; M. Auffray, once 'one of the most highly regarded young advisors of the Comte de Paris', watching over the juridical safety of the enterprise, in and out of the house of ex-General Mercier at all hours . . . and the frantic comings and goings between all these hotbeds of reaction![14]

If the possibility of being a witness is the sole guarantee of getting the 'true' measure of an event, it is essential to preserve it. And when it is achieved, it is still under threat, because, in spite of the materiality achieved by witnesses, which gives their words a content that is lacking in those of the rhetoricians, their words do not easily destroy the power of shallow rhetoric. This is the paradox: in spite of their immateriality, the words which are spoken at a distance carry considerable weight; flocks of crows are good at darkening the sky, to adopt a metaphor of Séverine in her article of 22 October: 'Open their newspapers for the last week: nothing but denials, provocations, bravado, prophecies of woe and warnings of a massacre! They are like famished crows at the approach of the hecatombs. They provoke them, they long for them, and, so as to increase the agitation, they darken the sky with their black wings and their gloomy flight!'[15]

The power of words is never better evoked than at the time of the attack on Maître Labori, Dreyfus's lawyer, which Séverine blames on the rhetoricians. This time, she addresses them directly; 'they' have become 'you':

> As for me, thinking of my collections in Paris, of the last two years' newspaper articles, assembled and filed alphabetically, of the stream of insults to which Labori was daily subjected, I wonder about the thought processes, the logic, of those who, dispensing hatred drop by drop, are surprised and shocked at the result.
>
> The man who fired believed he was doing the right thing; he thought he was slaying the monster you made him out to be. His act was simply a sign of his credulity; the fierce pledge of his faith in your sincerity. This leads to that; it is ineluctable![16]

This article is significant in a number of ways: first, it links an affirmation of the power of words – words kill – to a new reference to their vacuity, this article being clearly intended to claim that the current tears of the 'right-minded' press are worthless and reflect no true feeling: 'It was strange, yesterday, reading the "right-minded" newspapers. Which of these crocodiles would weep the most tears; which would express the strongest indignation; which would find the best way of saying: "it was the act of a madman . . . all parties condemn it." And other such humbug!' For Séverine, the words of today have scarcely more content than the lies of yesterday; but the lies of yesterday had prompted a crime. Vacuity does not, therefore, preclude power, and yet power is not evidence of any material content 'filling' these words. Further, Séverine seems ultimately to have been more indulgent towards the man who had committed the crime than towards those who had fomented it, the 'rhetoricians'. It is as if there was a sort of innocence in a man who was still happily naive enough to take words for what they ought to be, vehicles for 'matter', which encourage the transition to action.

Finally, the article reveals, literally, Séverine's opposition to this world of murderous vacuity. She presents herself as a direct eyewitness to the attack on Labori, on the spot, and in a position to reproduce the true emotions and hence to produce words which are not 'empty':

> I was there, yesterday, when they put his stretcher in the little ambulance which was to take him to an airier and a more rural place. Against the whiteness of the sheets, his kind, strong face stood out, overcoming his pain to smile at us all. His voice encouraged us still. 'Hello, Séverine! See, they haven't killed me! I will live, to fight on . . . and to win!' Faced with this marvellous bravery, tears of emotion and enthusiasm welled up in our eyes. This man is truly a 'teacher of energy'.

A radical sensualism

Does Séverine, in lavishing such praise on the figure of the witness, as opposed to the rhetoricians, never worry about the possibility of a 'bad' witness? Scarcely at all, it has to be said. For her, *all* feeling is good; the emotions and the 'felt' as a whole are unreservedly praised. As long as witnesses are 'truly' witnesses, entirely given over to their feelings and their emotions, no wrong can result.

It is not the 'bad' witness who is to be feared, but rather the partial or *inadequate* one, the one who is still a rhetorician, not enough of a witness, still all words, not enough feeling. So, during Zola's trial, Séverine exposed the rhetoricians beneath the witnesses, ironically observing, for example, of a certain witness who 'had seen nothing':

> Tall, dry, the coronet of a count on the back of his kepi, M. de Boisdeffre, Major-General and Chief of Staff, after taking the oath, subject to professional secrecy (like everybody else, for that matter), hid, before resorting to it, behind the Court ruling restricting the evidence.
>
> He knew nothing, he had seen nothing . . .

And she took pleasure in quoting the scathing words of Labori, who was already Zola's lawyer, 'The defence lawyer eventually says: "All the words which come out of the mouth of a general are not necessarily a matter of national security." '[17] In other words, everything you say is not evidence, much is rhetoric.

It is not sensitive testimony that deceives, but the fact that there is not enough of it, that it is not sufficiently present under and in the words. Conversely, all sensitive experience is genuine or 'true'. This leads Séverine into a veritable apologia for emotion, already clear in the first article of her coverage of the trial of Zola, on 8 February 1898, in *Le Petit Bleu*. This is how she presented her journalistic method:

> And if, in the account of my impressions, in the manner in which I express them, there is something displeasing to the enemy, let them do me the

honour of assuming I am always sincere, *incapable of in any way distorting the truth.*

I say what I saw and how I saw it.

And if I feel a little excitement, and if a little passion stirs under the desire to be impassive, let them not hold it against me.

I am neither neutral nor blasé, I am not entitled to renounce, at will, the fine fervours of enthusiasm.

Old-fashioned though we may be thought, there are still a few of us, perhaps more than is generally believed, who experience the noble passion. There is nothing to be gained by repudiating it or pretending to be ashamed of it!

A thousand times better admit it and confess it with pride.[18]

In short, excessive emotion is only the obverse of a passivity at last completely achieved – as the etymology of the word 'passion' suggests. It is not something to be afraid of.

And in her reportages for *Le Petit Bleu*, in 1898, Séverine constantly praised emotion as a mode of access to those facts to which language was so unreceptive. She defended even the most extreme emotions, the 'furies', which sadly remain unknown to some insensitive citizens. Thus, on 9 February, she waxed indignant about 'the terrible sadness, the dreary lassitude which cannot be dispelled by an upsurge of the furies', and deplored the way this marvellous instrument for evaluating a situation was in danger: 'Because, in the civilized world, there is not an honest man who, if the heightened state of excitement achieves its end, does not condemn it with horror.'[19] The problem is not so much the emotions, therefore, as the barriers which intervene, preventing them from playing their salutary role.

This defence of the most powerful emotions is echoed, eighteen months later, in her praise, mentioned above, of the 'passionate'. They are in contact with the event. Further, Séverine constantly pays tribute to the *capacity to be moved*, a sign that whoever has it can be a true witness, given over to felt reality. This capacity can never delude. It makes it possible to say what is and how it should be judged. Conversely, there is scarcely an event which can be revealed without the mediation of an emotion; and an event which concerns justice and injustice arouses the strongest emotions of all. In the face of an event of this nature, the insensitive no longer have any excuse: it is they who are at fault.

This is why her comment, at the time of the attack on Labori, to the effect that the event must have pierced even the hardest of hearts, is so significant. On 15 August, in her account of the event, Séverine notes: 'I saw men renowned for their phlegmatic disposition weep silently, their fists clenched.'[20] (The adverb 'silently' expresses once again the contrast between the silent register of the emotions and that of discourse.) On 23 August, she makes a similar observation in a passage in which she emphasizes the truth of emotion, and hence the greater reliability of the observer who is *touched* as compared with the one who remains at a distance and who, as a result, is presented almost as incapable of any 'understanding' of the situation:

> Those who did not walk with me, through that room with its guarded doors, the minute after the attack, cannot, will never be able to understand the extent of our present joy,[21] compared with our despair then.
>
> We admired him, we respected him, we applauded his courage and his ability, but no one, I am sure, realized how much they loved him. I saw men, hard men, renowned for their imperturbability, collapse into a chair at the news of the murder, and weep as for a personal bereavement which strikes straight at the heart.[22]

Since emotion is the yardstick of judgement and comprehension, the 'sensualism' of Séverine is clearly more than an empiricism which would leave to the senses the task of knowing and recognizing what is (the 'facts'): her sensualism extends to attaching value to *everything* that is felt; the witness is not only the guarantee of factual truth but also the guarantee of the proper way of evaluating it; the body both guarantees what is and indicates what should be thought about it. She values the sensitive, immediate and 'instinctive' relationship to the world so highly because it allows both (true) knowledge and (correct) judgement.

Conversely, it can be said that the world of Séverine is a world in which reality is *revealed*, in the full sense of the word 'revelation': it appears to the senses, but in so doing, it also offers the 'recipient' the tools for its evaluation. The adjective 'revealing', in the writing of Séverine, should be understood, therefore, in this strong sense. For example, in her article of 2 September, she once again appeals for the senses, as opposed to words, to be left to evaluate the situation; she makes a defence of 'instinct', then refers to the evidence which emerges simply from observing the protagonists in this trial. She writes: 'Just as, from the contrast between Labori, who incarnates the defence, and General Roget, who personifies the prosecution, it emerges that aesthetically, in moral beauty, and in clarity of gesture, once again arms yield to the toga, so, from a comparison of our side and theirs, *it emerges that we should feel a certain pride.*'[23] What 'emerges', therefore, is how we should judge what is. 'Masks betray, they reveal,' she adds, and what is *revealed* is not only a hidden reality but also what should be thought about it. In sum, reality prompts the feelings in the direction necessary to its evaluation; all you need to do is leave things to this marvellous tool, that is, allow this surrender to the senses. When, in this same article, Séverine evokes the 'fine wave of emotion' aroused by 'our side' that very morning, when they proclaimed their conviction of the innocence of Dreyfus, she is simply applying her evaluative tool: they aroused emotion, *so* they are 'ours'; they are what they appear and what they arouse.

We see that this apologia for emotion leads easily to redundancy, even tautology. What is it, in 'our' witnesses, that guarantees that they are 'ours', that they are authentic witnesses? Their capacity to be moved, that is, to be 'truly' witnesses, all *body*. But what is the proof of this? What proves that their expressions reflect an authentic surrender to the body, that they are pure emotions? The very emotion they arouse in other witnesses. They are capable of being moved, and this 'appears' in the form of a capacity to move. This authentication of the true, emotive witnesses by the very emotion they arouse is clear-cut, for example, in 'Goodbye to my Friends', the article Séverine wrote a few days before the verdict, in homage to all the observers who had shared her passion for the truth, and for whom the innocence of Dreyfus was, in a way, obvious to the senses. She writes:

> I see this audience trembling with confused passions, these writers come running from every point of the compass, who feverishly write up their despatches.
> This is not routine hackwork, the fixed-price labour which inevitably ends by dulling, if not excluding, the feelings. Eyes shine, mist over, or darken; fingers clench round pens and pencils; words flow, involuntary, brief, which very quietly reveal turbulent states of mind.[24]

The capacity of these observers to be moved is central to this paean of praise; we are back with the latent opposition between the old, blasé journalistic tradition and the 'true' journalism, full of emotion – between hollow, overly deliberate, words and the words that 'flow' from the heart and not from the will. But Séverine then guarantees the 'value' of these 'friends', and the trust that the public can place in them, by the fact that they move *her*; once again, as if at a second level, it is emotion which guarantees a proper appreciation; the emotion of these Dreyfusard writer-journalists is evidence of their proper relationship to the event, and the emotion of Séverine who observes them confirms that emotion has guided them well, and that they are wholly in emotion and hence in truth: 'I repeat, I who have seen them at work; *I who can testify* to the dignity and the serenity displayed by these representatives of the human mind, caught up in the sombre tragedy being played out here.'[25] *I who can testify*! In other words, I can testify to the fact that they were witnesses and not rhetoricians. In sum, if it is the capacity to be moved that characterizes the true witness, what guarantees the presence of this faculty is the emotion which the emotions of this witness arouse in another witness, in this case Séverine.

This is equally clear in the article of 18 September, which has the title 'Our own people!' Séverine establishes a frontier between 'them', or 'the others', who are insensitive and wordy, and 'us', or 'ours', that is, the witnesses moved by Dreyfus, such as, for example, Colonel Picquart. But what is it that guarantees the authenticity of their emotion? The emotion they arouse in the general public – 'it was the abnegation of Picquart, once again affirmed, which tugged at the heartstrings' – or, even more surprisingly, in the chief protagonist, Dreyfus, as in this passage in which Séverine watches Dreyfus watching Picquart:

> However, he [Picquart] got his reward; I saw him receive his wages.
>
> When he arrived, a fixed stare, high forehead, pale cheeks, with that way of walking I saw for the first time in the Cherche-Midi, during the travesty of a trial of Esterhazy, when he had walked to insults, to persecution – to glory – , I turned my eyes to look at Alfred Dreyfus.
>
> And suddenly (a miracle more touching than those of legend!) I saw in eyes glazed with pain, a flash of something ineffable, indefinable, an expression of relief and gratitude such as might be felt by a man being crucified for someone who would draw out the nails!

In other words, the emotion of one – 'pale cheeks' – arouses that of the other – 'eyes glazed with pain'.

The duplication, and hence the authentication, of one emotion by another does not stop there, if we read these lines closely. In fact, it seems necessary for this last emotion of Dreyfus itself to be authenticated. In the end, as in the previous example, the supreme witness, whose emotion is, as it were, the last word, is Séverine herself. It is she who *sees*, and is *touched* – 'a miracle more touching than those of legend!' – by the emotion of Dreyfus when he sees that of Picquart; it is she who feels in her flesh the emotion of a relieved and grateful Dreyfus. And we may note that this reality perceived by her senses is described as 'ineffable' and 'indefinable', a sign that she really is a perfect witness, who no longer says much, who is wholly given over to her feelings (even though it is she who is saying and writing all this . . .). In the last analysis, it is she who authenticates the other witnesses, she whose emotion allows her definitively to separate the 'heroes' from the traitors (the former arouse emotion, the latter do not), and it is she who is the body of bodies, arbiter of the other witnesses' emotion, according to the emotion they arouse in her.

Thus, the apologia for the witness, against the 'rhetoricians', finds its supreme justification in the affirmation of an ultimate witness, one who cannot be doubted, and whose body enables her to judge the value and authenticity of the other witnesses; if such-and-such a witness moves Séverine, it is because that witness is 'emotive' and so a true witness. It is she who knows if another witness is completely, or only partly, abandoned to passive feelings; she who decides what proportion of 'witness' there is in the speaker, or the real extent of the influence of emotion in a discourse. Séverine sees and feels if the others see and feel properly, that is, fully. We find a similarly high regard for the senses in her colleagues on *La Fronde*. Marguerite Durand, for example, in an article of 23 August, calls on her readers to 'watch' the witnesses produced by the prosecution; she evokes the scepticism they cannot fail to arouse in those who look at them with 'astonished eyes', the adjective evoking innocence, the position of the true and purely passive witness, without designs or preconceived opinions to influence their feelings:

> How terrifying to think that it is these men who were, who still are, in charge of the national defence. *Look at them.* They look as if they are all recruited according to a single model and with the aid of a single boss. Their individualities merge to the point of physical resemblance, so much so that they *make appear before the astonished gaze* a strange type, with receding forehead, vague gestures and hesitant words, all the external manifestations of a weak mind.[26]

It is all too obvious that they are monitoring and distorting their sensitive testimony as they speak. To the 'true' witness, the falsity of their testimony 'appears' without a shadow of doubt.

This mode of authentication, or of unmasking, clearly assumes that, as regards Séverine, there is no doubt; she herself can hardly be suspected of pernicious rhetoric, of controlling her emotions or of an insufficient surrender to passive feeling; she is the absolute witness, she is all *body*. But how can it be that Séverine feels no need to offer her readers any further justification of this certainty? So much implicitness surely demands some explanation, that is, some self-legitimation of the witness-ambassador before her public?

2. The body of the reporter

Woman-as-the-people

It is clear that the confident sensualism of Séverine is supported, in one article after another, obliquely, by a meticulous labour of self-legitimation.

Let us look, for example, at the article of 8 August, in which she paints a portrait of Dreyfus. It is the beginning of the trial, the perfect moment for justifying her role as journalist to the readers who will be her interlocutors for some weeks to come.

I see him clearly, I stare at him eagerly, as one does at an enigma; so Oedipus, on the road to Thebes, must have stared at the sharp-eyed Sphinx.

And this contemplation makes many things become understandable, and clear.

This is not the traditional, impassioned victim, whose protestations and vehemence would rouse the dead from their tombs. There is nothing of that externally: not the physiognomy, not the gestures, not the words! He is not ordinary enough to resort to them, he is disconcerting, disturbing: he is not at all pitiful! He does not have the voice of a cracked cello, the ingratiating gestures, the desolate or rebellious attitude which go with the role, which attract and compel ordinary compassion.

He is neat, precise, composed, master of himself, this convict, with an incredible strength of character and a disdain of play acting which *will deprive him of much easy sympathy and alienate, obviously, the mawkish.*

He is a graduate of the École Polytechnique, with everything that this implies, a cipher, a methodical and precise mind, a rational and disciplined being.

A soldier, too: full of respect for his leaders, of deference . . . I would almost say of regulation artlessness!

But for those who know how to see, for those who know how to penetrate to the very depths of the consciousness, what tragedy in this person of such apparent calm! *There are two signs of emotion which cannot deceive, because it is not in the power of the 'subject' to stop them or alter them:* the mechanical movement of the corner of the jaws, a sort of chewing which smothers a sob, and, at the nape of the neck, below the hair, a shudder like that of a horse stung by a horsefly.

This seemingly placid defendant holds back, suppresses, an unthinkable despair, a volume of pain which is beyond human endurance! His physical appearance is drab, his voice is flat – but his hair has turned white from so much indescribable suffering, and his eyes, behind the gleam of his pince-nez, are glazed with tears.

The first syllables he utters take the form of his perpetual cry: 'I am innocent! Colonel, I swear I am innocent!'

And I, *sentimentalist as I am, detaching myself from the usual melodramatic display,* am almost grateful to this wretched creature so unlike the innocents of the theatre; for raising the level of the debate and the significance of our actions by a dissimilarity which adds to our very intervention *intellectual disinterestedness.*

He is one of us only through the immensity of his misfortune, the inevitability of his ruin and the unleashing of so many passions – and interests! – conjured up to keep him in irons.[27]

So, there is ordinary seeing, and seeing by those 'who know how to see'. There are two sensibilities, in fact, one which reflects the singularity of the 'observer'(in this case a tendency to sentimentality: the 'sentimentalist'), hence fails to grasp the truth of what is seen, and one which goes beyond this singularity to achieve a sensitive, correct perception, a sort of universal sensibility. Yet this further step is far from obvious; 'sentimentalist as I am', admits Séverine, in an extremely rare reference to the possibility of an excess of sensibility, an unexpected appeal for moderation and 'intellectual disinterestedness' coming from an advocate of 'passion' and the 'furies'. But it is in order, ultimately, to reassure us: don't worry, she can 'detach herself from the usual melodramatic display', she is not ruled by too singular a sensibility, she is a true universal body. This text is an act of self-investiture.

But the self-legitimation does not stop there. In fact her most frequent method is to demonstrate a symbiosis between her and a people who recognize and mandate her, that is, who designate her as the universal body. This is the point of several articles on Rennes and the way the inhabitants welcomed Séverine and her friends. On 12 August, in an article with the title 'Good Homes', Séverine describes the hospitality received by those whom the anti-Dreyfusist Édouard Drumont had called 'the clique', to suggest that they formed a strange, closed circle. Séverine writes:

> Many stay in the homes of workers, the blue-collar families who threw open their doors . . . is it not moving, in its evangelical simplicity? It has been the custom among anarchists for many years. Events have extended it. In the coming together which was effected between the learned 'contemptibles' and the people, the former have learned from the fine, infectious hospitality of the latter.

In her description, we see an entire and numerous people welcoming and rallying round the 'old masters': 'And the old masters have descended on the houses of the former pupils, now masters in their turn; and friends previously unknown have found a place, like returning relatives, among the big books, in the peaceful home.' In her conclusion, Séverine gloats: 'So this is the "clique"? I've met no drunkards yet.' It was the people themselves that Drumont had insulted. And to show this made it possible to reverse the roles: the real 'clique' was Drumont and his friends.[28]

The way in which 'the people' recognize Séverine and her friends is presented in a particularly interesting way in the article of 4 September. Séverine seems to describe once again the symbiosis with the people of Rennes, but this time one senses that the ties had not been established from the beginning:

Feel the old Breton town, initially hostile (I do not speak, of course, of the gang of young scoundrels who will be sent after us, perhaps soon, but of the decent, sensible population, for whom the other is shame and terror), feel the easing of minds, which will soon spread to hearts. Looks have softened; stern faces relax into the beginnings of a smile; hands begin to be placed in our own outstretched hands . . .

What have we done for this to happen? Nothing.

Simply, they have seen that we are good sorts; that we wish no one ill; that we urge calm; that we pay what we owe without haggling. The coachmen and the delivery boys, all those who, as they go about their business, spread news, have been able to see, to hear and to tell that we are not monsters.

The persuasive power of this text lies in its presentation of this recognition as a change of heart; it had been far from assured; the people had been the first to accept the portrayal of the Dreyfusards as a 'clique'. But now, being true to their senses, it seems that they could not but recognize their own mistake – a mistake due to those 'rhetoricians', those manipulators of the people, those 'darkeners of the skies', as Séverine had called them elsewhere. Ultimately, truth had prevailed, forcing itself on the people, on their eyes, their ears and their senses in general, almost in spite of themselves. The marvellous power of sensitive passivity has frustrated the deceitful power of words.

It is this inevitable correction of popular judgement, this victory of feelings over words, which Séverine presents in the following anecdote:

Close to the former home of Labori, on the third day of my stay here, a good old woman, a huckster, was telling me of her troubles and how her house had burned down.

'It was a calamity: I was ruined! I don't think anyone started the fire on purpose. It's true, there was a Dreyfusard in the area . . . but all the same, I don't believe it.'

I said to her: 'I am a Dreyfusard.'

She almost dropped her basket. 'You, Madame, it's impossible. Not when you look so gentle.'

I stayed another five minutes, describing as simply as possible, so she would understand, the high ideal we serve.

Some distance away, when I had left her, I turned round.

She stood, immobile, in the same place, her eyes fixed on the ground, her hands folded across the front of her apron. A host of new ideas were milling round and round in her old brain, under that headdress of tulle.[29]

You could not but recognize them, then, 'our side', beneath the masks that 'they' had tried to make them wear – though you might emerge shaken from the discovery.

This theme of recognition by the people easily connects, in Séverine, with representations which display her femininity. The motif of the woman-people may well be one of the most powerful assets in her labour of self-legitimation. As a general rule, to evoke the people, their good sense and their 'obvious truths', Séverine often brings in a woman or some women, as in the anecdote above. In her article of 27 August, the voice of good sense and of courage is put in the mouth of the fiancée of the witness Freystaetter; Séverine recalls the risks run by those soldiers who testify in Dreyfus's favour:

> A future, promotion, favours, they would have sacrificed them all to . . . the fulfilment of a task which seemed incompatible with their profession.
> And I think with tender pride that a woman, a young woman, was behind the determination of Captain Freystaetter; that his fiancée replied to those who pointed out the risks of such an attitude: 'Better more glory and fewer stripes!'[30]

To this woman, this young woman, this priority seems obvious. She is the voice of common sense and fairness. Already, during the trial of Zola, in *La Fronde*, Séverine had taken care to note the clamour of the women in favour of the accused man: 'Around us', she had written on 9 February 1898, 'women of every rank, elegant or ordinary, braving the danger, carried away by their enthusiasm for justice, cried: "Long live Zola!" '[31]

This feminine good sense, that is, this sense of what is fair, is something that Séverine clearly believes she herself possesses. On 21 August 1899, discussing the violent demonstrations fomented in Paris by the 'rhetoricians', she explains that she had chosen to remain silent for a week so as not to add more blood to that which words had already caused to flow. And her wise and quiet disposition, contrasted with the verbal excesses of her Parisian colleagues, is clearly credited to her femininity – she also attributes it to the all-female editorship of *La Fronde*: 'From what goes before, you will fully understand', she writes, 'that I am not in the mood for irony. Any extravagance or any folly which might give rise to a massacre is hardly likely to cause laughter in women, from whichever side the blood flows.'[32]

There is a sort of female propensity, Séverine suggests, to be more witness than rhetorician, and this is what makes women the natural ambassadors of the people. We see, in fact, the transformation into an asset of what she herself has constantly referred to as a serious handicap in the journalistic circles of her day, that is, her femininity. Already, in a piece written in 1894, Séverine had noted her marginality with regard to the journalistic profession, due to her gender – she was not allowed, for example, to join the press gallery at the National Assembly; but it had enabled her to practise journalism 'differently' from her male colleagues, that is, to go beyond the old wordy, isolated, 'deaf and blind' journalism and seek 'new horizons', both more sensitive and more unifying, in short, closer to the people: 'Being a woman', she wrote:

> I never went to the Press gallery, a change of milieu which allowed me to start afresh; to escape the 'profession', escape its traditions, its customs, its preconceived judgements, its bias of denigration or praise, and everything that makes the journalist who is supposed to 'enlighten opinion' isolated, deaf, blind – not dumb, alas! – and imprisoned in his profession like Robinson Crusoe on his island, if he never, once in a while, escapes, plunges into the crowd or goes out in search of new horizons.[33]

Thus, Séverine turns into a tool for 'unifying' the very femininity which might appear – and appeared to her colleagues – as 'singularizing'. She turns feminine identity into an advantage in making contact with the community, because she sees it as a privileged proximity to the body, a firm anchorage in the sensibilities. If we reread in this light the article on the attack on Labori, discussed above, we may read something different into the name, *Séverine*, spoken by the lawyer from his stretcher: it is above all to a *woman* that he speaks, he, the wounded body, the person assaulted in his flesh; it is to *her* that he says that he recognizes her from among the others, as if they both shared the same battle by their nature, *as close as possible to the body*, in a way. And their exchange is certainly in marked contrast to the jokes in poor taste of the jesters and the rhetoricians, far away, *far from the body* in both senses of the phrase: far from their own bodies, because they had not 'felt' the assault, they had not been there, they had only spoken about it; but also far from the suffering body of the victim. And Séverine reproduces the song published by the *Libre Parole*, a song based on a not very subtle play on words – arsehole and bullet hole – about the body.[34]

The theme of the woman-people in the writings of Séverine is an obvious echo of a theme dear to her master, Jules Vallès, who frequently represented the people in the guise of a woman. The street, which was at the heart of his political imagination during his years on *Le Figaro*, was feminine, as one of the great specialists on his journalistic writing, Roger Bellet, emphasizes:

> The street is feminine in its songs and in its most fragile characters; in its toilettes; in its demimondaines; among them, what country beauties! Plain Janes from the provinces now the Fifis of the bars and dance-halls or choosy Ladies of the Camellias who scorn violets but are frantic for red camellias or the blue dahlia; the romance of passion, which always obsessed

Vallès, whether it comes from history, literature, the news or memories. The spirit of Emma [Bovary] is everywhere; Parisian adultery, an obsession, is in the air; in sum, a diffuse, profound femininity.[35]

Bellet recalls that, in Vallès, this feminization of the people relates to representations of the people as *suffering* rather than *fighting*. He notes the influence of Victor Hugo, but above all that of the popular novels of Eugène Sue; and he emphasizes that such a representation is not without a touch of bourgeois sentimentality:

> Vallès also long retained the image of a persecuted, immortal, ageless and wandering People, often conveyed in the nineteenth century by the mythology of the wandering Jew: it had marked the images of Épinal; even more, the 'popular' novels of Eugène Sue had encouraged this equation of Ahasuerus and the People, persecuted in its two personifications, the woman and the worker.[36]

Bellet also claims that 'femininity, or rather a certain very conventional and very bourgeois ideology of femininity, would long prevent Vallès from understanding revolutionary woman, insurgent woman, or simply the citizen woman'.[37]

However that may be, we find in Séverine a similar representation of femininity as closeness to the body, hence, in particular, to suffering, and so to the people. Her work of 1894, mentioned above, continued with an observation to the effect that all these male parliamentarians, beside whom she was unable to sit, 'are afraid of the people'. The deputies, she wrote, 'have a fear, an irrational, unconscious – but how proper! – fear of the people seeing what goes on inside, attending their debates, weighing them up . . . and judging them!'[38] Conversely, she called her own closeness to the public – 'the good public' – a 'sort of strange coquetry', a phrase in which one cannot but see an allusion to her femininity.[39] In an earlier article devoted to Paul Lafargue, she had defended, against the 'politicians', but also against the left of Jules Guesde with which she had quarrelled after Vallès' death, a less intellectual, and hence less domineering and disdainful, representation of the people. She wanted to find, in contrast to the male actors of politics and journalism, the suffering body which Vallès had made central to his imagery:

> They are disdainful of the people, these politicians, to an unimaginable degree; of the people, with their simple intellects and their warm hearts. They regard them simply as the instrument conferring supreme power on whoever can manipulate them: the people-as-means, and not the people-as-goal; the people-as-caryatid[40] of the statue of Karl Marx – the levels of

their distress are, under their implacable boots, the steps which give access to Parliament![41]

The memory of Vallès was central to the quarrels between Séverine and the supporters of Guesde within the editorial board of the *Cri du Peuple*: 'I am truly weary, and request a few weeks' holiday', she wrote on 31 January 1887; 'I take away with me the name of Vallès . . . I have taken charge of his memory and do not feel I have the right to entrust it to anyone.' But in this quarrel between heirs, it is clear that it is two representations of the people that are really at issue, as we see, for example, in the articles by both sides at the time of the anarchist attacks, in particular that of Auguste Vaillant against the National Assembly in December 1893. On 10 December 1893, Jules Guesde wrote, in *Le Journal*, that 'violence is in all circumstances odious'; whereas Séverine, as in the Duval affair a few years earlier, seemed almost to identify with the suffering people – 'the poor' – that is, an unconditional and, above all, a more carnal than intellectual solidarity: 'With the poor, always – in spite of their errors, in spite of their faults, in spite of their crimes!'[42]

Few would dispute that Séverine is here the true heir of Vallès. But it must also be understood that this heritage did not consist only of a few literary and political themes found, here and there, in the course of her writing; it was a profound and complex meditation on the political meaning of the business of journalism that Vallès transmitted to Séverine. Let us return briefly to this heritage, to which Séverine remained faithful, but which she also extended and enriched.

The heritage of Jules Vallès

'The little that I know, the little that I am, my never-forgotten Master, I owe to you. You taught me to see, to hear and to think – and above all to sympathize with the terrible hardships of the poor.' It is with these words that Séverine pays tribute to Jules Vallès at the beginning of her collection, *Pages Rouges*, in 1893. It is more difficult to define the relationship which bound Vallès to Séverine, although one (rather obvious) interpretation springs spontaneously to mind, in which the emphasis would be on the surely fascinating ambivalence of this young woman for Vallès. For a man who liked to see in even the most bourgeois or 'Bovaryenne' femininity a historical proximity to suffering – taking account of the fate reserved to bourgeois women in the nineteenth century – and hence to the people, this young woman from a bourgeois background, driven by painful experience to mount a radical challenge to the values and practices of her milieu, undoubtedly had a special charm.[43]

Vallès pays tribute to Séverine in 1883, at the beginning of *La Rue à Londres*, in these words:

> My dear child, I dedicate this book to you, not as an act of commonplace gallantry, but as a mark of sincere gratitude. You have helped me to see London clearly, you have helped me to convey its horror and its desolation. Born to good fortune in the Boulevard Gand – scion of the aristocracy, flower of the fusillade – you gallantly deserted to enter, on my arm, the camp of the poor, unafraid of dirtying your lace by contact with their rags, unconcerned by any bourgeois 'what will people say'. *Honni soit qui mal y pense*! as the motto of old Albion goes. You have made to my life the gift of a little of your grace and your youth, you have made to my work the offering of the best part of your mind and your heart. It is therefore a debt my grey hairs pay to your blonde locks, friend in whom I have found both the affection of a daughter and the ardour of a disciple.

The next passage brings out even more strongly, by the choice of metaphor, this ambivalence of Séverine: she was a 'bouquet of roses' in exile among 'poor women' (this feminizing is very typical of Vallès):

> Do you remember how, one day, in front of a workhouse, we saw a few blood-red roses nailed to the worm-eaten door, who knows who by or what for? This tiny fragment of nature, this foretaste of spring, brought a wan smile and a gleam of hope to the dead faces of the poor women who were waiting their turn. It gave renewed courage to us, too, and we crossed the threshold of that hellhole less sadly. At the beginning of my book, in which several chapters are, like 'The Refuge', full of sadness and misery, I want to place your name like a bouquet.[44]

It is clear from this tribute that Vallès recognized in Séverine a true sensibility, exceptional in its universality for someone born into the privileged enclave of the bourgeoisie. And this true sensibility was exactly what Séverine learned from Vallès, the model before whom she presented herself, at the time of their correspondence, as a humble disciple, distressed that she 'feels badly' – we find here, a few years earlier, the dread of being only a 'sentimentalist', subject to her body, certainly, but a very particular body, incapable of truly acceding to sensitive universality. Vallès, for his part, knows how to 'feel'; she is only the ignorant pupil who has everything to learn of this strange knowledge; or at least this is how she portrays herself in the correspondence. It is he, undeniably, who is the universal body, neither blasé – an indifferent, insensitive rhetorician – nor sentimental – tied to an ordinary sensibility, not sufficiently universal, not yet 'proper'. This is clear, for example, in a letter of 25 December 1882: 'You who have lived through the civil war, who have seen blood running in the gutters and heads split open like ripe pomegranates,' she writes, 'you cannot feel the great individual pity which shakes me to the core, I who am ignorant, who know nothing, who have no memories of slaughter.'[45]

It seems, in short, that Vallès had long been the model for the 'true' witness she claims to be at the time of the trial of Dreyfus, this pure body that is content to *feel* without seeking to produce a deliberate discourse, and which is therefore able to reach a unifying universality beyond the singular voices of the rhetoricians. It is a model in which we find the paradoxical dimension already noted: it is a demanding ideal, and difficult to attain, although it consists of no more than a surrender to the sensations, innocently and passively, far from any wordy and singular will.

In fact, Vallès wanted to achieve a *concrete, sensitive* writing which would be, as a result, truly *collective* and *unifying*. And journalism seemed to him to be a way of achieving this access to the 'concrete', this seizing of 'life', causing the 'I' who writes to lose his inevitable isolation and merging him, in a sense, into the community. As with Séverine some years later, Vallès had two closely linked and interconnected aims in his journalism: to touch reality and merge with the people; and to produce a lively style and a unifying text, as if without an author, written by a wholly collective 'I', pure ambassador of the people. In this sense, journalism should lead to what Vallès called 'liberation from ink', which he conceived as the emergence of a language that was at last affective and, above all, visual; a language full of *images*, because images would enable words, in his phrase, to 'return to life'. We find here, at the centre of the Vallèsian universe, the idea of *seeing* as more unifying than *saying*, because closer to life. Significantly, when Vallès mocked hollow French eloquence, he identified in it an inability to *see*, and hence to make contact with the crowd: 'Everyone', he wrote in 1865, 'deliberately puts their hand between the light and the crowd. They carry their convictions not like a torch, but like a muffled lantern.'[46] Whereas what was needed, in his eyes, was, in the words of Bellet, 'to abolish writing; not to write, but to make see; not to trace signs, but to create images: "to paint life without embellishments in the same way that Sieyès asked for Death without fine phrases"'.[47]

If Vallès pinned his hopes on a revolution in journalistic writing, it was because he believed that the ink of the 'Book', that object become institution which isolates its author, had become terminally dry. He was conscious, by contrast, of the way in which journalism is written – in the midst of life, in the present – and is received – also with an immediacy which prevents the text from congealing and the ink from drying. For Vallès, reading journalism 'transforms writing into life, ink into blood; the newspaper creates a new collective life'.[48] The iconoclastic journalist then joins, in the Vallèsian universe, marginal and rebellious figures like the street acrobat. Laughter, discontinuity and disorder: the sphere of the street acrobat is described with a vocabulary that is similar to that he uses to evoke the sphere of journalism, which ultimately leads back to the street.[49]

The main issue is always the street, which crystallizes all the great Vallèsian themes: the concrete, life, the collectivity, the present. It gave its name to several of his articles, then to his collection of 1866, and finally to his newspaper, *La Rue* (*The Street*), founded in 1867, and which subsequently experienced many deaths and rebirths. In an article of 1879, 'The Boulevardiers', which appeared in his third *La Rue*, Vallès described the birth of journalism as what had enabled the boulevard to enjoy 'its glory days'.[50] But they did not last; the boulevard, that is, the street of yesterday, was now policed and embourgeoisified; the street had moved away and set up elsewhere, now threatening the bourgeoisie of the boulevard just as the bourgeoisie of yesterday, from its boulevard, had threatened the Tuileries. Vallès thought that this displacement of the street, that is, of the 'true' street, ought to carry journalism along in its wake. Already in the 1860s, when he was editor of *Le Figaro*, he had been attracted by the more popular press.[51] More generally, he never ceased throughout his life to measure journalism by the yardstick of this 'passion', this desire and this ability to encounter the street. When, for example, in 1876, in spite of some scepticism, he was considering contributing to the paper of Naquet, *La Révolution*, it was in these terms that he expressed his doubts: 'The People will not read *La Révolution*. Naquet seems to me to be brave, methodical and honest, but he has neither the sacred fire nor the cursed flame of journalism.'[52]

The model of the newspaper-street is, of course, *Le Cri du Peuple*, which, according to Vallès, was its closest approximation. At that time, under the Commune, Vallès seemed to have attained his goal and fulfilled all the hopes he had pinned on journalistic writing. *Le Cri du Peuple* offered, not least in its title, multiple versions of the theme of the unified people, united at last in one great body (able, therefore, to 'cry' with a single voice). Significantly, he decided that the articles in *Le Cri du Peuple* would no longer be signed, as if to mark the emergence of a genuinely collective writing. A few years later, in an article for the new *Cri du Peuple*, he referred to this collective writing as follows:

> We had to ascribe to the people a language both simple and grand. Before history, they spoke, in the most terrible of storms, under enemy fire. We had to think of the Fatherland as well as the Revolution . . . we needed a phrase, only one, but it had to be one in which the heart of the People beat; we needed a word, also, to take a stand in the future.[53]

For Vallès, *Le Cri du Peuple* had truly reconciled ink and blood. At last, the street seemed to write and to write alone, unified and incarnated in the newspaper.

It is clear that this Vallèsian conception of journalism permeates the figure of the witness-ambassador as we have traced it in the writing of Séverine. The same desire for a heroic merging of the journalist into the people can be seen in her reporting. This raises the question of whether it is purely by chance that our archetype of the witness-ambassador came from the ranks of anarchism. Probably not; the fact that certain anarchist representations help us to understand modern journalism should come as no surprise when we remember that this journalism, as we saw in chapter 1, is rooted in the desire to create a 'we' beyond official representations of this 'we', and consequently to create space for a counter-power. Modern journalism naturally intersects with anarchist themes, just as anarchism – as the work of Vallès testifies with such distinction – confronts the question of journalism, grasping that it is a crucial issue.

Séverine, however, is more than just an heiress. She goes further than Vallès in defining what unifies, what constitutes the 'we'. In Vallès, the question of the 'centre' remained problematic: what exactly was the quality that enabled the writer-journalist to get access to the unifying 'concrete'? What was the lever, the focus of the unification? Séverine, however, explains this centre: it is the body of the journalist. It is Séverine's confidence in the senses, her sensualism, that enables her to be the fully formed figure of the witness-ambassador, perfectly coherent and clear, and in this way archetypal. Vallès did not take his ideas on the body as focus of a collective experience so far. The theme appears in his work at the end of his life, which is a period when he and Séverine were in frequent contact. For example, in an article from this period, in order to criticize opportunist republicans, forgetful of the heritage of the Commune, Vallès evoked as a counterpoint the heroes who had suffered *in their flesh*, and who were thus the authentic voice of the people, 'those who paved with their bodies the path which now takes the victorious opportunists to the Capitol'.[54] But it can be argued that his political thinking on the meaning of journalism was extended, in the sensualism of Séverine, in a way only hinted at in his own work.

Séverine makes it possible, therefore, to define the nature of the link which binds the journalist – the true and good journalist – to the people. It is more than a link of representation, more than a simple mandate. The body of the journalist, and in particular her own, when it is she who writes, is truly that of the people 'in miniature'. Séverine *resembles* the people as well as *representing* them; in this sense, she can be said to *embody* them; she is the people in person, and she enables them, therefore, to go where they had never gone and to have a sensory experience through her own body. The writing of Séverine is certainly indebted to several Vallèsian themes, such as that of the woman-as-the-people, but the radical sensualism in which all these themes take their place gives a new dimension to the Vallèsian figure of the unifying journalist, while demonstrating, in archetypal fashion, a fundamental act of modern journalism.

3. Unifying by orchestrating a conflict

Can we go further in our examination of this unifying process, as it is performed by Séverine in her writing? Should we see it as the negation of everything which, within the people, produces conflict, and as the creation of a *commonality* beyond the differences? Not at all; both Vallès and Séverine offer something much less simple, which is what gives the figure of the witness-ambassador its complexity.

Vallès never regarded the newspaper-street, the unifying newspaper, as something that *became established*. With every article, with every stroke of the pen, you had to begin again and win over the street. It is significant that during the Commune, hour of glory of the *Cri du People*, Vallès was strongly opposed to the restoration of censorship against other newspapers. Most notably, he defended his old newspaper, *Le Figaro*, when it fell foul of the censors: 'I wrote long ago, and I repeat today, that I am in favour of total and unlimited freedom of the press. I deeply regret, therefore, that *Le Gaulois* and *Le Figaro* have been prevented from appearing, even if it means they continue to laugh at our principles and call us pillagers! Freedom has no borders.'[55] Which would seem to mean: no press can ever institute itself as the definitive representative of the street.

It is as if to assert yourself as newspaper-street you needed enemies against which to fight; there is a world of difference between claiming something and instituting yourself as that something. *Le Cri du People* needed the laughter of *Le Gaulois* and *Le Figaro* so that it could claim that its own 'laughter' – and we should remember that 'laughter' was, in Vallès, a metaphor for the street, hence for the 'ideal' newspaper – was more unifying, the laughter that came from the belly of the People, from its flesh. We can then see the Vallèsian conception of journalism as an example of a desire to unify through and in permanent conflict. The body (of the People) is *always fighting*, even in its claim to be a *body*.

We find a similar conception of journalism in Séverine; indeed, the fact that she describes the centre, the focus of the unification, that is, the *body of the journalist*, even more precisely than Vallès enables her to go even further in representing unification as *conflictual unification*. It enables her to show this fighting body. In fact the body of the reporter always, in Séverine, affirms itself in the experience of struggle: the witness emerges *against* the rhetoricians, and never ceases, in affirming herself, to fight these enemies whose words are 'hollow', and yet so powerful. The body of the witness-ambassador reveals the world in all its materiality to its readers, it offers full proof, and yet it is constantly being called on to justify itself against the 'darkeners of the sky'. It is noticeable that it is extremely rare for the 'I' or 'we' in the writing of Séverine to appear without the counterpoint of a 'you' or 'them'. The construction of the 'we' is closely connected to a debate about frontiers, itself the expression of a never-resolved conflict. It is not that 'their' criteria and 'our' criteria are of equal value; 'ours', that is, feelings, are the only ones that count. But 'they' remain, in spite of this obvious truth.

It seems, therefore, that the explicit nature of the centre in Séverine – her body – also makes this conflictual dimension, inherent in this centre, particularly explicit. For Séverine, what unifies, what is 'obvious', is posed in a radical manner and never questioned; there is no real debate about this trust in the senses that underlies the writing. In contrast, however, because the proof is total, the hostility to those who do not recognize it, who continue to close their eyes to it, is also total; in Séverine, frontiers are *flaws*. The centre is obvious, and this determines the battle that is fought around it; it is a battle both simple ('them' and 'us') and total ('them' and 'us'). The conflict is exclusive, therefore, in the primary meaning of the word: it *excludes* 'them', those who no longer have anything in common with 'us', and who yet remain there, barring access to the centre and making it necessary for 'us' to go on defining ourselves in relation to them.

This conflict is neither co-operative nor multi-dimensional. And this is also its limitation: the exclusive conflict is, in the last analysis, a fairly simple, contained, ordered and predictable conflict. 'We' exclude 'them' without truly confronting 'their' values. 'We' are *put to the test*, but not threatened in our profound identity, not damaged, not undone. In other words, if the act of unifying allows a conflict to be expressed, it is a conflict which never questions the very existence of a centre; this centre remains obvious in spite of the obstacles it encounters in affirming itself, in spite of its lack of peace, and in spite of the endless tests it undergoes before it can prevail. The very idea of a centre is never questioned; there is a centre, and what is needed is to fight those who try to obscure it. The fight, in consequence, remains 'centred', it retains an organizing centre, and it does not lead to complete decentring. This is the crucial difference between the unifying journalisms, discussed here through the archetypal figure of Séverine, and the decentring journalisms, which we will discuss later, and in which the conception of the conflict operating is much more radical, and also much more dangerous for 'us'.

Nevertheless, as we have seen, the unifying journalisms are not complete strangers to conflict, even if the conflict is limited – it might even be said orchestrated – by a witness-ambassador whose ultimate aim is to reaffirm the centre. The figure of the witness-ambassador frequently bases its unifying method on a conflict it reveals and portrays: it constitutes or reconstitutes the 'we' by testing it and by confronting it with a 'them'. The witness-ambassador cannot be said, therefore, to *institute* the centre, because it makes it a place that is perpetually endangered, in fact inadequately instituted and in need of permanent reaffirmation. The witness-ambassador assumes this role of 're-centring' the political community against a backdrop of never-ending struggle.

3

Unifying through a Test:
Nellie Bly, Albert Londres and Edward R. Murrow

If we are to take our examination of unifying journalisms further, one question above all needs to addressed. How, in practice, do the journalists who are witness-ambassadors, in their gaze and in their writing, impose a test on the public they unify, on this 'we' they institute? Séverine has shown us how the struggle, or conflict, can be incorporated into the act of unifying. This conflict still needs to be described more fully, however, and we need to ask if it can take more than one form. In short, can the figure of the witness-ambassador, who offers a way in to a reading of the history of modern journalism, include what would be called, in the language of music, variations?

Obviously, we cannot hope to be exhaustive. But the process of defining figures can be taken further and will help us to come to a better understanding of this act of unifying, and so provide a few additional markers for travellers at sea in the immensity of modern journalism.

I propose here to present three witness-ambassadors who each, in their own way, put this 'we' to the test so as to help it to experience itself as a 'we'. The first is a reporter, Nellie Bly (1864–1922), who was close to Joseph Pulitzer and his *New York World*, in which, in 1887, she published a report on the psychiatric hospital for women on Blackwell's Island; it is this text that I will examine in some detail. The second is Albert Londres (1884–1932), a mythic figure in French journalism, though actually little studied; I will focus on three of his reportages from the 1920s: *Au Bagne* (*In the Penal Colony*), *Chez les Fous* (*In the Madhouse*) and *Terre d'Ebène* (*Ebony Land*). The third is a superstar of American journalism, Edward R. Murrow (1908–1965), who spent most of his career at CBS, where he experienced the transition from radio to television – he first became known to a wider public as London correspondent during the Second World War. For many years Murrow presented the television programme 'See It Now', prepared in collaboration with

Fred W. Friendly, a programme that played a large part in the downfall of Senator Joseph McCarthy, by broadcasting, in 1953–4, three documentaries which remain jewels of television journalism; it is these three programmes that I will discuss.

My study of these journalistic documents will not take account of their impact on the public or their social and political consequences. To do this would mean considering factors other than the 'effectiveness' of the reportage itself. The penal colony of Cayenne, for example, was closed after the reportage of Albert Londres, but the proof that other factors would have to be taken into account is that this went beyond the demands of the reporter: in the letter to the Minister for the Colonies which concluded his report, Londres asked not for the closure but the reform of the penal settlement. Similarly, the fall of McCarthy was certainly facilitated or even precipitated by the documentaries of Edward R. Murrow and Fred W. Friendly, but it clearly had other causes. And although Nellie Bly prided herself on the fact that her reportage ('on the strength of my story')[1] had persuaded the town to free an additional million dollars for the Blackwell's Island hospital, the reality was once again less simple: a budgetary rethink seems to have been under way even before her reports appeared, though it was no doubt confirmed as a consequence of the embarrassing publicity she gave to the hospital.[2]

It is clear that to venture into the territory of 'real effects' would raise many other questions, which go far beyond my concern here, which is to study the documents themselves, the type of journalistic approach expressed in them, and the relationship the journalists build with their imaginary public.

1. Nellie Bly or the test of the hidden

Stunt journalism

Nellie Bly (1864–1922) is very representative of a type of popular reporting in the United States, in the late nineteenth century, that used a range of stratagems to penetrate large institutions and reveal their hidden face, and for which the expression 'stunt journalism' was invented. Stunt journalism was part of what was called, more generally, 'exposure journalism' or the 'literature of exposure'; it set out to make visible, and 'expose' to the general view, what more often remained hidden away in well-protected centres of power, and to use any means to this end, even the most unexpected and dangerous.[3] In the 1880s and 1890s, many women reporters disguised themselves so that they could enter institutions about which little was known; they were often called 'stunt girls' or, as they tended to come up with notably tear-jerking reportages, 'sob sisters'. W. R. Hearst, for example, when he ran the *San Francisco Examiner* (before famously founding the *New York Journal* in 1896), sent one of these reporters to investigate the scandals in the town's public hospital. This reporter, Winifred Black, became for the purpose 'Annie Laurie', and pretended to faint in the street so as to get herself admitted to the hospital as a patient. Soon after, she told what she had seen 'inside'.

It should not be forgotten that it is these 'scandal sheets' that enabled the most rigorous investigative journalism to take its first steps. It is generally accepted by the experts that the stunt girls and other exponents of the exposure journalism published in the yellow press in the second half of the nineteenth century were the ancestors of a movement which is usually treated with far more respect, and which flourished in the first decade of the twentieth century: that is, muckraking.[4] It was the great owners of the popular press in the 1880s, such as Joseph Pulitzer, who bought the *New York World* in 1883, who were the real inventors of muckraking.[5]

This popular press made constant use of the figure of the witness-ambassador. In stunt journalism it was even taken to the point of caricature: the journalists invited their public to accompany them on a veritable journey into the innermost depths of an obscure place; they made them live by proxy a totally new experience; they gave them eyes to see where seeing seemed forbidden and, as they did so, presented themselves as the public's impeccable ambassadors. They freely manipulated the discourse of 'truth', which was understood as that which must be dragged out from obscurity, exposed to the full light of day, in fact made to 'shine for all', as the heading of the *New York Sun* famously proclaimed.[6] Unifying the public in contemplation of what had at last been brought out into the open was what stunt journalism was all about.

Inevitably, this had implications for the type of 'scandal' revealed: because it had to unify, this scandal had to conform to the canons of 'common sense', that is, not only be revealed according to generally accepted norms of truth, but also fall within a *common* conception of right and wrong. Some would say that it must always refer to something 'consensual'. This may be so, but the interest of this type of journalism lies in the fact that, precisely because it dealt in scandal, it still exposed a conflict at the very heart of the process of unifying. What was revealed to us, and united us, also questioned this 'us', cross-examined it and enlisted it to fight for what it was. The 'us' was appealed to and tested, not simply constituted. The gaze of the journalist indicated a sort of unexpected enemy, an intruder lodged within this 'us', which this 'us' had to fight if it was to measure up to what it wanted to be and had believed itself to be before the reporter had 'raked' all this 'muck' within it.

It remains to establish, of course, exactly what sort of conflict is operating within this type of journalism. It is certainly a fairly 'simple' one, as the example of the writing of Nellie Bly will show: a conflict that presents the 'we', centred or re-centred by the reporter (focus of unification), and a 'them', excluded but still very much there, at the very centre (a 'them' revealed by the journalist, and at last identified as such). Nevertheless, it is a conflict, and it is imbricated into the act of unifying; it makes it possible, is even its basis. This test which the journalist here makes 'us' undergo is *the test of the hidden*: it shows 'us' that there, where one never goes, there is a hidden and unsuspected 'them' which thinks it is 'us', when in fact it is nothing of the sort. The test of the hidden consists in showing that, in places usually concealed from view, it is necessary to reconquer a centre in danger.

Nellie Bly was probably the first 'stunt girl' in the history of American journalism, preceding Annie Laurie by several years.[7] Born in 1864,[8] Elizabeth Cochrane started her career on the *Pittsburgh Dispatch* in January 1885. It was then that she became Nellie Bly, a pseudonym suggested by the managing editor, George A. Madden, alluding to the heroine of a popular song of the day. It was also on the advice of Madden that she specialized in reporting 'the woman's sphere'. In particular, she wrote an article on the factory girls of Pittsburgh. In December 1885, she left Pittsburgh to become a free-lance journalist, travelling to Mexico; then, in May 1887, she went to New York. She tried everything to make a career in New York journalism. She managed to get taken on by the *New York World* of Joseph Pulitzer, in September 1887, on the basis of an idea which won over the managing editor of the newspaper, John Cockerill: she would pass herself off as a mentally ill woman by the name of Nellie Bly in order to penetrate the Women's Lunatic Asylum on Blackwell's Island.

Rumours were already circulating about the terrible conditions in which the patients in this hospital were kept. Two editorials in the *New York World* of 3 and 9 July 1887 had repeated these rumours. The place was in any case legendary for the air of mystery it exuded. This strip of land in the East River was exactly the sort of 'hidden' place about which nothing was known and around which fantasies bred. Charles Dickens had mentioned it in his *American Notes*, admitting that he had been there without really penetrating the place or its mystery. He offers a few brief descriptions of its strange 'madhouse air', passes quickly over the question of the degree of comfort or discomfort existing there (he says only, 'I cannot say that I derived much comfort from the inspection of this charity'), and simply expresses his surprise that the management of such a place was not entrusted to specialists but was subject to the vagaries of political appointment.[9]

For the purposes of her report, Nellie Bly first went to a hostel for working girls, where her strange behaviour got her taken by the warden before Judge Patrick G. Duffy; when all efforts to establish the identity of this confused young woman failed, she was sent to the Bellevue Hospital, then to Blackwell's Island, where she remained for ten days, until she was 'rescued' by the newspaper. She then published two articles in October 1887 in the *New York World*, followed, two months later, by a book with the title *Ten Days in a Mad-House or Nellie Bly's Experience on Blackwell's Island*.[10]

Nellie Bly's method, as it emerges in her writing and as she presents it herself, consisted of exposing what was hidden and shedding light on a shadowy corner, which led her to define two very distinct worlds: that of the patients, who are 'like us', and who arouse our pity and our sympathy; and that of the medical personnel, who torture, violate and despise the patients. On the one hand, there is a 'we' who recognize ourselves in (project ourselves into?) 'them', these very human patients, whose madness is not, in the end, so very strange or foreign; on the other, there are the real and terrifying 'others'. The shedding of light is then conceived as the source not only of a unification (we are there, in this hospital, alongside these patients who are so very 'us') but also of a conflict (through them, who belong to 'us', we confront 'others'). The conflict is a very simple one, certainly, appearing, as it does, in the form of an 'us–them' frontier. But it is intrinsically linked to the unifying process. In other words, the hidden reveals *us*, but reveals us *in conflict*.

This labour of revelation which the journalist performs has implications which need to be emphasized, and which also give this type of reportage a 'simplistic' character: the hidden is entirely exposed, the light shed is total, thanks to the journalist. In other words, the way in which the exposure is envisaged, with its power to reveal a conflict, and hence to reconstitute the 'we', means no vestige of strangeness can be allowed to remain. It leads to an understanding which claims to be perfect and total and eventually culminates in the contemplation of two clear and distinct worlds: 'ours' and 'theirs', the latter designated as an enemy. There are no grey areas, no strangeness that cannot be categorized (neither 'us' nor 'them'); everything that was hidden eventually becomes clear and is added to the 'simple' categories of identity and alterity-adversity.

It is this one episode in the itinerary of Nellie Bly that I will discuss here. Nevertheless, a few details about her subsequent career may help us to understand what sort of person she was in the process of becoming through her writing about Blackwell's Island. This reportage brought her instant fame, which she exploited and further enhanced a few months later. First she repeated her technique, getting herself hired as a domestic servant, for example, to reveal the practices current in the recruiting agencies for domestic help:[11] in fact, the *New York World* generalized the technique, taking on other stunt girls and training existing staff in the method.[12] Then, in the autumn of 1888, Nellie Bly was sent by the *New York World* on a world tour that was to be followed on a daily basis by the paper's readers. There is perhaps no better illustration of the figure of the witness-ambassador, with all its weaknesses, such as an undeniably superficial gaze at the countries visited; her journey resembled nothing so much as a race in which the chief focus of interest was Nellie Bly herself. The idea was, explicitly, to break the record of Phileas Fogg – in fact she met Jules Verne when she was in France. She returned on 25 January 1890, that is, after 72 days, 6 hours, 11 minutes and 14 seconds, to be welcomed by a crowd of admirers; she had become a celebrity.[13] In 1895, soon after writing a report on the strike of Chicago railway workers in May 1894, she abandoned journalism to marry a businessman. On her husband's death, she tried her hand at business, but with far less success than journalism, and came close to ruin; in the final years of her life, therefore, she returned to journalism, but without ever recapturing the success of her early career.[14]

Making us see what is hidden and making us see ourselves

The writing of Nellie Bly in her reportage on the Blackwell's Island asylum was directed towards two goals: to reveal the hidden, and to reveal those who were present at this disclosure ('us'). We may speak, therefore, of a twofold revelation, consisting both of *making us see something* and of *making us see ourselves*.

First, she aimed to make us see this *some thing*: to bring it out from concealment and put it on display. The first pages of her book are full of a discourse on 'truth', a discourse which derives from a more or less explicit trust in the senses, similar to, but much less developed than, that of Séverine – this is why Séverine and her representation of the body in her writing have served as my archetype, enabling us to see with special clarity something that is implicit in much of the reportage of the late nineteenth century. Nellie Bly assures her readers that she will write only of what she has seen and felt, but she explains that these feelings will not in any sense be singular, because she will avoid any 'sensational' excess and remain faithful to her role as ambassador for the sensibility of the public. She cleverly puts these preliminaries into the mouth of her editor:

> I was to chronicle faithfully the experiences I underwent, and when once within the walls of the asylum, to find out and describe its inside workings,

which are always so effectually hidden by white-capped nurses, as well as by bolts and bars, from the public. 'We do not ask you to go there for the purpose of making sensational revelations. Write up things as you find them, good or bad; give praise or blame as you think best, and the truth all the time.'[15]

The 'workings' which this text reveals are all characteristic of the figure of the witness-ambassador. Her ability to tell the 'truth' is linked to her privileged relationship with the public. Further, the figure is here presented in a totally 'sensualist' version, as in Séverine; that is, her eyes and her senses in general are presented not only as faithful reporters, but as excellent *evaluators*: see *and judge*, the editor tells Nellie Bly – with the implication 'because you are the public'. The need to distinguish between observation and interpretation (or judgement) is never referred to, because, as with Séverine, all emotion felt by a witness so thoroughly 'legitimated' is regarded as correct or truthful. It is the way to achieve an 'unvarnished' narrative,[16] getting at the truth, at its deepest levels: to go there, declares Nellie Bly, is at last to fulfil her 'desire to know asylum life more thoroughly'.[17] As we see, the witness never considers the possibility that her observations might remain superficial.

What gives this journalistic method its distinctive aspect, however, as compared with other versions of the figure of the witness-ambassador, is the insistence on the theme of the *hidden*. The witness-ambassador is presented almost as if on the threshold of an initiatory experience, which she is going to make us all experience by proxy. The object she is about to reveal is particularly well guarded, and the revelation thus has from the beginning a markedly belligerent dimension. This has implications for the nature of the unification which takes place through the journalist's gaze: it is clear that 'we' are going to be appealed to against enemies, 'them', the guardians of what is hidden.

This brings us to the second revelation: making 'us' see ourselves. If it follows from the first – revealing what is hidden – it is because that first exposure is conceived as the replacement of a strange and – or so we believed – wholly foreign world by two distinct worlds: 'us' and 'them'. In this way, we are there also, in these patients who arouse our sympathy, while, in contrast, a true *stranger* is at last revealed: the medical staff. The discourse of *truth* (revealing the hidden) performs, at another level, therefore, the function of a discourse on identity and on difference-adversity: here 'we' are, there 'they' are.

As is apparent, this double revelation involves a sort of attrition of the *strange*: in the end, everything becomes clear, that is, by the distinct categories of 'us' and 'them' being made one; even the finally identified *stranger* is 'clear' and, in the end, not so very strange after all. The fact that nothing is hidden seems to imply that nothing is strange: the light precludes the possibility of a mysterious, unclassifiable and disturbing 'third party' emerging from the 'us' or 'them' alternative. Right from the beginning of the book describing her experiences, Nellie Bly suggests that she is going to *reduce* madness and its mystery to something comprehensible, that she is going to assimilate it into the revelation. As early as page 8, she makes it plain that, by going to see these wretched women locked up on Blackwell's Island, she realized that the distance which she had initially imagined as separating them was an illusion; in fact, they are like us, they are *ours*, and their madness is a construction created by the veils that have shrouded that place and been lifted by the irruption of the gaze. Thus she writes of these 'unfortunate women who lived and suffered with me, and who, I am convinced, are as sound of mind as I was and as I am now'.[18] On a number of occasions in the reportage, she emphasizes that these women are not *really mad*. On the contrary, it is the authors of this construction who are unmasked as the true strangers, or true others. A vague strangeness, that is, the 'mad women', is replaced, therefore, by a true strangeness or a distinct otherness, the medical staff, as these false strangers are returned to 'us'. Her remark to the effect that 'they' – the doctors – invariably found her madder, the more normally she behaved, is significant: 'Yet strange to say, the more sanely I talked and acted the crazier I was thought to be.'[19] To her this was proof that a false otherness, the pseudo-madness, had been constructed by those who are the real true others, the doctors who work there. In a similar vein are her observations on the ease with which she is able to perform her role as 'madwoman'; the crudest of ruses are effective, because the doctors seem determined to project on to her an obvious 'madness'. The medical staff even supply her with stratagems, as when a doctor asks if she hears voices at night, and what they say.[20] Whatever Nellie Bly may say, for him she *is* mad.

We observe, in this last passage, a significant characteristic of the writing of Nellie Bly: the distribution of good and bad marks throughout her observations; this is, of course, exactly in line with the instructions of her editor, who wanted her to express her opinions and confirm, once again, the triumph of light over strangeness. Nellie Bly shows that, thanks to and through her, the public always recognizes its own. This is also why she is quite happy to record the names of a handful of individuals who are exceptions in this world of the 'others'. She several times praises the gentleness of Judge Duffy, for example, and emphasizes the kindness of one of the maids-of-all-work, Mary: 'I am glad to know that there is such a good-hearted woman in that place.'[21] Nellie Bly never loses her way on her voyage into the obscure, armed as she is by a truly all-powerful gaze.

This means that *we* never get lost either. We are always there, right behind her; she leads us, and she speaks to us as to accomplices, as, for example, when she tells us that she took a notebook in with her, partly to record her impressions, but also for strategic reasons: she wrote absurd sentences in it, for the express purpose of appearing crazy to anyone curious enough to inspect it.[22] When, later on, she describes how a nurse stole this notebook, it is the public itself which feels robbed and the thief is then naturally identified as an enemy. Further, the nurse in question lies about the incident to the doctor to whom Nellie Bly complains – or it might be the doctor who lies to Nellie; all of which places them even more firmly in the category of odious 'others' in our eyes.[23]

There seems to have been only a single moment of danger for the figure of the witness-ambassador. It comes at the end of the book, when Nellie Bly returns, accompanied by the jurors, to Blackwell's Island, in the course of the judicial proceedings that followed her revelations. In the intervening period, many things have changed. The boat giving access to the island is now new and clean, the food more appetizing, the kitchen at last salubrious. If *seeing* is regarded as proof, Nellie Bly's method now seems invalidated. In fact she says as much herself: 'I hardly expected the grand jury to sustain me, after they *saw* everything different from what it had been while I was there.'[24] But trust her they did. This ultimate confidence signifies the final triumph of the figure of the witness-ambassador, presented by Nellie Bly herself in her writing. We may see the moment of danger, consequently, as only enhancing this triumph, a weakness destined to become an extra strength: by admitting that she no longer sees today what she had once seen, she makes herself even more deserving of the confidence of her readers, appearing as a journalist who, manifestly, even against her own interests, always tells the truth about what she sees. Thus the story finishes on a self-celebratory note, scarcely disguised by this touching anxiety that she might no longer be believed. When she tells how one of the patients, a Mrs Neville, confirms her earlier statements by describing in detail the changes made during the last two weeks in the asylum, or when she sees as proof of the veracity of her story the fact that many of the women she had known during her stay had since been moved and were unavailable on the occasion of this second visit, Nellie Bly supposes that her status as witness-ambassador has actually been *preserved*. Because, after all, to accept the evidence of Mrs Neville, or her own observations on the subject of the disappearing patients, we must continue to believe Nellie Bly in *her* confidence in Mrs Neville, and in *her* assertion that these women really did exist . . . If her best weapon for 're-legitimizing' herself is to make her readers share her anger at these changes, this implies, clearly, that she *can* make them share it, hence that she was never actually wholly 'de-legitimized' in her role as confidential ambassador.

In general, then, the disclosure, by a reporter set up as a pioneer in this previously unknown territory, is *guaranteed* and never presented as problematic. The gaze of the journalist is *the* gaze, the true gaze, as opposed to the gazes of the doctors who institute and preserve the masks – they 'see' these poor patients, systematically, as 'madwomen'. Significantly, it is her colleagues, the reporters, and they alone, who are feared by Nellie Bly during her experience: if they enter and question her, she is lost; they will see through the hoax immediately. Judge Duffy – as if by chance, one of 'ours', who knows, therefore, that the reporters are our very eyes, that is, *the* very eyes – expresses regret that the reporters are not there to discover the truth about this strange unidentified young woman who presents herself before him:

> 'I wish the reporters were here,' he said at last, 'They would be able to find out something about her.' I got very much frightened at this, for if there is any one who can ferret out a mystery it is a reporter. I felt that I would rather face a mass of expert doctors, policemen, and detectives than two bright specimens of my craft.[25]

Later, having arrived at Bellevue, she declares: 'The reporters were the worst. There were so many of them! And they were all so brilliant and intelligent that I was terrified at the idea that they would see that I was of sound mind.'[26] In fact, she is able to deceive them, though only really by avoiding them, with one exception, who recognizes her. But the scene which then takes place between them is significant with regard to this 'we' in which they are each caught up, and which, in fact, constitutes the public and its interests: Nellie Bly manages to ask him not to give her away, for the good of the cause; after all, if they are both the ambassadors of the public, they can unite in this battle being fought in the name of the public. He agrees.[27]

This celebration of the gaze of the journalist, substitute for the gaze of the public, hence a correct gaze, quick to unmask, banishes all doubt from Nellie Bly's mind as to the value of her testimony. She spends ten days in an asylum and 'obviously' accedes to its profound truths; she sees through it, exposes it without any vestige of strangeness resisting her. In this regard, stunt journalism is a veritable apologia for *seeing*, including in its immediacy, when it consists simply of a 'glance'. We need only note how our stunt girl resolves the problem of time, that is, of the transformations the gaze might undergo over the longer term: 'I have described my first day in the asylum, and as the other nine were exactly the same in the general run of things, it would be tiresome to tell about each of them.'[28] The gaze is presented, therefore, as correctly oriented from the outset, empathetic towards those it recognizes, indignant towards the others. 'For ten days I had been one of them,' claims Nellie Bly without a scruple.[29] Such is the power of the gaze, as long, that is, as it is the gaze of a true ambassador of the public and not of a representative of specific interests or powers.

This omnipotence is due to the fact that, in the world of Nellie Bly, as in that of Séverine, everything 'appears', and probably fairly quickly. Nothing resists being *seen* for long, which then serves as definitive and full proof. The truth cannot remain hidden. Nellie Bly's observations on the cleanliness of the dining-room are significant here; at the beginning of the reportage she notes: 'Everything was spotlessly clean and I thought what good workers the nurses must be to keep such order. In a few days after how I laughed at my own stupidity to think the nurses would work.'[30] A few pages later, she gives the *visual proof* that had enabled her to correct the judgement:

After we were back to the sitting-room a number of women were ordered to make the beds, and some of the patients were put to scrubbing and others given different duties which covered all the work in the hall. It is not the attendants who keep the institution so nice for the poor patients, as I had always thought, but the patients, who do it all themselves – even to cleaning the nurses' bedrooms and caring for their clothing.[31]

In the end, therefore, everything is seen. The suffering of the patients has its *visible proofs*, as does the incompetence of the medical staff – the proofs provided by Nellie Bly are staggering: the nurses did not even know the correct temperature of the human body.[32] The journalist's method is always the same, therefore: to say exactly what she sees – as in the case of the food, for example, which she describes in minute detail throughout her reportage – but also to believe only what she sees. Thus, when she reports the words of patients who told her about their past sufferings, she tries to find visible traces, which would serve as guarantees: 'Mrs. Cofter [a woman who was describing the tortures inflicted on her by the nurses] here showed me proofs of her story, the dent in the back of her head and the bare spots where the hair had been taken out by the handful.'[33] The fact that Nellie could verify on her own account an experience recounted by someone else is also a way of authenticating, which confirms her function as witness-ambassador, the only figure able to claim an objectification of her lived experience. Consequently, she begins by reporting the words of a patient by the name of Bridget McGuiness, who herself speaks as a witness of the others, then as a direct witness: 'I have seen the patients wild for water from the effects of the drugs, and the nurses would refuse it to them. I have heard women beg for a whole night for one drop and it was not given them. I myself cried for water until my mouth was so parched and dry that I could not speak.'[34] Nellie Bly then confirms this: 'I saw the same thing myself in Hall 7. The patients would beg for a drink before retiring, but the nurses – Miss Hart and the others [this interpolated 'the others' is significant] – refused to unlock the bathroom that they might quench their thirst.'[35]

There is a concern, therefore, for material proof. But Nellie Bly also uses a more instinctive recognition: she 'feels' whether a discourse is true or false, feels who is one of 'us' and who is not. It is still a matter of sensitivity, but of a more complex and vague sensitivity, a feeling, an intuition, and not a 'cold' sensation which depends only on material traces. As in Séverine, it is always the body of the reporter which authenticates, recognizes 'our side' and identifies the others; nothing lies, all the emotions are 'true', and it is enough to let yourself be guided by them. And this remains true even if it means interpreting and imagining, rather than rigorously observing, what is. Thus, when Nellie Bly imagines a fire in the corridor where the patients are kept double-locked by the nurses, she is positive: 'Should the building burn, the jailers or nurses would never think of releasing their crazy patients. *This I can prove to you later* when I come to tell of their cruel treatment of the poor things intrusted to their care.'[36] This is a visual 'proof', certainly, but to validate something which nevertheless remains a fantasy; which is to say that the feelings of the witness-ambassador, sources of truth, extend easily into imagination and interpretation, without this presenting any problems.

'We' and 'the others'

The techniques which Nellie Bly uses to expose two worlds, 'us' and 'them', can be explained with the aid of the categories identified by Luc Boltanski in his book *Distant Suffering*. The reporter is constantly making use of what Boltanski calls the 'topic of sentiment' – tender-heartedness producing an identification with the patients, a recognition that they are 'ours' – and the 'topic of denunciation' – focusing attention on the persecutor, and the designation of the one responsible for the suffering observed, and hence the identification of an 'other'.[37]

Each of these topics, explains Boltanski, allows a spectacle of suffering to establish a link with action. In fact, this is the main question posed by his book: how can a spectacle of suffering instigate a 'politics of pity', that is, create, in the words and in the spectacle, the desire to react? How can the spectator 'point towards action by putting himself in the position of having to report what he has seen?'[38] Boltanski sees this as the purpose of the different topics he identifies in the gazes and discourses on suffering. He also explains, however, that each topic carries the risk of failing in the very objective it sets itself. In fact, the *topic of denunciation* orients the gaze towards those responsible for the suffering more than towards those who experience it; it indicates whoever is responsible and urges them to stop what they are doing; this is its way of forging a link with action. But this link can be weakened by the very tendency to neglect the suffering experienced: 'In the topic of denunciation the spectator's attention does not dwell on the unfortunate,' he writes.[39] This explains the weakness of certain discourses of denunciation, which are lacking in 'empathy', and struggle to re-create the singularity of the suffering. Conversely, the *topic of sentiment* is based on an intense empathy with the sufferer, often using the real or imaginary person of a benefactor with whom to identify; it urges us to sympathize 'with the unfortunate's *gratitude* inspired by the intervention of a *benefactor*'.[40] This explains this tender-heartedness, produced by the actual or imaginary contemplation of a benefactor who has just relieved the suffering. From this point, says Boltanski, this topic 'dispenses with denunciation and accusation',[41] in order to remain as close as possible to the sufferer. This is how it hopes to produce a reaction. Once again, the weakness of the topic is not hard to spot: it can also turn into 'sentimentalism' and a possible unavowed and unavowable enjoyment of it: that is, pleasure at being moved, emotion for emotion's sake, which is hardly likely to lead to action.[42]

The conclusion Boltanski draws from the respective ambivalence of these two topics is that they each have an interest in not operating without the other. The best way of avoiding the respective pitfalls of each of the two topics, that of denunciation and that of sentiment, is to combine them and make them work together, in fact rely on their complementarity. Because the topic of denunciation carries the risk of turning into an obsession with 'them', forgetting to forge an affective link with those who suffer, that is, to portray a sensitive 'us', the topic of sentiment is a powerful corrective. Conversely, the topic of sentiment, which empathizes with 'sufferers' systematically recognized as 'ours' but risks indulging in sentimentalism by ignoring the causes of the suffering, gains by appealing to the topic of denunciation to, in a sense, compensate. Perhaps, therefore, it is by using them both in tandem that each topic works best and avoids its own pitfalls. This leads to a representation of suffering designating both an 'us' and a 'them' and avoiding the hypertrophy of one of the two worlds – that hypertrophy which makes the spectacle of suffering less 'effective', less likely to provoke a reaction in the spectator.

It seems to me that in the writing of Nellie Bly we find both these topics in all their complexity, their principal strengths but also their respective ambivalences, which is precisely what makes them complementary. Indeed, Nellie Bly is constantly using them in combination. This is perhaps at its clearest in the passage where, immediately after describing the torture inflicted by a nurse, Miss Grupe, on a freezing cold patient who asks for a blanket – Miss Grupe runs her cold hands all over the patient's body, laughing 'savagely', and the other nurses join in[43] – she goes on to describe another patient, Miss Tillie Mayard, who also suffers greatly from the cold, and who inspires intense pity in Nellie Bly and the other patients; one of these, Miss Neville, takes Miss Mayard in her arms, in spite of the sarcastic remarks of the nurses.[44] The topic of sentiment here succeeds that of denunciation. In fact, in this last scene, which presents a benefactor, as required by the topic of sentiment, we already see a topic of denunciation combined with it, because, just before Miss Neville's gesture of affection, Nellie Bly herself, no longer able to endure the spectacle of Miss Mayard's suffering, went to complain to the three attendants who were sitting there, with their coats on, and accused them of cruelty: ' "It is cruel to lock people up and then freeze them," I said.'

This passage is also revealing with regard to the political implications of the respective use of these two topics: denunciation aims, ultimately, to indicate a world of 'others', whereas sentiment gives substance to a 'we'. In other words, the topic of denunciation defines the frontier – a conflictual frontier – and the topic of sentiment defines the centre. And the use of the two in association makes it possible to effect a unification, a re-centring, by linking it closely to the representation of a frontier and a conflict: it is 'we' who are in conflict with 'the others', and 'we' who are disclosed in this struggle; our centre makes itself visible through the vision of these 'others', who cannot pretend to be linked to this same centre, and who must therefore be excluded from the 'we'. The adverb 'savagely', used to describe the attitude of the cruel nurse, should probably be read as a strong mark of exclusion from 'us' while, significantly, Nellie Bly explains that the pity and the horror at Miss Mayard's misery were shared ('every patient looked frightened'), which emphasizes the unification of a 'we' round the reporter.

More generally, Nellie Bly's book is full of observations which divide the asylum world into two in this way. The empathy with the patients is absolute, and never really questioned: they are 'ours', they belong to 'us', that is obvious. The journalist is forever telling us how her heart bleeds for these poor women, whom she calls her 'sisters'.[45] Conversely, the medical staff are presented as a world of complete strangers. She does everything she can to demonstrate the unbridgeable gulf between 'us' and the medical staff, with whom empathy is impossible. Already, on her journey by ambulance from the hospital of Bellevue to Blackwell's

Island, she paints a dreadful picture of the two attendants: they are true 'others', 'coarse, massive women', spitting out tobacco juice and glaring at the patients 'in a way that was simply terrifying'.[46] In fact the two topics are still complementing each other, since the sympathy with the patients is served both by the representation of a benefactor – Bly refers, for example, to her own desire to comfort these 'poor creatures' and herself tries to relieve the cold of a patient by taking her in her arms[47] – and by the constant references to the persecutor; thus the topic of denunciation is never far from the topic of sentiment. What most tugs at her heartstrings is seeing the cruelty of the staff; she describes pityingly the almost unconquerable revulsion the patients feel for the food, even though they are famished with hunger, in the very same passage that she describes the appetizing food that is being prepared for the staff, before the very eyes of the patients.[48]

There are rare moments when Nellie Bly seems to question her capacity for real empathy with these women, amongst whom she lived for only a few days, and who might well, after all, be afflicted with an illness that erected an insurmountable barrier between them and her; however, they are soon eclipsed by her constant emphasis on her ability to be one of them, because they themselves are so very much 'ours', that is, essentially sane. So the references to the 'savagery' of the patients are never related to the same inhuman savagery which, by her account, characterizes the nurses. When she says, for example, that in the refectory, the patients, who have to eat without proper cutlery, 'looked fairly savage', it is significant that she goes on to note that she herself ends up eating in the same way.[49] They are still, therefore, part of 'us', or at least might possibly be 'us'. Similarly, when, a few pages earlier, she describes the way in which the patients ruthlessly steal from each other at table, behaviour which might well have destabilized Nellie, she says only that she was 'amused'.[50] She seems to have wanted to avoid recognizing the divide between these patients and her. From the beginning, she locates herself 'inside', as close as possible to these women and, in parallel, does everything she can not to locate these women in a strangeness inaccessible to 'us', that is, 'us' the public, represented by Nellie Bly.

This implies, on the one hand, that it is not difficult for her to be 'inside'. She says, in fact, that it was enough for her to enter to empathize, hence understand: 'People can never imagine the length of days to those in asylums,' she writes,[51] a sentence which assumes that it is enough simply to enter an asylum, as she did, to understand. On the other hand, however, this proximity is clearly facilitated by the fact that these 'madwomen' hardly constitute, in reality, a profound or disconcerting otherness. She avoids dwelling on any cases of frightening madness, radically strange to her, that she might have encountered.

She is certainly confronted with it, now and then. There is the occasion when she sees some patients chained one to the other, horribly dirty, their eyes dazed. But she describes them as 'the most wretched collection of humanity I have ever seen', and once again it is pity that takes priority, as if in a last burst of the capacity for empathy which drowns out the initial distant horror ('My heart contracted with pity'). Even if there is something here that seems out of kilter with the rest of her account, it has to be said that these patients appear as *something beyond the remit of this reportage*; it is not about them that Nellie Bly primarily speaks, it is not them that she is 'covering'. What she is really 'covering' are these false madwomen, those who are less mad than the doctors who examine and torment them.

In the case of these patients who are so similar to us, Nellie Bly certainly makes several comments that allow a feeling of distressing strangeness to show through. There is, for example, the passage where she hears the cry of a baby which has just been born in the basement; so babies are born in this strange, inaccessible world! She seems shaken.[52] It is significant that the baby's cry is heard coming from down below, that is, from a 'hidden' world that she does not see. This is perhaps the only time that she contemplates the possibility that she has not revealed everything, and that it is just possible that real strangeness exists, simply hidden from her view. On the other hand, however, it confirms the implicit idea that, once exposed, everything becomes clear: perhaps if she went to look . . . And this episode is immediately associated with another anecdote about a woman who had become terribly agitated, distressed beyond measure, at the sight of a visitor with a baby in her arms, which reminded her of her own children, from whom she was separated.[53] Nevertheless, it cannot be said that Nellie Bly really pursues the theme of extreme, inaccessible and alienating suffering, 'strange' to her. Admittedly, there is the bathroom scene in which Nellie seems for the first time to exclude herself: she watches 'them', horrified to see that they all use the same towel in spite of the rashes she can see on some of their faces; one of them passes her a minuscule piece of soap, which she refuses. She excludes herself, in a way, on the grounds, she says, that 'they' had greater need of the soap than she, but we may reasonably wonder whether this self-exclusion had other causes, more difficult for Nellie Bly to admit, such as revulsion or self-protection.[54] But the problem of what may be an irreducible distance between 'them' and 'I' or 'we' is not really addressed in this reportage. At most, it is just perceptible in a brief interior monologue in which she admits that it needed an effort of the imagination on her part really to put herself in the place of these patients who, unlike her, do not see things with the eye of someone who will be leaving in ten days' time.[55] That is all.

In fact, such questioning would belong to another type of journalism, which would be aiming to unsettle 'us' much more deeply, and make 'us' see limitations which would radically decentre us; here the aim is still to remind us of our centre, even if this centre involves conflictual frontiers. Here 'we' are not too deeply disturbed, the test re-centres us more than it decentres us. Nellie Bly remains firmly committed to a journalism of unifying and not of decentring. There are risks she does not take.

As a result, her journey into what might have proved a 'different world' remains remarkably serene. She is never threatened by the possibility of losing herself, or of becoming other, 'truly' mad. Her whole method consists of uncovering the false otherness that people usually believe to be madness, whereas the 'true' other is elsewhere; or of frustrating, in a way, the naive curiosity of the crowd who watched her get into the ambulance for Bellevue, and who thought that what they were seeing was the stranger, the disquieting other, when, as she wants to show, this is not so.[56] There is a scene in the hostel for working girls where this strange Nellie Brown frightens everybody, and a certain Mrs Caine agrees to sleep in the same room and look after her, and even shows signs of motherly affection;[57] this scene is as if premonitory of what Nellie herself is going to do on Blackwell's Island, that is, recognize her sisters and support them.

There is a single moment when she seems to have an extreme experience, that is, when she is forced by the nurses to take a cold bath in front of the other patients; her misery makes her say that, at that moment, she appeared truly mad.[58] But in whose eyes? Those of the watching patients, she writes. It is interesting that this moment when she thinks the extreme (a decentring, it seems . . .), under the impact of torture and humiliation (and she says, in fact, that the cases of 'true' madness are actually largely due to the treatment received),[59] she continues to think it through the eyes of a constituted 'we', the patients and she herself. Yes, some people 'drop out' of this united community, perhaps I myself, here, she seems to say; but in general, like me, here, we are recovered by the 'we', still caught in its field of perception. This asylum is above all, therefore, a community where one recognizes and understands oneself, not a fragmenting or shattering of the 'we' under the influence of extreme and alienating suffering. There are, furthermore, many scenes of warm complicity between the patients, for example, when they all laugh at their own clothes, in particular the hats they are made to wear.[60] The true otherness in the scene of the cold bath is still, ultimately, that of the nurse, who is described as 'fiendish'.[61]

The gaze of Nellie Bly thus offers a particularly revealing example of a unification inseparable from confrontation with a 'them'. And the test that produces this constitution of a 'we' in conflictuality is the test of the *hidden*. The journalist is then presented as the figure who passes – and so makes 'us' pass – this test until it achieves its end: the exposure of the hidden, and the related and clear definition, in this place long concealed from view, of a 'them' finally identified as such and of an 'us' properly revealed.

Of course, it might be argued that the conflictuality here is distinctly perfunctory. There are goodies and there are baddies, and all that is needed is to fight the latter. We remain at the level of *the obvious*, or of the cry: It must be stopped! Let us liberate 'our own' from these 'others' who torture them! This is not without echoes of the slogans of the reporter Jacob Riis, who was writing his reports on urban poverty at about the same time as Nellie Bly (his *How the Other Half Lives* appeared in 1890), and whose slogans were incisive, definitive and never entirely free of moralizing. Think, for example, of his famous sigh, punctuating a bleak description: 'Mulberry Street must go!' The ambivalence of the relationship between Lincoln Steffens, next-generation muckraker, and 'Father' Riis – a father to be venerated for some of his rigorous descriptions, but also a father to be 'killed' for his intolerably maudlin, moralizing and simplistic gaze – is revealing as to the frustrations created by this sort of reporting and the complexity that the muckraking movement would try to inject into the heritage transmitted by the sensationalist press. But this is jumping ahead – these questions will be discussed in the next chapter.

For the moment, let us pursue this analysis of the tests that the witness-ambassadors inflict on 'us', with the intention of constituting this 'us' and making it experience its collective identity. These tests will probably always be of a fairly 'simple' type, asking us to consider a 'them' who must be fought so that we can recover the centre. But there is one point on which, compared with Nellie Bly, this method might turn out to be different. In her, as we have seen, the exposure of the hidden led to an attrition of the strange. This is not the case with other reporters, even though they too journey into obscure places and want to *reveal*. It is possible for the exposure to lead, on the contrary, to a disturbing strangeness, at the very heart of what there is to see, and for this strangeness to be the lever of the unifying process – a strangeness appearing as 'other', but in the sense of a bizarre, mysterious and unfathomed otherness, quite unlike the 'them' of Nellie Bly, a limpid adversary. We might call this the test of *strangeness*. We will examine this variation on the same theme – that is, another version of the figure of the witness-ambassador – through the writing of the French reporter Albert Londres.

2. Albert Londres or the test of strangeness

The gaze as emergence of the strange

Some famous words of Albert Londres (1884–1932) on the role of the journalist would seem to suggest a conception of journalism as a test of the hidden: that is, as a gaze penetrating into all the secret places of society in order to reveal them and confound all those disturbed by this revelation. Having declared, in the foreword to his reportage on colonial Africa, *Terre d'Ébène*, 'Our métier is not to give pleasure, nor is it to do harm, it is to dip our pens in the wound . . .',[62] he declares in the epilogue:

> Was it in the interests of France to deepen the obscurity which still con-
> cealed this country from us? I did not think so . . . It is said that the first
> necessity of colonial life is for it to be conducted in secrecy, or at least out
> of sight of the mother country. Whoever has the audacity to look behind
> the screen is guilty of an abominable sacrilege in the eyes of the pure colo-
> nials . . . it is not by hiding one's wounds that one cures them.[63]

Yet the method of Londres seems to me to be very different from that of stunt journalism. In the work of Londres, the exposure is not designed to reduce strangeness. On the contrary, it is strangeness as such that he sets out to reveal, with all the complications that such a revelation entails: that is, as a *difficulty* in dividing the world into two – 'ours' and 'theirs' – and, in this sense, a gaze that is politically less clear-cut. The route from the emergence of the strange to a questioning of or appeal to 'us' is a more sinuous one.

Perhaps, to describe the method of Londres, we should prefer another formulation of his, taken from *Chemin de Buenos Aires* (*The Road to Buenos Aires*): 'I wanted to descend into the pits into which society throws what threatens it or what it cannot foster; to see what no one wants to see; to judge what has been judged.'[64] The theme of the hidden is present here, clearly, but it assumes a very indeterminate, heteroge-neous character, difficult for the gaze which confronts it, perhaps pre-venting a dispassionate judgement. Londres does not speak of 'wounds' here, a word which suggests perpetrators and remedies, but of a return to the final judgement, whose outcome is not necessarily clear. The exposure is more disquieting in Londres than in Nellie Bly, where it was, in a sense, intended to do away with mystery, and to reduce a strange-ness which was due only to the veil which concealed it.

We should probably, when discussing the writing of Londres, not allow ourselves to be too influenced by the reactions provoked by his reportages at the time, or by the 'Albert Londres myth' as it is often evoked. The scandals caused by his articles had many and complex causes, which went well beyond the texts themselves; it is interesting to note how often they have led to a clarity being attributed to his writing that it is far from easy to detect on a subsequent close reading. Let us take as an example a piece which has direct echoes of the writing of Nellie Bly, the reportage of 1925 on psychiatric asylums, *Chez les Fous*.[65] The shocked reaction of the psychiatric profession[66] should not blind us to the fact that this reportage is very far from expressing the same type of clear indignation as that of Nellie Bly. What dominates in it is a representation of madness as a harrowing, inaccessible and incomprehensible world, which baffles both its observer and those who treat it. Londres is scared by it, but also sometimes laughs at it, remaining always, either way, in a position of exteriority, with no empathy at all with the madmen and madwomen. He manages to steer his way between exposing the strangeness and questioning 'us': what are we doing there, with these mad people? What is an asylum? Are the doctors really doing what they claim, that is, providing treatment? But this interrogation has none of the clarity of the denunciation of a Nellie Bly.

The problem is that Londres himself creates confusion. At the end of this reportage, he launches into a ferocious diatribe against the doctors, whom he accuses of incompetence and of bullying instead of caring;[67] but this diatribe seems somehow at odds with the general tenor of the descriptions which have preceded it, whereas the indignation of Nellie Bly is wholly justified by everything she describes. In Londres, the sharpness of his sudden denunciation rather obscures the complexity of his way of throwing light on things: he invests the mad persons with a frightening and painful strangeness, which the doctors probably *should* have controlled and, above all, relieved, but which nevertheless has the effect of at least partly excusing a body of carers who are 'overwhelmed', especially the nurses. Take the scene called the 'Meal of the Furies' (chapter 5). The sisters of this asylum in the west of France are shown in a situation of almost moving impotence in the face of these unruly, inhuman and cruel creatures. Londres uses one of his favourite techniques to bring out the strangeness, that is, metaphors which animalize or reify the creatures he describes, and the chapter ends with the image of a patient biting a nurse deeply enough to draw blood. The nurses are overwhelmed, as is the reporter himself, who indulges in fantasies of violent control: 'Some thirty furies sit on the benches, but their posteriors are on springs, or so at least it seems. To stop them moving, you think of pressing down on their shoulders. At last! Surely, when their mouths are full of macaroni, they'll stop moving?'[68] As a result, when, later in the chapter, he describes the sisters beginning to feed the furies with tubes,[69] it is difficult to come to a 'clear' (indignant) judgement regarding this constraint.

By letting all the strangeness of madness show, Londres oddly complicates his denunciation of the medical practices. This is the case also in the scene of the madwomen of the Salle de Pitié, where we may wonder whether the dread aroused by these creatures leaves any room for indignation about the way they are treated:

> At the far end is the Salle de Pitié. It was unexpected and incomprehensible. Perched on a platform, eleven chairs were fixed to the wall. Eleven women tied to eleven chairs. For which entrepreneur of horror were they 'on show'? One wept! Another shrieked! Their bodies rocked from left to right, and seemed, like metronomes, to beat a gloomy time. You would have said they were mechanical dolls of the sort ventriloquists take on to music-hall stages. Their hair was unkempt. Their noses ran . . . their chins were wet with spittle. 'Puddles' formed under the seats. What prehistoric animated museum had I come upon? The smell, the sight, the cries made one's gorge rise.
>
> They are senile old women who no longer know how to behave.
>
> Why not leave them in bed?
>
> They are tied up because asylums are short-staffed.
>
> All the same![70]

We may note the emphasis on the incomprehensible nature of the scene, as well as the ambiguity of the image of the gorge rising. As for the final 'All the same!', it is certainly more complex than the shocked indignation of a Nellie Bly. For his indignation to be aroused, Londres has to go beyond his first reaction ('Why not leave them in bed?') and gradually introduce considerations regarding treatment into the general feeling of strangeness and horror that overwhelms him.

The atmosphere is similar in the bathroom scene, where he paints a strange picture of heads swimming in a single bathtub, and where the unease of this vision gradually questions the conditions of care: why were there not more bathtubs, and more staff? How could the restraint be justified? Here is the scene:

> One day, my innocent footsteps took me into a room. I saw heads which looked like cabbage heads in a vegetable garden. This vision destroyed on the spot all my capacities, except one: that to count. I counted: one, two, four, six . . . fourteen heads . . . It was from a bathtub that these heads emerged, not from the stocks. What amazing bathtubs! They were completely covered by a plank of wood which, fortunately, had an opening just where it reached the neck.
>
> How clever! The bathers will not escape from the bathtub.
>
> Some heads were calm; but one swore at me. And another, with a gesture of the chin, asked me to scratch its nose.

A hole for the head, what a splendid idea! But, please, another for the hands, at least for one!

Baths are expensive, staff are few, so instruments of restraint, cells and lock-ups appear. Tie someone who is mad to a bed and watch their face: they grow angry, they swear. The nurses get more peace, but the sick get more agitated.

If asylums are there for the peace of the attendants, and not for the treatment of the mad, I take my hat off to them, they are serving their purpose.

Pinel, a century ago, freed lunatics from their fetters. Good for another portrait in the Paris Medical Faculty! Well, well! They've made a mockery of Pinel.

Straitjackets, wristbands, bonds and straps replace fetters.[71]

Londres progresses from one surprise to another, gradually including the medical staff and the attendants in a feeling of strangeness initially created simply by observing the mad persons; this is very different from an immediate and clear identification of the carers as true 'others', odious and malevolent. Instead, the medical staff are questioned about their contradictions – is this treating people? – rather than designated, from the outset, as in Nellie Bly, as total strangers. In fact we find the sphere of the strange extended, rather than a clear revelation of the good and the bad, of 'ours' and 'theirs'.

In any case, the 'good' and the 'bad' are hardly fixed categories in Londres. As well as his insistence on the cruelty of the mad, he seems to take a malign pleasure in creating unease with regard to the few doctors who might spontaneously appear as 'good'. Dr Dide, for example, who was much readier to listen to the sick than any of the others, and much more competent, nevertheless proves to be a strange character, cutting brains 'into thin slices like Parma ham in Italian delicatessens' and keeping them in chamber pots 'because the chamber pot is the ideal shape of the brain'.[72]

The exposure in Albert Londres thus takes the form not so much of *scandal* as of *unease*, which is a very different matter, even though the unease aroused at the time did also give rise to a scandal (the scandal has its sociology!), and this differentiates Albert Londres from Nellie Bly. Where stunt journalism says 'I understand' (which is the constant presupposition of Nellie Bly, as we have seen), Londres is constantly saying that he does not understand what he sees. 'It was unexpected and incomprehensible,' he says, early in his description of the Salle de Pitié. And it is this disquieting incomprehension that he makes his readers share. And this does not necessarily have a political 'outcome' or a clear political significance. With all due respect to devotees of the 'Albert Londres myth', he is impossible to categorize politically; even the vague adjective 'rebel' is too precise. His gaze is above all one which is surprised and which surprises – which has political implications, certainly, but they are complex and ambiguous.

Let us recall an episode which did much for the construction of the 'Albert Londres myth', his report on the Ruhr under French occupation, in 1923. Londres had been sent by *Le Quotidien* to cover the revolts of the German workers (encouraged by the Communists) against the French. The owners of the paper had a clear ulterior motive, to weaken the French premier, Raymond Poincaré, by this means and force him to abandon the Ruhr. In this light, the reportage of Londres was found to be too bland; true, he emphasized the Francophobia of the Germans, but without mentioning any particularly intolerable tensions or any absolutely scandalous treatment of the German workers. Londres refused to change his text, making his famous statement: 'Sirs, you will learn to your cost that the reporter knows only one line, the railway line.' What better defence could there be of the right of the gaze not to be politically 'clear and distinct'? Londres is not defending the right of a reporter to have a line politically different from that of his employers, but the right not to have a line at all. It is a statement not on the right to commitment, but on that to remain, in a sense, uncommitted.[73]

According to Pierre Assouline, his biographer, we should nevertheless note a turning point in the itinerary of Albert Londres. He was certainly, in the beginning, a 'poet'; he wanted above all to write literature, which he conceived of as removed from political considerations. Assouline describes him, on his arrival in Paris in the early years of the twentieth century, as a young 'belated romantic, half Byronic, half "Young France" in the manner of Théophile Gautier',[74] indifferent to all the political debates of the day. According to Assouline, however, 1923 was 'the decisive year', that, in particular, of his reportage on the penal colony of Cayenne, the origins of which apparently remain mysterious. Is there really, however, a complete break at that moment between the old 'salaried *flâneur*' and the new 'righter of wrongs'? Assouline seems to hesitate in his analysis: 'Albert Londres was a witness. He reported. More than a role, it was a duty when lives were at stake. But he was moved by a poetic, romantic, even chivalric instinct, all generosity and altruism. This natural inclination became more pronounced after 1923, when the salaried *flâneur*, employed by an editor to inform his readers, turned into a righter of wrongs.'[75] In fact, when one examines these new, more committed texts (of which *Chez les Fous* is one, in the line of *Au Bagne*), to speak of a break seems to be going too far. Perhaps the expression 'righter of wrongs' is itself also mistaken. These new reportages, whether it is *Au Bagne* (1923), *Chez les Fous* (1925) or *Terre d'Ébène* (1929), which were sensational in their day, all retain this element of strangeness, of ambivalence and of something, dare I say, 'unjudgeable', producing an undeniable feeling of frustration in the reader who is looking for this clear figure of the 'righter of wrongs'. That he entered the realm of the political may well be the case, but it is, it seems to me, on the same basis as before, that is, a curious disengagement, a detached surprise, an external gaze, which makes the strangeness emerge. It is a gaze which gradually builds up and questions 'us' in the face of the strangeness, tracing a sinuous route from 'I don't understand' to ' "It" makes an appeal to us'

From 'I don't understand' to ' "It" makes an appeal to us'

Londres' method was always to begin by discovering an 'it' that was indefinable, shocking and unthinkable according to pre-existing categories. Take, for example, this extract from *Terre d'Ébène*, in which he discovers a logging site in the hands of the slavers:

It is half-light.
Axe on shoulder, a naked man descends towards the road. His eyes are defeated, his body broken. It is the first time I see a Negro tired. He looks at me with surprising interest.
'The site?', I say.
He points back the way he came. A tornado is blowing up. The wind begins to attack the treetops. Above me, all is agitation.
I walk for an hour. No more railway track. The fresh footprints are guide enough.
Another Negro appears. For him I am a boss, and he comes over and sticks a crushed and bleeding finger under my nose, by way of passport. I say: 'OK', as if I had to say something!
Suddenly the forest speaks. At first, it is a muffled rumbling. I go on. It is as if someone is chanting a litany. The forest, however, remains voiceless, yet the cries grow louder.
'Ah ya! Ah ya! Ah ya! Ya! ya! ya! Yââââ! yââââ!'
The cries tell me which way to go. I find it. A hundred naked Negroes, yoked to a felled tree trunk, are trying to pull it.
'Yââââ! yââââ!'
The boss beats time with his whip. He seems to be in a state of frenzy. He roars: 'Yaho! Ya-ho ko-ko!' and even 'Ya-ho! Ro-ko-ko!'
In their exertions, the men-horses are all muscle. They pull, heads lowered. A hail of blows from the whip rains down on their tensed backs. Creepers lash their faces. The blood of their feet marks their passage.
There is a general bawling. A pack at the kennel gate. Groom, valets, whip, baying.
A white man! He is delight to see me. I go up to him.
'I'm interested in the life of the forest,' I say. 'I wanted to see the logging.'
And I introduce myself: 'Londr. . .'!

'Martel', he replies.

He was thin and harassed; he was 26 years old. His eyes gleamed as if from the sockets of a skull. A whistle hung from his belt. He was streaming with sweat.

'What a job!'

He says: 'It's a job for a convict. But you survive! And you make up for it on furlough!'[76]

The text is very clearly employing the figure of the witness-ambassador, in a wholly 'sensualist' version: the writing is focused on the feelings and emotions of this 'I'. But this concentration on the feelings has as a consequence an inability to define: there is a constant indefiniteness and vagueness. A forest that 'speaks', a 'rumbling', animal cries, 'it'. Animal metaphors, and an 'I' whose naivety seems to be sustained as long as possible – the naive eye is surely, by definition, the eye of 'everyone', or of 'no matter who'? – an 'I' that is passive, even submerged by what it sees.

It is from this indefiniteness, passively experienced, and from the contemplation of this nameless 'it', that the appeal to 'us' comes. There is no outright denunciation, no clear-cut recognition of an 'us' and a 'them'. This is because there is a little of 'us' in these slavers whom he meets and who are at the heart of this 'something' revealed. So, faced with 'it', in order to *feel completely ourselves*, 'we' must at the same time *define ourselves*, establish a conflictual frontier with a 'them' who resemble us, a frontier which is far from clear at the outset. 'They' are lodged in us, or are at least fairly close to us! That is why this revealed strangeness creates unease. Séverine and Nellie Bly, each in her own way, did more to preserve 'us' from a compromise with 'them'; they demanded that 'we' fight and confront a 'them' clearly designated and unmasked, and, in a way, therefore, they asked 'us' to prove that we really are at the level of what we claim to be. The sense of unease was not so strong; the appeal to the 'we' lacked the complexity it acquires in the writing of Londres, where, on the contrary, nothing is clear, where the 'we' is asked who exactly it wants to be – is it, or is it not, this white man with the mysterious eyes and a whistle hanging from his belt?

One might conclude from this that the gaze of Albert Londres, after 1923, belongs less to the journalisms of unification than to those of decentring. Does he not boldly create uncertainty with regard to the centre, far from re-centring around it? Should we not see him as a precursor of that American journalism of the 1960s and 1970s known as the 'New Journalism', which would reveal the disarray of the 'we' in the face of many forms of otherness? This comparison is made, most notably, by the French writer Didier Folléas, in a short book on the African reportages of Londres.[77]

I do not share this view, for a number of reasons, some of which will only appear fully when we discuss the New Journalism in chapter 5. The main reason for my opinion that Londres remains a unifier is the relationship he establishes with the strangeness he reveals. That this puts 'us' to the test is clear; but the purpose of the reportage is not, as in the New Journalism, to probe this strangeness or seek to understand it, whatever it is (at the risk of a partial failure), or to shift the frontiers between 'us' and 'them', inasmuch as this is possible. Londres makes no attempt to question in depth the category of 'strange' and then go beyond it. He postulates the strange and then keeps his distance, observing the effects that 'it' produces. He protects himself and protects us behind him; he does not really confront us with an otherness explored, does not seriously endanger us, does not decentre us. He questions us – that is all – so as to make us feel an identity that has to be reaffirmed but is neither uncertain nor in need of radical reinvention. In its own way, the gaze of Londres remains at the level of *the obvious*, in this way resembling that of Nellie Bly. For her, there was no difficulty in empathizing or excluding; it was easy to recognize her own side and her enemies, the only possible categories. Londres is different in the way he sees strangeness everywhere. But if this strangeness disconcerts 'us', it is never to the point of engulfing us; he himself, in his surprise, remains a focus, the centre. He calls on 'us' to make ourselves heard, to say what we want; but the fact that we *can* say it, and so remember the irreconcilable difference between us and this strangeness revealed, is not in itself challenged.

This brings us to another reason for the unease and the frustration produced by the writing of Londres: the profusion of stereotypes he conveys, and the way he keeps a distance that is never questioned (unlike the New Journalism) between 'us' and those who trigger the interrogation of 'us', the 'mad', the 'convicts', the 'Negroes' and their whole environment. The appeal to 'us' is based on our relationship to these strange creatures without the legitimacy of the category of strangeness itself ever being called into question. The only question the text of Londres poses, and its aim remains to unify, never to decentre, is this: knowing what we claim to be, and believed we were before a reporter poked his nose into unknown places, can we truly recognize ourselves, or at least recognize something of ourselves, somewhere in such strange places, somewhere in 'our' relationship to these strange creatures? Is it really us here, here also, is it really us before these strange people, in these odd places, this bizarre Africa, this lunatic asylum or this penal colony, the 'world's cul-de-sac'?[78] Is there not something wrong here? Londres does not place the centre under serious suspicion; he only 'tests' it; he affirms us capable of this reaffirmation of the centre through him; he makes sure, in any case, to re-centre us in these places where we had ceased to ask ourselves about our frontiers, these places where we no longer saw the strangeness which threatened us. And what remains certain in this re-centring is that these strange creatures, these 'lunatics', 'convicts' and 'Negroes', *they* have nothing to do with us; they are only there to put us to the test, so that we will ask ourselves if we can still be ourselves in our contact with them.

Albert Londres had read not a single line on Africa before going there.[79] His approach was very definitely not that of an ethnologist, or of those very 'ethnology-minded' journalists of the New Journalism, who tried to penetrate the otherness and probe it, and call into question the established categories of 'us' and 'them'. The gaze of Londres remains amused and stereotyped when directed at the 'logic' of his servant, for example, so very strange and so very 'Negro',[80] and, more generally, when it is directed at these strange people among whom wives were rated lower than animals:

'Your father OK?'
'Yes, he OK.'
'Your mother OK?'
'Yes, she OK.'
'Your boy OK?'
'Yes, he OK.'
'Your dog OK?'
'Yes, it OK.'
'Your wife OK?'
This greeting had gone on for a minute.
   This Negro, meeting this Negro, asked him for news of everything he possessed: of his *lougan* (field), his horse and his pirogue. His wife came last.[81]

He describes how 'the Negroes are changing', but not in order to lessen the feeling of strangeness they inspire, and which ought increasingly to make the French think about the attitude they should adopt towards them. In Senegal Londres refers to the aspirations for independence without either supporting or criticizing them, simply to indicate the unexpected nature of what he sees and pose the question of the consequences for France. ' "You beat me?" said the Black. "Ah! you beat me? This isn't France, it's Senegal, do you understand? Senegal, my country, here, my home, do you understand?" '[82] He notes that the French prefer not to see these developments, preferring the figure of the 'good Black', and believing it to be immutable:

Look at the Blacks, the real true ones, not the children of universal suffrage, but those of the old Cham. Aren't they lovely! They come running from the bush to say 'Hello'! They wave their arms with such sincerity, they have such great beaming smiles that you have to believe it gives them pleasure to see us. They look at you as if, in the past, they had been dogs and you had given them a lump of sugar. Among them, you feel like a sort of kindly god on parade.[83]

What exactly are we meant to understand by this? Who is he mocking, if not everybody at the same time, the naive French, the 'lovely Negroes' who pander to this naivety, and the emancipation movements themselves, busily engaged in 'conjuring tricks, boxing and kick-boxing'?[84]

In Londres, Africa never emerges from its strangeness. But this is not the point; what matters is that it makes us ill at ease. It is what this strangeness does to our 'we', the questions it raises for this 'we', the test it administers to it. For example, Londres reminds us that it is these strange beings who have constructed 'us' here, in Africa; it is 'they' who have done it, and yet we say that it is 'us' here.[85] Or he makes us see 'our' strange behaviour in that country: for example, in an equally ambiguous and disquieting passage on the people of mixed blood, in which he emphasizes that we lack even the decency to let them alone, and that we create, consequently, rootless figures who belong neither to us nor to them.[86] Or he asks us, incidentally, if their strangeness entitles us to treat them like currency, or kick them about like a 'football'[87] between the administrators and the businessmen:

> Ah! the beautiful roads! You can't imagine anything better. I'm not joking. The roads are magnificent; ask the natives! They are all the more remarkable in that they didn't cost us a single cowry shell.
> All we spent was Negroes! Are we so poor, then, in Black Africa?
> Not at all! The central government's budget has a reserve of I don't know how many hundreds of millions![88]

So what is questioned or tested here is the humanist, universalist and noble 'we', but not the 'we' who has prejudices and stereotypes. Actually, Londres repeats many of them, but he pushes them to the point where they risk contradicting other aspects of the 'we'. His text booby-traps not the principle of colonization, which he never challenges, but the 'noble' discourse of colonization, its certainty of being absolutely generous. As a result, the ' "it" makes an appeal to us' can never touch more than a part of 'us', sometimes a very small part: that part which can be sensitive to the fact that there might, nevertheless, in all that, be something strange, and that this strangeness might reveal contradictions inside the 'we'. And for this 'we' to experience such a test, there is no necessity for deep empathy with those who suffer.

The limitations of this procedure are obvious. Londres comes up against them in certain reportages where his astonishment before the 'strange' has great difficulty in questioning 'us', and which are not, as a result, among the texts I have chosen to illustrate the *test of strangeness*. In them Londres finds no 'handle', it seems to me, by which to trigger a test for 'us', and his gaze remains confined to an 'I do not understand' full of comfortable stereotypes for the 'we' who mandate him.

His reportage of 1920 on Soviet Russia – before the 'turning point' of 1923 – is a case in point. It is full of amazement, both amused and severe, at this 'revolution' he has before his eyes. 'And your purpose?', he had been asked on his entry into the USSR: 'To see,' he had replied.[89] This raw *seeing*, which required no prior understanding of the context (true to his habits, Londres had read nothing), could have been a courageous approach only in a context where a fiercely pro-Communist ideology obstructed the view of the majority of observers. Thus, a few years later, their ideological sympathies meant that many travellers to the USSR would no longer see anything, and in this context the raw seeing of Londres could have been a salutary shock. But in Londres' time, when the prevailing ideology tended rather in the other direction (fear and loathing of Communism), we may wonder whether his gaze was not extraordinarily conformist and predictable.[90] He sees women who do not carry handbags, as they do in Paris, but empty baskets and pitchers;[91] he sees poverty and hunger,[92] but makes no attempt to seek the causes, never refers to the international situation, and his point of comparison is always France and not, for example, pre-Revolutionary Russia. As his Franco-centrism requires, he likens Bolshevism simply to monarchy,[93] without exploring in any greater depth the nature of the regime he has before his eyes. In fact, he questioned only a small part of the 'we' of his time, not to say of those excluded from 'us', a few already marginalized dreamers. To the 'we' of the French in general, the everyday anti-Communist French 'we', he administered no test, but confirmed them in the stridency of their ignorance and their contempt.

This illustrates the intrinsic problem of a unifying gaze. To introduce a conflict at the heart of this unifying movement, to appeal to 'us', is perilous by nature, because it cannot, at the same time, be a conflict which destabilizes 'us' too profoundly. So it needs also to strengthen some common ideas of the 'we', and the conflict it raises in this 'we' is of necessity a 'simple' and contained conflict – a test. Sometimes, as in this reportage on the Soviet Union, the conflict does not emerge at all, and the test fails. But it is the successes which are of interest to us here, and the reportage of Albert Londres which employs *the test of strangeness* in exemplary fashion is that on the penal colony of Cayenne.

Au Bagne *(1923)*

If the theme of strangeness succeeds in appealing to 'us' in *Au Bagne*, it is because it is posed from the beginning in relation to what France is, or what we generally believe France to be; it is the permanent backdrop to the 'I do not understand', and it creates an unease that raises questions. There is something strange, something incomprehensible, and *in our territories*. Even before the descriptions of the penal colony, the text teems with observations regarding this lost and inhospitable place, Cayenne, kingdom of crow-vultures and of wandering. From the beginning, everything is different from how one might imagine a French territory to be. Londres points out that, in this town which lacks even a port, he is welcomed by a statue of the abolitionist Victor Schoelcher, and a fine phrase on the Republic and Equality: 'Perhaps, in five years, there will be a second statue in Cayenne, that of the man who built a port.'[94] He assumes, naturally, that he will be able to find a hotel and a road. Isn't this the very country where they build roads, in fact, where they're supposed to do nothing else? 'For half a century, naughty children have been told: "If you go on like that, you'll end up breaking stones on the roads of Guiana", and there isn't a road; that's how it is! Perhaps they make soup with all those stones they break?'[95]

The power of the reportage consists in applying this same technique to the observation of the prisoners: so this is what they do with them? I don't understand . . . Londres thus puts 'us' to the test without making us feel any sympathy, still less empathy, with the convicts. They are strangeness personified, that is a given. But the experience of strangeness does not spare us; rather, it affects us and tests us because it indicates our contradictions. Finally, as he watches, he always has in mind the statue of Schoelcher and the fine phrases on the Republic, and he makes the strangeness emerge, without needing to go beyond it by an authentic encounter.

The way in which Londres plays on the theme of distance from the convicts is worth noting: this distance is manifest in his descriptions, quelling the rare – though barely perceptible – impulses of pity, but he also makes the question of the proper role of the journalist the subject of an underlying debate which can be read between the lines of his reporting. The distance is established from the time of the boat journey which took him to Cayenne: also on board the *Biskra* were eleven escaped convicts, the first our reporter sees. He describes them in a wholly exterior manner:

Four were without shoes. Chiggers and spider crabs had ravaged their feet. The flesh round these wounds looked like meat that had gone off, in summer, after a thunderstorm. On the cheeks of ten of them, the beards had re-grown in a bristly stubble; the eleventh was still at the downy stage, being 20 years old. Dressed like tramps whose one outfit had been ripped to shreds by the teeth of every guard dog along the route, they were as white as candles.[96]

If they elicit, nevertheless, a 'Poor devils!', or if, a few paragraphs later, he risks mentioning a 'feeling of pity', he still, when he finds himself with two of them in the same small boat, a little later, after it had become dark, admits to turning round 'to be sure the two convicts behind him were not going to knife him'.[97]

Once in the colony, the distance persists. Admittedly, there are a few passages where Londres seems to get closer: he calls them 'lost children';[98] he describes one particular ex-convict, condemned for white slave trading, who is so honest that he returns to Londres the money he had forgotten;[99] and he describes another convict, Ullmo, in tears, overcome by a suffering and penitent humanity.[100] But, against this, there are so many aloof descriptions, teeming with animal metaphors which distance the reporter even further from these creatures on the margins of humanity. We are told of men 'fifty to a cage', with bare, tattooed chests, hiding their money in a tube in their rectum;[101] of a 'Sodom and Gomorrah – between men';[102] of men sick with a fever, afflicted with ancylostomiasis ('they are tiny little hookworms, which destroy the intestine'), inadequately dosed with quinine, who 'tremble on their beds like those little mechanical rabbits when you press the switch';[103] of men likened to dogs, 'who are no more than mangy, snotty-nosed, hairless, anxious and abandoned animals', who it comes as a surprise to find don't bark;[104] of a 'bear', Ginioux, an ex-convict who shares a house with Londres in Saint-Laurent, who had strangled his ex-boss's daughter, and now breaks the backs of cats every night with a stick;[105] of an 'ostrich';[106] of a terrifying creature nicknamed Hespel the Jackal; and of lepers Londres claims he daren't even describe.[107] Nor do the warders really escape this gaze which animalizes to express strangeness;[108] there is even one who is quite mad, who rolls meat in camphor to send to his mistress in Cayenne.[109] But, just as the dehumanizing of the convicts fails to encourage empathy towards them, so, in the case of the warders, it fails to arouse antipathy. The world of the penal colony is so strange that it blocks affect and leaves the reporter – and hence 'us' – at a distance.

The reporter appears always as someone who is not part of the scene, a situation which is his privilege and which Londres never ceases to emphasize. Whereas Nellie Bly made haste to put herself (and along with her, the public, 'us') in a place, that of the poor women in the asylum on Blackwell's Island, Londres fiercely defends his non-place. This trope is probably a way of strengthening his implicit pact with the public: he is of no party and is on no one's side. But it is chiefly developed as the necessary precondition for seeing, because if lucidity is achieved in Nellie Bly through the attrition of the strange, in Albert Londres it is produced by its advent. Seeing requires this exteriority, this place which precludes understanding. When you are in the place of one of the actors, in contrast, you understand; but this is because you see nothing.

This reportage is particularly successful in developing this theme of the *seeing* which necessitates a distance with regard to the actors, a fundamental incomprehension. It begins by presenting the journalist as a neutral receptacle for the words of the actors: Londres goes to see Ullmo in the house of M. Quintry, and says to the former convict: 'This is who I am; I have come to see you for nothing, really, to chat. Perhaps you have something to say to me?'[110] This way of presenting himself itself implies a withdrawal from the actors, but Londres wants to go further, and Ullmo's reply can already appear as a first criticism of this simple role of midwife to words: 'Oh no! All I ask is silence.' A few pages later, the same role is evoked by the warder who introduces Londres to the convicts with the following words: 'There is someone over there, who comes from Paris; he will listen freely to those who have something to say!' Londres then waits in a cell for the convicts to visit him. One arrives:

> The man looks at me and says nothing.
> 'Have you something to say to me?'
> 'Nothing.'
> 'But you knocked.'
> '*It's not for us to say, it's for you to see.*'
> And he stood motionless, eyes lowered like an erect corpse. He was like a ghost against a black background who haunts me still.[111]

It is a lesson in journalism which Londres receives here: let him use his exteriority to do something other than listen passively to words which will not come! Let him do the very thing that cannot be done from 'inside': see! It is significant, also, that the man who really is inside is described as having his 'eyes lowered'.

The same themes are found in another scene, where similar words are placed in the mouth of a very unusual convict, a former journalist:

> He weeps. His emotion makes him stammer. He wants to kneel down before me. Like Brengues, he said to me:
> 'Look! Look!'
> He answers me: 'I'm not weeping, it's joy!'
> He begs me: 'Tell everything! Everything! So that things change a little . . .'

'Here are the blind, in this case. They sit with their hands on their laps and wait.'
There are some who makes themselves blind on purpose with grains of liquorice. At least they no longer see![112]

The discourse of the journalist-convict contrasts the reporter who sees and the actors who do not see, and who, in any case, if they still have eyes to see, do everything so as no longer to see. Significantly, the terrible anxiety of the convicts, that of having to face poverty after their release, as they were obliged to remain in Guiana for as many years as they had spent in the penal colony (what was called 'doubling'), is expressed in the form of a fantasy about a blind man recovering his sight. This is the metaphorical story recounted by the ex-convict Marius Gardebois:

'Hell! That bastard *has pulled it off.*'
It was his benefactor of whom he spoke in this way. In restoring his sight, the man of science had plunged him into poverty. This is the story of the convict.[113]

But the journalist has to confront these visions, intolerable for those who are 'inside'. So he should not try to get close to the actors, to enter into their condition. That might be to understand, but it would be to blind himself. *Au Bagne* is a defence of exteriority and of distance, because they are a guarantee of light, a precondition for seeing.

A few pages later, Londres signals the failure of the position of listener, which is still, in one way or another, too closely linked to an empathic approach. What he would have heard would in any case have been incomprehensible, he seems to say. He pretends to complain to the convicts: 'Listen to me. For a month now I've been asking questions, and you all say the same: "If we told you the truth, you wouldn't believe it." On the other hand, you claim that the management will hide everything from me. What do you expect me to do?'[114] The reply is in the text, in the scenes we have just described: he must stop trying to find meaning by appealing for words; he must rely on the fundamental incomprehension in which the reporter flounders, so as to be able to *see* – to see the strangeness as such, incomprehensible and source of a test for 'us'.

The way in which Londres represents himself in this reportage applies this defence of distance and refusal of empathy. In a strange scene, he presents himself in the process of observing the convicts, unknown to them, through a peephole:

In the evening, at eight-o'-clock, on the Île Royale, the governor says:
'Would you like to take a look into a hut, at night?'

'Yes'.

'If you go in, you won't see anything; they'll put on a show. I'll take you to a judas hole. Stay there as long as you like'.

They were lying on two long bed-boards, their feet shackled. Little lamps cast haloes of light. What they showed was sardine tins. They were not playing cards. A few of them were walking about, those who had been able to escape from their fetters. The shackles are all of the same diameter and some ankles are thinner than others. They were swearing at each other. I heard:

'Hey! Nord-af! Is it true that your mother . . .'

They talked about the big event of the day, the visit of the journalist.

'You think he'll do something? Nothing, take it from me. In any case, we don't have anything in common with men, now; we're a cattle-pen.'

'It can't go on for ever, though.'

'You shouldn't have killed someone.'

'What about you, who did you kill?'

'Get on the boat and ask the judge in Le Mans, if he'll be so kind as to see you.'

No one slept. You saw some couples. There was a constant dull hubbub, occasionally broken by an outburst of harsh shouting. The smell and the sight were redolent of a zoo.

'I'll go and see him, tomorrow, to show him I'm not mad. The screw says I'm mad! I'll go and see him, that journalist.'

'So what! He's one of them, remember, like all the rest.'

And one convict, in a working-class voice, got my position to a T:

'Well then, why don't you go? You don't have to be afraid, he's in with them, for what that's worth.'[115]

He hears them talking about him, 'the journalist'. For them, he is clearly an 'other'; perhaps also for the management; or perhaps not . . . In any case, Londres emerges sure of the distance at which he was kept: there is no point in even trying to get closer. But it is distance that is fruitful. It is what makes things strange, so it is what makes it possible to see in a way that questions those who are unified behind the reporter.

This external point of view seems to be something the journalist shares with the doctor. In Londres' text, there are analogies between these two persons. Like the journalist, the doctor sees man in all his nakedness, he can make raw diagnoses independently of any empathic approach; he objectifies as abnormal and pathological, therefore, symptoms that are no longer seen as such in the penal colony, so commonplace are they. The behaviour of one of the convicts, Roussenq, towards Londres, is revealing with regard to this analogy between the doctor and the journalist. The convict says to him spontaneously: 'I'm going to show you my body.' Londres continues: 'He bared himself completely. Passing his hand over his stomach, he says, "Cachexia!" He is so thin that you would have said he was shivering.'[116] The convict wants to be objectified in an external gaze; he puts the journalist in a position to make a diagnosis, as if to help him to grasp what there is to see, and so what there is to be told.

The test of strangeness, in the writing of Albert Londres, does not consist, therefore, in an attempt at empathy, far from it; it consists in keeping his distance from the situations with which the journalist is confronted, so as to bring out this *strangeness* which questions us at the same time as it unites us behind the witness-ambassador.

3. Edward R. Murrow or the test of the usurpation of the centre

'See it now' versus McCarthyism: 'Americanness' at stake

When McCarthyism was at its height in the United States, in the years 1953–4, Edward R. Murrow (1908–65) was the perfect incarnation of a figure of the witness-ambassador, or of the 'centre'.[117] He had been the courageous CBS radio correspondent in London during the Second World War, and his 'This is . . . London', spoken amidst the constant racket of the bombardments, had entered into the legend of war journalism; present at the liberation of the Buchenwald concentration camp, he had embodied the values of an America of freedom in the face of a barbarism described with undeniable literary skill. He was a heroic figure, then, though in the eyes of some he had lost a little of his lustre. His loyal and admiring colleague Fred W. Friendly had been the first to regret that Murrow had seemed to be compromising himself in entertaining and worldly programmes, to which he lent his fame and his ability to 'unify' the public; had he nothing better to do than conduct interviews with Hollywood stars, in his weekly programme 'Person to Person'?

On the other hand, these broadcasts had maintained and even enhanced a popularity which was later, at the time of the programme 'See It Now', necessary to give full impact to his commitments. This was emphasized by the programme's reporter, Joseph Wershba, in an article published in 1979 for the fifteenth anniversary of Murrow's 'battle' against McCarthy:

> But it was precisely the popularity of 'Person to Person', which had millions more viewers than 'See It Now' could ever claim, that made Murrow's attack so powerful in terms of reaching a broadbased audience. For it was inconceivable to these starry-eyed millions that the commentator who had taken them into the boudoirs of Hollywood sexpots could be anything but a true-blue American.[118]

Murrow possessed, therefore, all the attributes to prove particularly dangerous to McCarthy; he, more than anyone, could assume the stature of incontrovertible representative of the collective American identity (of 'us').

The programme 'See It Now', broadcast on CBS, consisted of heavily 'written' documentaries – voice-over commentary on images themselves meticulously edited, the whole introduced and closed with a text read by Murrow facing the camera – and was in the tradition of the written journalism most concerned with factual accuracy and impartiality. The aim was certainly to bring the American public together, by a journalism which would make them see generally accepted 'truths'. Television was regarded as an additional tool in the establishment of the 'truth'. Thus, in the first broadcast of 'See It Now', on 18 November 1951, Murrow emphasized that television offered unprecedented potential for broadening the gaze, and hence for the emergence of the truth; this first programme began with a simultaneous view of San Francisco's Golden Gate Bridge and Brooklyn Bridge in New York, while, in voice-over, Murrow declared: 'For the first time in the history of man we are able to look out at both the Atlantic and Pacific coasts of this great country at the same time.' 'No journalistic age', he continued, 'was ever given a weapon for truth with quite the same scope as this fledgling television.'[119]

But Murrow was not one of those who saw 'truth' (unifying) as synonymous with absence of conflict. The 'truth' might allow a generally shared gaze, but this did not necessarily exclude an appeal to 'us' against an enemy, and hence the introduction of a conflict at its very heart. Murrow seems to have been well aware of this possibility, as is revealed by a conversation with Friendly at the beginning of the 'battle' against McCarthy (which had begun with a documentary on an army lieutenant, Milo Radulovich), Friendly writes:

> We were both mindful of an old CBS news adage laid down by Paul White, the dynamic wartime head of the CBS news department: 'Ideally, in the case of controversial issues, the audience should be left with no impression as to which side the analyst himself actually favors.' In the case of Milo Radulovich, Murrow doubted that such an attitude was possible. 'We can't make the Air Force's case if they won't help us. Besides, some issues aren't equally balanced. We can't sit there every Tuesday night and give the impression that for every argument on one side there is an equal one on the other side.'[120]

Murrow had always denounced the hypocrisy of the confusion of 'truth' and 'neutrality', a denunciation which was based, I believe, on his conception of the journalistic method of establishing the 'truth'; this was rarely, he believed, the product of an unanchored gaze, but rather was established on the basis of an axis, or a centre, that is, the journalist, whose duty was to be an impeccable representative of the values and needs of the community. It is because Murrow's relationship to the 'truth' is linked to the figure of the witness-ambassador, that is, is sustained by the need for a centre that shows itself, that he was particularly open to the possibility of conflict in the very process of establishing the unifying truth. In fact, the centre served both as a mechanism for bringing 'us' together and as a pointer to possible obstacles to this bringing together: it might expose the existence of an intruder within 'us', hence of a conflictual frontier.

In other words, it is because he was such a perfect version of the figure of the witness-ambassador that Murrow was in a position to open the bringing together to the possibility – perhaps the necessity – of a test for 'us'. And it is the nature of this test which is of interest to us here, as we examine his three famous documentaries of 1953–4 on the subject of McCarthyism, made with the assistance of his collaborator Fred W. Friendly.[121]

The first of these documentaries, broadcast on 20 October 1953, had the title 'The Case of Milo Radulovich, A0589839'. It should be remembered that, since the autumn of 1953, McCarthy and his Senate committee of inquiry had been investigating the army. Milo Radulovich was a 26-year-old lieutenant who worked in a department of meteorology in the Air Force Reserve, while studying physics at the University of Michigan. He had been asked to resign from the army in August 1953 because he presented a 'security risk'. When he refused to resign, he was made the subject of an official inquiry by the Air Force Board, which established that, though his loyalty was not in question, the security risk remained and required his removal from the army, because his sister and his father were suspected of engaging in 'Communist activities'. Murrow and Friendly had been planning to 'do something' on the subject of the pernicious atmosphere of McCarthyism for some months and, in particular, had begun to collect recordings of speeches by Senator McCarthy. The case of Radulovich provided them, at last, with the 'little story' or 'little picture' they had been waiting for. The notion of 'little picture' was central to their method at 'See It Now'; Murrow and Friendly liked to tackle big issues through a 'case', which revealed the nature of these issues 'in miniature' and concretely, in a way that brought things home to the viewers.[122]

This documentary allows Milo Radulovich, members of his family, and friends and neighbours from the little town of Dexter (Michigan) to speak. The programme patently takes the side of the young lieutenant, raising numerous problems regarding the methods of McCarthyism:

investigations disregarding the right of defence; an 'extremist' application of the notion of 'security risk' (requiring resignation even when loyalty was not in question); confusion of the individual and his family; and lack of proof regarding the reality of the activities of the father and sister of Radulovich. At the same time, the principle of an investigation into the political convictions of individuals is presented as contrary to the American conception of the freedom of the individual. In this regard, the problems raised are not without their own contradictions; the documentary does not follow through any particular argument: it attacks both the inadequacy of the investigation and the principle on which it was based. Should only the father and the sister have been investigated? Or should there have been no investigation, so as to respect their freedoms, even that to be Communists? Or an investigation, but without the results having any implications for Milo, their son and brother? Or an investigation and, if the father and the sister proved to be 'real' Communists, a review of the question of the security risk represented by Milo? The documentary does not come down clearly in favour of any one of these.

In any case, following this programme, it was announced by the Secretary of the Air Force, Harold E. Talbot, in a statement made at the beginning of a later broadcast of 'See It Now', on 24 November 1953, that Radulovich was to remain in the army.[123] This episode had not escaped the attention of McCarthy and his friends. In November 1953, when Murrow's reporter Joseph Wershba was covering the sessions of the investigating committee in Washington, he was taken on one side by friends of McCarthy, who threatened to reveal that Murrow had been a lackey of the Soviet Union in the 1930s. Their 'proof' was a list of teachers and students who had participated in exchanges with the Soviet Union during that period, a list which included Murrow's name. In spite of, and angered by, this threat, Murrow finally decided to make a documentary devoted entirely to McCarthy himself, composed of a montage of his speeches, intended to expose both the man and the danger he represented.[124] This would be 'A Report on Senator Joseph R. McCarthy', broadcast on 9 March 1954. The documentary reveals the system of accusation and intimidation employed by McCarthy, particularly his technique of 'guilt by association', without tangible proofs, and his use of lies to destabilize suspects. The programme went out in the middle of the Zwicker affair: in February 1954, McCarthy had accused General Zwicker of having agreed to promote an extreme left-wing dentist-captain, Irving Press, and then of protecting him. McCarthy had abused the general, but also the Secretary of the Army, Robert Stevens, whom he had managed to intimidate with increasing success and make cede to his demands.[125]

Murrow had announced at the beginning that McCarthy would have the right of reply. The senator used this, two weeks later,[126] but another

'See It Now' documentary had meanwhile hit home: 'Annie Lee Moss Before the McCarthy Committee', broadcast on 16 March 1954. Once again, it was a 'little picture', as Murrow emphasizes in his introduction: 'Good evening. On "See It Now", we occasionally use the phrase "the little picture". Tonight we bring you the little picture of a little woman, Mrs Annie Lee Moss. . .' McCarthy had just made new 'revelations' about Communist infiltration of the army: a civilian employee, responsible for sending and decoding coded messages, by the name of Annie Lee Moss, had been listed by the FBI as a member of the Communist Party. This was on the basis of statements made by an FBI agent by the name of Mary Stalcup Markward, who claimed that she had seen Annie Lee Moss at a Party meeting some years earlier. A woman by the name of Annie Lee Moss, who worked in the Pentagon cafeteria and claimed that she had never set foot in a code room, was brought before the senate committee. The documentary is largely composed of film of this hearing, in which viewers see, facing indefatigable questioners, a lower middle-class black woman, who obviously has no idea what she is doing there, claiming that she had never engaged in any Communist activities and did not even know 'who Karl Marx was'. She is a woman with whom one could easily identify. And it is this 'little woman', increasingly sympathetic as the programme progresses, who destroys the credibility of the investigators. In any case, McCarthy left the hearing in the middle of the session, leaving an empty chair on which the 'See It Now' cameraman, Charles Mack, gleefully lingers. McCarthy's deputy, Roy Cohn, casts increasingly black looks at the defendant, who is winning general sympathy.

When, eight days later, McCarthy counter-attacked, in a badly filmed programme, made in a dark studio, he had already been badly wounded by Murrow and by other events: on 11 March, the army, in its turn, had put McCarthy in the dock, 'claiming that he had tried to obtain preferential treatment for one of his deputies called up for military service in July 1953'.[127] It is not the consequences of these three documentaries that are of interest to us here, however, but rather the type of gaze they offer, and the way they present both a movement to bring an 'us' together and, in so doing, a test for this 'us'.

In Nellie Bly and Albert Londres, the tests were, respectively, that of the hidden and that of strangeness. In Murrow, the test is of a different type: that of the usurpation of the centre. If 'we' are appealed to here, it is because here it is 'our' very centre, hence our identity, that is at stake; what there is to be seen, what the journalist exposes for 'us', is a usurper who speaks in 'our' name, hence in our stead. The way in which Murrow presents the conflict into which he plunges 'us' is, therefore, as follows: 'we' cannot not see, here, on the spot, a threat to what we are. There is no need to journey into obscure places to test 'ourselves' in the face of an unexpected enemy or a disquieting strangeness; the enemy is here, under our very noses, at the centre of the very people – 'us' – this enemy claims to be unifying. This enemy has assumed the features of a witness-ambassador. The theme of 'Americanness' is never off his lips, and he claims to embody it. This usurpation means that 'we' have to reconstitute ourselves in a confrontation with the intruder. We have to recover this 'Americanness' which McCarthy has confiscated.

Murrow's aim, therefore, like that of Nellie Bly and Albert Londres, is to recall the centre, to re-centre, but on the basis of a specific test which is different from that administered by Bly or Londres: an acknowledgement that this centre has been usurped. Once again, the aim is to re-centre, not to decentre. For if Murrow contests the nature of the American/un-American divide as it is conceived by McCarthy, and seeks to 'reintegrate' many Americans 'excluded' by the senator – the purpose of the unifying theme of the documentaries on Milo Radulovich and Annie Lee Moss – he is not ready to kill off the issue which sustains McCarthyism, the existence of an 'Americanness'. Murrow confronts McCarthy on his own ground. This limits his own room for manœuvre with regard to McCarthyism, as he himself is reliant on a certain conception of 'Americanness', which involves, in particular, a far from negligible dose of anti-Communism. It should be noted that Murrow never defends a real Communist; it is because Radulovich is not a Communist, and is therefore 'loyal', that he is reintegrated into 'us', against the accusations of McCarthy. With regard to his relationship with the 'suspect' members of his family, two lines of approach coexist in the documentary, in which, as we have already noted, there are several internal contradictions, because Murrow was fighting on several fronts; each of these approaches contains a latent anti-Communism. On the one hand, the documentary presents, with an insistence which tends to legitimate it, a discourse by Radulovich on the family, an entity no one wants to do away with (to demand that a young lieutenant cease all contact with his father and his sister is absurd, for the very reason that they are his father and his sister) and which, in any case, respects the freedom of the individuals who constitute it (in other words, Radulovich, though in contact with his father and his sister, was not influenced by them); on the other hand, the documentary emphasizes that, in any case, the charges made against the father and the sister have not been proved.[128] Both these approaches, therefore, assume that the fact of being a Communist would have been a problem in respect of 'Americanness': the second shows that this eventuality has not been proved in the case of the members of Milo Radulovich's family, which makes it possible to get round the problem;

the first admits it, but represents the family in a way that, because it combines a defence of solidarity based on affection and an affirmation of the autonomy of thought of the individuals composing it, protects the son and the brother from this potential 'evil' surrounding him.

In general, Murrow and Friendly are here using to their own advantage a certain ambiguity in the notion of 'Americanness', in which a strong attachment to individual liberty coexists with a manifest dose of anti-Communism. Thus the documentary on Radulovich emphasizes that the investigation of the father and the sister had been contrary to the American principle of individual liberty, but also asserts that it had, in any case, been inadequate – the second point suggesting that, in spite of everything, if it had been adequately proved, their Communism might well have merited attention. One has the impression that, though Murrow clearly made himself the defender of individual liberties, the basis of 'Americanness', he still does not go so far as to assume that this means you need not be concerned about the danger represented by the Communism of some individuals. He clearly prefers, therefore, to defend victims of McCarthy who are not Communists, which allows him, as we have seen, to sustain the discourse on individual liberty without confronting its ultimate problem: are individuals free to be Communists? It can surely be argued that this way of using his characteristically 'American' freedom, in spite of everything, calls 'Americanness' into question.

The 'unifying' process by which an Annie Lee Moss is reintegrated into the 'us' from which McCarthy wanted to exclude her is also based at least in part on the very obvious fact that she is a woman as remote from Communism as it is possible to be. The most tangible evidence of this is her innocent amazement, which causes warm and affectionate laughter and destroys at one go the malevolent suspicions of McCarthy: to the question, 'Did you ever hear of Karl Marx?' she, an average American above all suspicion, answers, 'Who's that?' Senator Symington, who was conducting the interrogation, smiles: 'I'll pass the question.' He goes on to ask her if she sees herself as a 'good American', and then says, 'Would you ever do anything to hurt your country?' 'No, sir,' replies Annie Lee Moss.

A few minutes earlier, she has been seen, before the Senate, stumbling through the text which summarized the reasons for her dismissal. Murrow, voice-over, ironically observes: 'This woman, under suspicion because of charges made by Senator McCarthy and Roy Cohn, alleged to have examined and corrected secret and encoded overseas messages, attempted to read the uncoded words of her suspension notice.' It is apparent that she can scarcely read or write. If this fact makes Murrow's victory certain, it should nevertheless be noted that the person defended here as emblem of the individual liberty threatened by McCarthy is particularly obviously not 'dangerous', that is, hardly likely to use her freedom to think subversive thoughts with regard to a certain conception of 'Americanness'.

A similar observation may be made with regard to a key passage in the 9 March documentary on McCarthy. To demonstrate the accusatory techniques of the senator, the documentary includes a filmed extract from the interrogation before the Senate of Reed Harris, for many years employed by the State Department, Director of the Information Service, and accused of using his office to assist the Communist cause. Before the Senate, McCarthy asks him about a book he had written in 1932, when he had still been in the academic world, teaching at Columbia University. This makes it possible to see how McCarthy operated, that is, by association of facts, rather than a concern to establish the truth of the accusation in question. This book, written when Harris was a young man, seems to have been sympathetic to hard left ideas and to have included some fairly subversive remarks about certain pillars of 'Americanness', in particular the institution of the family. It had cost Harris his job at the university, even though he had been defended by a lawyer from the American Civil Liberties Union. Harris does not dispute the facts. McCarthy then introduces a lie into his interrogation, intended to intimidate his interlocutor: he states that the ACLU had meanwhile been 'listed' as an association working for the Communists, which Harris says he is unaware of. In voice-over, a few minutes later, Murrow notes that this statement is untrue; the ACLU does not appear on any list of 'subversive' associations, of the Attorney General, of the FBI, or of any government body. It is sheer intimidation. McCarthy then reads an extract from this book attacking marriage as 'an antiquated and stupid religious phenomenon' which should 'be cast off of our civilization', and asks Harris if, at the time he wrote the book, he believed that professors should be permitted to teach such things; Harris replies that, at the time, he did indeed believe this, in the name of complete freedom of teaching. But it is clear that, throughout the interrogation, Harris is thrown on the defensive: he emphasizes, on the one hand, that this isolated extract gives a biased picture of the general argument of the book and, on the other, that this general argument itself should be put in the context of a period when the Communist threat was not comparable to what it has since become. He goes further; he no longer believes, he says, like Senator Taft, for example, 'that Communists and Socialists should be allowed to teach in the schools'.

In other words, the documentary once again presents a 'perfect' victim, now a fully paid-up subscriber to all the shared values of 'Americanness'. In the documentary on Radulovich, Murrow suggested that an individual should not be confused with his family – even if he was

close to them, he retained the freedom to think for himself, so if he said
he was not a Communist, he should be believed; now he argues that an
individual today should not be confused with what he had been twenty
years earlier – you are free to change, and to invoke the past is to deny
this fundamental individual liberty. 'Americanness' is thus not challenged today by these individuals accused by McCarthy. The conception
of 'Americanness' which emerges in the documentary is hardly subversive. The voice-over commentary of Murrow is revealing: 'Senator
McCarthy succeeded only in proving that Reed Harris had once written
a bad book which the American people had proved twenty-two years ago
by not buying it, which is what they eventually do with all bad ideas.' The
'American people', safe from 'bad ideas': the unifying intent is clear, as
are its implications, that is, the exclusion of certain ways of thinking from
the definition of 'Americanness'. The attack on McCarthy, consequently, takes the following form: do not think of yourself as more
American than the Americans themselves; listen to the regrets of the
'true' Americans who were once cast out from the innermost circle. Do
not take yourself to be the centre; the centre decides spontaneously, and
more flexibly than you, who is close to it, who strays from it, and who
returns to it. As for the fact that the ACLU is not 'suspect', we see that
this, too, is, if anything, reassuring; not only does it make it possible to
denounce the use of lies in the intimidatory techniques of McCarthy, but
it also makes it possible to guarantee the 'Americanness' of the victim.

In a similar vein, we should also note how Murrow is constantly legitimating himself during his confrontation with McCarthy, in particular
when responding to his counter-attacks: he is at pains to guarantee that
he himself is very definitely not a Communist or a sympathizer with the
extreme left, again so as to be able to present himself as a 'true' American.
The way in which, a quarter of an hour after a forceful intervention on
the part of the senator, he describes his political 'position' in his own
radio programme shows a strong desire to maintain his position in the
centre, implying the impossibility of any sympathy for the hard left. 'I
have a little difficulty', McCarthy had declared, 'answering the specific
attacks . . . because I never listened to the extreme left-wing bleeding-
heart elements of radio and television. However, after you invited me to
come over . . .' Murrow's answer is: 'I may be a bleeding heart, being not
quite sure of what it means. As for being left-wing, that is political short-
hand; but if the senator means I am somewhat to the left of his position
and of Louis XIV, he is correct.' In an article in the *New York Times* on 13
March 1954, Murrow goes further in asserting his own anti-
Communism, and concludes by issuing a challenge to McCarthy: 'The
record would soon show who had served the Communists – You or I.' In
his 'Reply to the Reply', broadcast on 13 April 1954, Murrow invokes his

dignity and his 'responsibility' as a journalist, which has often led him to fight the Communist cause in the name of truth; in his radio broadcasts during the war, for example, he had asserted that the Russians were responsible for the massacre of Katyn. 'I require no lectures from the Junior Senator of Wisconsin as to the dangers or terrors of Communism,' he declares.

This in no way detracts, of course, from the courage of Murrow in this battle against McCarthy. Those who lived through this period, friends of Murrow and Friendly I have spoken to, are emphatic that the necessary precondition for an effective fight at that period was for it to be based on just such a common (in the sense of 'the most commonly accepted') conception of 'Americanness'. Here, once again, we see the difference between a unifying journalism and a decentring journalism, which might have challenged the very existence of a centre – for example, by directly confronting the question of the 'otherness' represented by Communism in relation to 'Americanness', that is, by a more fundamental questioning of such categories, their foundations and their consequences.

'Un-American': the situation reversed

This measure of anti-Communism, necessary to unify his audience around him, does not prevent Murrow from having what is, in the last analysis, a very different approach to Communism from that of McCarthy. This difference emerges most clearly in the way Murrow defends himself against the accusation of having been on the 'suspect' list of academics who had relations with the Soviet Union in the 1930s: 'I believed nineteen years ago and I believe today that mature American graduate students and professors can engage in conversation, controversy, and the clash of ideas with Communists anywhere under peacetime conditions without becoming contaminated or converted.'[129] Admittedly, the 'conversation' must seemingly be a robust one, avoiding the spectre of conversion to such a profoundly un-American cause, but it is still, nevertheless, considered a possibility. We find here the very balance which is defended at one point in the documentary on Radulovich, a balance expounded by the young lieutenant himself, which brings into play a whole representation of the individual: one can, up to a point, not be Communist and associate with Communists, without this implying 'influence', that is, an absence of loyalty with regard to America.

In fact, so as to be able both to differentiate themselves from McCarthy and to remain on his ground, that of 'Americanness', it is essential for the Murrow–Friendly team both to present themselves as anti-Communist and to make it clear that their anti-Communism is of a very different type from that of McCarthy. Indeed, it is in this interstice that their re-centring, their recovery of the 'centre' from its usurper, takes place. Admittedly, the interstice might be very small – a risk which seems literally 'lived' by Friendly in the days which preceded the broadcast of the documentary on McCarthy. As described by Wershba a few years later, Friendly seems to have been acutely aware of the difficulties of the defence of 'Americanness' adopted by Murrow against its usurper, McCarthy. He was understandably anxious that no one in the 'See It Now' team could be suspected of Communist activities, which would have invalidated the team's work: the documentary might then have appeared as no more than the voice of an extreme left splinter group – precisely how McCarthy wanted it to be seen. It was necessary, therefore, in a sense, to enter into the logic of McCarthy to be able to attack him on his own ground, that is, to make sure that the team contained only true-blue Americans. But at the same time, Friendly was manifestly ill at ease during the staff meeting at which he asked his colleagues to declare if they had a suspect past. In a way, he did not want to know. This ambiguity emerges in Wershba's account: 'Friendly assembled the staff and grimly warned that if anyone in the room felt he had any associations, past or present, that would hurt 'See It Now', he should speak up. But before anyone even had a chance to respond, Friendly rushed ahead: "And I'll brain whoever says anything." '[130] Friendly could not bear the idea, obviously, that his question might make him sound like McCarthy. In any case, again according to Wershba, Murrow declared a few days later: 'If none of us ever read a book that was "dangerous", had a friend that was "different" or joined an organization that advocated "change", we would all be just the kind of people Joe McCarthy wants.'[131] Implicit here is: this is stupid; ultimately, would we be free, thinking, individuals? Would we be the true heirs of the ideals which built America?

The interstice in which Murrow and Friendly operate is thus the following: it is necessary, admittedly, as a position in the 'centre' (or as witness-ambassador) requires, to be concerned about the 'un-American', but this concern should not go to the obsessional lengths to which it goes in McCarthy. It is necessary, admittedly, to recognize the existence of an American/un-American divide, but without seeing it, as in McCarthyism, as a rupture, or a radical and fearful exclusion. This is the position of Murrow, located in this interstice: what is truly 'un-American', ultimately, is the constant obsession with un-Americanism. More un-American than the Communist himself – the Communist being, it should be emphasized yet again, the great absentee from these documentaries, the tacit untouchable – is he who is obsessed by un-Americanism: namely, McCarthy. Because the 'Americanness' which Murrow here represents, though it may imply a divide, something un-American, of which the Communist is part, still implies a certain relationship to this divide, one which permits dialogue and confrontation, and precludes the permanent sense of threat and the creation of a climate of fear and hatred. And it is the application of this idea of 'Americanness' which exposes the usurper of the centre: he is the true un-American.

So Murrow, ultimately, turns the situation on its head, designating as the true 'other' the very person who is haunted by otherness. This attitude is neatly summarized in the words of a priest quoted in another 'See It Now' documentary of the same period, 'An Argument in Indianapolis'. This programme was broadcast on 24 November 1953 and deals with events which had occurred a few days earlier in Indiana: a group of some seventy citizens had reserved a room, the auditorium of the Indiana War Memorial, for a meeting of the ACLU; four days before the set date, the reservation had been cancelled, officially because the meeting appeared too controversial. It was suddenly impossible, apparently, to reserve a room anywhere in the area, that is, until a Catholic priest offered his parish hall. These events did not involve McCarthyism directly, but they were still revealing as to a certain atmosphere of wariness towards associations which might, from one day to the next, be classed as 'suspect' and so compromise those who had agreed to provide them with accommodation. It is this atmosphere that Murrow and Friendly bring out in their documentary. They allow the priest to speak, and this is what he says on camera: 'When the climate is such that so many people are so quick . . . to deny to others the right to peaceful assembly and free speech – then somebody certainly has to prove to them that they are, in their activities, actually un-American.'

At the same time, if what constitutes the 'other' is this very obsession with the stranger, the logic of this reversal implies that the relationship established towards this 'other' should not itself be characterized by obsessiveness and a desire to exclude, as is that of McCarthy with his own phantoms. Effectively, in the gaze cast by Murrow and Friendly on McCarthy in the documentary directly devoted to him, we see that the method is the exact opposite of his: they confront him on his own ground; they allow him to speak; and they set out to designate him as the enemy 'in its own words and pictures'. In other words, they take him seriously as 'centre' in order, on his own ground, to expose the flaws in this discourse of Americanness, that is, to get at what it is in him that is a negation of the most obvious heritage of America, the right of the individual to freedom of speech and thought. This is the opposite of the logic of McCarthyism, which establishes right from the start a conflictual frontier with 'others' who are never confronted, but excluded from the outset.

The consequence of this designation of the true un-American on the basis of a confrontation regarding the very question of the centre, and not, as in McCarthy, by an a priori decision about who is excluded, is that this un-American is conceived as much closer to 'us'. He appears as a possible deviation from the centre or from 'Americanness'. Thus McCarthy, in his monstrousness, in his perversion of Americanness, questions the 'us' whose centre he has so easily usurped; this is the significance of the quotation from Shakespeare used twice by Murrow in his final comments: 'The fault, dear Brutus, is not in our stars but in ourselves.'

At the same time, Murrow is teaching America an important lesson: the centre is always open to conflict, it is at stake, it is not permanently fixed. We should mistrust those who fix the centre, when the centre is something which both *makes itself felt* and *puts itself to the test*. Murrow's unmasking of the usurper of the centre, by showing the proximity of the enemy, simply urges 'us' to a vigilance which should never have been relaxed and to an Americanness conceived as a perpetual alertness on 'our' part against our own tendency to forget ourselves in the mechanical obsession with the enemy. The famous connection established by McCarthy between the external and the internal enemy – the idea that the Soviets are here, in our midst – is suddenly denounced as a comforter which feigns ignorance, so that we need not recognize the true proximity of the 'non-us'; it is to be forever chasing after an 'other' which does not come from 'us' ourselves, but is heterogeneous to us. Murrow, in contrast, makes us see the dangerous connection between the intruder and the 'us' this intruder infiltrates and deceives; he sees McCarthy as a sickness of Americanness itself. Thus, for Murrow, what is un-American is the permanent challenge which threatens the obvious 'us', which then has to be both restored and made uneasy – one might even say restored *in its unease*.

Exposure to the public

In this method, the crucial role is played by public exposure, because it is this that makes the 'obvious' emerge – the turning of the usurper into an un-American at the same time as the restoration of the true 'us'. Just as the Americanness of McCarthy cannot withstand the public exposure of his words and behaviour (a test which is precisely the technique of the documentary 'A Report on Senator Joseph R. McCarthy'), so, but the other way round, the Americanness of a Milo Radulovich or an Annie Lee Moss is revealed by the simple fact of their appearance.

One scene in the documentary on Annie Lee Moss is particularly revealing in this regard. The unifying impulse which operates in the documentary culminates, finally, in the speech of Senator McClellan, who rises to defend the accused woman against unacceptable methods. Roy Cohn has just concluded, notwithstanding all Mrs Moss's answers, that there is still the testimony of Mrs Markward, an FBI agent, stating that Annie Lee Moss is well and truly a member of the Communist Party. This conclusion is an obvious negation of everything Mrs Moss has said and, more generally, of the 'innocence' which the hearing has so clearly demonstrated. Senator McClellan then asks to speak, and Murrow, in voice-over, gives us his name. Both Murrow's intervention and the method of filming – Charlie Mack, the cameraman, makes the camera slide gently from the interrogators towards this individual who is about to speak from the hall – seem to guide the television viewer towards something obvious and necessary: the voice of the revolt of the public itself against the methods of McCarthyism. The impropriety denounced by Senator McClellan is this very invocation by Roy Cohn of a hidden witness in the face of a witness who is present, who has agreed to expose herself, and who is denied the right to be confronted with this witness who, even though she is concealed, is set up as arbiter of her fate. If Annie Lee Moss is recognized as obviously one of 'us', it is particularly by her courage in exposing herself.

We may note, furthermore, that Senator McClellan here takes on the role of the witness-ambassador. To be more precise, it is the scene itself which, delivered by the Murrow–Friendly gaze, presents a succession of such figures: Murrow presents himself as the witness-ambassador, spokesperson for the public, which then presents us with another witness-ambassador. Senator McClellan constantly refers to the 'public' and to its right ultimately to decide who is 'one of us' and who is not. In applying this criterion, he designates the witness here present, A. L. Moss, as another witness-ambassador, symbol of a public robbed and defeated by the illegitimate triumph of the hidden.

The public, the essential authority, reaffirmed in its unique status as arbiter of what is the 'centre' – hence the necessity, for whoever claims this centre, to expose themselves publicly, because such is the test – is literally put on show in the documentary on Milo Radulovich: many people from the lieutenant's neighbourhood state in front of the camera their confidence as to his loyalty. In the eyes of Thomas Rosteck, who has studied these documentaries, the neighbours here play the role of Greek chorus, which represents the spectators and displays their emotions.[132] In this case, it recognizes Radulovich as 'self-evidently' one of its own. There is no voice to express the slightest doubt with regard to this young man; in fact, Wershba has told me that the production team was genuinely surprised, especially at a time when suspicion was rife, to find no one in the neighbourhood who would speak ill of the young lieutenant.

To the extent that journalism consists of the labour of exposing things to the public, Americanness is thus erected into a fundamentally journalistic matter. This is because identity ('we') is conceived as something which is revealed: what is 'ours', what is not, and what usurps the centre – all can be seen. We find here a constant in the figure of the witness-ambassador: confidence in the omnipotence of the gaze, of its gaze, to apprehend the truth and in this way bring together; it is this gaze that sets a test for 'us' and at the same time passes this test and reconstitutes 'us'. Everything 'appears', as we saw in the world of Séverine; in Nellie Bly, the gaze was erected into a force for exposure, which overcame the challenge of the hidden; in Albert Londres, the same theme of the omnipotent gaze took the form of a power to make strangeness appear, and then to draw out all its power to question 'us'. Here, with Murrow, the gaze is what makes it possible to determine identity: the gaze of the journalist, who represents the public and enables this public to recover its rights, that is, enables us to recover 'our' identity from whoever has stolen it and whose status as usurper also *appears*.

Murrow *exposes* the victims of McCarthyism in order to prove them innocent. He does this, for example, with the father of Radulovich, to reveal the obvious fact that he belongs to 'us', that is, to an America of immigration, but also and at the same time to an America of the values of honour, dignity and respect for democratic institutions, almost of devotion to the common good. The letter from this father to the president of the United States, written in poor English, read with a strong Central European accent, with the assistance of his wife, sitting alongside him on a settee facing the camera, is the supreme 'proof':

> I am American citizen who come here thirty-nine years ago from Serbia. I served America in the Army in the first world war. . . My whole life, my whole family, is American. Mr. President, I writing to you because they are doing a bad thing to Milo. They are wrong. The things they say about him are wrong. He has given all his growing years to his country. He is good for this country. Mr. President, I am an old man. I have spend my life in this coal mine and auto furnaces. I ask nothing for myself. All I ask is justice for my boy. Mr. President, I ask your help.

But Murrow also exposes the usurper, in order to unmask him. The fact that he takes McCarthy seriously, in 'A Report on Senator Joseph R. McCarthy', is never clearer than when he pretends to take as his own a statement of McCarthy's, or when he compares it to a statement of President Eisenhower's. Was McCarthy, perhaps, the 'centre'? Murrow leaves the question open. But he immediately makes us see the contradictions of the senator, through his body language, through his almost pathological aggression towards the very person who sometimes spoke

like him (Eisenhower), and through his relentlessness and general inco-
herence. For example, at the beginning of the documentary, Murrow
quotes an apparently reasonable statement, only later mentioning its
author (McCarthy): 'If this fight against Communism is made a fight
against America's two great political parties, the American people know
that one of these parties will be destroyed and the Republic cannot
endure very long as a oneparty system.' Murrow shows that it is precisely this destructive fantasy which motivates McCarthy in his relentless hostility to the Democratic Party, and that his whole behaviour is in
contradiction with this statement. He then shows an extract from a
highly anti-Communist speech made by Eisenhower when he was
a presidential candidate, and follows it with several speeches of
McCarthy's: this comparison ultimately reveals a degree of overkill on
the part of McCarthy, an absolute will to destroy – including the
Republican Party and even all those who share many of his ideas. In this
way, taken seriously as the centre, McCarthy ultimately emerges as its
usurper. In one of his speeches, McCarthy explains that after his interview with the candidate Eisenhower, he cannot 'report that we agreed
entirely on everything', which sounds moderate enough, but he inter-
rupts himself with an unpleasant laugh, a catching of the breath which
reveals a sort of exultant destructive folly. This passage in the documentary is often referred to by contemporaries as a key moment. In any
case, we see clearly in this passage that it is precisely when McCarthy
claims to represent the 'American people' – because he claims, in this
speech, to be addressing the 'American people' as one of its representatives in the Senate – that he is revealed, by his terrible laugh, to be a
dangerous usurper.

The way Murrow and Friendly conceived the documentary on
McCarthy seems, therefore, to rely on the fact that Americanness, the
true Americanness, *can be seen*, and that McCarthy could not but, as a
result, be exposed, a man who, what is more, spends his days making
connections, interpreting and accusing without ever offering visible
proofs. For example, he makes a habit of deliberate slips of the tongue:
in a speech of 1952 devoted to the Democratic presidential candidate
Adlai Stevenson, shown in the documentary, McCarthy calls him
'Alger', an allusion to Alger Hiss, one of the first victims of the witch-
hunt in the United States. This is McCarthy's technique: he sees something else behind what is there to see, without ever seeking to justify it
or to make it really visible. We have already observed this procedure in
the interrogation of Reed Harris, notably in McCarthy's mendacious
insinuation on the subject of the ACLU. The methods of McCarthy are
the opposite of those of Murrow, who wants to show McCarthy as
McCarthy presents himself.

Murrow also repeats a quotation used by McCarthy in his speech against Adlai Stevenson – 'Upon what meat doth this, our Caesar, feed?' – and applies it to McCarthy himself. In doing so, however, he changes the tone: full of insinuation in the mouth of McCarthy, remote from any concern for evident proof, when used by Murrow the quotation becomes one which encourages the observation of tangible facts. Murrow shows that McCarthy's insinuations regarding Stevenson lead nowhere, to no visibly compromising truth: there is no 'meat' to speak of to be discovered in Stevenson's secret larder. What they reveal, however, are the methods of McCarthyism: this particular meat is ultimately seen for what it is: rotten.

Nellie Bly, Albert Londres and Edward R. Murrow are three versions of the figure of the witness-ambassador, through whom we can see how journalists, erected as 'our' representatives, bring a community together behind them by making it undergo a test. The journalist is both origin and hero of this test, because it is the journalist who enables 'us' to pass it in order to reconstitute ourselves.

These witness-ambassadors show, therefore, that the act of unifying, which operates through their gaze, does not abolish all conflict, but is able successfully to base itself on the exposure of a conflictual frontier between 'us' and a 'non-us', requiring the former to fight to affirm itself. The form this conflict assumes is fairly simple, admittedly, but it nevertheless indicates something that is important if we are to understand the methods of the unifiers in modern journalism.

We must now examine the limitations of this very position, that of the witness-ambassador. An analysis of the limitations and the frustrations inherent in this figure is latent, though not necessarily formulated, in the methods of those who 'decentre', for whom it is imperative that journalism has other aims. It is important, therefore, to make this analysis with care as a preliminary to understanding the journalists who decentre.

4

The Limitations of the Position of the Witness-Ambassador:
The Case of Lincoln Steffens

However fundamental the figure of the witness-ambassador may be to modern journalism, however solid it may appear, it has to be admitted that one need only express a few doubts regarding the gaze of this supposed representative of 'us', or detect in it something 'constructed' or biased, for the certainties on which such a figure is based to collapse; and for this to cause what we may call the *crisis* of the witness-ambassador.

To demonstrate this crisis, I will trace the itinerary of a famous muckraker,[1] Lincoln Steffens (1866–1936), who came to question this pact with the public, even though it had been the basis of his own work as a reporter. Two decades after Nellie Bly, this master of exposure journalism experienced a crisis, in the very name of the values of muckraking: truth, identifying the enemy to be fought, and unifying a public finally enlightened. Steffens asked himself this question: what if the journalistic gaze were doomed to remain on the surface of things, to miss the profound truth, to substitute simplistic divides for complex realities and, as a result, to 'unify' on an erroneous basis?

This return to Steffens in order to show, through him, the figure of *the witness-ambassador in crisis*, is a useful way of explaining difficulties which continue to dog journalists, and which expose them, in particular, to the criticism of sociologists. The question we need to answer is this: does this crisis condemn journalism itself, or does it enable us to conceive, within journalism, an alternative figure to that of the witness-ambassador?

1. The ease of the recourse to 'I saw'

Having returned from Macedonia, Serbia and Kosovo, it is my duty to give you my impressions: I am afraid, Monsieur le Président, that we are making a bad mistake. You are a man with his feet on the ground. You have scant regard for the intellectuals who fill our columns with grandiloquent and peremptory suppositions. That is fortunate: no more do I. So I will stick to the facts.

This extract is not from a piece of late nineteenth-century journalism, but is the beginning of the article published by the French author Régis Debray in *Le Monde*, on 13 May 1999 ('Letter of a Traveller to the President of the Republic'), in which he declared his opposition to the war in Kosovo. All the devices of the figure of the witness-ambassador are present: the rejection of empty editorializing and hollow words, the cult of 'facts', seen as what has been *lived* or *experienced* and the position of one who is *mandated*, and who returns from a journey with an urgent truth to tell; one might even say, reading these first sentences, the position of the journalist who sees as against that of the intellectual who discourses.

Of course, the author takes a few precautions. He lets us know that he is aware of the relativity of 'facts':

> To each his own, you will tell me. Those I was able to observe on the spot, in a short stay – a week in Serbia (Belgrade, Novi, Sad, Nis, Vramje) from 2 to 9 May, of which four days in Kosovo, from Pristina to Prej, and from Pritzen to Podujevo – do not seem to me to correspond to the words you use, from afar and in good faith.

But the figure of the witness-ambassador quickly reappears, in this affirmation of the impartiality of the spectator: 'Do not think me biased,' declares the witness, firmly basing himself in a collective 'I'. Even the most 'classic' sensualism is present, that is, faith in the *lived* and the *felt*: 'I spent last week in Macedonia, was present at the arrival of the refugees, and listened to their statements. I was devastated, like many others. I wanted at all costs to go and see "from the other side" how such infamy was possible.' The witness tells us that he is not a tourist, nor is he an average journalist, wedded to the singularity of an over-fabricated gaze; he is the representative of the universal sensibility: 'Distrusting Intourist-style visits, or journalistic coach trips, I asked the Serbian authorities to let me have my own vehicle and the opportunity to go wherever, and speak to whoever, I thought fit.'

We do not know if Debray was conscious here of deploying the most traditional tools of unifying journalism, even in his sarcasms at the expense of journalists. This, at last, is 'true journalism', he seems to be saying, as opposed to 'journalistic' coach trips. The discourse of the concrete, of the evidence of the senses and of the feelings, allows him to guarantee that he is giving his audience ('us') the absolute truth, not only the 'facts' but also the way to evaluate them. 'Do you not know that in the heart of old Belgrade the children's theatre Dusan-Radevic is next door to the television studio and that the missile that destroyed the latter hit the former?' The 'I saw' is the foundation on which the article stands:

> I saw, in the hamlet of Lipjan, on Thursday 6 May, a private house demolished by a missile: three little girls and two grandparents slaughtered, and not a military target within a radius of 3 kilometres. I saw, next day, at Prizren, in the gypsy quarter, two other civilian hovels reduced to ashes two hours before, with many victims buried.

At the same time, Debray occasionally permits himself to break the 'I saw' rule, which only brings out more clearly the way he instrumentalizes it. 'Three hundred schools, all over the place, have been hit by the bombs,' he assures us, a claim which can hardly be an eyewitness statement: you do not *see* 300 schools. He also mentions many things he has not seen, simply so as to mention them: 'I was not a witness, admittedly, to the carnage inflicted by the NATO bombers on the buses, the columns of refugees, the trains, the hospital at Nis, and elsewhere.' But many other things – other acts of violence, especially in the other direction – do not figure in the list of things not seen. There are also the extrapolations of 'I saw', not unknown, admittedly, even among the greatest travellers (we noted the tendency of Albert Londres to rush to the hasty conclusions of political theory with regard, for example, to the USSR): 'There is no "totalitarian" charisma over minds,' Debray assures us. 'The West seems a hundred times more obsessed with M. Milosevic than his fellow citizens.' Can such a thing be *seen*, at a glance, on a journey of a few days?

So here we see in action, once again and in spite of a few permutations, the omnipotence of the 'I saw' of the gaze that claims to give the lie to things, without itself ever telling a lie, even by omission. The declarations of modesty only expose more clearly the arrogance of this world of certainties:

> Much may have escaped my modest observations, but the German Minister for Defence lied, on 6 May, when he declared that 'between 600,000 and 900,000 displaced persons had been concentrated in the interior of Kosovo'. In a territory of 10,000 square kilometres, this could not go unnoticed by an observer who travelled, that same day, from east to west and from north to south. In Pristina, where tens of thousands of Kosovans still live, you can eat in Albanian pizzerias, in the company of Albanians.

Had Régis Debray really seen everything? And what was his *seeing* worth?

This contemporary text, written from the position of the witness-ambassador, is an excellent demonstration of the weakness integral to it.

What makes one uneasy is the 'obviousness' implicit in it: this particular witness is *the* witness, the one who, in a manner worthy of a Séverine, defines the 'true' and the 'false' witnesses. Yet the models of impartiality offered by Debray leave one perplexed: 'Could our ministers not question, on the spot, cool-headed witnesses – Greek doctors from Médecins sans Frontières, churchmen, popes?' The devices of the witness-ambassador are, in a way, so crude that they are all you see; they make it possible to offer, through a 'pure', 'innocent' and 'true' testimony, the opinion of a manifestly closed mind on the situation in the former Yugoslavia.

If the weakness of the method shows through the text, it is not without also, and at the same time, reminding us of its undeniable power: as the self-confident tone of the article suggests, there is nothing like adopting the posture of the 'simple witness' to persuade, to affirm that you are speaking the truth, and hence to unify over and above partisan divides. It is simply that if this power, which is that of 'I saw', is overused, it ends up exposing its own flaws. In short, the article is open to the same criticism as that which is so cavalierly addressed to 'journalists' in the first paragraph – and which finally points to the Achilles heel of the figure of the witness-ambassador. The unification suffers by appearing largely constructed and artificial; the test it administers – because it appeals to 'us', through 'our' President of the Republic, 'we' who are in Kosovo through the intermediary of NATO – appears too simple not to be the product of this construction. The claim to go beyond the singularity of the point of view only serves to make this point of view singular.

How do the journalisms of 'unification' contend with these problems, which seem destined to threaten the figure of the witness-ambassador, even when this figure is their strongest asset? By criticizing the figure of the witness-ambassador, are we not putting modern journalism in the dock? If we put this major figure in crisis, how are we to avoid the ultimate outcome of simply abandoning journalism? These are the questions which are explored, in a work plagued by doubt and anxiety, by one of the greatest witness-ambassadors in the history of journalism, Lincoln Steffens.

2. The itinerary of a muckraker in crisis

The muckrakers

Lincoln Steffens was part of the 'muckraking' movement that became famous in the first decade of the twentieth century in the United States of America. In fact he is regarded by some specialists in the field as the first of the 'muckrakers',[2] because his first article on the corruption of American municipalities ('Tweed Days in St Louis') was published in *McClure's* in October 1902, a month before the first 'exposé' of the other journalist who might equally lay claim to this status of pioneer of the movement, Ida M. Tarbell. Tarbell studied the capitalism of her day through the example of the Standard Oil Company. The investigations of Steffens resulted in a collection of articles, *The Shame of the Cities*, published in 1904, that is, a few months before the appearance of Tarbell's big book on the Standard Oil Company.

The magazine *McClure's* was a beacon of muckraking. It had been founded in 1893 by Samuel S. McClure, the son of an Irish immigrant. In 1902, he recruited Steffens, who was then editor of the *Commercial Advertiser*. In an editorial of January 1903, McClure defined the objectives of the type of journalism developed by his magazine, and which, we should remember, was not given the name of 'muckraking' until 1906.[3] McClure declared that three of the articles in this 1903 issue were part of a common project: those by Steffens on corruption in Minneapolis ('The Shame of Minneapolis'), by Tarbell on the Standard Oil Company, and by Ray Baker – another great name in muckraking – on working conditions and the trade union world ('The Right to Work'). In each case, he said, the aim was to trace one same evil, law-breaking, in particular of the anti-trust laws which should have made it possible to protect the working conditions of wage-earners and shelter government officials from the corrupting pressures of over-mighty capitalist groups. 'Capitalists, workingmen, politicians, citizens – all breaking the law, or letting it be broken. Who is left to uphold it?', he asked. A lengthy list of those corrupted (lawyers, judges, the Churches and so on) followed, and then:

> There is no one left; none but all of us . . . We forget that we all are the people; that while each of us in his group can shove off on the rest the bill of today, the debt is only postponed; the rest are passing it on back to us. We have to pay in the end, every one of us. And in the end the sum total of the debt will be our liberty.[4]

Once again we find the notion of the need to bring the people together in a new collective awareness. This was what the muckrakers laboured to achieve, in a clear line of descent from the large circulation press of the nineteenth century. Like it, they combined a desire to reveal the 'truth' – in the sense of the accuracy so dear to Joseph Pulitzer – with a desire to stimulate a general curiosity and offer something of interest to the largest possible number.[5] The magazines which published the muckrakers, however, had varying conceptions of 'factual' reporting. Historians of the press distinguish, for example, between *McClure's*, which offered reportages 'based on painstaking investigation at great expense', and a magazine like *Everybody's*, which had a conception of reporting of 'the most impressionistic kind, full of sound and fury'.[6] Even the former, however, was anxious to 'entertain':

> It would be pleasant to think that all this crusading against corruption in government, in industry, in finance, and even in religion and education, was motivated by altruism; but it seems clear that S. S. McClure, in the inspired experimentation that was a characteristic of the man, discovered a formula of exposés which was found so immediately popular that it was followed at once by the editors of the competing popular magazines. This does not mean that there was not much sincerity on the part of writers of this 'literature of exposure', or that the whole movement did not perform a great service to the people. It means only that the materials and skills to get a quick popular response are commonly necessary to any significant performance by the magazines.[7]

Lincoln Steffens: from 'the facts' to 'the system'

The practice of journalism, in the life of Lincoln Steffens, was part of a tortuous itinerary which he himself retraced, in 1931, in his huge 800-page autobiography. Steffens had studied a wide range of subjects, both in the United States and in Europe, until he was nearly 40, and been patently and perpetually dissatisfied. In particular, he spent many months as assistant to Wilhelm Wundt in Leipzig. It seems to have been a letter from his father which issued an ultimatum and so finally forced him to choose a career, that is, in his father's words, to move from an apprenticeship in the 'theory of life' to one on the 'practical side'.[8]

Steffens's response was to choose journalism. Such a choice probably reflected certain concerns he had already expressed in his time as an assiduous student. The question of 'the practical side', of the concrete, of 'pure factuality', beyond abstract intellectual constructions, had pre-occupied the young Steffens, even when, according to his father, he needed only to learn the 'theory of life'. In the part of his autobiography devoted to Wundt, it is difficult not to see his interest in journalism pre-figured: 'and then there were Wundt's lectures and the hard scientific spirit of the experimental laboratory. "We want facts, nothing but facts," he used to declare. The laboratory where we sought the facts and measured them by machinery was a graveyard where the old idealism walked as a dreadful ghost and philosophical thinking was a sin.'[9] Obviously, for such a comparison with journalism to be justified, the journalism in question would have to be, in Steffens's eyes, as scientific and rigorous in its discovery of the 'facts' as the practices of Wundt in his laboratory.

It is precisely this that Steffens seems to have had in mind when he took up the profession of journalist; he wanted to push to the limit the cult of 'facts', to make journalism, in a sense, 'scientific'. And he prepared himself to experience a possible failure as an intense personal crisis.

This crisis, which is undeniable, has fascinated more than one commentator. Some see it as a retrospective disillusionment with regard to 'the Progressive Movement', in which the ideals of muckraking reigned supreme. The 'progressiveness' of these years certainly deserved such a critique, because the word had ended up no longer saying anything in particular, so 'pervasive' had it become.[10] But for others, including Christopher Lasch,[11] Steffens's crisis cannot be reduced to a syndrome of retrospective disillusionment, as this disillusionment was present very early in his itinerary; even in his 'muckraking' years, Steffens incarnated a 'radicalism' distrustful of the wooliness of 'progressive' ideas. 'It is a mistake, in my opinion', says Lasch,

> to take the literature of disillusionment . . . at its face value. The radicals and bohemians of the twenties claimed to have lost their illusions about the world, but if their own earlier testimony is to be believed, they had never had any illusions to begin with – not, at any rate, the particular illusion they later claimed to have lost. Certainly they had never been progressives in the sense in which they later used the term. On the contrary, men like Walter Lippmann, John Dewey, Briand Whitlock, Fremont Older, Frederic C. Howe, and Lincoln Steffens had attacked progressivism all along as a variety of 'puritanism'.[12]

According to Lasch, the way in which Steffens shed light on the evils of his day, in particular corruption, already revealed a fundamental pessimism regarding the possibility of the people as a whole ever truly becoming aware of the deep causes of these evils, and consequently regarding the real importance of his role as witness-ambassador. The question, even the crisis, was already present: what if the journalists who denounced, and the public who delighted in their revelations, were themselves only cogs in a machine so deeply tainted that it laughed at muckrakers and their audience alike? And what if the journalistic gaze, even at its most combative, was by its very nature deprived of the clear-sightedness which makes it possible to see to the heart of a society's problems, because this very clear-sightedness is something *the public unified behind it is unable to receive*?

Reading Steffens's autobiography, it is difficult not to conclude that Lasch is right: the crisis was already taking place during Steffens's muckraking period, at least according to the old muckraker himself. In his first reportages on Wall Street, for the *Commercial Advertiser*, he claims to have understood just how far the facts he was expected to report were conditioned by the expectations of the public; he had perceived a gap between the facts he revealed as a journalist – the 'news' – and the information he would have had to reveal for a fuller and deeper understanding of the business world. He tells how he had already begun to wonder to what extent the search for 'facts' must result, in the end, in the contemplation of a true 'system' – the very thing that the journalistic 'facts', both scattered and oriented by the expectations of the public, never achieve.[13] He wondered what lay 'behind' the words he heard spoken by the players on Wall Street, and what made them speak and act: 'I could never be satisfied with a fact or a phrase; it was a picture I needed, a diagram of the connection between the saloon business and the banks, just as I had one of the nervous system that linked up my lower and upper extremities.'[14]

Thus, for Lincoln Steffens, the 'facts' involved a vertiginous search for the 'hidden', which the position of the witness-ambassadors of the preceding generation could not entirely satisfy. We have referred to Nellie Bly, but here the major figure with whom Steffens never ceased to engage was Jacob Riis, author of the famous reportage on urban poverty, *How the Other Half Lives* (1890). For Steffens, it was necessary to go further, to ask if the picture was complete and to expose the 'system'. He claims that it was this need, perhaps the same need that drives sociologists and novelists, that led him to write *The Shame of the Cities*: 'What reporters know and don't report is news – not from the newspapers' point of view, but from the sociologists' and the novelists'. It enabled me, when I learned a little of it, to write my *Shame of the Cities*.'[15] He emphasizes the extent to which his own way of looking at crime, corruption and the city had always been different from that of a Jacob Riis. In fact, Steffens was in the habit of accompanying Riis and his informant, Max Fischel, to the parts of the district of New York which this master of reportage covered. In this regard, Steffens was truly a pupil of Riis; he had watched him in action and admired him. But the lessons he learned hardly encouraged him to erect Riis into an ideal model. Riis had a way of looking at things that rendered him incapable of recognizing those that did not suit his combative generosity. He practised a sort of denial; he never addressed the profound causes of the phenomena he observed. At least, this is what Steffens emphasizes in his account:

Though I had nothing to do, professionally, with criminal news, I used to go out with the other reporters on cases that were useless to my paper but interesting to me. Crime, as tragedy and as part of the police system, fascinated me. I liked to go for lunch to the old Lyons restaurant on the Bowery with Max Fischel or some other of the 'wise' reporters. They would point out to me the famous pickpockets, second-story men and sneaks that met and ate there; sometimes with equally famous detectives or police officials and politicians. Crime was a business, and criminals had a 'position' in the world, a place that was revealing itself to me. I soon knew more about it than Riis did, who had been a police reporter for years; I knew more than Max could tell Riis, who hated and would not believe or even hear some of the 'awful things' he was told. Riis was interested not at all in vice and crime, only in the stories of people and the conditions in which they lived.[16]

Nevertheless, it cannot be said that this sort of criticism of Riis led Steffens to question the figure of the witness-ambassador. In fact – and this is what makes the personality of Steffens so complex – it was more a case of perfecting it, of taking it literally and pushing it to extremes: if you wanted the 'truth', the 'facts' and all the facts, the image that would faithfully reflect reality, beyond the singularity of one point of view, you must also be careful not to be a prisoner of the 'we' which, collective though it was, still remained one point of view. In many regards, Steffens simply defined a more demanding and 'better' figure of the witness-ambassador: he had to be *even more* of a witness-ambassador, that is, be the representative of an ever-wider community; he must be so concerned for the 'facts' that this of itself would lead to the search for the 'system' or the 'true image'. Later, in his autobiography, Steffens writes:

> Facts. It seems to me now that facts have had to beat their way into my head, banging on my brain like bullets from a machine gun to get in; and it was only by being hit over and over again that I could let my old ideal and college-made picture of life be blown up and let the new, truer picture be blown in.[17]

Steffens confirms that he saw this ideal as an extension of the demand for factual accuracy, and without abandoning the position of witness, observer or journalist; his dissatisfaction required him to go further, but not, it seems, to behave differently (for example, by leaving journalism and switching to the analytical methods of the sociologist and/or the economist).

There was apparently no break, therefore, with this journalism 'in crisis'; unless, that is, you read between the lines and detect an even deeper pessimism in Steffens. In fact, there are many passages which suggest that this *better* journalist, this perfect witness-ambassador, who would truly achieve a universal (or a de-singularized) gaze, might well *no longer unify anyone*. By achieving perfection in his role, he would abolish himself and lose the public which is the ultimate purpose of his gaze. In short, he would cease to be a journalist. This is surely the meaning of an anecdote he tells in his autobiography: one day, in that part of New York where Riis was king of reporters, and where Steffens himself operated for the *Evening Post*, Steffens went to East 35th Street, scene of a raid by a band of toughs. Steffens describes it in the driest possible way, without 'a single syllable of indignation'. The facts, nothing but the facts: he seems to be pushing this doctrine of the journalism of his day as far as it will go. However, the editor of the *Post* received a stream of letters indignant at the detached tone of the reporter who had recounted these facts. There followed a discussion between Steffens and his editor. Steffens sees this as a lesson, to the effect that it is precisely this minimalism in the expression of the 'I' which makes this 'I' more likely to unify – and appeal to – the 'we': better than ever, thanks to this self-effacement, he had been the witness-ambassador; for once, it is the 'system' in its purest form that an article had let the public see, and this intolerable truth had made the public react. Yet Steffens was well aware that he had also gone too far, hence the disquiet of the editor: the 'we' so successfully aroused by the gaze of the journalist turns against him, casts him out, and withdraws his mandate.

Let us look at another anecdote which follows immediately after, and which also concerns a crime in the Murlberry Bend district. We find the same theme: the ideal of the journalist is at the same time a furthest point, a point where one leaves journalism behind. This time, Steffens describes the differences between the way Riis reported crime and his own way of covering it. Steffens had once again tried to achieve a distanced tone, slightly cynical, in order to re-create the ordinariness of this violence; he painted a picture which restored to these 'facts' their 'logic', their deep meaning, which inevitably made them banal. Riis, in contrast, as usual, had got carried away; he was equally precise in his factual description but very far from effacing himself; he punctuated his description with his famous and indefatigable cry of indignation which was also an appeal for 'our' unification: 'Murlberry Bend must go.' What did the *Post*, where Steffens worked, do? What else could it do than turn 'crime' into news, notes a pensive Steffens: it, too, spiced it up with sensational facts and cries of indignation.[18] In other words, the lesson of Steffens – to be as little indignant as possible, precisely so as to maximize the indignation of the readers – was not sustainable for a newspaper: it was a furthest point, the point where the 'facts' were so successfully restored to their logic or system – the system of organized crime – and, as a result, to their banality, their lack of novelty, and hence of interest for the normally curious, that they lost any reason for being presented to the public. It is the culmination of the work of exposure, which at last achieves a full understanding of reality (so that's what it is, a whole system) but which, at the same time, and for this same reason, leads to indifference (so that's all it is). It is a point which no newspaper owner can contemplate.

The depth of Steffens's crisis is now easier to understand: there is no journalistic solution to his dissatisfaction. The ideals of journalism cannot be achieved 'journalistically'. Journalism is doomed to a lie in relation to its own ambitions, because it has to heed the curiosity of its readers. All journalists, Steffens seems to say, are aware of this lie, and of the impossibility of getting beyond it: when he tells the earlier anecdote, the one about the article written so coolly, which aroused so much indignation, he claims only to have restored the gaze of someone in the business, Max Fischel, the informant who sees such things on a daily basis: that is, the cynical gaze of a man who knows better than anyone that Murlberry is a 'system' into which the 'facts' routinely recorded fit. But this sort of gaze cannot be published in a newspaper – in any case, the journalist who wrote and signed the articles is Riis, not Fischel. Otherwise, you reach a furthest point of journalism, where the public no longer follows; a point where its indignation eventually causes it to rise up against its representative, who no longer gives it the 'facts' with the freshness and innocence of the surprised and horrified witness, but presents it, in a cold, scientific and blasé style, with the 'system'.

At this point, in the depths of so serious a crisis, one might expect, in spite of everything, a desire to have done with it and abandon journalism. In fact, it is only in his worst moments that Steffens contemplated such a move, for example in 1908, when he moved closer to sociology, which seeks the causes of the 'evils' in structures and 'things' rather than in individuals. For Steffens, as his biographer, Justine Kaplan observes, 'the cause of Adam's fall was not Adam or Eve, or even the Serpent, but simply the apple'.[19] It was also in 1908 that he moved even closer to socialist circles. Something like a break with journalism seems to be contemplated in the article he published that year in *Everybody's*. In it, Steffens describes his interviews with the candidates for the White House.[20] The article begins with these words, put into the mouth of an 'average American': 'I'm tired of exposure. I know something is wrong; something big. But what is it? Don't go on proving the evil over and over again. Tell us what to do about it. That's what we want to know.' More than ever, Steffens shows the emptiness of 'facts' and the impotence of journalism. Where are the men who will really take on the 'system'? Men who really *see*? The candidates think only of representing the people and their gullibility. 'Who is looking for that Evil which is the source of all our superficial evils? No one. We are all fighting the consequences, not the causes of our corruption.' (We should note this possessive: '*our* corruption'.) In this way of asking, almost despairingly, who is ready to attack the real structures of the 'system', instead of being content with the illusions of the battle against the symptoms, Steffens is also, obviously, engaged in muckraking. When he describes the incomprehension of the outgoing candidate, Theodore Roosevelt, the question he puts to him, 'Do you see it now?', strangely resembles the question put to Steffens himself, some years earlier, by one of his fellow muckrakers, Upton Sinclair, who hoped to persuade him to convert to socialism instead of continuing to engage in an incomplete, superficial diagnosis of the evils of the society of his day: 'One day, Upton Sinclair called on me at the office of *McClure's* and remonstrated. "What you report", he said, "is enough to make a complete picture of the system, but you seem not to see it. Don't you see it? Don't you see what you are showing?" '[21] In fact, Steffens seems to suggest, the muckrakers had perhaps not equipped themselves with the means actually to *see* better than Theodore Roosevelt (whom they had, nevertheless, considerably embarrassed) . . .

It cannot be said, however, that, in his itinerary, Steffens truly worked out a way of emerging from this crisis. He remained perplexed in the face of the impasse which journalism represented for him, and this, in the last analysis, is what his autobiography is mostly about. He continued to feel the ambivalence which characterizes, for example, his portrait of Jacob Riis in 1903:[22] the fierceness of his criticism is tinged with a sorrowful, unavoidable feeling, that of seeking an ideal of journalism which remains, quite simply, antinomic to the nature of journalism. Thus, in this portrait, Steffens emphasizes the blindness of Riis, his incomprehension of certain deep 'logics' of poverty – for example, the behaviour of a family who return to the city when, thanks to the assistance of various bodies with whom Riis had worked, they had been sent into the countryside. He shows that the gaze of Riis was full of projections, and that the profound nature of 'vice' remained alien to him, a man known as 'the pious Dane' (he was of Danish origin).[23] 'Riis was never really "wise",' he wrote; 'the power to conceive evil in its vicious form was always lacking in Riis.' He was certainly not without admirable qualities; his imagination and his capacity to be moved enabled him to order the 'facts' better than anyone else, and in this field he was hardly in need of a lesson from the editors who sometimes criticized him for the omnipresence of the 'I'; his extraordinary capacity for emotion and for empathy gave him a penetrating vision of poverty and crime. But he did not, for all that, see as well as *it was possible* to see; though head and shoulders above the ordinary journalists of his day, Riis was still far from the journalistic ideal. On the other hand, however, Steffens knows that realizing this ideal would mean losing the public. He honours Riis as the best possible representative of the public, and of their reforming or 'progressive' aspirations, which were at that period growing fast. 'The big, jolly, sentimental Dane took his adopted citizenship literally, and literally "worked for the public good" – "worked" like a political rascal,'[24] says Steffens, referring to Riis's underground work in the community, in parallel with his work as a journalist. Riis was both the eyes and the strong right arm of the public, a man who saw his work as a journalist as a perpetual harassing of politicians, supported by close links with charitable organizations. Riis was the witness-ambassador *par excellence*, that is, a very great journalist.

In essence, the nub of the crisis experienced by Steffens is the public: it is the public which imprisons the gaze of its 'ambassador', and it is the public which you cannot lose if you wish to remain a journalist. The most interesting, or at least the most touching, aspect of this muckraker is perhaps his stubborn and persistent revolt against an authority from which he could never really be free. The public itself did not really want the ultimate truth; it unites only around a construction which leaves the deep origin of the 'facts' it reports in obscurity. Yet this remains the ultimate goal of journalists.

The public, a prison

'A newspaper', writes Steffens, rather scornfully, in his autobiography, 'to advertize itself and build up circulation and power, has, now and then, to do something besides print the news: help elect or defeat a party, force a public improvement through or stop an outrage, bring to justice some public enemy or rescue a popular hero from the machinery of the law.[25] In which case, to be a witness-ambassador was inevitably to share this puerile enthusiasm and to support those who supported "the people's cause".'

Very early on, Steffens wanted to attack all this, but he was conscious that, in so doing, he would destroy the basis on which journalism rests. The tensions with McClure, which he describes in his autobiography, represent the impasse he was backing himself into. The more Steffens investigates the corruption of the municipalities, the more his gaze adopts the coolness of science which understands the necessity of laws;[26] and the more he distances himself from the myth of the 'saviour', of the 'good man' who will come to the rescue of these towns in distress, the more McClure is irritated. He writes:

> I wanted to study cities scientifically and I argued with Mr. McClure that it would heighten the interest in the articles we were planning to start out with blank minds and search like detectives for the keys to the mystery, the clews to the truth. He would not have it so. Science did not interest the readers, except as a source of wonders; and besides he was sure of that which he had learned by experience on *McClure's Magazine* and by observation in all other business – that the dictatorship of one strong, wise man . . . would abolish our political evils and give us a strong, wise administrator of cities.[27]

Thus, the newspaperman thinks of the readers and believes in the saviour, whose arrival should be hastened by the angry reporting, whereas the tormented muckraker dreams of taking his demand for the truth to its conclusion, bringing to light the profound logics that are not susceptible to quick reform, even if it means breaking with the public. 'My mind was on my theory,' he recalls, 'but Mr. McClure's was on our business.'[28] What McClure incarnates in Steffens's account, deep down, is the public itself, the 'innocent' public: an incarnation which this newspaperman had, in fact, proclaimed, saying to Steffens:

> I want to know if you enjoy a story, because, if you do, then I know that, say, ten thousand readers will like it. If Miss Tarbell likes a thing, it means that fifty thousand will like it. That's something to go by. But I go most by myself. For if I like a thing, then I know that millions will like it. My mind and my taste are so common that I'm the best editor.[29]

McClure, as a unifier, reminded his reporters of the 'facts', and therefore of a certain truth; but it was a truncated truth, as Steffens had already begun to realize: 'Mr. McClure was interested in facts, startling facts, not in philosophical generalizations.'[30] The whole of Steffens's personal crisis is contained in this adjective 'startling', which implies a dramatic and anarchic (not ordered) factuality, unsatisfying for someone who wants to attack the 'system' itself.

In this confrontation with McClure, Steffens does not deny being, 'journalistically speaking', dare one say, in the wrong – guilty in some sense of abandoning his mandate as witness-ambassador. In the paragraphs of this autobiography that follow the extract just quoted, he recalls how he himself had been an excellent journalist, *when he still shared the innocence of the public*: 'The reporter and the editor must sincerely share the cultural ignorance, the superstitions, the beliefs, of their readers, and keep no more than one edition ahead of them. You may beat the public to the news, not to the truth.'[31] But, as we see, these words also suggest that, for him, the age of innocence was coming to an end.

It was succeeded by the age of shame. In fact, as he uncovered the 'shame' of American cities, that is, this 'system' which implicated not only the individuals directly responsible but the community as a whole, Steffens felt his own shame grow, shame at not being able to tell it like it is, because journalism demands something different; shame at not telling the whole truth about corruption, because he needed 'public approval'. Steffens was becoming a celebrity, thanks to these reportages of 1902–3 on the municipalities, but he remained ambivalent with regard to his fame:

> I looked at the men who were giving me my taste of fame, and, business men, I thought that if their town were investigated they might be caught bribing or backing the bribers. But suppose they were honest men, what of it? What did such men know? Fame wasn't what it was cracked up to be. That I thought, with a feeling of shame which grew month by month as my disappointment grew – the feeling that there was something positively offensive about public approval, that it liked the wrong part of your work, made you out to be other than you were, and then tried to keep you up or down to expectations.[32]

The locals who fête me, he seems to be saying, do not know that they are tomorrow's corruptors, perhaps even today's – that they are themselves part of the 'system'.

The Shame of the Cities, this book of 1904 which brings together and presents his various articles on the cities, thus offers the striking image of a witness-ambassador who is constantly attacking those he represents, though also without succeeding in wholly renouncing his mandate. The introduction to the collection is revealing: 'The people are not innocent,' he says:

> That is the only 'news' in all the journalism of these articles, and no doubt that was not new to many observers. It was to me. When I set out to describe the corrupt systems of certain typical cities, I meant to show simply how the people were deceived and betrayed. But in the very first study – St Louis – the startling truth lay bare that corruption was not merely political; it was financial, commercial, social; the ramifications of boodle were so complex, various, and far-reaching, that one mind could hardly grasp them . . .[33]

Steffens then explains how the same analysis was applicable to each of the cities examined: corruption is a global phenomenon, with multiple ramifications. This is why he decided, in March 1903, to write a new article ('Shamelessness of St. Louis') on the first city he had studied, in which he revisited the 'facts' presented and denounced in his original article of October 1902 ('Tweed Days in St Louis'). He attributed the failure of the reforms that had been embarked on to the strength of the 'system', itself related to the way the 'people' condone it and always, in the end, stop over-zealous reformers.[34] This is how he justifies, in the next section of his introduction, his choice of the word 'shame', which is the key to the evils he describes.[35]

Also present in these pages, however, is Steffens's terrible indecision, his difficulty in following through his criticism of the people on whose behalf journalists labour. In the last section of the introduction to *The Shame of the Cities*, he finally makes his peace with the figure of the witness-ambassador and re-establishes the link with this public he had begun, nevertheless, to put in the dock:

> We Americans may have failed. We may be mercenary and selfish. Democracy with us may be impossible and corruption inevitable, but these articles, if they have proved nothing else, have demonstrated beyond doubt that we can stand the truth; that there is pride in the character of American citizenship; and that this pride may be a power in the land. So this little volume, a record of shame and yet of self-respect, a disgraceful confession, yet a declaration of honor, is dedicated, in all good faith, to the accused – to all the citizens of all the cities in the United States.[36]

It is clear that Steffens seems to halt in midstream – in a way, to remain a journalist.

We observe a similar impulse, an indecision full of ambivalence, in the case of his fascination for 'bad men'. To break with the naivety of the 'good people' who, like Riis, their impeccable representative, have a 'single and simple' mind,[37] Steffens often says that he prefers the corrupters themselves, the 'real men'. His search for lucidity brings him closer to the outlook of the crooks, the direct source of the evils, warped but at least without illusions. But Steffens lives a strange tragedy, a painful incapacity to stop being, himself, a 'good man'. He denounces the hypocrisy of the 'good' reformers, who tackle everything except anything that might affect them personally, and who end up by retreating, leaving the system intact. Steffens detests them, and yet, 'with all my growing contempt for good people', he confesses in his autobiography, 'I was one of them. Unconsciously I wanted to be one of them . . . I was preferring the conscious crooks; *and yet I was one of the righteous.*'[38]

This explains the permanent state of *crisis* that marks Steffens's itinerary, and which does not really, ultimately, contrive a clear *way out of this crisis*. In his book of 1906, *The Struggle for Self-Government*, he is still speaking of the need to see corruption as a 'system' and so see the complicity of 'good' people, but he still returns, in the end, to a certain optimism – that same optimism which emerged at the end of the introduction to *The Shame of the Cities*. In the words of one of his biographers,

> Steffens's first book [*The Shame of the Cities*] began with cautious optimism but seemed to move on a zigzag course toward warning and doubt. The second book [*The Struggle for Self-Government*] began with doubt (transformed into sarcasm in the dedication to Czar Nicholas II), then attempted to return to optimism. The question of reform was still open, obviously, and for Steffens it would remain so for a long time to come.[39]

There was, as we have seen, the time of extreme tension in 1908. But Steffens never found a clear outlet for his exasperation. We should not be surprised, therefore, by his development in subsequent years, when he turned not so much towards socialism as towards a social Christianity, based on trust in a few exceptional men, 'saviours' of the Good beyond the systematic organization of Evil. This is the atmosphere of his book of 1909, *The Upbuilders*, in which he reinvests, in a sense, the theme of the witness-ambassador in this idea that the salvation of the people depends on a handful of heroes.

We will leave our examination of this itinerary here, an itinerary marked by a moving confusion and ambivalence, which throw a particular light on the limitations of the position of the witness-ambassador. This figure is imprisoned by the very thing that is its greatest asset: its link with the public, a public which it has to make 'feel' events, situations and problems. For Lincoln Steffens, the search for truth was inevitably limited by this context. The 'unifying' truth was only a partial truth; the 'facts' brought to light by the journalist were only elements in a 'system' which remained opaque in the 'innocent' eyes of the public. Nevertheless, the clear-sightedness of Lincoln Steffens did not lead to a complete break with this figure of the witness-ambassador. This is what makes his case so interesting; through him, we can see the witness-ambassador in crisis, leaving open the question of ways out of this crisis.

3. Saying good-bye to the witness-ambassador?

It is up to us, then, to answer the question. Does this grave charge against the witness-ambassador constitute a last word on modern journalism, a final judgement from which there is no appeal? Or does it allow us to envisage 'resistances' to the dominant journalism, that is, to find other approaches in modern journalism than that of unifying?

For one intellectual heir of Lincoln Steffens, the issue was not in doubt: he was led by the muckraker's crisis to pass a disenchanted and definitive judgement on journalism as a whole. Steffens's personality left its mark on Walter Lippmann, who was at one time his assistant. And it can be argued that Lippmann's own analyses of public opinion, though certainly 'cooler' and more conceptual than the prose of Steffens, are nevertheless a logical continuation of them. Lippmann was clearly a steadier and more moderate character than Steffens.[40] This probably explains why, in spite of the real admiration he felt for the old muckraker, he kept his distance, especially towards the end of Steffens's life; the turbulent spirit of Steffens, prone to extremes, and his way of thinking *in crisis*, were alien to Lippmann.[41] The intellectual heritage between the two is undeniable, however, and it will be helpful to trace the itinerary of Lippmann, because he took the disillusionment of Steffens to its logical conclusion. And then, of course, we will have to ask whether a way out exists . . .

In May 1910, the young Walter Lippmann (1889–1974), brilliant assistant of George Santayana at Harvard, decided to embark on a career in journalism and wrote to Steffens to say that he would very much like to work for him. He had met Steffens for the first time in the autumn of 1908, in Boston, where the famous muckraker was giving a series of lectures. Lippmann was 21 years old when he became assistant to Steffens, who had just joined the editorial team at *Everybody's* in order to publish a series of articles on financial power. Many things brought the two men together at this stage in their respective lives. Their relationship to socialism was one: they were both, at that period, attracted by socialist thinking, which attempted to organize the 'facts' into a coherent representation of capitalism, but also equally irritated by the dogmatic mind-set it produced in many militants. In short, the desire to integrate the observed facts into a complex representation of reality, while also thinking of ways of emancipation, led both men into the temptations of socialism, but left both ultimately frustrated.

However, what in Lippmann most strongly echoed the thinking of Steffens was the way he himself was beginning to question public opinion and the role of the journalist. Indeed, echoes of the 'crisis' of Steffens can be detected in all Lippmann's published work, from *Drift and Mastery* (1914) to *The Phantom Public* (1925), by way of *Liberty and the News* (1920) and *Public Opinion* (1922). The echoes are sometimes very faint, especially in the early texts, because it is only really with *The Phantom Public* that a more serious disillusionment set in. But there is always something of the master in the way Lippmann questions journalism; like Steffens, he puts his finger on the limitations of a unifying journalism, and hence of the figure of the witness-ambassador, if always resignedly.

Before *The Phantom Public*, the works of Lippmann express a reforming optimism which reveals what was still rather a 'soft' way of apprehending the problems. The young Lippmann believed that one *could* reform journalism, bring it out of its crisis and make it into an authentic means of access to the profound truth of the phenomena it describes. These early texts introduce doubt and criticism only to define the 'ideal' journalism, with a faith, and also a composure, that have little in common with the tormented questioning of Steffens. Lippmann brings journalism out of its crisis, but, for him, the crisis had never been so acute in the first place. Let us take the example of *Drift and Mastery* (1914), in which he offers an analysis of the 'themes of muckraking' which is certainly hard on this movement. Like Steffens, he emphasizes the dependence of the muckraker on the public and its consequence: a gaze under constraint. 'But the mere fact that muckraking was what people wanted to hear is in many ways the most important revelation of the whole campaign,' he declares.[42] Muckraking 'was itself considerably more of an effect than a sign of leadership'.[43] It is easy to understand, therefore, why, according to Lippmann, the movement died out: the public had gradually grown tired of this unending stream of denunciation of the evils of society; people did not really want the muckrakers to go further than this process of accumulating the 'facts'; they certainly did not want them to move on to an analysis of the 'system'. As a result, reduced to accumulating facts, the movement ran out of steam as it were.[44] Lippmann seems, therefore, to be putting his finger on precisely what had led Steffens into the 'crisis' I have described. But his approach stops well short of this. In fact, *Drift and Mastery* is a book full of increasingly high hopes for science as an instrument of emancipation: Lippmann believed that the concern for truth and scientific knowledge ought to make it possible to 'master' the 'drift' which is responsible for the ills of our democratic societies. Such a conviction assumes the possibility of a way out of the crisis for journalism: it too, must break out of its prisons (including that of the public), its 'routine' and its 'drift', thanks to a rigour worthy of scientific rigour. This optimistic scientism is at its height in the works of 1920: that is, the article written with Charles Merz, 'A Test of the News', published in *The New Republic*, and the book, *Liberty and the News*.

In this long article, Lippmann and Merz criticize the reporters of the written press who had covered the Soviet revolution in a way that was 'nothing short of a disaster'.[45] But the two authors are not content with identifying the weaknesses integral to any gaze in the present; they do not seek to show, for example, that biases of observation can only be corrected by historical distance. They accuse, indeed denounce, a journalism which sees 'not what was, but what men wished to see'.[46] They are assuming, therefore, that the journalists could and should have seen properly. The ideal is accessible. And they launch an appeal for a journalism that will at last be worthy of the name: that is, rigorous and professional, prepared, in the name of the 'truth', to go against its own wishes and those of the public it represents.[47] Their criticism of contemporary journalism does not, therefore, condemn journalism itself to a definitive crisis: the alternative to 'poor' journalism exists; *it is possible* to emerge from this bias which is what the public wants, *it is possible* to impose on the public what does not please it. In other words, the model remains the witness-ambassador who *truly* unifies, not by being content with rumour or the general will, but by uncovering the 'real' truth. The resistance of the public, which drove Steffens to despair, is not analysed in any detail. Instead, the article urges journalists to use force, to make the public recognize the very thing it is reluctant to see and listen to the sources it would not hear of its own accord.

All these themes reappear in *Liberty and the News*, in a form less buried in empirical analyses. The 'truth' is erected into a journalistic ideal, but without, like Steffens, questioning whether this ideal can ever be fully realized. 'There can be no higher law in journalism', Lippmann asserts, 'than to tell the truth and shame the devil' (the evil here being that inherent tendency of the journalist to be economical with the need for truth behind that which the public wants to see and hear).[48] Lippmann urges journalists to emancipate themselves in a way that, in spite of the unease which can be detected in the text,[49] seems possible; he appeals to them to have the courage not to write anything that their rigorous observation means they cannot 'truly' believe. The solution to the unease is, therefore, a *voluntarism*: '. . . resistance to the inertias of the profession, heresy to the institution, and the willingness to be fired rather than write what you do not believe, these wait on nothing but personal courage.'[50] Further, in *Liberty and the News*, it is clearer than in 'A Test of the News' that the model of access to this 'truth' remains the figure of the *witness*, the person who has direct and sensitive access to the event. In other words, to correct the bias characteristic of 'poor' witness-ambassadors, let us all be 'good' witness-ambassadors; the figure itself is not seriously attacked. In parallel, the notion of public is not treated nearly as harshly as in Steffens: according to Lippmann, it is possible to make a clear-sighted public emerge, 'created', as it were, by the voluntarist journalist.

This triumphant scientism in Lippmann's youthful works tends, consequently, to stifle at birth the sort of anxieties experienced by Steffens. It culminates in the distinction between 'news' and 'truth' put forward in *Public Opinion* (1922): professional journalism, he says, should be capable of *making people see* the truth behind the news, which is what *sells* newspapers.[51] This truth is accessible to the eye, and now. Journalism has abundant resources. It can, from the surface of events, reach what lies below: this capacity to dig is what distinguishes the 'good' from the 'bad' reporter.[52] The possibility that this truth eludes sensitive observation by its very nature, and demands other methods of analysis, such as sociological, is not envisaged – whereas, as we have seen, this possibility haunted Steffens, even if he never dared to make the radical break. We may also note that the notion of distance has negative connotations in Lippmann: it is direct and sensitive access to the event that gives the truth the opportunity to emerge, whereas distance, on the contrary, favours the protections which are themselves a breeding-ground for the elaboration of 'fictions'.[53] In this way, the difficulties inherent in the sensitive perception, which are discussed at length in *Public Opinion*, do little to stop Lippmann believing that they can be surmounted by the observer himself.

Public Opinion too, therefore, stops well short of the 'crisis' of Steffens. In fact, it is not until several years later, in *The Phantom Public* (1925), that Lippmann really confronts the problem of the blindness inherent in the public and risks criticizing the scientist voluntarism which had hitherto dominated his approach to journalism. He finally poses questions worthy of his master: what if the need for rigour, knowledge and science, laid down for professional journalism, is based on a total misunderstanding of what it is actually *possible* to achieve from a body which addresses a public? And what if this reforming enthusiasm, which requires that you, as it were, 'create' the public, by forcing it to contemplate the 'real truth', amounts to taking the public for something different from what it can ever be?

The Phantom Public provides a veritable theoretical overhaul of the notion of 'public', and it is for this reason that I believe that this text should be seen as a turning point in Lippmann's itinerary. Instead of thinking of the public, as in *Public Opinion*, as an ideal which has to be fulfilled – created, in a sense – beyond ordinary 'public opinion', the product of a pernicious routine, Lippmann seems here to resign himself to a fundamental imperfection in the notion of public, hence to the frustration it causes. *The Phantom Public* takes account for the first time of a profound and irreparable disillusionment, worthy of that felt by Steffens. Chapter 1 has the title 'The Disenchanted Man', and chapter 11 is entitled 'The Unattainable Ideal': Lippmann accepts the pointlessness of demanding from a public access to the 'truth' that he himself has previously considered the objective of a 'reformed' journalism. He sees the public as condemned to a crude, limited and simplistic grasp of problems: 'We must assume that a public is inexpert in its curiosity, intermittent, that it discerns only gross distinctions, is slow to be aroused and quickly diverted; that, since it acts by aligning itself, it personalizes whatever it considers, and is interested only when events have been melodramatized as a conflict.'[54]

Thus, not only does he accept the validity of the 'crisis' of Steffens, but, in so doing, he develops concepts which explain with great clarity the limitations of a unifying journalism. We find in this book the very same questions I have raised with regard to the simplicity of the conflict presented by the witness-ambassador (the simplicity of the us/them divide). The theme of personalization, in particular, echoes my earlier analyses: the 'unifying' reportages we have studied are full of *characters*, on which the us/them opposition was constructed. Nellie Bly opposed medical personnel and patients. Albert Londres presented us with 'strange creatures', who provoked the question: who are 'we'? Murrow and Friendly opposed 'heroic' individuals like Radulovich and Annie Lee Moss to the diabolic person of McCarthy.

Lippmann makes this tendency to personalize and simplify issues, tests and conflicts the destiny of journalism – a journalism conceived of as unifying by nature, since he scarcely considers any other journalistic approach. He relates the problems he identifies to the very structure within which the journalistic gaze operates: journalists are the eyes of the public, they are connected to it and mandated by it. In sum, journalists are themselves a personification of the public; themselves the product of this simple relationship, mediated by *persons*, to factual reality. Thus, themselves needing, in self-justification, to make their legitimacy *seen* (visibly, I represent you), journalists share in the public's search for the 'objective signs', to use Lippmann's own words, by which it can identify those who represent it and those who betray it. In other words, the disenchantment seems here to become resignation: yes, journalism, inasmuch as it is unifying, and inasmuch as it tries to unify the public behind it, has its limitations. But that is how it is: it seems that you have to accept it. Lippmann formulates the crisis of Steffens in more conceptual terms; but, like Steffens, he does not make it lead to a simple abandonment of journalism. He reveals and assumes the limitations of a figure that I, for my part, call that of the witness-ambassador.

In fact, in this way of acknowledging the limitations inherent in any appeal to the public, Lippmann offers a particularly successful theorization of the unifying journalisms. His diagnosis is complete, without a definitive condemnation, but also without illusions. He explains exactly what is involved in the journalistic act of 'unifying' a public. On the one hand, he confirms that the unification does not mean the end of all conflict; he even suggests that unifying always requires engaging in conflict, because the public demands that journalism dissect a problem for it by presenting different 'characters', each of whom claims to represent it, and who confront each other before it. The public can then make up its own mind and in this way experience itself as a 'we', represented by one of these characters. It is this 'operation', in a way, that Lippmann describes. On the other hand, he shows that the conflict taking place is necessarily a simple one, too simple: to make a small part of reality visible to the public is inevitably to betray its complexity.

The only thing missing from such an analysis is this question: is there another type of journalism? To what extent has the history of journalism produced counter-models to the dominant unifying model? To what extent has what should properly be seen as a journalistic 'counter-culture' broken with this simple conflict, the only one the unifying jour-nalisms allow themselves to represent, the 'us/them' divide, and been able to present, in the journalist's gaze, a conflictuality that is richer, more tumultuous and more dangerous for 'us'? How, concretely, can the very notion of 'centre' be challenged, and a more dispersed representa-tion of conflicts and identities made to emerge, in the journalistic gaze?

These are the questions I propose to discuss next. There would be no point in denying the difficulty of the decentring approach: it is complex and risky, dogged by pitfalls, and I prefer to recognize these at the outset. My investigation will therefore be characterized by a benevolent suspi-cion: is it possible to decentre? Or are the attempts I will describe per-manently in danger of going astray? To describe the figures of decentring journalism will be, therefore, at the same time, to show the obstacles these figures have encountered.

5

The Difficulties of Decentring:
The New Journalism and the Early Years of *Libération*

The two periods in the history of journalism that I have chosen to focus on here in order to examine the decentring process are both from the 1960s and 1970s: the first is the New Journalism movement in America; the second is the '*Libé*' project in France, that is, the creation of the new French newspaper, *Libération*, in 1973, and, to be more precise, '*Libé 1*', which lasted from 1973 to 1981. In both cases, the aim was to challenge the dominant journalism, but to challenge it by means of a journalistic practice. Both projects were an attempt to invent *another journalism*.

How did they set about it? What do these projects tell us about the decentring process? Did they keep their promise to decentre their public? As a close examination will show, they each reveal a temptation to abandon the ambition to decentre – a temptation which speaks volumes with regard to the difficulty of achieving a decentring journalism.

1. The New Journalism and the temptation of ubiquity

A journalism in the first person

The New Journalism was a journalistic – perhaps one should say 'literary' – movement, originating in the United States in the 1960s, on the border between the novel and journalism. It fitted the general mood of those years: that is, what has been called an 'adversary culture'.[1]

It was closely linked to parallel developments in the writing of fiction; indeed, it was in this context that the expression 'adversary culture' was coined, in 1965, by the critic Lionel Trilling. Trilling believed that modern literature, since the end of the eighteenth century, had been a vehicle for a 'subversive intention'; it was constantly urging its readers to criticize the habits of thought of the dominant culture of the day. This anti-establishment dimension had reached its apogee, he claimed, in the first decades of the twentieth century, and then been endangered by the growth of the consumer society. The writers of the 1960s, troubled, plunged into what others have called an 'apocalyptic mood',[2] were trying to rekindle the flame of subversion. Indeed, literature was central to the 'adversary culture' of the 1960s. A whole school of writers decided to launch a root-and-branch assault on the dominant representations of reality. They used literature to question the conventional divide between fact and fiction, and they took as their subjects events customarily regarded as 'non-fiction' and reserved to journalism. This led to the appearance of the 'Nonfiction Novel', which rejected the conventional frontier between fact and fiction, and so challenged the frontier between journalism and literature.

The Nonfiction Novel and the New Journalism were two sides of the same coin: a complete revolution in writing, which led to the previously distinct fields of fact and fiction being treated in a similar manner. Literature broke out of fiction and its straitjackets; journalism emerged from its belief in its own 'objectivity', and from the rigid and hollow writing that this belief had produced.[3] The writer thus became a journalist as well, and the journalist a writer. This revolution was to liberate both journalism and literature, as these distinctions lost their meaning, since both had suffered from the prevailing stereotypes regarding 'reality'. The critic John Hollowell has helpfully explained, for example, how the literature of fiction felt constrained by the narrow and stereotyped definition of the 'real':

> Generally, for a novel to succeed, the writer must first comprehend a social 'reality' and then create a plausible fictional world that bears some resemblance to that world. During the sixties, however, when the differences between 'reality' and 'fantasy' had blurred, novelists were often unable or unwilling to claim such knowledge. Even the adoption of the technique of omniscient narration commonly found in realistic novels implies a comprehensiveness of knowledge that many writers refused to accept. In contrast, the writer of the nonfiction novel says, in effect: '*This I saw and this I did and felt.* My book implies only whatever impressions and observations I can make about my own experience.' If reality and even the 'facts' become suspect, then the writer of the nonfiction novel chooses a confessional tone.[4]

It was not, therefore, in order to anchor themselves in a confident 'reality' that the writers of the Nonfiction Novel turned their attention to events customarily dealt with in newspapers; it was precisely because these events revealed the imbrication of reality and fantasy, in fact confounded the certainties about what reality was. 'Everyday events continually blurred the comfortable distinctions between reality and unreality, between fantasy and fact,' writes Hollowell.[5]

As this discussion would suggest, the form of writing that seemed naturally to result from this questioning of frontiers was a writing in the first person, fully accepting the singularity of the point of view. In fact, if I can no longer say what is true and what is fiction, and if what I write is postulated as the inextricable mixture of the two, then I regard my writing as a simple discourse in the first person, the expression of a singular subject, refusing any attempt to distinguish the 'objective' from the imaginary. The challenge then takes the form of expressing, even rehabilitating, an 'I', in place of a pseudo 'we' which had claimed to hold the key to the truth/fiction divide, and in which the subjective voice was effaced.

It was the 'subjectification' of writing that constituted the great originality of the New Journalism in the eyes of the movement's first defenders. In an article of 1966, 'The Personal Voice and the Impersonal Eye',[6] the journalist and writer Dan Wakefield acclaims the way in which this type of journalism has destroyed the myth of the 'impersonal eye', which *always*, in practice, conceals a singular voice. Wakefield uses a formulation from Thoreau's *Walden* to summarize the New Journalism project: 'It is, after all, always the first person that is speaking.' Wakefield quotes, in particular, the personal tone of Tom Wolfe's article 'The Kandy-Kolored Tangerine-Flake Streamline Baby', published in 1965, which, with Truman Capote's nonfiction novel of 1965, *In Cold Blood*, is traditionally regarded as marking the beginning of the era of the New Journalism. Wolfe had been sent to California by the magazine *Esquire* to cover an exhibition of trendy motorcars. As he himself explains in the preface to the collection of articles to which this famous text gave its name,[7] he found he was unable to order his ideas in a form suitable for a formal article. His managing editor, Byron Dobelle, asked him simply to write up his notes and send them to the magazine for another journalist to turn into an article. Wolfe spent many hours noting down his observations in the form of a letter beginning 'Dear Byron'. Dobelle was delighted with the result, and it was finally this very text, this letter on a personal note, that was published in *Esquire*. The power of the article lies in the re-creation, through a plethora of personal observations, of the values of the consumer society of which these little 'kandy-kolored' cars were the emblems. It is impossible to distinguish between the 'facts' and Wolfe's own personal impressions: 'reality' is grasped only through the fantasies it generates, and it is this that explains the fantastical punctuation, the repetitions, the ellipses and the extravagance which characterize Wolfe's style.

In his article, Wakefield shows that the New Journalism essentially set out to dismantle the whole 'objectifying' project that characterizes modern journalism. As we have seen, this project tends always to value the eye more highly than the voice. Wakefield specifically denounces this eye, which he regards as a tool for achieving a mystifying 'depersonalization'. The gaze should be restored to its inevitable subjectivity, and the story returned to discourse: you should listen to the voice which is, in any case, always there. It is this very imbrication (eye/voice) that the New Journalism wanted to get down on paper. It set itself up, therefore, against the myth of a 'we' and represented, on the contrary, the sphere of points of view as the home for a plurality which resists unification. It is a profound, insoluble conflict, which is hinted at in Wakefield's article, and can also be detected in the first pages of his *Between the Lines: A Reporter's Personal Journey through Public Events*, of 1966 (a year after Wolfe's 'founding' article, 'Kandy-Kolored'). Wakefield explains at the beginning of his first section, entitled 'The Shadow Unmasked', that his book is intended for readers 'who have grown increasingly mistrustful of and bored with anonymous reports about the world, whether signed or unsigned, for those who have begun to suspect what we reporters of current events and problems so often try to conceal: that we are really individuals after all, not all-knowing, all-seeing Eyes, but separate, complex, limited, particular "I"s'.[8] Thus, according to Wakefield, the New Journalism urges its readers to disunite, in contemplation of what can never unify: a singular point of view, in which it is a unique voice that is heard.

It would seem, therefore, that we should see the New Journalism as a direct descendant of the first-person journalism, or 'personal journalism', which had older origins. It is significant that Ronald Weber gave the title 'Personal Journalism' to the first section of his collection of articles on the New Journalism. For Weber, the New Journalism is essentially a journalism in the first person, accepted as such, whether the 'I' is explicit in the writing or not. Among the important models for the 'New Journalists', according to Weber and many others who have studied and admired the movement, is the book of James Agee and Walker Evans, *Let Us Now Praise Famous Men*, published in 1941, and generally regarded as a true monument of 'personal journalism'.[9] This reportage of the late 1930s on the poor whites of Alabama combines photographs taken by Evans and a text by Agee which accepts the total singularity of the point of view, hence also its limitations. 'I am telling you what I see and only what I see,' the reporter-writer seems to say. The rejection of any unifying gaze is obvious from the first pages of the book. Agee emphasizes the importance of questioning *his* relationship to these individuals, so as to avoid the 'obscenity' of those ordinary journalists who think it a simple matter to 'pry intimately into the lives of an unde-fended . . . group of human beings'; it seems to him 'curious', he goes on, that people 'should be capable of meditating this prospect without the slightest doubt of their qualification to do an "honest" piece of work, and with a conscience better than clear, in the virtual certitude of almost unanimous public approval'.[10]

Personal journalism is in a sense a 'classic' model of decentring by the gaze. But it should be added that, by definition, this journalism in the first person decentres only in one direction, that defined by the 'I' who deploys his singular perspective in the writing. Agee, for example, never makes any claim to be presenting several singular gazes at the same time, only his own. This modesty, and this sense of the limitations, is the obvious and fully accepted counterpart of the claim to an absolute sin-gularity. Thus, in this passage quoted by Wakefield, Agee writes about one of the peasant farmers, George Gudger: 'But obviously, in the effort to tell of him (by example) as truthfully as I can, I am limited. I know him only so far as I know him, and only in those terms in which I know him; and all of that depends as fully on who I am as on who he is.'[11]

Among the great names of personal journalism who left their mark on the New Journalism movement, we may also mention Lillian Ross, who, with Joseph Mitchell and A. J. Liebling, was one of the pillars of the *New Yorker* in the 1940s and 1950s. The 'Profiles' section of this magazine, devoted to portraits of celebrities and written in a free style, in the form of personal accounts, has often been seen as a journalistic project that was a precursor of the New Journalism. A close reading of a report by Lillian Ross of 1960 entitled 'The Yellow Bus' will help us to understand how personal journalism can decentre.[12] Ross directs a personal gaze, whose bias is fully accepted, at a group of Indiana schoolchildren she accompanied on a bus trip to New York. Their visit, as tourists, and their first discovery of New York, lasts two days and three nights. The reporter never explicitly says 'I', yet this is certainly first-person reporting: that is, a singular gaze which gives brief sketches of all the stereotypes into which these schoolchildren remain locked, and of their inability to be open to what they see, even just *to see*. Ross gives selections of their conversation, in which we hear, as well as their drawl, their determination to be inter-ested only in what reminds them of Indiana, and so reinforces their instinctive hatred of this strange city. She notes the way anything in the least surprising is related to their unique point of reference, home, and takes a malign pleasure in describing in detail the stereotypical presents they buy (a salt cellar with the Statue of Liberty on top, a pepper pot with the Empire State Building on top, a teapot with the George Washington Bridge, and so on); she makes no attempt to be impartial. You also sense that the words she reports are often answers to questions she herself had put; thus she observes that, during the full hour they spent on Coney Island, not one of them goes to walk by the seaside, even though none of them had ever seen the ocean before in their lives; she must have asked them about this to elicit this pathetic reply: 'We knew the ocean was there, and anyway we aim to see the ocean on the tour tomorrow.' With surprise, mockery and perhaps also pity, this article exposes for the benefit of the reader, in order to demolish them, the values of this little group of young Americans from the Midwest. They are 'typically American', and it is this which makes this reportage a decentring text: 'Look,' she says to the public, 'come with me to see *yourselves*; get out of that.'

It is also necessary, of course, for the public to feel itself concerned for the decentring to take place. But is this not a text addressed to readers who already share this mocking vision of the 'American backwoods', and on whom this writing, consequently, ultimately has little effect? I was present at a class in the Department of Journalism at New York University a few years ago, when there was a collective reading of this text, and I witnessed a revolt on the part of a student from Texas who found her friends' laughter malicious and arrogant, and the text intolerably 'New Yorker': she denounced a sort of unavowed 'unification', a solid and unquestioning 'we', laughing at a strangeness which is itself never questioned. She had put her finger, clearly, on a key issue, which allows me to make the point that we have barely started on our analysis of the 'decentring' journalisms before being presented with the risks that lie in wait for them, chief among them that of continuing, in practice, to be 'unifying' texts, perhaps even in spite of their best intentions. Nevertheless, if we accept that Ross was not writing only for scornful New Yorkers, and that the rebellion of this Texan student was itself an 'effect' of her text, 'The Yellow Bus' remains a good example of 'decentring' writing.

It is reasonable to regard the New Journalism as a first-person journalism, in direct line of descent from a rich and already anti-establishment American tradition, if only for the type of writing it advocates. The qualities that enable it to decentre would then be the same as those of personal journalism – and involve the same limitations and the same risks. This is too hasty an analysis, however. The New Journalism cannot be reduced to this apologia for the subjective voice of the reporter-writer.[13] Its 'decentring ambition' goes further. Whereas Wakefield emphasizes the personal and deliberately subjective elements in the New Journalism, one of its most important representatives, Tom Wolfe, insists that it is equally motivated by a quite different ethos, which he sees as far more original. We then have to ask whether this other ethos, which gives the

New Journalism other tools with which to decentre, involves other difficulties and other risks of the decentring project being led astray.

The 'chameleon' journalism of Tom Wolfe and its ambivalence

Let us look at 'The New Journalism', the article written by Tom Wolfe in 1973 and published that same year.[14] It introduces an anthology of texts of the New Journalism, and it is an appraisal at least as much as a programme: it explains what this movement, both journalistic and literary, is, and what it was intended to be. The 'subjectivist' interpretation of the New Journalism is rejected in the name of a more ambitious vision of decentring.

What is at first surprising is Wolfe's attachment to the notion of *realism*, which seems to run counter to the desire, discussed above, to blur the frontiers between reality and fiction. In fact, in the preface to the collection, preceding this article, Wolfe compares the introduction of realism into literature to the discovery of electricity. 'It raised the state of the art to an entirely new magnitude,' he declares: 'And for anyone, in fiction or nonfiction, to try to improve literary technique by abandoning social realism would be like an engineer trying to improve upon machine technology by abandoning electricity.'[15] Then, at the beginning of his article 'The New Journalism', he describes his entry into the world of journalism, emphasizing his desire to join the 'real world', abandoning his academic studies[16] – a piece of self-analysis which has striking similarities with the motives cited by Lincoln Steffens to justify his own abandonment of the academic world and choice of journalism. Wolfe also sings the praises of Jimmy Breslin, that leader-writer who dared to leave his office and go out into the streets to find subjects for his newspapers, that is, who understood that reporting was the only way to get access to 'real' things.[17]

Wolfe seems, therefore, to be opposing the characterization which has so far been central to my analysis of the New Journalism: he refuses to see it as the advent of a pure first-person discourse, which would undermine the very definition of reality. But it is when he explains the four essential 'devices' of the New Journalism that he most clearly articulates his hostility to all purely subjective writing; in fact, what he rejects is the arbitrariness and the relativism inherent to the strongly subjectivist position. To him, the New Journalism still bears some relation to a certain properly journalistic search for 'objective reality'.

Some of the procedures he describes do not appear to be directly at odds with the principle of writing in the first person. They are primarily devices which rehabilitate a more literary and a freer style, contrary to the rules of writing of the journalistic profession. For example, the first device indicated by Wolfe, scene-by-scene construction,[18] involves a departure from the golden rule of conventional journalism. This dictates that you begin an article with a first synthesizing paragraph, the 'lead', condensing the substance of the news and noting its source, then gradually develop the elements or ingredients which comprise this news, from the essential to the more anecdotal. In opposition to these conventions, which banish chronological narration in favour of an approach through a series of choices of what is essential (by virtue of what is called 'news judgements'), the New Journalism rehabilitates the narrative *thread*. Scene-by-scene construction makes it possible to rediscover an authentic dramatization, to which all the sorts of detail ignored by conventional journalism often contribute. This leads on to the fourth device: attention to the details of everyday life, which rediscover, therefore, a place in the account.[19] The second device is the frequent use of realistic dialogues,[20] which should be preserved as far as possible – contrary to the practice of conventional journalism when selecting quotes – in order to re-create the ambience the reporter has found.

There is nothing here, so far, that runs counter to the principle of a singular, deliberately subjective gaze, but rather the contrary. That said, it needs to be spelt out that, in Wolfe's own writing, these literary procedures are already in themselves devices which tug the narration in the direction of a *realist* ideal. For Wolfe, they are not just any old literary devices, but tools bequeathed by the tradition of the *realist* novel. The first device is simply the transposition of the device of scenic depiction, which Henry James – for Wolfe, one of the great models of the realist novel[21] – saw as properly characteristic of the novel as opposed to the historical résumé.[22] The importance of detail, for its part, recalls the procedure dear to Dickens and acclaimed by George Orwell,[23] himself frequently referred to by Wolfe, which consists of studding the story with observations unrelated to the narrative thread for the purpose of creating atmosphere – what Roland Barthes was later to call the 'reality effect'.[24]

It is the third device, however, that constitutes the undeniable originality of the New Journalism as presented by Wolfe and also constitutes the most fundamental assault on subjectivism. This is *variation of point of view*, which, according to Wolfe, should allow the writer to break out of the confinement of a single subjective gaze. In explaining his third device, he does not refer directly to the *variation* of point of view, but only to the need to break away from the 'classic' vision of things from the single standpoint of the journalist. Wolfe enjoins the New Journalist to tell the story from the point of view of at least one of the characters.[25] Then, later in the article, it emerges that the aim is never to be limited to a single point of view: if journalist-writers leave *their* seeing and *their* experience, it is not to imprison themselves in that of a single other:

> If the journalist wants to shift from third-person point of view to first-person point of view in the same scene, or in and out of different characters' points of view, or even from the narrator's omniscient voice to someone else's stream of consciousness – as occurs in *The Electric Kool-Aid Acid Test* – he does it.[26]

In other words, Wolfe does not want to maintain a coherence of *focus*, to adopt the terminology of the French critic Gérard Genette. It is even clear that he favours the widest possible variation of point of view, either by the introduction of multiple dialogues, in which different voices make themselves heard, which reveal something of the personal perspective of each character (a sort of plurivocality in direct speech), or by the use of free indirect speech (*style indirect libre*), by which the narrator slips into the skin of the characters.

This variation of point of view allows the journalist-narrator to see the same scene from a number of different angles. Journalist-narrators blend in everywhere and see from everywhere because they adopt every perspective. So, the metaphor Wolfe uses to evoke the 'new journalist' is that of a chameleon: 'Eventually, a reviewer called me a "chameleon" who instantly took on the coloration of whomever he was writing about. He meant it negatively. I took it as a great compliment. A chameleon . . . but exactly!'[27] Wolfe is clearly trying, by this metaphor of the chameleon, to differentiate the New Journalism from the tradition of personal journalism:

> Many reporters attempting to write the New Journalism use an autobiographical format – 'I was there and this is how it affected me' – precisely because this does seem to solve so many technical problems. The New Journalism has often been characterized as 'subjective' journalism for that very reason . . . in fact, most of the best work in the form has been done in third-person narration with the writer keeping himself absolutely invisible, such as the work of Capote, Talese, the early Breslin, Sack, John Gregory Dunne, Joe McGinniss.[28]

Wolfe keeps his distance, therefore, from the claim to subjectivity hailed by Wakefield in the New Journalism. The distance turns almost to scorn when Wolfe discusses Agee's book, *Let Us Now Praise Famous Men*. Everything that Wakefield, eight years earlier, had admired and seen as a fundamental 'precedent' of the New Journalism (the recognition that the point of view is subjective, and that it leads to prejudices and limitations in apprehending things, and in particular other points of view) is here dismissed by Wolfe; for him, it is being imprisoned in the subjective viewpoint of the single journalist:

> After all the enthusiasm I had seen critics generate over James Agee's *Let Us Now Praise Famous Men* – a book about poor folks in the Appalachians during the Depression – reading it was a great disappointment. He showed enterprise enough, going to the mountains and moving in briefly with a mountain family. Reading between the lines I would say his problem was extreme personal diffidence. His account abounds in 'poetic' descriptions and is very short on dialogue. It uses no point of view other than his own. Reading between the lines you get a picture of a well-educated and extremely shy man . . . too polite, too diffident to ask personal questions of these humble folk or even draw them out.[29]

So, the only 'autobiographical' literature which seems to interest Wolfe is that in which *the 'I' decentres itself*, crosses a threshold that Agee does not cross when faced with the peasant farmers, enters into the minds of other actors, and merges into them by empathy, even metamorphosis. It is significant that one of the examples Wolfe quotes is *Down and Out in Paris and London,* the book-reportage in which George Orwell tells how he turned himself into a vagabond and wandered from Paris to London.[30] Wolfe acclaims in this text a decentring in relation to the self, a novel experience that opens a door into the interiority of poverty. (As we will see in the next chapter, this was indeed the aim of the young Orwell in writing this book; however, he was harsh in his judgement of this enterprise a few years later, revealing that, unlike Wolfe, he had a clear vision of all the difficulties, even contradictions, involved when the decentring technique is equated with the experience of metamorphosis.) Among his contemporaries, Wolfe clearly admires those motivated by the desire to go where it is generally believed it is forbidden or impossible to go. For example, he is particularly warm in his praise for the work of Hunter S. Thompson on the Hell's Angels:[31]

> One of the strengths of *The Hell's Angels* is the skill with which Thompson depicts the milieu not only of the Angels themselves but also of the people whose lives they invade . . . Thompson's use of the first person – i.e., his use of himself, the reporter, as a character in the story – is quite different from the way he uses the first person later in his Gonzo Journalism; here he uses himself solely to bring out the character of the Angels and the locals.[32]

On the other hand, Wolfe criticizes Truman Capote for an insufficient capacity for empathy:

> Capote does not use point of view in as sophisticated a way as he does in fiction. One seldom feels that he is really inside the minds of the characters.

One gets a curious blend of third-person point of view and omniscient narration. Capote probably had sufficient information to use point of view in a more complex fashion but was not yet ready to let himself go in nonfiction.[33]

At first sight, therefore, Wolfe's desire to avoid being confined within a single point of view reveals an ambition to decentre in a more radical manner. The modesty of authors conscious of their prejudices and of the limitations of their perspective does not impress him. For him, this sort of decentring has little appeal. Journalists should aim higher; they should expose a far wider conflictuality, demonstrate that there are many perspectives, and make their text a veritable cacophony. In this way, the 'chameleon' shows that there is no fixed point of anchorage, no 'centre', for the gaze. In reality, however, this very aim makes the decentring project suddenly ambivalent – much more so, in fact, than the strictly subjectivist approach of the New Journalism. The motif of the journalist-chameleon raises a number of problems, which reveal that Wolfe's conception of decentring assumes a fairly bland approach to alterity and to conflict, and that it might well, in fact, conceal a unification without realizing it.

This ambivalence takes many forms. First, the motif of the chameleon implies a capacity for the gaze to go everywhere, prompting the question: is this not a fantasy of ubiquity, implying a refusal to envisage a truly unfathomable and incommunicable otherness? Agee's confession of failure in his attempt to enter into the minds of those he observed showed, in a sense, more respect for this incommunicability; his decentring might have been more modest and limited in its aims, but it was ultimately less prone to the deception which can be detected, in contrast, in Wolfe's motif of the journalist-chameleon. It should also be noted that Wolfe never *justifies* this motif. He assumes a capacity for total empathy on the part of the journalist, but he never explains, even less defends it. He never asks whether journalists really *can* emerge from confinement in their own subjectivity. Even if he recognizes that the labour of empathy primarily involves an effort of the imagination on the part of the journalist-narrator, he is quite clear that it is not the journalist's own fantasy about the psychic interiority of the actors, but their *real* interiority that the journalist grasps and re-creates. The potential theoretical and practical problems of empathy are never mentioned, which is surprising; it is as if to import into journalism the Joycean desire to reconstitute 'stream of consciousness', with regard to the psychic interiority of characters who are not invented by a novelist, poses no problems.

The second aspect of this ambivalence is connected to the first: the device of variation of point of view is mentioned by Wolfe not as a way of yet further eroding the reality/fiction frontier, by exposing a wholly disorganized conflictuality, a general confusion offering no reference point to the reader, but rather as a way of defending or reconstituting the notion of 'reality'. Wolfe seems determined to shrug off the accusation of subjectivism because he knows it to be dangerous to the New Journalists: it allows their detractors[34] to deny them the title of 'journalist' because their writing cannot claim to be anything other than pure fantasy, an imaginative fancy from the mind of a single writer, a construction of literary value at best, but of no journalistic value: 'The bastards are making it up!' as Wolfe himself put it.[35] The assumption of real empathy – the idea that the journalist accedes to the true psychic interiority of the actors – follows from this ferocious realism: he needed to claim that journalists reached a reality which existed and would exist without them, and that *they hadn't therefore made it all up*. More generally, however, the way in which Wolfe evokes the device of variation of point of view results in it being made a complete 'antidote' against this subjectivism and all its dangerous implications: there is a 'common world', Wolfe seems to say, there is a *reality*; hence what we, the 'new journalists', do *is journalism and not novel*.

Further, it is significant that it is precisely when Wolfe is evoking this device of variation of viewpoint that he suddenly differentiates himself from the 'novel', rediscovering the classic distinction between fiction and reality. Certainly, he says, in substance, we employ the techniques of James and Joyce, we enter into the minds of the characters, but we do it better than they, because *everything is true* – that is, because the characters are absolutely *real*. What we write is not, therefore, a novel; *it is more real than even the best realist novel*. Here is the relevant passage in full:

> The result is a form that is not merely *like a novel*. It consumes devices that happen to have originated with the novel and mixes them with every other device known to prose. And all the while, quite beyond matters of technique, it enjoys an advantage so obvious, so built-in, one almost forgets what a power it has: the simple fact that the reader knows *all this actually happened*. The disclaimers have been erased. The screen is gone. The writer is one step closer to the absolute involvement of the reader that Henry James and James Joyce dreamed of and never achieved.[36]

This claim – the assurance that one is writing journalism, that is, that one accedes to *reality* – is in many ways a retreat from one of the aims of the New Journalism, which I emphasized early in our discussion: namely, the blurring of the frontiers between fact and fiction, between journalism and literature. Hence this paradox: it is precisely when Wolfe claims to be aiming at a more radical decentring than ever – it is not *one* new, singular point of view that the New Journalism offers, he declares, but a vast array of conflicting perspectives, a general decentring of the gaze, a journey into the most varied points of view – that he retreats from this very aim. The journalist-chameleonot Wolfe, aside from his formidable and enigmatic capacity for empathy, never loses his way; he always knows where he is, that is, in the *real* internal world of such-and-such a person, and he always knows how to differentiate between these two worlds. He even knows, when he penetrates the psychic interiority of such-and-such a person, how to differentiate between what is a fantasy that distorts external reality and what is faithful to 'objective' external reality. In fact, and it is not the least of the paradoxes, Wolfe, in his realism, even goes so far as fully to rehabilitate the idea of a common 'objective' reality: that is, a reality which is external to all these interior worlds and which is in no way challenged by conflicting interpretations of it. 'The idea', he acknowledges, 'was to give the full objective description . . . plus something that readers had always had to go to novels and short stories for, namely: the subjective or emotional life of the characters.'[37] In sum, they will show all, the 'inside' as well as the 'outside'. The fantasy of the *total gaze* could hardly be clearer, implying that this gaze remains capable of accurately distinguishing, at every level of reality it embraces, between what is objective reality – 'true reality', in a sense, universally valid – and what is subjective reality – the fantasy reality of such-and-such an actor regarding 'true reality'.

One sees the extent to which this claim to realism, however understandable its polemical purpose (to demonstrate to its detractors that the New Journalism really is journalism), plunges the project into ambiguity. Everything the decentring had dared when it had been presented as the work of a deliberately subjective point of view, that is, this challenge to the idea of a common reality, is now invalidated: it will not, says Wolfe, attack 'our' reality; it will navigate between interpretations and the fantasies of this or that person regarding it, but it itself will not truly be questioned; there really is an 'outside', and there is an 'objectivity', valid beyond the subjective experiences that apprehend and may possibly transform them.

In the end, and it is troubling, worn down by the attacks of their detractors, the New Journalists were driven to the extreme of appealing, against all assaults, to their accuracy and the reliability of their reporting;[38] they *too*, they claim, work and investigate according to the most classic criteria of their profession, in order to discover the 'facts'; their originality is then presented as simply an additional labour, intended to grasp the subjective lived experience of which these facts are a part. In other words, they then claim not to transform the classic notion of 'fact', but to give it an extra dimension, access to what Norman Mailer calls 'intimacy', and what Ronald Weber calls 'interior states';[39] not to challenge the empiricist principle of determining the facts, but *also* to enter into the minds of all those who perceive, experience and distort these facts; not to amend the journalistic aim to objectify but to add a 'bonus', dare I say, a little more soul.

In this regard, the discourse on the importance of adding many different techniques, often advanced by the New Journalists, has a regressive, even a defensive, feel about it. We find this, for example, in the work of Gay Talese, who writes, in a note published in his collection, *Fame and Obscurity*:

> The new journalism, though often reading like fiction, is not fiction. It is, or should be, as reliable as the most reliable reportage although it seeks a larger truth than is possible through the mere compilation of verifiable facts, the use of direct quotations, and adherence to the rigid organizational style of the older form. The new journalism allows, demands in fact, a more imaginative approach to reporting, and it permits the writer to inject himself into the narrative if he wishes, as many writers do, or to assume the role of a detached observer, as other writers do, including myself.[40]

To Ronald Weber, this discourse denotes an inability to go all the way in pursuing the challenge to the very notion of journalism:

> The New Journalism, however, tries to draw together, or draw closer, the conflicting worlds of journalism and literature . . . obviously the New Journalists attempt such blending in varying degrees. Most position themselves on one side or the other – as journalists trying to extend journalism's reach or as literary types using fact for artistic purposes. But however the New Journalists view themselves, what they are up to is neither exactly literature nor exactly journalism, but a rough mixture of the two – and that's the heart of the critical problem. The New Journalism is vulnerable on both sides.[41]

Beyond Weber's own judgement, this argument puts its finger on the double discourse of the New Journalists regarding themselves, a double discourse which is meant to resolve, by addition, something that remains, nevertheless, highly problematic. Instead of facing their own contradictions head on, they tend to say: we write *both* novels *and* journalism, and the one does not really invalidate the other. They continue, in particular, to claim that they do not *only* write novels, even though their whole project is motivated by a desire to blur the frontiers between the novel and journalism.

In Wolfe, this double discourse takes a particularly arrogant form: we do better than both the traditional novel and conventional journalism, he says, precisely because we combine the two. We 'complete' journalism with the aid of the techniques of the novel, that is, a more meticulous observation of external reality (the Balzacian model), but also, and above all, a labour of intropathy, of entering into interiority, which was alien to traditional journalism (the Jamesian and Joycean models);[42] and in so doing, we 'complete' the realist novel itself, we go one better, we follow through the dream of the realist novelists, because we finally apply their techniques to true 'reality'. Wolfe is here clearly displaying a fantasy of the *total gaze* (exteriority and interiority, journalism and the novel, etc.).

This fantasy is highly suspect when applied to the decentring enterprise. It supposes an ultimately rather bland conception of the conflictuality in the sphere of points of view: not only is no 'other' perspective sufficiently 'other' to be completely inaccessible, but there remains, beyond the plurality of points of view, a 'common reality'. In other words, something is salvaged from the general confusion. Radical subjectivity had not been particularly concerned to salvage anything. Journalist-chameleons, in contrast, restrict the extent of the conflict while claiming to reconstitute and expose it; and to the point where we may wonder if the 'other' points of view through which they navigate are perceived in their deep otherness, and the conflicts exposed in their full intensity. The chameleons, and their readers with them, never get lost, as if these different worlds always form simply one single great world in which we are all unified.

Further, the fact that, for Wolfe, no otherness and no conflict can withstand the reporter's gaze is demonstrated by his confidence in the complementarity of the various devices he describes. He never asks if these devices are all mutually compatible, or if the multiple focuses he encourages are mutually contradictory. One might well be more doubtful, when it is actual as opposed to invented characters that are at issue, as to the possibility of employing all the devices he describes at one and the same time. For example, can one really apply the imperative for wholly external observation, which includes, in particular, attention to detail and attentive listening to conversations (words spoken), at the same time as the requirement to focus on the interior monologues (not explicitly spoken) of the characters? To the question of whether one really can be *inside* (the enigma of perfect empathy, so quickly resolved by Wolfe), there is added the question of whether one can be inside and outside *at the same time*. For Wolfe, there seems not to be a problem: there is no need to choose to prefer this or that perspective on a situation, all perspectives being possible at the same time; ideally, all these devices complement each other, broaden the gaze, and bring it closer to this totality to which he seems to aspire.

His own texts, which delight in sudden shifts of focus, express this confidence in the possibility of a total gaze. Let us take *The Electric Kool-Aid Acid Test*, his book on the hippie group 'The Pranksters', which inspired *On the Road,* Jack Kerouac's novel about the Beat Generation. The writing of Wolfe is often highly empathic; he seeks to reconstitute the 'stream of consciousness' of their leader, Kesey. He does not, however, want to lose the advantage of an external focus, a detached gaze – his own, Tom Wolfe's – unless, in line with a theory he preaches more often than he practises, he presents one character through another. This is what the critic Robert Scholes called the 'double perspective':

> Wolfe also has the double vision it takes to see Kesey as a genuine religious leader and a projection of a comic book fantasy . . . keeping his own cool, Wolfe ranges from strong empathy with Kesey's group to detached skepticism. This double perspective, simultaneously inside and outside the object of his investigation, is typical of his method.[43]

This comment confirms a sort of desire for totality (the interior and the exterior) linked to the device of variation of point of view. And it is thanks to this addition, it might be said by depending on it, that Wolfe can consider the New Journalism (or the Nonfiction Novel) as what brings both the novel – the only one of any value in Wolfe's eyes, the realist novel – and journalism to perfection, that is, as what finally gives access to total reality.

A nagging suspicion remains, however: is there no inner door that remains truly closed to the journalist, no perspective that remains irremediably alien, no conflict so fierce that it cannot be serenely navigated? The journalist-chameleon is too reassuring a figure, too anxious to safeguard the idea of a 'common world', not to be suspected of failing to face up to the idea of a conflict that is incommunicable. What, after all, does Wolfe say: that if there is no 'pure factual', outside subjective experiences, if the real and the imaginary are inextricably mingled, and if there can only be 'constructs' – in sum, if the old objectivist belief in access to the 'facts' has crumbled – there remains, nevertheless, against radical and frightening subjectivism, this ability of the journalist not to remain confined within a single lived experience (his or her own), and this possibility of entering into the multiple constructs, the fantasies, the ideas and the 'stream of consciousness' of all the characters; perhaps not access to the 'pure factual' (though, as we have seen, the New Journalists do not wholly rule this out), but at least the ability to travel infinitely in the plurality of constructions. Here we see the full extent of the ambition of the New Journalism, but also, whether it likes it or not, its ultimate flaw, its contradiction.

Because, if everything is construction, and if all the actors are some 'I' who build their own world, mingling reality and fantasy, then surely the

journalist's journey into the interior worlds of all the actors is also a construction, by an 'I' which imagines at least as much as apprehends,
incapable of differentiating between the objective and the subjective,
between the real and the imaginary. Not to acknowledge that journalists
themselves are prisoners of a subjectivity that is limited, and may even
distort reality, is surely to defuse what was most subversive in this movement with regard to traditional journalism. And what is to stop us from
thinking that this certitude of empathy does not conceal, in practice, an
inability to grasp the depth of the gulfs and the contradictions, that is,
to confront profound otherness? It is the assurance of this chameleon,
both omnipotent (able to go everywhere and enter every interior world)
and protected against 'folly' (never lost or confused, always knowing
what is 'real' and what is a fantasy of an actor), that can give rise to
doubts. Is the New Journalism, as it is presented by Wolfe, really a model
of decentring journalism, or the symptom of the very pitfalls which the
decentring project encounters in its most triumphant version?

Misunderstandings, the incommunicable and the questioning of reality in the New Journalism: a reading of Norman Mailer's The Armies of the Night *(1968)*

A journalistic movement cannot be evaluated, however, on the basis only
of the text that defines its programme. Many typical products of this
movement confront the questions which the self-confidence of Wolfe
tends rather to gloss over.

The paradox is that the most interesting texts of the New Journalism
are perhaps those which question the programme from the inside, and
those, in particular, which cast doubt on the possibility of applying
simultaneously all the devices described by Wolfe; those driven by the
anxiety of not managing to become 'chameleons'; those which accept
that they are only a singular and limited perspective, a *situated* gaze; and
those which try to achieve access to the interiority of the actors, but
know at what cost – for example, that the act of reconstituting the
'stream of consciousness' may only be possible after the event, and not
simultaneously with the events described, or, conversely, that a wholly
exterior apprehension of the dialogues and actions may preclude a
simultaneous understanding of the 'interior worlds'.

It is not without some amusement that one finds Wolfe, when he discusses the texts of his fellow New Journalists, expressing surprise at the
seemingly antithetic character of some of the techniques he favours.
Thus, in his short introductions to the texts printed in his anthology of
the New Journalism, he remarks that those texts which successfully
engage in intropathy (I will refer here indifferently to empathy and

intropathy) and the reconstruction of the interior monologues of one or more characters are very often less rich in dialogues, and vice versa. Let us take, for example, his introduction to the article by Robert Christgau, 'Beth Ann and Macrobiotism', a foray into the 'inner world' of a young woman who had been indoctrinated into a no-protein diet from which she had eventually died: Wolfe praises the labour of intropathy in this article, and attributes its high quality largely to this closeness between the journalist and his subject. Christgau was at the time (1965) a young 23-year-old reporter working for the Dorf Feature Service in Newark, which supplied local papers with news stories; he had been the only reporter on duty in the office one evening when the *New York Herald Tribune* had appealed for information about the death of Beth Ann Simon, a young girl who had apparently died as a result of Zen Macrobiotic Diet No. 7. It was Christgau who telephoned the dead girl's father and conducted the investigation, of which the article was the result. Wolfe quotes Christgau's own words, in which it is clear that he had something in common with this girl of his own generation, if only a shared language – for example, he was familiar with the word 'macrobiotic', which probably put her father at ease during their conversation. But Wolfe thinks that the article lacks living dialogues, a shortcoming he attributes, logically enough, to the fact that the journalist had had to reconstruct this story, not having seen it unfold before his eyes.[44] It seems not to have occurred to Wolfe that these two requirements, on the one hand, the immediate reproduction of the action, and, on the other, intropathy, might well not be compatible, and that these devices might belong to different timescales. Perhaps it is only afterwards that it is possible to reconstruct the psychic interiority of the characters; conversely, a reporter who is present at the scenes he describes might have more difficulty in immediately penetrating the experiences of those who, for the moment, are primarily part of his own experience. Is not Wolfe, in his ambitious programme, wanting to synthesize two timescales of writing that are, in reality, different? We again find this desire for totality (to be in the present *and* in the afterwards), which in practice invalidates the few moments of insight when Wolfe seems to see that his desires, far from being so easily combined, might be contradictory.

It is noticeable in this connection that Wolfe is far from precise about his conception of realistic dialogues. He seems to have been insensitive to the possibility that a 'living' text, which contains many instances of dialogues, hence a sort of plurivocality, may be something very different from the text of a true 'chameleon'. Plurivocality is not the same thing as a multiple focus – perhaps is even its opposite. The confusion between plurivocality (many dialogues, 'it speaks a lot') and variation of point of view (which requires a labour of intropathy) is very clear in Wolfe's over-hasty reading of Michael Herr's article on Khe Sanh. We will show in chapter 7, when we analyse in more detail the writing of this reporter of the Vietnam War, that the question of intropathy is central to his approach, but *in the form of the question*: am I able to 'enter'? Am I not doomed to failure, by the very fact that, in order to be able to see, I protect myself from the violence? In reality, if there is a lot of speaking in Herr's text, it is often a sign that *there is no intropathy*, that he has not got into the heads of the Marines alongside whom he lives in Vietnam, in fact, that the chameleon has failed. And the interest of Herr's text is that it demonstrates, in this way, the impossibility of a real encounter, since the violence leaves everybody confined in his own present and in incomprehension of the other: the other, the Marine, is presented as a total enigma, who speaks, certainly, but who remains an impenetrable atom.

Wolfe remained patently blind to this dimension. He sees the plurivocality of 'Khesanh' as the sign of a true penetration of psyches:

> In terms of technique, then, one of the interesting things about 'Khesanh' is that Herr did not give in to the temptation to make the story autobiographical . . . Little Me 'n' No Man's Land . . . Instead he attempted the far more difficult feat of penetrating the psyches, the points of view, of the line troops themselves, using the third as well as the first person.[45]

My reading of this text will be very different, showing that Herr, in applying the devices of the New Journalism, exposes the contradictions which Wolfe does not recognize. In Herr's writing, one technique (the dialogues, the 'it speaks') works against the other (the entry into otherness); further, Herr makes us wonder whether intropathy may only be achievable after the event, which would signify that it is not, strictly speaking, the business of journalism. It would not be surprising, consequently, if the finest examples of intropathy are, as Wolfe himself recognizes, texts in which journalism reconstructs events at a later date.

It may be, therefore, that there is, within the New Journalism, a more complex and more concrete debate than that exposed in the programmatic texts, on the very possibility of being this chameleon lauded by Wolfe. It is possible that, by demonstrating the failure of the chameleon in the writing itself, or by demonstrating the cost of such a model (the time lag required by the labour of intropathy and the working out of a deeper communication which is absent at the time of the spectacle itself), some journalists say more about decentring, and even go further in this direction, than by an unquestioning adoption of the model. Their writing is then constantly posing the question of how to reconstitute the asperities of this sphere of points of view, the incommunicability of the 'inner worlds', and the depth of the misunderstandings. At the opposite pole from the serene metaphor of the chameleon, the New Journalists worry away at this question, revealing a keen sensibility to everyday suffering, inner solitude, obstacles to communication, and the illusions of the common world and sharing. In this sense, their texts are more significant than the programme of Wolfe.

The text of the New Journalism that I have chosen for a detailed study of this decentring, a difficult and hardly 'chameleon-like' decentring, that is, alien to triumphant ubiquity, is *The Armies of the Night* by Norman Mailer, the famous book-reportage on the 1967 march on the Pentagon, against the Vietnam War, in which Mailer himself participated.[46] This book, like the whole of Mailer's *œuvre*, is haunted by the question of *conflict*, which takes place between different points of view as much as within one same subjectivity.[47] Here, the conflict concerns the relationship to the event: who sees? Who perceives the truth about this militant march? What confidence can one place in the observer's perspective? Every point of view can be contested and made to conflict with another. Mailer's method, as a result, is something of a sapping operation: every anchorage of the gaze is cast doubt on, challenged and relativized.

The writing exposes this permanent conflict between different perspectives. This explains this theme, developed from the beginning and running counter to the 'realism' of a Tom Wolfe, namely, that all testimony remains inextricably of the novel, that is, the point of view of a subject who inevitably adds elements of the imaginary, itself full of internal contradictions. Book One of *The Armies of the Night* has the title 'History as a Novel: The Steps of the Pentagon'. It introduces us to the witness, 'Mailer', referred to in the third person. It is he who constitutes the point of view from which the narration unfolds, the anchorage. The purpose of this distancing – Mailer-the-narrator speaks of Mailer-the-witness – is primarily to sow doubt: is he any good, this so very singular witness? In sum, the narration draws attention to its point of anchorage, the singular gaze of Mailer-the-witness, and at the same time undermines it, destroys its foundations, and reminds us that the story it tells remains a novel.

It is first the way Mailer exposes the egotism of Mailer that discredits him as a reliable witness. The relativity of his perspective is constantly emphasized, at the same time as his narcissism, which renders him incapable of grasping the significance of an event. For example, when he speaks at a meeting, he experiences it in an exclusively narcissistic manner: 'Just as professional footballers love sex because it is so close to football, so he was fond of speaking in public because it was near to writing. An extravagant analogy?'[48] Mailer-the-narrator takes an obvious pleasure in letting us know, in the middle of the book, that his Mailer-the-witness is the champion of 'cock-ups', always missing what matters most in the events he attends:

> Mailer had an instinct for missing good speeches – at the Civil Rights March in Washington in 1963 he had gone for a stroll just a little while before Martin Luther King began 'I have a dream', so Mailer – trusting no one else in these matters, certainly not the columnists and the commentators – would never know whether the Reverend King had given a great speech that day, or revealed an inch of his hambone.[49]

On top of the typically Mailerian provocation (the racist overtones, a historic event juxtaposed with a banal physiological need), the attack on the objectivist beliefs of conventional journalism is clear. What can we be sure of? Nothing; so not the gaze of this Mailer-the-witness either.

When Mailer-the-narrator declares, 'It was one of the little inconveniences, one of the sewed-up pockets of modern history that no one was capable of counting the crowd',[50] it is not at all clear whether this impossibility of an objective testimony distresses or delights him – the latter seeming, if anything, more likely. Mailer-the-narrator seems intent on emphasizing the extent to which all testimony is an inevitable mix of 'vision' and 'imagination', as, for example, in this passage on the muddled gaze of Mailer-the-witness:

> Mailer had then that *superimposition of vision* which makes descriptions of combat so contradictory when one compares eyewitness reports – *he did not literally see* any uniformed soldiers or marshals chasing this civilian army down the embankment, there was nothing but demonstrators flying down toward them now, panic on their faces, but *Mailer's imagination so clearly conceived* MPs chasing them with bayonets that for an instant he did literally see fixed bayonets and knew in some other part of himself he didn't, *like two transparent images almost superimposed.* Then he saw nothing but the look of terror on the faces coming toward him and he turned to run in order not to be run down by them, *conceiving for one instant MPs squirting Mace in everybody's eyes.* Then panic was on him too. He didn't want *Mace.* He sprinted a few steps, looked over his shoulder, stepped on a drainage trough where the parking lot was hollowed, almost fell with a nasty wrench on his back and abruptly stopped running, sheepishly, recognizing that some large fund of fear he had not even felt for a minute these three days had nonetheless lived in him like an abscess quick to burst now at the first mean threat.[51]

What is 'real' here, except the confused feelings of Mailer-the-witness himself, who 'conceived' the army firing on the crowd, and who discovers in himself a fear he had not admitted, although it clearly permeates his point of view? In which case, what difference is there between a testimony, particularly a journalistic account, and a 'novel'? None, Mailer-the-narrator seems to say, as this passage, heavy with irony, confirms:

> Some time in the early morning, or not so early, Mailer got to bed at Hay-Adams and fell asleep to dream no doubt of fancy parties in Georgetown when the Federal period in architecture was young. Of course, if this were a novel, Mailer would spend the rest of the night with a lady. But it is history, and so the Novelist is for once blissfully removed from any description of the hump-your-backs of sex. Rather, he can leave such matters to the happy or unhappy imagination of the reader.[52]

A brief dialogue between Robert Lowell and Norman Mailer reported in the book turns on this very question of the difference between journalism and literature; and it is a clever reader who can detect a clear-cut opinion:

> 'Yes, Norman, I really think you are the best journalist in America.'
> The pen may be mightier than the sword, yet at their best, each belongs to extravagant men. 'Well, Cal,' said Mailer, using Lowell's nickname for the first time, 'there are days when I think of myself as being the best writer in America.'
> The effect was equal to walloping a roundhouse right into the heart of an English boxer who has been hitherto right up on his toes. Consternation, not Britannia, now ruled the waves. Perhaps Lowell had a moment when he wondered who was guilty of declaring war on the minuet. 'Oh, Norman, oh, certainly', he said, 'I didn't mean to imply, heavens no, it's just I have such *respect* for good journalism.'
> 'Well, I don't know that I do', said Mailer. 'It's much harder to write' – the next said with great and false graciousness – 'a good poem'.
> 'Yes, of course'.
> Chuckles. Headmastermanship.[53]

This dialogue could hardly be more ambivalent. It seems to reveal a certain contempt on the part of Mailer for journalism as compared with literature – he is keen to spell out that the true pride is that in being a great writer, and certainly not in being a great journalist – but also contempt for anyone who feels such contempt . . . His apparent distinction between journalism and literature is actually full of irony, and he mocks Lowell, who adopts it on his own account, with his headmasterly manner. In sum, this passage is in itself a play on points of view.

The discrediting of Mailer-the-witness appears definitive at the point – towards the end of Book One, which in this way is revealed as fundamentally damaging – when readers learn that 'their' witness is, in fact, using the event as a way of achieving stardom. Mailer gets himself filmed by a TV crew during the march. Something of the sort had seemed to be on the cards when Mailer-the-narrator had noted, with regard to his own character: 'if his head was to be busted this day, let it be before the eyes of America's TV viewers tonight.'[54] But the news comes a little further on:

> It must now be admitted – the reader does well to expect a forthright shock – that the Participant was not only a witness and actor in these proceedings, but was being photographed as well! Mailer had – in what he considered an inexcusable weak moment – agreed to the request of a young English filmmaker named Dick Fontaine to have a documentary made of him for British television.[55]

The observer is observed; and who knows what is then seen; perhaps the very bias which is inherent in his gaze, that self-satisfaction which is constantly showing through.

Mailer is very fond, in general, of imagining what one would see if one changed one's viewpoint: 'From above, from the helicopters, it must have looked like the pulsations in the progression of a caterpillar,' he remarks, for example.[56] Or he presents 'his' Mailer-the-witness reading an article about himself, that is, the point of view on the point of view on the point of view. Mailer-the-witness is, of course, revolted by what he reads:

> He remembered the reporter who had been running in front and behind of Leiterman's camera. He had had neatly combed hair and had asked polite questions. The reporter had hung on his words. It had been his own best moment in all these days – he had never felt so fair a moment of dignity in his whole life, and now they had him smiling wanly, saying, 'I am guilty.' Were they incapable of giving any enemy a fair chance?[57]

His revulsion must be understood, clearly, as a revulsion against ordinary journalism. Oh, these journalists! Yet at the same time, we realize that these journalists have seen something in Mailer, something Mailer cannot bear, but which is there. His point of view on their point of view is just as correct and as false as their point of view on him. In other words, the enemies are inseparable: their battle is without end, and then, they are the same, they go together. Mailer-the-narrator clearly reveals the failure of the desire to correct the point of view when he confronts his Mailer-the-witness with a young boy, who is beside him in the cell in which he has been locked up, and is in the process of reading the article aloud so as to make fun of Mailer: "The novelist smiled wanly," said the boy in a mocking tone. "Wanly," said Mailer and said no more for he could feel the amusement of the others at his anger.'[58] There is always a third point of view, therefore, to laugh at the very one who is in conflict with another. In the eyes of this boy, Mailer is little better than the journalist, and it is because Mailer-the-witness feels the same that he holds his tongue.

This relativism, and the sapping operation that signals his triumph, seem, therefore, to be at the heart of the reportage. Yet there are passages in which the reliability of this Mailer-the-witness is lauded. Mailer-the-narrator then seems, curiously, to turn the weaknesses of his character – his egotism, his unbounded imagination, his 'foolishness' – into assets. 'To write an intimate story of an event which puts its focus on a central figure who is not central to the event', he remarks, 'is to inspire immediate questions about the competence of the historian.' And yet, he goes on, this is the best way, that is, not to take as 'centre' the principal actors, deeply involved in the events, torn between their contradictory testimonies. He goes on to praise this strange distance of the comic hero, the complete egotist, in fact 'Mailer' the character:

> For that, an eyewitness who is a participant but not a vested partisan is required, further he must be not only involved, but ambiguous in his own proportions, a comic hero, which is to say, one cannot easily resolve the emphasis of the category – is he finally comic, a ludicrous figure with mock-heroic associations; or is he not unheroic, and therefore embedded somewhat tragically in the comic . . . so if the event took place in one of the crazy mansions, or indeed the crazy house of history, it is fitting that any ambiguous comic hero of such a history should be not only off very much to the side of history, but that he should be an egotist of the most startling misproportions, outrageously and often unhappily self-assertive, yet in command of a detachment classic in severity (for he was a novelist and so in need of studying every last lineament of the fine, the noble, the frantic, and the foolish in others and in himself) . . . once History inhabits a crazy house, egotism may be the last tool left to History.[59]

In fact, it is clear that Mailer-the-narrator is preparing a change of direction: he is finally going to show that he who is most self-centred, and the least reliable of observers, is, in fact, closest to the intimacy of History; the more you are in the novel, the more you are doing history. Book Two of *The Armies of the Night* has as its subtitle 'The Novel as History: The Battle of the Pentagon'. The turnaround is effected by means of an almost Nietzschean apology for the egotist's thirst for power:

> He had been born to a modest family, had been a modest boy, a modest young man, and he hated that, he loved the pride and the arrogance and the confidence and the egocentricity he had acquired over the years, that was his force and his luxury and the iron on his greed, the richest sugar of his pleasure, the strength of his competitive force.[60]

But what he salutes most in the egotist, and what he links directly to his narcissism, is the unbridled imagination. He makes the following comments, for example, in connection with Mailer's arrest and the almost megalomaniac state of mind it inspires in him:

> He had the conviction that his early arrest might excite others to further effort: the early battles of a war wheel on the hinge of their first legends – perhaps his imagination, in lockstep to many a montage in many an old movie, saw the word going out from mouth to ear to mouth to ear, linking the troops – in fact cold assessment would say *that was not an inaccurate expectation*. Details later.[61]

The key to this paradox – it is the 'inaccurate' imagination itself which gets to the heart of history – lies in the fact that the egotist is by definition, in Mailer, the man of conflict; he whose imagination is both focused on the self and constantly comparing this self with all others. In its very narcissism, the imagination opens the self up to grasping the misunderstanding in which it is constantly embroiled. It makes the witness peculiarly capable of what Mailer called, in an extract quoted above, the 'superimposition of vision', to which, we should remember, he attributed a certain 'clarity'. Mailer imagined the bayonets which he knew were not there in *fact*, but the clarity of this constructed image nevertheless reached the intimacy of this event, that is, the heart of the representations of the participants regarding the event: for the demonstrators, the bayonets were there, illustrating the violence of their battle with the army. One might think, admittedly, that any eyewitness could have used his imagination to grasp, that is, to construct, this image, but the difference between the egotist and the average witness is that the latter would have taken it for fact. The egotist, in contrast, establishes a distance – thanks to his self-centredness – in relation to the event, which allows him to perceive *the moment when reality gives way to fantasy*, the superimposition itself between the image received and the image already distorted, the construction into a real act by the imagination. The egotist, Mailer-the-witness, sees himself fantasizing in the very act of observing. He imagines the clash of contradictory representations which is taking place in the situation. He knows that this conflict is not in the 'facts', but in the atmosphere, and it is this atmosphere that he catches in fantastical manner.

In other words, 'intimacy', in Mailer, is the conflict that is at the heart of the event. The observer who confines himself to the 'facts' does not really apprehend it; to get close to it, there has to be a witness who is only too well aware that he is fantasizing. Mailer-the-witness is only too well aware that his own viewpoint is limited, so he is constantly imagining all the others – hence the superimposition of images. He accepts the contradiction in imagination, and so he 'sees' all the misunderstandings generated by the situation, the irresolvable conflicts between points of view, the superimposition of images which do not fit together. He 'sees' that no one sees the same thing, that the very notion of reality loses its meaning.

We can then understand that, for Mailer, the reconstitution of pure facts is vain – possible, maybe, but completely pointless. The truth of this march cannot be reduced to the simple 'facts', and this truth will never emerge in a single story, because it actually consists of the contradiction between stories. This pointlessness of the search for the 'true' story is nicely brought out when Mailer, after quoting two contradictory eyewitness statements regarding the violence (one emphasizing the aggression of the demonstrators towards the soldiers, the other the unprecedented brutality of the soldiers towards the demonstrators), writes: 'It may be obvious by now that a history of the March on the Pentagon which is not unfair will never be written, any more than a history which could prove dependable in details!'[62] The intimate truth of this event consists, therefore, of these very distortions that characterize the representations of the actors and make them collide with each other in an irresolvable way; and it is so as to be able to understand these distortions – what he called these 'crooked towers'[63] – that the novelist labours, and is therefore recognized as the best possible journalist. 'An explanation of the mystery of the events at the Pentagon cannot be developed by the methods of history – only by the instincts of the novelist,' he declares.[64] It is not that the facts can never be established:

Forget that the journalistic information available from both sides is so incoherent, inaccurate, contradictory, malicious, even based on error that no accurate history is conceivable. More than one historian has found a way through chains of false fact. No, the difficulty is that the history is interior – no documents can give sufficient intimation: the novel must replace history at precisely the point where experience is sufficiently emotional, spiritual, psychical, moral, existential, or supernatural to expose the fact that the historian in pursuing the experience would be obliged to quit the clearly demarcated limits of historic enquiry. So these limits are now relinquished. The collective novel which follows, while still written in the cloak of a historic style, and, therefore, continuously attempting to be scrupulous to the welter of a hundred confusing and opposed facts, will now unashamedly enter that world of strange lights and intuitive speculation which is the novel.[65]

It is primarily to journalists, clearly, that these words are addressed. Mailer calls on them to leave behind the simple, sterile cult of 'facts', and welcome the gaze of the novelist; which is tantamount to asking them to cease to be *unifiers* in order to become *decentrers*, who will grasp not what one can understand, but the misunderstanding itself.

It is in this way that Mailer-the-witness, though so unreliable, appears, against the odds, *because he is writing a novel*, and better than anyone else (thanks to an imagination peculiarly well suited to constructing the conflict of perspectives even within his own perspective), as a journalistic model. This raises the question, obviously, of the extent to which Mailer-the-narrator has made his 'hero', Mailer-the-witness, the model for exactly the sort of journalism he achieves in this account. Perhaps there are two levels here: the definitively discredited level of the simple witness, that of Mailer-the-witness; and a second level, that of Mailer-the-narrator-and-novelist, observing the witness, all the witnesses, and, over and above all their points of view, himself constructing the novel of the march on the Pentagon. But perhaps also Mailer-the-narrator, who is the true author of the novel of this march on the Pentagon, hence the true journalist, is paying tribute, all the same, to he who anchors his novel, this very special witness, this Mailer-the-witness, a funny sort of hero, egotistical and tragi-comical, already a journalist-novelist or on the way to becoming one.

In any case, if the novel-history is ultimately written by Mailer-the-narrator and not by Mailer-the-witness, it is clear that the latter recognizes that he is only continuing the work of the former. It is always, after all, 'Mailer'. In other words, Mailer, unlike Wolfe, never claims wholly to leave what is the point of departure for the activity of journalism: the singularity of a point of view, and of a situation, which implies limitations and distortions. Simply, the journalist-novelist pursues to the end this game of contradictory images which already characterizes the point of view of the egotist-witness; he continues his work of fantasy. Thus, contrary to the Wolfean model of the chameleon, which invited us to see the New Journalist as a traveller who is scarcely anchored and who is already, from the outset, above conflicting perspectives, the model of the journalist-novelist in Mailer remains anchored in a perspective. Mailer-the-narrator never denies that his novel is the product of a singular point of view, on which basis the conflict of points of view he presents is *imagined*.

Let us take, for example, the long description of the encounter between the demonstrators and the police, which comes late in the novel. Every sequence is described assuming there is an element of the imagined mixed in with the observation. Mailer never denies, therefore, that the conflicts described are imagined by a witness, and not reconstructed through real empathy with all the actors in the events. For example:

Earlier in the day, a couple of Negro demonstrators were reported to have taunted a Negro soldier until he had finally been obliged to hang his head, turn it away. *One can conceive of the dialogue.*

'Hey, nigger, how long you going to kiss Mr Charlie's who-who-who? Going over to Vietnam, going to be a nigger hero, huh? Going to have your photograph in a honkie paper, that right, is that right? Hey, Mr Big, give us some skin, take your fat black hand off that honkie asshole rifle and give us some skin. You're the man! You're the man![66]

The dialogue is *imagined* by Mailer-the-witness (and reconstructed by Mailer-the-novelist); the conflictuality is constructed by a singular imagination, accepted as such. Mailer does not pretend to reconstruct *real* interior worlds, in which he would *really* be merged like a chameleon. He is considerably more cautious than Wolfe in manipulating the categories of 'real' and 'fictive', and he accepts that his reconstruction is still fantasy. In the following extract, he presents a dialogue between the police and the demonstrators and, once again, it seems clear that he is imagining it:

Sex, fear, the lift of first courage, the lightness of freedom, the oncoming suffocations of dread, the wild swinging ache or the somnolent drift of pot, the biting cold of the night, the Civil War glow of the campfire light on all those union jackets, hippies on the trail of Sergeant Pepper – the U.S. Army looking out on a field of fires heard demonstrators talking to them, crying, 'Join us, join us,' demonstrators talking in low voices. 'Why do you stay in uniform? Do you like the helmet on your head, is that it? Do you like obeying officers you hate? Join us. We have everything. Look. We are free. We have pot, we have food we share, we have girls. Come over here to us, and share our girls' – a generosity of Eskimos and the New Middle Class which these soldiers of the working class and the small town would not be quick to comprehend – who gives his girl away, would be their question. And the answer – a fag! Yes, the hippies offered much, perhaps they offered too much.[67]

In general, therefore, Mailer is not seeking to make us feel that the dialogues he reconstructs are 'true' in the factual sense of the term; they are 'true' in a different way. They have similarities with what is called, in the writing of the French novelist Nathalie Sarraute, the 'subconversations',[68] that is, what is not said, but is said all the same: the French literary movement of the 1950s and 1960s known as Le Nouveau Roman, to which Sarraute belonged, tried to reconstruct them, to make them heard in the text. These constructs are quite unrelated to some empathic approach which sees it as vital to prove its access to the real – to the reality of the inner worlds of the actors. There is no such justification or guarantee in Mailer. He is beyond the real/fiction divide, which he wants to contest, true to the 'subversive intention' of the New Journalism. He accepts that his labour of the imagination, which is the source of his journalistic method, contains holes, halts and contradictions: you are always,

in fact, 'outside'; you are never sure of truly entering into the other
points of view you imagine.

Take, for example, the 'subconversation' between the soldiers and the
'girls'. These last provoke the soldiers, scoff at them, and exasperate
them. Here is the 'logic' of the soldiers as it is reconstructed – that is,
constructed – for us by Mailer:

> The logic here speaks of the old misery of the professional soldier, cen-
> turies old. He is, at his most brutal, a man who managed to stay alive until
> the age of seven because there were men, at least his father, or his broth-
> ers, to keep him alive – his mother had drowned him in no oceans of love;
> his fear is therefore of the cruelty of women, he may never have another
> opportunity like this – to beat a woman without having to make love to
> her . . . yes, and they beat the women for another reason. To humiliate the
> demonstrators, to break them from their new resistance down to the old
> passive disobedience of the helpless sit-in waiting one's turn to be clubbed;
> they ground it into their faces that they sat there while their women were
> being taken off and no one of them or group of them dared to charge for
> all that hour.[69]

Mailer does not really 'enter' anywhere; he is content to imagine, he
makes no attempt to 'guarantee'. And it is because he does not really
enter that he can imagine freely, travel *in the imagination* among different
points of view. To do this, you have to remain outside, to remain in what
he himself calls the 'gulf' between the different internal worlds of the
actors.[70] This is the most interesting place to be, because it is from the
'gulf' that you see what is important: that is, the conflict between these
worlds, the misunderstanding, and the incommunicable. What Mailer
calls the 'gulf' is what separates the American middle class from the
working class, and he constructs their respective worlds for us. Because
it is Mailer who constructs, however, it is Mailer who indicates the points
of conflict, who draws attention to the gulf and places himself in it, so
that he can work up the internal worlds of the classes in his imagination,
like a painter does his colours.

Not only does Mailer accept that this is a labour of the imagination,
and hence abolishes the myth of ubiquity, but he also takes his hesitations seriously; he begins again, tests hypotheses, and contradicts
himself. For example, are the demonstrators rebels? Or petit bourgeois?
Or 'soldiers' without knowing it? His gaze is constantly shifting, both
ironic and tender, for example, in the following passage:

> Standing against them, the demonstrators were not only sons of the middle
> class of course, but sons who had departed the middle class, they were
> rebels and radicals and young revolutionaries; yet they were unbloodied,

they felt secretly weak, they did not know if they were the simple equal, man for man, of these soldiers, and so when this vanguard confronted soldiers now, and were able to stare them in the eye, they were, in effect, saying silently, 'I will steal your élan, and your brawn, and the very animal of your charm because I am morally right and you are wrong and the balance of existence is such that the meat of your life is now attached to my spirit, I am stealing your balls.'[71]

In fact there is something destructive in the writing of Mailer, which protects him against the fantasy of ubiquity that can be detected in the programme of Wolfe. Whereas universal empathy is always suspect of exposing the conflict so 'well' and so 'completely' that it amounts to a sort of 'euphemizing', the decentring gaze which escapes this temptation of ubiquity truly *experiences* the conflict, that is, is constantly in conflict with itself within its writing, switching from point of view to point of view and reproducing the clashes these switches involve.

This explains the decentring power in the writing of Mailer: it is not so much that he leads the public *everywhere*, as that he shows it that, wherever it goes, it can still locate itself *elsewhere* and see differently; and that this possibility is not a very pleasant one, because it means a permanent conflict of points of view, as well as the impossibility of ubiquity. Within the New Journalism, Mailer is clearly one of the figures most tormented by the need to make people see the depth of the misunderstandings and the intensity of the conflicts which disturb the sphere of points of view.

2. *Libé 1* and the temptation to unify the dominated

Multiplicity of voices or common voice of the dominated?
The double discourse of the early years of Libération

We come now to another decentring journalism, threatened by a different temptation from that of ubiquity. The daily newspaper *Libération* was born on 22 May 1973, also with the intention of mounting a challenge to the dominant journalism. 'In a France occupied by "bastards", it was necessary to create liberation zones and support movements that emerged,' declared Philippe Gavi, one of the founders of the paper, according to one of *Libération*'s 'biographers', Jean-Claude Perrier.[72]

The new paper relied on the work of the Agence de Presse Libération (APL), founded on 18 June 1971, whose director of publishing was Maurice Clavel. The APL had undertaken to seek news everywhere in France, in the factories, the universities and the militant movements; it

was a Maoist propaganda organization, controlled by the Proletarian
Left (Gauche Prolétarienne). However, the daily newspaper *Libération*,
brain-child of Jean-Claude Vernier, seemed anxious not to be known
exclusively as a 'Maoist rag'. Indeed, the 'Maoists' suggested to other
militant groups that they join them in their journalistic venture: small
leftist groups, who called themselves, within the editorial board of *Libé*,
the 'désirants'. They all seemed to want to reach a wider public, the
'people' to whom they claimed they wished to 'give a voice'. *Libé* was
published by a limited liability company (the Éditions Libération) with
a capital of 20,000 francs, divided between four co-directors, Jean-Paul
Sartre, Jean-Claude Vernier, Jean-René Huleu and Serge July. It was initially financed entirely by popular subscription and gifts from well-
wishers; among those who made a financial contribution was Michel
Foucault. Sartre was chairman of the editorial board.

The first issue having been announced for 5 February 1973, a first
press conference was held on 4 January of that year. Number 0, of
5 February, proved a disappointment, and was followed by several other
false starts (22 February, 14 March and 18 April). In the end, it was
the paper of 22 May 1973 which was the first real number; it was on
sale in kiosks, it had a print run of 50,000 copies, it sold at 0.80 francs,
and it was distributed by a press distribution service, the Nouvelles
Messageries de la Presse Parisienne (NMPP). The first phase of publication ended on 29 July; the editorial team was restructured during that
summer, and Serge July became editor-in-chief. A special number
appeared on 10 August devoted to events in the Lip factory. Daily publication was resumed in September 1973.[73]

The early days of the newspaper *Libération* provide an instructive illustration of the difficulties of the decentring project. The aim, clearly, was
to provide *another gaze* than that dominant in 'bourgeois' journalism. As
in the New Journalism, the challenge to the pseudo-objectivity of the
dominant journalism meant giving priority once again to the notions of
'speech' and 'voice': the dominant gaze was denounced as the expression of no more than a singular voice, against which other voices must
be made heard. In fact, there must be a return to questioning and to conflicting points of view – of the 'I' – in order to fight against this consensual eye which claimed to unify an 'us' by smoothing out disagreements.
The initial manifesto of the paper, of 2 November 1972, is revealing with
regard to this vocabulary of the 'voice':

> Those who are responsible for the material or moral poverty in which the
> majority of the inhabitants of our country live shroud themselves in the
> strictest secrecy and impose silence on the majority. They make a great
> brouhaha, nevertheless; they bombard us with news, images and ideas

which distract us from essentials, and denature even our faces. It is time to attack secrecy, and help the people speak.

This 'speaking' is understood not as a single voice, but as what will open up the possibility of a debate: 'Without shutting our eyes to the strength of the prejudices which still divide the population (racism, men's oppression of women, puritanism, respect for hierarchy . . .), by relying on the direct expression of the people, *Libération* will provoke a debate.' The manifesto goes on to call for a new gaze at reality, a 'daily critique of daily life', which will provide a forum for all those voices that are never heard: 'Everything that is discussed at work and in the community will be at the heart of the newspaper.'[74]

Yet it is by no means certain that the explanation of the project manages wholly to rid itself of a rhetoric of unification, which has crept even into the decentring purpose. In many regards, the desire to 'give the people a voice' implies the constitution of a new 'us' against the official 'us': a 'we-the-dominated' against the dominant, and one may ask whether, in the end, the paper really tried to address the latter. In other words, the *Libé* project seems to have been particularly threatened by the temptation to see the union of the dominated as more important than the decentring of the dominant. This ambivalence – ambivalence, yet again – was particularly visible at the press conference of 4 January 1973; indeed, it was even one of Sartre's major concerns on that occasion. He speaks above all of the importance of making visible the 'contradictions' that exist within the population, in order to avoid what he calls the temptation of 'leftist journalism', in-turned, motivated by a sectarian spirit. It seems that Sartre was conscious from the beginning of what might be called the risk of clannishness, of a retreat into an 'us' of the dominated who will no longer confront anything that might imperil their unity. He urges the editors to be as open as possible to the multiplicity of voices that emanate from the people. The paper must be 'leftist', he says, but in the best sense of the word, that is, the sense that implies an attitude of permanent challenge ('on the left of the Communist Party'), and not in the narrow and negative sense that derives from sectarianism.

It is piquant to note, however, that, in this statement at least, Sartre himself notes that this policy of 'listening' to the contradictory voices emerging from the population implies, nevertheless, something like a unification. Sartre may reject the narrow sort of unifying which is the 'sectarian spirit', but he accepts and even promotes another: the sort that would bind together the people as a whole through the exposure of their conflicts. His statement continues: 'And inasmuch as this is what we are all working for, as has already been said, there are contradictions and conflicts which *should be publicly resolved in the newspaper*, through articles which are in opposition to each other and which should lead, eventually, to *an even stronger bond*.'[75] The resolution of conflicts, a bond: the proposal is hardly what one might expect from Sartre, who, in his philosophy, promotes a radical conception of the alterity of other people, and argues against the idea of a 'connection between consciousnesses'.[76] His philosophy even urges deep distrust with regard to the project for a decentring gaze, hardly disposed to adapt to the fundamental paradox of decentring, illustrated in chapter 1 by the anecdote told by Francis Déron; a hard-line Sartrean would have been more likely to denounce decentring as a process which inevitably betrays the otherness of whoever decentres, since, by definition, it *reconnects* to the decentred and so misses what, in this otherness, eludes any possible connection. When the Sartre of *Being and Nothingness* describes the 'decentring' which each individual produces in another, he emphasizes that this does not in any way connect them;[77] rather, it mires them in misunderstanding and the impossibility of communicating, and leaves them with the prospect only of 'sadomasochistic' relationships, since no one can make contact with another except by absorbing them into their own point of view or letting themselves be absorbed into theirs. But perhaps, when he took on the editorship of *Libération*, Sartre was faced with a requirement which, in spite of his philosophical radicalism, he now had to find some way of accommodating. So he returns to this theme of the connection, effectively accepting that even conflict, the decentring of some by others, creates a bond between these some and these others. Not only does he return to this theme, but he goes further than one might have expected, because he appeals explicitly for a 'unification', which would emerge from the cacophony:

> We have nothing to restrain us because we have no advertising and hence the information must be total. It must at the same time be the beginning of a *popular unification* – this is the essence of our thinking, which will permit the unified *people* to demand from the State and the administration control of everything that goes on within these organizations. The government must no longer have any secrets. We must demand this. We may be sure that it will hang on to its secrecy, the secrecy of its deliberations, unless we wrest it away. This is precisely what is needed now, to wrest it away, and it is in this manner that we will try to create this *unification*, that is, by trying gradually to provide the *common elements which are desired by all*, such as, for example, the absence of secrecy in a given sphere, etc.

These 'common elements', brought out by the debate, allow even Sartre to describe this 'popular thinking' as 'objective': 'They have spoken to you about objectivity. Objectivity is a real situation as it is expressed by popular thinking. It is people who think about a situation, their own situation. And this is what we must record.'[78]

This unification is clearly of a very particular type: produced by a conflict between the voices finally freed from their political straitjackets and at last able to express themselves fully, it is based on the contemplation of 'contradictions' that are not in any way glossed over. Sartre is firm that there will be absolutely no glossing over of contradictions, and he emphasizes that the editorial board which will orchestrate this great coming together will not itself be consensual but, on the contrary, riven by deep disagreements. 'In sum,' he goes on:

> we are far from splinter groups, you will see, because *we are not wholly in agreement amongst ourselves*. We are in agreement on specific points, that is, the absence of secrecy, information by the people, popular unity, but on other points we are not. Moreover, *we know that there are deep contradictions among the people*, which the system uses to its advantage, and we also want to try, not to accept one or other thesis or anti-thesis of these contradictions, but to confront them one with the other and see what emerges.

It is above all, therefore, the *unifying* effect which results from decentring that Sartre is describing. It is yet again a far from obviously Sartrean point of view; he is suggesting that the forging of a link, and even the achievement of a new unification, remain the ultimate aim of the project which seeks to make people move on from otherness and all-out conflict. The cacophony *reconnects*, with a power that challenges the artificial unification orchestrated by the powers-that-be (that is, by the dominant powers).

However, we may be more Sartrean than Sartre here, and pose some crucial questions (which, in any case, would continue to haunt Sartre, and ultimately lead him to judge the early days of *Libération* harshly): to what extent does this theme of the *bond*, in the first years of *Libé*, lead to a betrayal of the project to make a generalized conflictuality emerge within the sphere of points of view? To what extent did the newspaper, in spite of everything, make the unification of the dominated its chief priority? Or, to use the vocabulary of the Sartre of those years, to what extent was *Libé 1* impregnated by the 'sectarian spirit', which aims to unify the dominated more than to expose the multiplicity of the contradictions?

Everything depends, in fact, on the way the theme of the bond, or encounter, was treated in the first years of *Libération*. It may be that the newspaper meant by it only that bond created, ultimately, by the confrontation of voices that are customarily strangers, that is, an encounter that doesn't really cancel out the differences and disagreements and that is, therefore, part of the paradox inherent in the process of decentring: what challenges 'us', that is, challenges the 'we', remains connected to this 'we' simply because it has an effect on it; the decentring undoes fixed identities, but still reconnects all those involved in the vast conflict of points of view it presents, but in a different way from in the original artificial unification; it makes them listen to each other, speak to each other, and confront each other, hence, whether they wish it or not, meet each other.

This is the type of bond referred to, for example, in Number 0 of 22 February 1973, where the word 'link' appears explicitly in an article on the 'Libé Débat' page. Here the theme of the bond refers only to that forged by the conflict itself, by the debate the journalist is expected to reveal and then orchestrate. 'Until now', we read in this article:

> there have been many failures; the articles produced exposed the errors: they are often like questionnaires. For example, a journalist, with three colleagues, approached a young worker from the Cité des Marguerites in Nanterre with a tape recorder and asked him a series of questions without giving his own point of view; the journalist remained totally passive throughout the interview. The result: snatches of conversation placed end to end. The watchword of *Libération* at the beginning was 'Information comes from the people and returns to the people.' This watchword is gradually becoming clearer. *The journalists try to be a link* [my emphasis]: to ask a person questions which other people are asking, to reflect with the people so as to be able to shed light on the contradictions which divide them. It is not enough to return to the scene of the investigation and see how the article was received and how it helped those who had participated in its production. It is necessary for the people interviewed to guide the journalist at the scene of their struggle, of their daily life, while formulating their problems more clearly. We need gradually to establish new relationships between journalists and the people; the information must come from the people and not end its life on a telex, it must constantly open and reopen debates which will be more than just a page of letters to the editor.

The idea pursued here is that *the conflict itself produces community*; if not, it is because it has not been fully exposed, but remains at the stage of the juxtaposition of points of view in a totally random manner, a sterile and superficial *cacophony*.

We find the same idea in the expression 'bringing together of voices', used, for example, in the paper of 18 April 1973: 'In every letter', we read on the page devoted to correspondence from readers, 'the birth of a thought, that which is never expressed, that of the lowly and the oppressed . . . this is the bringing together of voices which will make *Libération* the echo of a people who fight and who live. *Libération* should not only be the cry of a free press, but of a press that frees.' This theme of the bond created in the population at large, by the very fact of exposing its internal contradictions, is found in a statement by Michel Foucault in an interview with José, an unskilled worker at the Renault plant, published in *Libération* on 26 May 1973. Foucault considers the *exchange* introduced by the gaze of the intellectual – seen as very similar to the journalist – as the counterpart of the capacity of the intellectual to provoke conflict and debate:

> We are agreed, the workers have no need of intellectuals to know what they do, they know this perfectly well themselves. For me, the intellectual is the guy who is plugged in, not to the productive system, but to the information networks. He can make himself heard. He can write in the newspapers, give his point of view. He is plugged in to the information networks of the past, too. He has the knowledge that comes from reading a certain number of books, which others do not have at their fingertips. The role of the intellectual, therefore, is not to form the consciousness of the workers, because it exists, but *to enable this consciousness and this knowledge of the workers to enter the information system, to disseminate it and, in consequence, to help other workers or people who are not workers to become aware of what is going on.* I am ready to talk to you as if I was a mirror [Foucault is here responding to José], if we mean by mirror a means of transmission.

And it is for José to start things off: 'And from then on, *the intellectual encourages the exchanges.*'[79] Here, the aim does not seem to be the unification of the dominated; in any case, in Foucault's formulation, the new exchange affects everybody, the dominant included. The aim is a debate which will finally integrate the point of view of those 'dominated', those forgotten by the general information system, a debate which will, therefore, 'decentre' gazes, but without a re-centring announced a priori: the debate and the decentring must at last put the question of the centre on to the agenda and at last leave it open; who knows what will be the result of this dissemination which helps 'other workers or people who are not workers to become aware of what is going on'.

So, when the theme of the *encounter* or the *exchange* is simply incorporated into the idea of the debate, it is 'complicated', and emphasizes the *paradoxical nature* of the decentring movement, but it does not pose the problem of the *distortion* of this movement into something quite different. On the other hand, certain uses of the theme of the bond, the exchange and the encounter certainly do slide into something else. Thus, in the editorial of 22 May 1973:

> Our fellow journalists who struggle to get the truth into their newspapers know how, after one mutilation after another, their articles end up on the

spike. This is why a new daily newspaper was necessary. Because our poverty is also, perhaps paradoxically, our strength. That of being able to say anything. That of being the spokesperson for the population, for its debates, for its contradictions, as for its hopes, for its inventions, as for its revolts. *Libération* is a little like David in the land of Goliath . . . the existence of *Libé*, its presence in the kiosks every morning, is a breath of freedom, a clearing in the jungle of the press, an open space where people can meet and talk. The France of the lower orders, the France of the big housing estates, the fields and the factories, that of the Métro and the buses, speaks.

The method described here consists, it is true, of decentring the bourgeois public by making an 'other' voice emerge and portraying their confrontation – David against Goliath. It also assumes, it seems, taking criticism of the centre as far as possible, since the paper insists that it wants to be 'the spokesperson for the population . . . [and] its contradictions'. The exposure of the contradictions seems to take priority, which might suggest that the only 'bonds' referred to are those which are forged in confrontation, thanks to the creation of an 'open space where people can meet and talk'. But the expression which follows, 'the France of the lower orders', is ambiguous. It is clear that it is primarily the 'Davids', that is, the 'others' of the bourgeois public, who are meant to be unified here, and not the 'Davids' *and* the 'Goliaths'; 'the population' is not the *whole* population, it is 'the France of the lower orders' as against 'the France of the upper classes'. In other words, the theme of unification does not relate solely to the bonds forged by the decentring movement; it is not a matter of linking the bourgeois and their 'others' (those who decentre); nor is it, or at least not only, a matter of linking all those whose conflicts will be exposed (the whole population). The theme is more precise: it is the 'others', the dominated, who must be unified, to help them to experience themselves as an 'us'.

Imperceptibly, this concern to unify the 'dominated' tends to neutralize the *general* or *all-out* nature of the decentring project. One has the impression that they, the dominated, have not so much to be unmade as constituted; that the internal contradictions of 'the France of the lower orders' ultimately become secondary; and that the Sartrean concern for all the contradictions to be exposed and for the paper to orchestrate a decentring in many directions, is as if overtaken by the desire to constitute a circumscribed 'us'. As a result, the journalistic figure of the decentrer shifts towards something that is closer to a new witness-ambassador, representing the 'we' of the dominated. In this case, you can no longer claim to decentre altogether, you accept that you now decentre only to be able to *re-centre*.

The 'Lili Blues' column of Philippe Gavi, which appeared daily from 30 May to 22 June 1973, is very revealing with regard to this tendency to turn the decentring process into a unification of the dominated. The column owed its title to a juvenile delinquent, a young girl who faces the courts, hospital and a variety of ordeals, and whose story Gavi wants to tell 'as a soap opera'. From the beginning, 'their' speech – that of Lili herself and that of the many who resemble her, victims of a society that excludes them – is presented as 'ours': 'Lili Blues is a sort of soap opera,' we read in the preamble, on 30 May 1973:

> Only, there is no need to invent the characters. They are there, they exist. Over the coming days, they will speak and tell their stories. Our story, too. Every misfortune, every injustice is shared, like night time or tenderness. We are on the same road, weak and at sea, dreaming of a world that does not exist. That of freedom.

After introducing Lili and Aïcha, another young girl, who has suicidal tendencies, Gavi ends his first article with the words, 'So, each hanging on to the other, between life and death, they are also what I am, what we all are, a few details apart.'[80] The way the 'I' expands into a 'we' here is so explicit as to constitute a near-textbook example of the figure of the witness-ambassador; as is the empathic treatment, coolly announced and causing the journalist-ambassador to recognize these girls excluded from the 'us' as 'ours'. It is of Nellie Bly that we are reminded here, that is, of a journalistic attitude that ultimately reduces otherness to identity: 'we' are there, alongside those whom we thought were 'others'.

What is different from Nellie Bly, however, is that the column allows the characters to speak at length. We hear a lot of *their* voice, which might well have a decentring effect; this voice could make us hear the singularity of an experience difficult to share, an otherness, something truly strange in relation to us, especially, for example, if it began to designate a 'you', to speak to us from a position of exteriority and of non-belonging. But this would require the journalist, when he made us hear this voice, to position himself outside it, between it and we who hear it, and not inside it; to be the mediator who allows the conflict to be expressed. However, it is the position Gavi adopts that often prevents the decentring from happening. His questions to Lili, for example, immediately put him alongside her, and his use of the familiar 'tu' allows him, in practice, to reduce Lili's otherness and constitute a 'we' through her. In the interview of 9–10 June 1973, for example, he begins by asking her a question which reveals her in her singularity, in her separation from the dominant 'we'. 'You began to have sex when you were 11. That's rather young, isn't it?' Lili's voice could appear here as the 'other voice'. But the next question immediately turns this 'other' into a representative of the real 'us' – just as Nellie Bly turned psychiatric illness into a representative of 'us' (in her case, 'us', the American public): 'The fact that they are determined to make us ashamed of our bodies, of our desires and of having to make love on the sly, didn't it spoil your pleasure?'[81] The manifest empathy and the evidence of his understanding of Lili negate the decentring effect, the 'speaking to', the questioning. The interview speaks only of 'we' who are with Lili from the start.

Further, it has to be said that the voice of Lili is highly predictable right from the start, that it is closer to stereotypical and cliché-ridden propaganda than to the original story of a unique life, which would seek to understand domination in its singular intimacy, would question the possibility of this voice ever making itself heard and understood and would exploit its own conflictual strength; and which would, as a result, make the encounter something debatable rather than a statement of the obvious. For example:

As soon as a human being feels the need to make love, to communicate with people in this way, they have to do it straightaway, and I mean straightaway! It's fucking great, so simple . . . I can understand why people have problems in their social life, or at work, or with housing, but why sexual problems. Shit, it's ridiculous . . .[82]

The journalist who 'absorbs' the young girl's singularity in this way is not orchestrating a conflict between her and a shocked bourgeoisie; he is losing sight of the 'you' to be decentred and contenting himself with unifying the 'dominated' – characters who are, what is more, transparent and lacking in complexity – with whom he merges, happily forgetting the 'dominant'.

These examples make it possible for us to see that the decentring project depends to a large extent on the position the journalists adopt through their gaze. It is the journalists' own exteriority, in relation to 'us' the public (to be able to make us encounter an otherness), but also in relation to the 'others' (to make 'us' hear them), which makes them decentrers, that is, journalists who reveal and orchestrate conflict between two poles distinct from themselves. It is this position which is compromised in certain episodes of 'Lili Blues'.

It was equally compromised in some of the reporting on the strike at the Lip watch factory in Besançon in 1973, which illustrates with particular clarity this temptation to unify the dominated.

The headline on the front page of the *Libération* of 22 June 1973 reveals how the journalists identified with the struggle they 'observed':

'Lip: our readers are the France of the lower orders.' As early as 20 June, the joint signatures of the Lip workers and journalists of *Libération* ('P. A. and D. G. and the Lip workers'[83]) had appeared at the end of an article openly celebrating the sense of community among the strikers. On 27 June, an article appeared with the headline 'At Lip, the journalists experienced something new', signed 'A group of journalists present at Besançon'. In it we read:

> An unskilled worker using the familiar 'tu' to the tie-wearing special correspondent of *Le Monde*, and an Italian journalist having the company's position on the financial markets explained to him, in the office of Fred Lip, by the employees; these are only two examples of a mutual trust which has developed between the journalists and the Lip workers. One of the women who works there says to us, 'We would never have believed that a bronzed lady-journalist from *Paris-Match* could live with us for several days'.

And, further on:

> The consequence is a series of situations in which, for once, the contact was genuine and no longer self-interested. So we see the INF 2 team, like most of our colleagues, eating in the Lip canteen.
> This is why it was impossible for the special correspondent of the Agence France-Presse to spend the first night anywhere else but inside the factory with the workers: 'We want by our mark of confidence to win his,' explains one female employee.
> And when the appeals for solidarity immobilized the switchboard, a worker made his own telephone available to a journalist.
> The Lip workers have experienced something new, but so have the journalists! Perhaps the batons of the anti-riot police served a purpose. Most of the journalists became purchasers of stolen goods [the watches the factory produced], out of solidarity.

The article expresses a veritable desire for fusion between journalists and strikers, in other words, for the destruction of the specificity of the observers so that they merge into the world of the actors. In which case they would not betray those who were fighting: '. . . trust was further strengthened by the appearance of the first articles which had, in general, not misrepresented the meaning of their fight.'

Admittedly, the article emphasizes that this trust should not prevent the journalists from seeing the 'contradictions' which exist within the group of workers: 'From the first days, the reporters, the only outsiders admitted into the factory, could, accompanied by a hostess, circulate through the workshops, talk to whoever they wanted, and even attend the meetings of the action committee. The workers were not afraid, therefore, of revealing their contradictions, like their unity.' But the overall tone still leads one to question the true significance of this remark. To be more precise, it is clear that the journalists are hardly being encouraged to seek out other 'contradictions' than those that would be obvious to the workers themselves; their point of view is not regarded as constituting a new point of view in relation to that which the strikers have of themselves.

Many articles on this episode show that it was, in fact, the aim to keep to this wholly insider viewpoint. The point of view of management is usually evoked solely from the standpoint of the workers; the journalists do not introduce a third point of view, do not position themselves 'between' the two poles of conflict. We see this, for example, in an article of 26 June, signed 'Daniel Grignon, Edmonde Morin, Lip workers', in which the policy of the owners is 'summarized' by a quotation whose author is not named, but who is clearly one of the strikers: 'The policy of ÉBAUCH S. A. might be summarized as follows: "We don't need intelligent people to make watches, stupid ones will do." ' In fact, the very idea of an autonomous journalistic gaze at those who are, after all, being observed, seems odious; it is the very status of observer which is then perceived as dangerous, to the point where the legitimacy of the observer depends on having 'Lip workers' alongside their signature.

It would seem that this temptation to fuse with the dominated was so powerful in the first years of *Libération* for it to be, as we will see, a major issue in the debates which rocked the editorial board of the paper in the years 1977–9, and which led to the break with leftism. During the 23 October 1977 occupation of the offices of *Libération* by readers from the extreme left unhappy at the way the paper had distanced itself from the Red Army Faction, Serge July made comments which, in many ways, constitute a reminder of the 'decentring' role of the newspaper, a role that implies being perpetually 'elsewhere'. In an interview given to *Le Nouvel Observateur*, he declares:

> In the beginning, it is helpful to spell out that *Libé* is a serious newspaper, a cultural object, if you like. But not a newspaper of the extreme left, as is often said. If we were, it would mean that we position ourselves in the polit-ical arena, whereas we are outside it. It is an expression that others have over-used, but we are 'elsewhere'. We do not believe that everything happens at the centre, at the head of the State.

July also puts a particular emphasis on the 'internal differences' within the editorial team, which 'the paper greatly values'; this 'diversity in its expression and its thinking', which makes *Libé* the instrument of a 'social experiment', constitutes, he says 'a questioning of all the terms of revolutionary action'.[84] To unmake rather than to create, and to rediscover the taste for cacophony: this would seem to be the meaning of these words, which represent a break, therefore, with a certain leftist attitude for which Sartre had already voiced his mistrust some years before.

Perhaps the most significant aspect of this interview is the fact that July raises questions regarding a requirement which had been accepted as self-evident in the early days of *Libé*: the need to listen to the readers. 'The journalists of *Libération* will share the lives of the readers of the newspaper in the cities, in the suburbs and in the villages,' said the first manifesto of 2 November 1972. 'To found a press in the service of the public and the readers, in other words, for the People,' declared the press release of 5 February 1973. To be a 'newspaper where people speak', declared a column of December 1973.[85] In 1977, however, July speaks of the need to consider limits to this attitude, or at least, finally to spell out its meaning: 'No media constructs its news with its readers more than *Libération*,' he says, 'but this endeavour has its limits: with Lip, for example, it didn't work.'[86] What exactly does he mean? It is far from clear. Nevertheless, the context in which the remark appears seems to indicate that it was a comment on the role of the observer and on the importance of not confusing the requirement to listen with pure and simple self-effacement, empathic fusion with those seen both as objects and audience of the journalistic gaze. July emphasizes the impossibility of empathizing with everybody, and even the undesirability of such an attitude, because it risks making the journal a permanent hostage, instead of an organ of the free press. To be 'in the service of the readers' and to present their various and conflicting points of view may require an attitude that is not one of permanent and shifting empathy. Another approach – the 'real labour of information' to which July refers – has to be developed if it is to be a decentring newspaper.

It is not, therefore, in order to renege on this decentring purpose but rather, it would seem, to defend its radical nature, that July expresses the wish to change the journalistic practice which had previously been regarded as inseparable from it, empathy; an empathy which amounted, in essence, to 'unifying' many different groups of readers, and which carried both a risk – that of creating malcontents – and an intrinsic weakness – was this all-embracing empathy even possible? We seem here to be back with the difficulties associated with the figure of the 'chameleon' as described by Tom Wolfe. But the example of *Libé* restricts the practice of empathy rather more: it had been the margins, the places where the dominations are practised, that the newspaper had primarily wanted to reconstruct, as if from the inside. Nevertheless, the problem is analogous to that faced by the chameleon: is this really the model for the 'decentring journalist'? Perhaps, rather than see the decentrer as an enthusiast for permanent metamorphosis, we should see the decentrer as an 'I', who is, after all, singular, with all the limitations attached to the fact of always taking up a position somewhere (whatever is said), even if it means assuming this journalist to have, at the same time, a capacity for permanent self-criticism and for 'change' (which is not the same thing as doing away with oneself)? Because what July seems to be describing here, in essence, is the very impasse which consists of the desire to be *everywhere* where there are dominated, margins and challenges. It is also a form of ubiquity, if more limited, that is being denounced here, a ubiquity which always produces discontent. Instead of urging the newspaper to be ever more ubiquitous, July asks it to rethink its method: to conceive of the decentring differently, that is, on the model of 'elsewhere' rather than that of 'everywhere'.

Since journalists cannot avoid taking up a position, they need to construct a situation which is 'elsewhere' – what, in a long article of 22 May 1978, July later called the situation of the 'nomad'. In this later article, he suggests that the concern to be away from the centre, close to the margins and the dominated, carries the constant risk of settling into a new fixed position.[87] In other words, it is the very nature of the 'place' – the non-centre – that needs to be rethought. Consequently, if the 'coming together of voices' (July would also, in an interview given to *Esprit* in May 1978,[88] speak of the 'coming together of challenges') was not to be simply a coming together on new foundations, that is, the construction of a new centre (which inevitably tends to smooth over the contradictions which obstruct it, hence to restrict, even neutralize, the project to decentre), there needs to be a different conception of the relationship of the decentring journalists to those challengers of the 'official' centre to whom they give a voice. In this same interview for *Esprit*, July notably declares: 'It was essential to rid ourselves of the old problematic of leftism and bear the burden of reality ourselves, without institutional or ideological referent.' One of the points he emphasizes is the importance of the absolute autonomy of the 'observers': they are to investigate everything, he says, with a freedom which seems also to imply a freedom with regard to those to whom they listen. They are to do this without categorizing, and constantly on the lookout for what he calls the 'homogenization of thought'. It is as if July is reconstructing what an older interpretation of the imperative of listening to the dominated had abolished, that is, the autonomy of the gaze; as if, at last, the rejection of pure empathy, and the horror of a relationship of fusion, has been clearly articulated.

It should be noted, furthermore, that Sartre was himself, in 1979, fairly harsh in his judgement of the first years of *Libé*, suggesting that his fears on the subject of 'sectarianism' had been premonitory. His criticisms, which came in an interview published in *Les Nouvelles Littéraires*, are not, it must be admitted, altogether clear. However, one can detect criticism of a style which tried to be working class, when the real test had been to invent a style which spoke to the workers as well, which is not the same thing:

> We needed to speak to the workers who read us as we would have spoken to them face-to-face. That should have been the style of *Libération*. In my view, the paper tried, but that is not what it did; it went in more for the style of 'La Semaine de Suzette', that is, an infantile style. That is not what was needed. We should have tried to find a mass style so that it would be as clear and as audible as possible.[89]

Nevertheless, Sartre emphasizes the advantages as well as the disadvantages of the 'exit from leftism', that is, the exit from 'bad', 'sectarian' leftism so as to achieve a more interesting, more 'nomadic' 'leftist' approach. His interview raises a problem which also helps to explain why *Libé* clung for so long to the militant and empathic position. Sartre's comments on the gradual evolution of the newspaper run as follows: 'It was a jumble and then, bit by bit, something emerged which was better done and which showed what *Libération* might have been as a leftist paper.' But he also notes that something was lost in this evolution: 'The articles are better written. But you no longer sense the will behind them. There is good work, but you no longer sense rebellion. Many things have disappeared.' Is this a cause for regret? Sartre seems not to have wanted to expand on his comments: he was ready to criticize anything, unafraid of contradicting himself. But we may take up the problem in his place, a problem which takes us back once again to the paradox of decentring: true rebels, Sartre seems to say, cannot be good decentring journalists; they 'cling' to those they support, they are incapable of observing them and 'showing' them to others, their main concern is to unify behind them and construct a new centre against the centre they fight. The truly decentring journalist, in contrast, restores distances, always looks for the 'non-place', that of the nomad from which the conflicts can be exposed; this can only be done, however, by losing a little of the intensity of the revolt. This is another way of expressing the dilemma of the decentring project: the more it is willed with the vehemence of the rebel, the more it fails; but can the distance of the nomad be a model for decentring, when it has lost the vehemence of the rebel? The recognition by Sartre of *Libé*'s 'progress' remains tinged with disillusionment, itself very Sartrean. But there is no way out; this is the paradox at the heart of the decentring project.

It is interesting to note, furthermore, that the fiercest supporters of an exit from 'leftism' – so as finally to enter 'journalism' – often also had their moments of nostalgia, conscious that this 'progress' inevitably meant that something was lost. Serge July himself was nostalgic for that feeling of 'fusion' which had characterized the first days of *Libé*. Further, he uses, in this context, the Sartrean expression 'group-in-fusion', which emphasizes, if it still needed to be spelled out, that the temptation to unify the dominated, in spite of Sartre's warnings, actually constitutes an eminently Sartrean temptation:[90]

> What was *Libération*? A team. What constituted *Libération*'s capital? A team. *Libération* existed, was possible and lasted, *Libération* could play the role it played, create new journalistic forms and even make journalism an entirely separate culture, only inasmuch as the different people who came together over the years managed to gel, blend and create a crucible, a matrix. *Libération* helped to support the 1970s only inasmuch as this team was both an authentic creation and a creator. The 'miracle' of *Libération*? No, a 'group-in-fusion', like Sartre in the *Critique of Dialectical Reason*. I am keen to quote Sartre, because his old age mingled with our birth, our development and our life, without our always being aware of it. Let us follow Sartre in the revolutionary Paris of 14 July 1789 which prefigures, in its way, the success of *Libération*: 'And this group, though still unstructured, that is to say, entirely amorphous, is characterized by being the direct opposite of alterity: in a serial relation, in fact, Unity as the Reason of the series is always elsewhere . . . in the Apocalypse . . . that is to say, the dissolution of the series into the group-in-fusion.' And later, 'a group being constituted by the liquidation of an inert seriality under the pressure of definite material circumstances'. This was the *Libération* team until 1978. Two hundred individual histories produced by the multitude of experiences in the aftermath of May 1968 which dissolve in a 'totalizing totality': a desire for a newspaper made communally.[91]

These words are, to say the least, surprising, explicitly evoking the importance of unifying, in its most extreme form, in order to create a common culture, that of the dominated for whom *Libération* was spokesperson. The conflicts and the presence of an otherness introducing contradiction into the heart of this unification are all here treated as of little importance, or at least regarded with fear. July adds:

> The team no longer pursues this 'totalizing totality' totally. The contradictions insurmountable yesterday have become mountains. The fusion slows down. Until the time when the fusion no longer happens . . . when the wishes of this one or that one diverge to the point of opposing each other, but their oppositions are no longer positive. They become systematically negative, always negative . . . then we have to realize that the *Libération*

team is no longer a group-in-fusion, that it is on the way to becoming a 'Fraternity-Terror', still quoting Sartre. That is, a collectivity where the initiatives of this one or that one have become damaging to both. Where the differences will end by wounding. For a long time the role of the editors of this newspaper had been to manage the consensus, to enable the team to surmount all the internal contradictions. Then the moment came when this was no longer possible.

This is how July justified his own resignation, on 6 February 1981, and his proposal to cease publication in order to prepare for a rebirth. 'In a way', he adds, 'we are embarking on the search for a new fusion.'[92]

Over and above any matters of personal strategy, which should not be ignored (this is an eminently 'political' article), such a discourse raises a fundamental problem. It seems that the very thing that had constituted the weakness of *Libé 1*, the temptation of 'clannishness' or of fusion with the dominated, *at the same time* constituted its profound originality, the key to the subversion the paper represented with regard to the official 'centre'. It is the very fact that it unified so strongly that put it in danger, even if this *at the same time* meant limitations for the decentring project. This is why, paradoxically perhaps, the metaphor of 'public letter-writer' which was often used to characterize *Libé 1*[93] – a metaphor astonishingly reminiscent of Jules Vallès,[94] which shows clearly how the process of decentring meets up with that of unification – is a subject of criticism and nostalgia *at the same time*. It was felt that it had to be left behind for the project for a decentring newspaper to succeed, while it was also recognized that the decentring gaze can no longer have the militant enthusiasm or combativeness of the 'public letter-writer'.

The search for the 'wandering word': Marc Kravetz, reporter in Iran

Just as many New Journalists were well aware of the pitfalls that threatened their movement, so the *Libération* team of the 1970s offers concrete examples of extreme caution with regard to the process of unifying the dominated and of hard thinking about what it means to *decentre*. Let us take as an example the work of Marc Kravetz, who encouraged the developments desired by Serge July in the years 1978–9 and who, as a reporter, offers a gaze at the opposite pole from empathic fusion.

Kravetz never ceased to emphasize the extent of his debt to *Libération*, this newspaper he had joined only a few years after its foundation, where you could debate, disagree and invent. Kravetz was the paper's correspondent in Iran in 1979–80; his reportages, especially his article 'Portrait of Iran through a Young Woman', published in the 8 March 1979 number, earned him the Prix Albert Londres in 1980. At the end of *Irano Nox*, his book of 1982, he describes how he got the idea for this article, a text so surprising that he himself only uses the word 'article' in inverted commas.[95] The editors had asked him to write an article on the position of women in Iran; to prepare for it, he had met an Iranian architect, Nasrine T. But, after his conversations with her, he found it impossible to write his piece.

> The article did not come . . . so I wrote instead of the article this 'Portrait de l'Iran en jeune femme' as one writes a letter. It was neither Iran, nor Iranian women, only Yasmine [in the original article of 1979 she is Nasrine T, in *Irano Nox* she becomes Yasmine] and a little of her story, a way of describing the great vertigo of the Iranian revolution through one exceptional gaze, even if it was not typical.

And Kravetz paid homage to his newspaper: 'Never was I so happy to work for this newspaper, *Libération*, the only one which could publish such an "article".'[96]

This story is remarkably similar to that of the genesis of Tom Wolfe's article 'The Kandy-Kolored Tangerine-Flake Streamline Baby', as described above. It also makes one think of another figure of the New Journalism, Gay Talese, and an article of his on Frank Sinatra: unable to obtain an interview with the star himself, because Sinatra had a cold, which preyed on his mind and depressed him, Talese ended up writing the story of his attempts to get the interview, which turned out to speak volumes on the subject of Sinatra.[97] Kravetz is one of the figures of *Libé* who best illustrates the analogies between this French press venture and the American movement of the New Journalism: like the New Journalists, he poses the question of what journalism is as he practises it. What is more, as we will see, he was familiar with the work of Norman Mailer.

His gratitude notwithstanding, Kravetz very soon highlighted the weaknesses of the first years of *Libération*. He agreed with the diagnosis of Serge July in 1978, believing that the newspaper, in spite of its sympathy for those who fought, and for the 'dominated', must stop seeing itself simply as their 'voice'. His words ring like an appeal to break with the very thing that many people saw as the newspaper's profound originality. In the same supplement of 22 May 1978 in which the 'farewell letter' of Serge July appeared (the article quoted above, in which July called for a return to the 'nomadic' spirit), Kravetz offers a piece on 'the happiness of being a journalist', in which he declares that it is time for *Libération* to become a 'newspaper', even if it means being to some extent 'a newspaper like the others'. He goes on:

> A newspaper without journalists, a newspaper which 'let the people speak', a 'different' newspaper: I have not myself either lived through this adventure or shared this illusion. I evoke them, therefore, free from nostalgia and

I believe, inexplicably, that the idea remains salutary. And I also believe that
the newspaper indirectly described by the readers who aggressively and
rancorously criticize our 'treason' is everything one would wish except a
possible newspaper, a 'readable' newspaper. To be a 'different' newspaper,
Libération had to learn to be a newspaper like the others. This is not a
renunciation but a contradiction. One more, which we have to live with,
unless we give up, unless *Libération* is to die.[98]

Kravetz is emphasizing here the risks associated with the desire to break
with the violence of the dominant gazes: by continuing to contest what
is dominating in the 'gazes at', by continuing to seek out the point of
view of the dominated themselves, wholly internal and non-violent,
there was a risk of ending up with, quite simply, an 'impossible' newspaper, that is, the abolition of every point of view, the pure and simple
effacement of the observer and the death of the journalist. *Libération* had
no choice: if it wanted to be a *newspaper*, it would be a 'gaze at'; it could
hardly practise empathy with all the dominated in whose name it claimed
to write.

This text is also, therefore, a very Mailer-like recognition of the *fiction*
that journalism necessarily is, because it always involves a gaze which fixes
on reality – a necessarily singular gaze, and necessarily conflictual for
others, for example, for those it observes. 'In the field or in their offices,
journalists always write fiction,' Kravetz goes on in the same article. 'The
reality about which they speak is not *the* reality. No more in *Libération* than
elsewhere.' What Kravetz is exposing is the contradiction inherent to the
original approach of the first years of *Libé*: the radicalness of the revolt
against the dominant gazes had a tendency to reproduce the same arrogance, that is, the conceit of wishing to be *the* reality. It is, in short, a way
of seeking subversion which reverts to conformism, as Kravetz again suggests when he writes: 'We pay dearly for this contradiction. To the point
of sometimes forgetting to assert our difference other than by deriding and
caricaturing the more traditional journalism.' The decentrers then turn
into the unifiers, who claim to apprehend *the real*, to be 'objective', even
though their approach is rooted in a heightened awareness of the vanity of
such a desire, and the domination it engenders. The ambition to decentre is distorted if its result is the enthronement of a new dominant gaze.
You have to try, instead, to observe 'against', as Kravetz also says: 'But at
Libération more than elsewhere we have the means to think and to write
against, not to succumb to the conformism of the code, to decipher in
reality the signs of its subversion, and to take pleasure in thinking and
writing without constraints.'[99]

But how is this to be done? Not, certainly, by abandoning the critical
distance or the fiction introduced by the singularity of a gaze. The
formula used by Kravetz to define the journalist is 'the decoder of the

other side of things and words',[100] an expression suggesting that the journalist is not 'in' this other side from the outset. The notion of decoding evokes a certain labour, an effort which is poles apart from self-evidently being, at once, in the middle of the dominated. Kravetz here evokes a gaze which would not do away with itself in the act of observing, which would accept itself for what it is, *one* point of view, born of a singular situation; and which would question and test itself, and introduce conflict into itself so as to take 'decoding the other side' ever further, and so as gradually *to decentre itself*. Not without analogies with Mailer within the New Journalism, Kravetz, in order to avoid the temptations which undo the decentring process, proposes a gaze which is constantly self-critical – as if, as they see, the decentring journalists would constantly ask why they see like this and if they could see differently.

This does not therefore assume the rupture with the official centre to be obvious and immediate, but constructs its separation, and its access to an alterity, while full of a doubt and a modesty that are never denied. '*Libération* suffers like other newspapers – and sometimes more, thanks to its poverty – from the constraints of the mass media system,' writes Kravetz, still in this article on 'the happiness of being a journalist':

> You can find ways of getting round it, but you cannot escape it. Nor can the readers of *Libération*. The language of newspapers, that of radio, that of television, is our language. To recognize this is not necessarily to agree with it. And it is here that the adventure of *Libération* begins, our adventure, mine, the happiness of being a journalist.

One feels how the 'we' ('our' language . . .) gradually falls apart, but not in rupture and the obviousness of another and immediate 'we'. The 'adventure' Kravetz describes is that of the decentring journalist, who gradually designates the 'we' as a 'you', never loses sight of this 'you', and continues to speak to it, on its own terms, far from postulating a rupture which would lose sight of the very purpose of the decentring, the 'speaking to'.

Mailer, as we have seen, accepted that he was offering only a 'novel', in many ways as false as the 'novel' of the 'official' journalists; yet he still sought a solution in the fact of being a journalist who was *all novelist*, that is, a journalist who made his imagination *work* better than most and who was, as a result, able to get to the heart of the contradictions. Unlike the 'chameleon' of Tom Wolfe who claimed to be *everywhere*, Mailer's journalist-novelist plotted a route with difficulty, with the aid of his imagination, less in the interior worlds themselves than in the 'gulf' which separated them; he constantly criticized himself and destroyed every point of view, including those he had presented as his own over several pages; he presented the conflict of various points of view rather than peaceably reproducing them one after the other. Kravetz too seems to call for a gaze that is situated, limited and careful to make this situation 'shift'. This is ambitious, but also more modest than empathy, precisely because the journalist is not claiming to be already 'with the dominated', even to be the dominated; he understands the risk inherent in such a claim, that of constructing a new domination, a fixed and indisputable point of view, a 'settling down' as July put it; he prefers to seek, gradually, and a prey to doubt and perpetual self-criticism, a way of refusing to be anchored, even though he knows he is anchored with every glance. He prefers to destroy and keep on destroying the point of view, even though he knows he has nothing to offer, at every line, but a point of view.

This evokes a sort of 'wandering' which must constantly be gained and regained in the face of the temptation to settle down. The theme of wandering is significant in the representations of Kravetz, to the point where he frequently equates the ' "true" word' that he claims to be seeking with the 'wandering word', an expression he borrows from the French poet, playwright and ex-reporter Armand Gatti.[101] And there is no better illustration of this 'labour' of wandering than *Irano Nox*, the book Kravetz published in 1982, which is a study of the status of the reporter at least as much as a reportage on Iran, all the more so in that it reproduces and revises reportages that had appeared in *Libération* in previous years. The time lag and the 'book' format bring an extra degree of introspection to the gaze – an introspection which, that said, is already apparent in his reporting at the time. Let us spend a little time on this book, in which every point of view, every look, dare we say, is scarcely proposed before it is questioned, discussed and relativized. It is this very questioning which makes it possible subsequently to change the point of view; and so on, and so on, in a long process of 'wandering'.

The photographer Alain Bizos, with whom Kravetz talks on the plane on his return journey, nicely defines the relativity and the contingency of the point of view:

> An interesting subject: you show a girl in jeans or cream trousers, a girl who has a pain in her eye and who gets herself examined by a woman who is perhaps your wife, and you say: I saw this in Iran. I ask you what on earth this has to do with Iran and you reply: what it has to do with Iran is that nowhere else would I have wanted to make use of such a cliché.[102]

These words also emphasize the introspection which should be that of the journalist: 'I ask you,' said Bizos; it is the journalist questioning himself that he describes. To look is then to ask yourself why you see *that*;

why the relation to the event 'gives' this point of view rather than another. For example, Kravetz tries to understand what it is that induces a feeling of 'malaise' when he walks through the streets of Teheran; he tries several times to define this malaise, which finally amounts to this: he sees women, but, at another level, he sees that there aren't any women. It is this conflict within the gaze which produces a malaise, which the reporter has to re-create for his reader:

> It took me some time to understand the source of this malaise when I walked through the streets of Teheran. Shiite Islam and urban squalor were not enough to explain this dreary sadness which permeated the town and the people. One day, I wrote: 'Teheran is a world without women.' The phrase was hasty and inaccurate.
>
> In statistical terms, the two sexes were almost equally represented on the pavements. A world of men perhaps, but of men who were sick, frustrated, ill at ease, and as if haunted by these phantoms in black they passed without ever meeting them. The women were there, but they had no bodies, no speech, no gaze. It was not a world without women but a world without femininity, a univocal world, without charm, without tenderness, from which desire was banished, a world ruled by shame and fear, where you dared neither to look nor to touch.[103]

If the practice of journalism consists of this introspection regarding an initially contingent point of view, it is clearly solitary: it is the work of an exile who represents no one. Inasmuch as the reporter is he who detaches himself from the 'we' that is the public, in order to designate it as a 'you', he is effectively condemned to a solitude which is the solitude of wandering. You get a strong sense of this solitude from the way in which Kravetz evokes his relationship to Iran; this relationship has its own logic, in which the readers, the public, scarcely intervene. Admittedly, it is in the public eye that the correspondent lives his own point of view and asks questions, but Kravetz totally rejects the idea that the journalist can *represent* the public. In these lines, for example, he explicitly rejects the figure of the witness-ambassador:

> I do not know . . . journalists – *bis repetita*, with all due reservations – who write or at least work 'for' their readers . . . the courage to speak is not in question, a matter of temperament, but the passion to know is an end in itself . . . even when we have served up in an acceptable form all the small beer from our collection of *facts*, the readers will be none the wiser. Unless they are themselves specialists or professionals with an interest in the subject, they will never know what we know or what we think we know because the reasons, the principles and the circumstances which govern the choice of the information we offer, and make it possible at a pinch to give it a meaning, are not supplied. Nor will they ever know what they want to

know, for the excellent reason that the question which fully occupies us is, even at best, no more than a subject of passing curiosity for them, and its manifestations rarely synchronize with the stopovers of the special correspondents who wear themselves out trying to follow the twists and turns of current events. The result, because newspapers are written to be read, is an unholy compromise between oversimplification and abstruse pointillism. The reporter chases rainbows, and the readers grow increasingly frustrated.[104]

When the reporter accepts that he has long split off from the public and its 'we', he discovers his solitude. If the solitude is absolute, however, it is because the journalist is also excluded from the 'others' he seeks to meet. Accused by those he observes and encounters of understanding nothing, the reporter portrayed by Kravetz has truly been abandoned by the 'we'; this is because he is an agent of conflict, he is what causes the misunderstandings to emerge. It is the notion of something *incommunicable* that is immediately obvious in the description by Kravetz of his profession. It is as if this profession consisted, not of overcoming the incommunicability, of giving the lie to those who are constantly debating it, but of recognizing it so as to see what can be done with it – for example, formulate it.

'Formulating' it enables the reporter to say, in particular, that the incommunicable in Iran is not of exactly the same type as elsewhere. More than ever, it signals an ill will, even a declaration of war on the West, through the intermediary of the journalist the West has sent to Iran:

> 'It isn't your fault, but you can't understand.' This is a sentence the foreign (let us say 'Western') journalist in Iran has heard so often that he no longer even hears it. He is resigned to the obvious: he doesn't speak the language; he isn't a Muslim; he has neither twenty-five centuries of Persia or fifteen of Islam in his head and in his veins. He knows that he does not come from the jails of SAVAK or the shanty-towns of Teheran. He is not particularly proud of it, nor is he any longer inclined to be ashamed of it. He is used to it. Change the date and the place, the situation remains the same. He is not Iranian, so be it. Nor was he Vietnamese, Algerian, Lebanese, Bengali, Kurdish or Chadian. The eternal problem of occidentalo-centrism? No.
>
> In Iran, the 'you're not from here, you can't understand' is not a way of signalling difference, even immeasurable difference, but of signalling exclusion. In the wrath of God against Taghout, the Devil makes no concessions. Khomeini makes no allowances.[105]

But what is important is that there is always, even in a less hostile atmosphere, an irreducible difference between the reporter, 'the other' who is observed, and the public for whom this observation is intended. In other words, Kravetz's representation of the journalistic gaze is strictly triangular: the reporter ('me') is alone faced with those he observes ('them') and faced with those for whom he observes ('you'). There is no fusion, not even a relationship of *representation*, either with those he observes or with 'his' public. This tripartite relation, which never manages to tame, much less absorb, one of the other two terms, completely prevents the figure of the 'us' from emerging. The reporter will be no one's witness-ambassador; he will be the exile or nomad, conscious of his profound strangeness, of the uniqueness of his gaze, and of what it contains that cannot be shared. The strangeness the journalist feels does not, as in Albert Londres, for example, have the virtue of ultimately reconstructing the 'we' of the public: it is without end, in every sense of the word, and it generates in the reporter a permanent and solitary frustration. He addresses his public in the accusative, as 'you', with the uncertainty such a questioning contains – what will the public retain? He cannot really control the effects of his gaze and, above all, does not claim to.

In these circumstances, the title of the reportage of Kravetz, 'Irano Nox', the 'night of Iran', is highly significant; it emphasizes the element of incommunicability and incomprehensibility which is always present in the relation of journalists to what they 'cover'; and it seems to announce that, at the same time, in spite of the journalist's efforts to extend the 'light' by shifting his singular point of view, the public may well remain faced with night – a night which will, in any case, always be darker than it is for the journalist. The title concentrates the uncertainties and frustrations induced by the triangular relationship:

> I will not brandish my torch in the night of Iran. I will offer neither solutions nor light. I will no longer say: 'Here is the Truth, do with it what you can.' I will describe a journey . . . I will say what I saw, what I knew or could verify, what I learned, but also everything else: what I was unable to see, what I thought I understood, what went through my mind, even if you might conclude that the mind was decidedly sick. It will be a sort of *roman-vérité*. The hero will be a country in the grip of one of the most devastating storms in history. Neither positive nor negative.[106]

This depiction of the journalist as anti-hero, author of a *roman-vérité*, but not of *the* truth, and tied to the relativity of his point of view, tinged with fiction and so ceding the role of hero to *what is observed*, and which always overflows and escapes the control of the 'observer', has obvious echoes of the method of Norman Mailer. We should not, therefore, be surprised to find Kravetz referring explicitly to the American journalist-novelist, in a way that is both collusive and teasing. The name of Mailer comes up during a conversation with an Iranian friend, Abbas. The conversations with Abbas are frequently an occasion for revealing the conflicting points of view on the confused situation in which Iran is mired: every time Kravetz thinks he has a point of view, it seems that the exchange with Abbas reminds him that it is always more complicated than he thinks. Thus in this dialogue, which begins with a 'joke' on the part of Abbas:

> Three militiamen were saying their prayers in a car park. Abbas smiled.
> 'What is the difference between the Shah's regime and Khomeini's regime?'
> I muttered that I didn't know but that he was soon going to tell me.
> 'Well, it's this: before, people went out to drink and returned home to pray, now it's the same except it's the opposite way round. It's a joke, but it's good, isn't it?'
> 'Abbas, what do you think really?'
> 'Really about what?'
> 'About all that.'
> 'I think that America has only got what it deserves. That international law is only hypocritical crap and that I don't care a fuck for their stupid hostages.'
> 'These are words. I would like to know what someone like you who has lived in America thinks. You know that America is not the devil. You can't believe that. I saw you in the procession. You were behaving like all the others. Yet you're not one of them. Or perhaps you are, when it comes down to it. I wonder if everybody isn't pretending. Like you. Two hundred metres from here they're wearing mourning for Hossein, and in this street people are walking about as if nothing had happened in the last ten years.'
> 'That's Iran for you! We have different faces, but no one is pretending like you say. If you really want to know, I think you still haven't understood a thing about what is happening in Iran.'
> We had arrived at the hotel. I was pretty depressed.
> 'Do you think Carter is going to extradite the Shah?' asked Abbas suddenly.
> 'No, I don't think so. Why do you ask me that question?'
> 'Because I thought the same as you. But I wanted to have your opinion.'
> Abbas thinks for a moment before adding, 'But, if they don't hand over the Shah, what will happen to the hostages?'
> 'I don't know any more than you. Perhaps they'll be tried. Perhaps there'll be an agreement.'
> 'I don't think the students could kill them,' says Abbas.
> 'Me neither.'
> 'So what?'
> 'So nothing. You're right, I think I haven't understood much.'
> 'One of these days, I'll take you to the South', promises Abbas.[107]

The contradictions which are apparent in this exchange illustrate the difficulty of finding a firm point of view and, as a result, make the journalist primarily *the one who doesn't understand*, who is unable to fix his point of view. One of these conversations with Abbas ends with a reference to Mailer:

'If I'd gone back to university [it is Abbas who is speaking], today I'd have been a fedayee or a mujaheddin, or some such. I'd have been kicking up a stink against the mullahs, against their stupidity, and against their fatuous rules. Or I'd have been concocting shitty theories about Islam and the revolution. Here I don't care a toss for all that. If I want a drink, I know where to find some alcohol; if I want to smoke a pipe, I buy some opium on the street corner. I don't know what's going to happen. But I want it to happen here. I want Khomeini to succeed.'
'If he fails?'
'Poor us. Then we'll have both the mullahs and the Americans. Or the Russians. It will be a thousand times worse than before. But don't worry, it's not over yet.'
'In other words, the shit is going to hit the fan.'
'Too right. You're beginning to get it. Are you going to write that in your paper?'
'That's not from me, that's from Norman Mailer, an American.'
'Yeah, I know. They're amazing, the Americans. They know everything and they understand nothing.'[108]

This dialogue can be interpreted in many different and overlapping ways, which sustain the sad irony with which it is permeated. The way of referring to Mailer is a typically Mailerean piece of provocation (to reduce Mailer to a vulgar 'American'!). One might also find in the question 'Are you going to write this in your paper?' an echo of a passage in *The Armies of the Night*, where Mailer emphasizes that his point of view would never, alas, be published in anything as left-leaning and proper as, say, the *New Yorker* magazine, 'because they wouldn't let you use the word "shit" there'.[109] There is also in this dialogue a play on 'understand' (or 'get it') and 'understand nothing': it is when Kravetz uses an expression of Mailer's that he seems to understand something, but, at the same time, provocatively reduced to his Americanness, Mailer is he who understands nothing. Thus, exactly as in Mailer, every point of view and every angle which affords some understanding is then demolished, if possible with maximum provocation. Further, at the heart of the 'understand nothing', there is perhaps the 'correct' position or the 'true word'. After all, it is towards this truth of incomprehension that Abbas is always steering Kravetz, as if to enable him to be truly a good journalist, that is, one who demolishes, rebuilds and demolishes again; one to whom, once he is yet again in despair at his incomprehension, you can say, 'I'll take you to the South'; hence one who, thanks to his constantly renewed incomprehension, is still capable of seeing something new, something different – which will no doubt later be demolished in favour of yet another and different point of view. In fact, it is this renewal of incomprehension which allows the journalist to *see* again. Hence, if Mailer is he who, as an American, 'understands nothing', this may, paradoxically, be a compliment – a very Mailerean compliment, furthermore, since in Mailer, too, it is the witness who understands nothing who reaches the intimacy of the event.

The 'understands nothing' means, therefore, that the point of view has not become fixed, that an 'elsewhere' is constantly emerging, and that the work of decentring, or of putting one point of view in permanent conflict with another, can continue. The incomprehension is not, therefore, something to go beyond: *you have to be permanently unable to understand in order to be able to continue to see.*[110] This is particularly clear in the way that Kravetz unashamedly presents his own 'incomprehension' in his conversations with the representatives of religion in Iran: it is because he understands nothing of what they say to him that he sees what is happening.[111] The conversations with Abbas enable him to keep on renewing this fruitful incomprehension, which makes the point of view 'shift'.

This way of making the point of view 'shift' within the reportage itself was already the most striking characteristic of 'Portrait de l'Iran en jeune femme', the article that appeared in *Libération* on 8 March 1979. This article is reprinted in *Irano Nox* as its last chapter, but slightly revised and also extended by the addition of a few pages describing a further meeting with Nasrine T. (called Yasmine in the book) two years later. It is here that we see that, for Kravetz, to be a journalist is never to cease the labour of questioning the point of view; indeed, his portrait of two years later tends, by its style, to play up even further the contradictions which had been central to the article of 1979.

Let us return for a moment to the original article. The gaze of the journalist at this Iranian woman finds three concomitant modes of expression: Nasrine is sometimes referred to in the third person, sometimes in the second (in this case it is the 'you' of the epistolary form), and sometimes, finally, it is the voice of Nasrine herself that we hear, her own words, in the first person. There are two voices, therefore, that of Nasrine on herself and that of the journalist, which itself takes two forms: sometimes it evokes Nasrine by referring to her in the third person ('she'), sometimes it addresses her in the second person ('you'). These three parallel discourses which, in the *Libération* of 8 March 1979, are reproduced in three different typefaces, are in practice three modes of access to the painful but also fascinating contradictions of this emancipated, Westernized and revolutionary young woman, who loves her country and is uneasy at the way events are turning out. Each of these discourses has its contradictions, including, of course, that of Nasrine on herself. But each also harbours a desire for unity. And it is at this very point that another discourse intervenes as if to demolish the preceding one: each makes it possible to demolish ever further the unity which, in spite of everything, emerges from another discourse, by the very fact that there is discourse.

For example, Nasrine refers to the importance of her experience in the West – she had studied in the United States – to explain her sympathy for the women's movement, a movement which had emerged under the Shah. She calmly sets out, almost synthesizes, the contradictions of those first emancipated women, who were both grateful to the regime for having granted them citizenship and who inevitably, once liberated, came to challenge that regime. It is at this point that the discourse in the second person intervenes, in which the journalist describes how the young woman behaves in the restaurant; he then communicates the con- tradictions of the present day, the most painful, perhaps those which still elude the self-analysis of the young woman:

> You say I would like to travel, you tell me about the Italian district in New York. You say I have nothing to do in this revolution. This evening, you would like to be from nowhere. You ask me how one becomes a jour- nalist. You envy this superficial availability, this absolute and short-lived passion. But you don't really think this. You conscientiously spread the caviar on the warm, crispy biscuit, disdaining the onions and chopped egg served in the American fashion. Difficult to marry the revolution and caviar, and without vodka, what is more . . .

This voice gets to the heart of the fault line which runs through Nasrine today, and which is as if hidden under her own voice.

But it also introduces fault lines into the third-person discourse, that is, into the more 'classic' journalistic discourse, which tidies Nasrine up, synthesizes and objectifies her. Because even if it exposes her contradic- tions, it introduces a degree of unity, in spite of everything. It tries to bring the painfulness of the contradictions alive by a staccato and binary rhythm (she likes this, she hates that), but it is always the 'and' which ultimately prevails: Nasrine is this *and* that. The discourse unifies, neces- sarily. The accumulation conveys the anxiety and the frenetic search for identity, more than the personal heartbreak:

> Nasrine doesn't want to lose anything. Not the wealth accumulated in the past. Not the recent victories, even if they were granted by an execrated regime . . . Nasrine wants to rediscover her culture and not lose her freedom . . . Nasrine rejects what Koranic law has done to women. She loves the femininity of Koranic culture. She loves the woman who wears the veil and is able to eroticize the world with a single glance. She loves the

fact that the movement has awakened Iran down to its inner depths, that the revolution is that of the whole community. She does not want the individual to be swallowed up in it, or women to be victims of this return to the roots. She loves the fact that women are engaged in the struggle. She does not accept the ambiguous homage that turns them into 'sister Mujahidin' so as not to recognize them as women. She loves the Islam of rebellion, she does not love Islam's power.

The second-person discourse then intervenes. It proceeds by small touches, which say little, but penetrate to the heart of things, further into the world of fantasies and their complicated logics:

> The woman the Iranian man dreams about is always, you say, a dream woman, a fantasy woman, the heavenly 'houri' promised by the Koran to true believers. The amorous discourse is always a discourse of conquest . . . you tell me that on your return from abroad your militant friends criticized you for having lost 'that tremendous tension you had in you when you were a true revolutionary'. Eventually you understood and made them admit that what they were criticizing you for was really your freedom, sexual, but not only that. You tell me that freedom is indivisible, that you do not separate your professional life from your political choices and your happiness at being a woman. This unity is your victory, your 'revolution in the revolution', a victory for which no one can criticize you.

Significantly, this discourse, the one which disintegrates most fully, which touches where it hurts most, also ends with the theme of unity ('This unity is your victory'). It is here that we see the extent to which, for Kravetz, the labour of the gaze remains fundamentally a labour to *demolish*: three years later, in his book, this phrase has disappeared. The sentence which follows the reference to her 'happiness at being a woman' is much more chaotic: 'You said to me: it's only a half-life, the worst is yet to come, I don't regret having believed what I believed, what I lived was beautiful and if I no longer believe, I'm not ashamed of having believed.'[112] In general, this later version tends further to complicate the situation, that is, the person who incarnates it, this young woman. The gaze of the journalist itself gets confused; it is not even he, now, who identifies 'your' ultimate fault lines, which is still a way of getting at an order – the order hidden 'under' the voice of the young woman. Further, the sentence on the caviar and the revolution, with its irony – a way of saying 'touché' – has also disappeared, to be replaced by a sentence which puts the intuition of irresolvable contradictions into the mouth of the young woman, and no longer into that of the journalist: 'The caviar without the vodka, you said . . . and so as not to become gloomy again, you added: at least we still have the vodka.'[113] Yasmine now serves something of the same function as Abbas: her own voice questions the journalist more than in the 1979 version. Thus, after describing the paradox of the Iranian women who had been liberated by the Shah but had finally turned against him, Yasmine says this time: 'Nothing is simple, my little French friend.'[114]

Like Mailer, therefore, Kravetz offers an example of journalistic writing which both accepts its anchorage in an 'I', with its limitations, its fiction and its 'novel', and sets out to make the point of view shift, by self-criticism and by constantly creating conflicts. The journalist tries to *demolish* what he has done, and all he really produces is his interminable wandering, which protects his capacity to *see*. In Kravetz, there really is a radical challenge to any centre, from which 'we' might serenely see; there really is a *decentring*, and not simply a *re-centring*, that is, the creation of another centre and another 'we', against the 'official' centre.

This method is the antidote to the temptations which threaten the decentring journalisms. Against the *temptation of ubiquity*, which minimizes the conflict of points of view by espousing them all, the true decentring journalists apply the conflict within their own gaze; they do not think they are 'everywhere', they think of themselves as needing constantly to try to change their 'place', which is not the same thing. Against the *temptation to unify the dominated*, a temptation which amounts to creating another centre, decentring journalists accept the absolute singularity of their gaze, whose attempts at empathy can only ever be partial and provisional, particular moments in the story they impose on their gaze by working on it and criticizing it from the inside; they flee any fixed point, which would mean that they had forgotten that seeing implies wandering; they work on their perpetual 'non-belonging' as the condition for continuing to be those who *see*, that is, those who establish a gulf in relation to the *already seen*.

The key to the decentring method is therefore the acceptance that one is always located in a singular situation. Decentring journalists see from somewhere, from a singular place, their own, not from everywhere, or from wherever they 'ought' to see. By accepting this situation, they can try to change it, sow conflict in it, and work on it. As soon as they claim to travel in otherness as easily as they would travel in a 'we', chameleons merging everywhere they go (the temptation of ubiquity), or as soon as they claim to fuse with an instituted 'other', to the extent of becoming their representative (the temptation of unifying the dominated), they betray the singularity of their gaze, which is the keystone of their decentring method. Because it is this singularity, accepted and constantly worked on, which enables the gaze to define an interstice between the 'we's' – the 'we' of the dominant and the 'we' of the dominated – an interstice in which their mutual confrontation can take place, a confrontation liable to endanger and undo them.

The two temptations I have distinguished share one point in common. Each in its own way, they deny the singularity, and therefore also the natural limitations, of the perspective of the 'observer'; they seek to go beyond the fact that it is always an 'I' who sees, in order to merge it into the totality of points of view (the chameleon model) or else into a particular collective point of view (the gaze of the dominated, considered as *one*). They re-position this 'I' in a total or a particular 'we', which ultimately neutralizes the most formidable weapon of this 'I' against 'us': its singularity, always renewable by a return to nomadism, a permanent challenge to fixed, collective identities.

The journalistic method of decentring is therefore, in the end, an apprenticeship in this nomadism and wandering; an apprenticeship, because temptations always threaten. It is an apprenticeship which is retraced, in archetypal fashion, by the itinerary of the writer-journalist George Orwell, as we will see in the next chapter.

6

An Archetype of Decentring:
George Orwell

An examination of the itinerary of the writer-reporter George Orwell (1903–1950) will enable us to rediscover the principal difficulties we have noted in the decentring process. Orwell hardly shirked these difficulties, but rather struggled hard with them in an attempt to overcome them. In this sense, studied from our chosen perspective, and after the analyses of the previous chapter, Orwell's itinerary seems to offer an 'archetypal' story of the decentring gaze.

What Orwell was seeking, in a way, was a different gaze at 'the others' (the colonized, vagrants, the unemployed, men in war), that is, a gaze other than the dominant one. In the course of this quest he tried a number of approaches, in particular that of the empathic gaze; Orwell went to great lengths in his desire to 'see differently' since, at one point, he actually underwent a metamorphosis (into a down-and-out). Then, abandoning the temptations of his youth, he engaged in self-criticism, reinstated the distance necessary 'to see something', and went on to base his ability to decentre on this very distance and the absolute singularity of the 'observer'. His self-analysis gave Orwell a masterly grasp of all the problems in the act of decentring; indeed, it turned it into a morass of difficulties and temptations.

If Orwell can appear as the archetype of the decentrer, it is also because he believed that decentring was the real purpose of the activity of observing: if you did not decentre, you saw nothing, you were blinded by ideological constructions. And this decentring required a permanent exile, a refusal to enter fixed communities, those of the 'we'. This theme of exile haunts his reportages of the late 1930s, while the hero's discovery of his ability to see, hence decentre, hence resist, is a key theme of his last novel, *Nineteen Eighty-Four*.

1. The question of the other gaze

The desire for metamorphosis: Down and Out in Paris and London *(1933)*

Largely on the basis of some autobiographical passages in *The Road to Wigan Pier*, published in 1937, many Orwell specialists emphasize the importance of guilt feelings as one of his motives for becoming a writer.[1] Writing allowed him to metamorphose into 'George Orwell', the pseudonym he adopted for the publication of *Down and Out in Paris and London*, in 1933; that is, it allowed him to expiate the sin of having been born Eric Blair, to a bourgeois family, and of having become a colonial officer in the service of the British Empire. Writing allowed him, finally, to join the ranks of the oppressed.

To attribute a political mission to literature implies having a broad definition of it, not overly concerned about the gulf between fiction and nonfiction.[2] For Orwell, the problem was not whether to write novels or reportages: he had to succeed in the very act of writing, to expiate the original sin. Pinning his hopes on literature would not, of course, liberate Orwell from his anxieties. As Raymond Williams justly observed, ' "Being a writer", in one definition, had been a possible way out. But being the writer he was, the real writer, led him into every kind of difficulty, every tension that the choice had seemed to offer to avoid.'[3] In fact, he still needed to discover *what sort* of writing would enable him to expiate the sin of having been born among the dominant, with the gaze of one of the dominant. How was he to change his gaze?

Orwell was well aware that the eyes, and the senses in general, always lag behind ideas. In spite of his sympathy for socialist ideas, he confesses that he was aware, during his time as a colonial officer in Burma, that is, from 1922 to 1928, that he saw the workers through bourgeois eyes:

> I loosely described myself as a 'Socialist'. But I had not much grasp of what Socialism meant, and no notion that the working class were human beings. At a distance, and through the medium of books – Jack London's *The People of the Abyss*, for instance – I could agonize over their sufferings, but I still hated them and despised them when I came anywhere near them.[4]

The same was true of the Burmese he had encountered as a colonial officer, for whom, he admits he felt deep contempt.[5] What sort of writing could change that?

What it could do, in expiation, was describe this very time lag of sight in relation to thought, that is, describe the deep guilt of the young man. Orwell tells how the officer, Eric Blair, had already scanned innumerable

Burmese faces for signs of an awareness of his sin: 'I was conscious of an immense weight of guilt that I had got to expiate.'[6] At a later stage in his colonial experience, Orwell was to force himself to meet those he called the 'lower classes'. By this guilt-inducing immersion, he hoped to find expiation and the metamorphosis of the gaze: 'I wanted to submerge myself, to get right down among the oppressed, to be one of them and on their side against their tyrants.'[7]

So, having abandoned his career in the imperial army, Blair decided, in 1928, to live by his pen and to become George Orwell; he went to Paris and then to London, where he led the life of a down-and-out and mixed with the poor, the oppressed and vagrants. This experience would provide the subject-matter for his book *Down and Out in Paris and London*, though it was not published until 1933. This book had its origins, therefore, in the desire to reach the interiority of poverty, to see, at last, 'from the inside'.

The cult of 'lived experience' and the high value placed on inner experience are evident in the book. Orwell describes his feelings in minute detail, presenting them as peculiar to someone who was 'there', for example, his hunger.[8] Was he acting as the public's ambassador, somewhere where the public was not present? If this had been the case, he would hardly have tried so frequently to make his readers feel the deep singularity of what he saw, from the other side, closer to 'them' than to 'us'. In fact, the 'us' that shows through here in the writing of Orwell is primarily the 'us' he forms with his companions in misfortune, an 'us' forged in a concrete shared experience. The public, on the other hand, is designated as a 'you', to whom he tries to explain things, even if they are probably inaccessible to it. The public is both a 'you' and the indefinite 'one'.[9]

Orwell takes a delight, consequently, in this book, in talking about 'your' incomprehension, 'your' stereotypes and the stupid ignorance of 'your' scornful gazes. For example, he describes, from the inside, his experience of 'your' fear of the tramp, through that of a young maid in a middle-class household who had been instructed to bring a cup of tea out to Orwell and his fellows: 'I remember the terrified way in which she brought it out, and then, losing her courage, set the cups down on the path and bolted back to the house, shutting herself in the kitchen. So dreadful is the name of "tramp".'[10] The part he most enjoys, perhaps, is his account of his arrival in a hostel for vagrants. When asked what he did, Orwell says he is a 'journalist', which attracts the attention of the Tramp Major:

'Then you are a gentleman?'
'I suppose so.'. . .

He gave me another long look. 'Well, that's bloody bad luck, guv'nor,' he said; 'bloody bad luck that is.' And thereafter he treated me with unfair favouritism, and even with a kind of deference. He did not search me, and in the bathroom he actually gave me a clean towel to myself – an unheard-of luxury. So powerful is the word 'gentleman' in an old soldier's ear.[11]

Orwell is taken for a journalist like 'one of you', which enables him to denounce the inevitable blindness of ordinary journalists, because they remain on the outside; to understand anything in the world of vagrants, it is necessary to enter it, change identity and attain interiority, leaving 'you' outside. And just as he as ironizes at the expense of journalists, so Orwell mocks novelists who, so as to 'be of the people', make their characters speak a slang that is actually never used, is outdated; they, too, are not 'there'.[12]

The only way to achieve 'another gaze' than this blind gaze is, therefore, his own metamorphosis: he goes away, he transforms himself, and as a result he will *see*. The key moment in *Down and Out* is the account of his own transformation, the metamorphosis. These pages are all the more crucial in that, ten years later, it is exactly this type of experience (the loss of his identity) that Orwell will criticize:

I had worn bad enough things before, but nothing at all like these; they were not merely dirty and shapeless, they had – how is one to express it? – a gracelessness, a patina of antique filth, quite different from mere shabbiness. They were the sort of clothes you see on a bootlace seller, or a tramp. An hour later, in Lambeth, I saw a hang-dog man, obviously a tramp, coming towards me, and when I looked again it was myself, reflected in a shop window. The dirt was plastering my face already.[13]

He does not immediately recognize himself. From now on, this story of his metamorphosis is also the story of the metamorphosis of his gaze: for a further moment, he sees in himself 'the other', the time it takes truly to become this other, from whose point of view otherness will in future have another definition – indeed, will be reversed: 'My new clothes had put me instantly into a new world. Everyone's demeanour seemed to have changed abruptly. I helped a hawker pick up a barrow that he had upset. "Thanks mate," he said with a grin. No one had ever called me mate before in my life – it was the clothes that had done it.'[14]

A passage where the narrator makes us feel clearly that he is now 'inside', whereas we remain 'outside', is that of the 'lunch in the Tuileries': his friend Boris, who has found work in a restaurant, finds him in the Tuileries Gardens and presents him with a large package wrapped in newspaper, full of food he has managed to steal: 'It is disagreeable to eat out of a newspaper on a public seat, especially in the Tuileries, which are generally full of pretty girls, but I was too hungry to care.'[15] There is hunger, which is 'ours', there is the gaze of the pretty girls, which is 'yours'.

The gaze is seen as entirely dependent on identity, especially bodily identity, which gives it its anchorage: to change gaze is thus to change the body which is the source of the feelings. In fact, *Down and Out* is the story of a bodily education: by rubbing shoulders with a world which, on first contact, gives a sensation of strangeness, the body becomes habituated; experience is transforming, and 'the other gaze' comes at the end of this initiation by physical experience. It is a sort of mix of voluntarism and passivity; in fact, the will leads to a revival of the passive feelings. Raymond Williams emphasizes the importance of the motif of *passivity* in Orwell, a paradoxical motif since this passivity both feeds on itself and leads to struggle – to the 'true' struggle, finally marked by the bodily experience of domination. It is this passivity, explains Williams, that characterizes Orwell's characters in the novels of this period; they accept and they suffer the surrounding social world. In *Down and Out*, Orwell resembles them in that, like them, he is a 'victim' who experiences domination in his flesh, but in his case it is he himself who has made himself a victim.[16]

Nevertheless, even before taking account of the self-criticism of *The Road to Wigan Pier*, we may question the metamorphosis presented in *Down and Out*. In particular, we may ask whether the account of the metamorphosis does not suppose, at least in part, that it will fail. This failure is due not to an original exteriority of Orwell to the world of the tramps, but to his status of observer-narrator, which demands a form of exteriority throughout this immersion in the life of the tramps. Orwell can only describe the 'hang-dog man' he has become at a time when he has not yet fully assumed this new identity. This account of the metamorphosis is also, therefore, and contradictorily, an account of the circumstances in which the gaze is possible (it is not by chance that it ends with a 'mirror' scene): it is only inasmuch as the metamorphosis is unsuccessful that it still allows something to be seen. It is only its failure, its incompleteness, that could be *seen*. Conversely, for the metamorphosis to be judged to be complete, it would have to be such that Orwell lost, at the same time, all capacity for surprised and curious observation of what happens to him, so any account of it would be impossible.

All the pages of meticulous observation and description of the milieu in which he finds himself in *Down and Out* can be read, therefore, in a sense, as the expression of this failure or incompleteness of his immersion in the interiority of this new world. Let us take as an example this description of the Hôtel X, where the last sentence totally betrays the narrator and his *actual* exteriority, because it clearly reveals that he is *surprised* at finding himself there: 'On the wall, under one of the lights, someone had written in a very neat hand: "Sooner will you find a cloudless sky in winter, than a woman at the Hôtel X who has her maidenhead." *It seemed a queer sort of place.*'[17] Equally significant are the many passages where Orwell notes just how dirty a place is, while at the same time recognizing that those who are on the inside either fail to notice it or no longer notice it. For example:

> The dirt in the Hôtel X, as soon as one penetrated into the service quarters, was revolting. Our cafeterie had year-old filth in all the dark corners, and the bread-bin was infested with cockroaches. Once I suggested killing these beasts to Mario. 'Why kill the poor animals?' he said reproachfully. The others laughed when I wanted to wash my hands before touching the butter.[18]

Further on, Orwell emphasizes that even though he 'used to wonder whether there could be a restaurant in the world as bad as ours', the others 'all said that they had been in dirtier places'. Worse, one of them, Jules, 'took a positive pleasure in seeing things dirty' and mocks Orwell for his constant cleaning up.[19] Their criteria are far from being the same, and Orwell is quick to record this. Lastly, in the bathroom of a London hostel, Orwell notices everything that separates him from the other tramps, emphasizing his disgusted reaction:

> The scene in the bathroom was extraordinarily repulsive. Fifty dirty, stark-naked men elbowing each other in a room twenty feet square, with only two bathtubs and two slimy roller towels between them all. I shall never forget the reek of dirty feet . . . when my turn came for the bath, I asked if I might swill out the tub, which was streaked with dirt, before using it. He answered simply, 'Shut yer – mouth and get on with yer bath!' That set the social tone of the place, and I did not speak again.[20]

In these extracts, the 'we' he forms with his companions in misfortune seems a good deal less solid.

In his attempt at immersion, his very position as observer seems, therefore, to be an obstacle. And an obstacle he is aware of; the young Orwell of *Down and Out* is constantly racked by doubt, as revealed, most notably, by the last lines of the book. It is still troubling, however, that at the end of such a plunge into the interiority of poverty, Orwell articulates a wish which seems to signify that his book has not achieved its objective:

I can at least say, Here is the world that awaits you if you are ever penniless. Some days I want to explore that world more thoroughly. I should like to know people like Mario and Paddy and Bill the moocher, not from casual encounters, but intimately; I should like to understand what really goes on in the souls of *plongeurs* and tramps and Embankment sleepers. At present I do not feel that I have seen more than the fringe of poverty.[21]

Had he missed, then, this intimate understanding, although it had been precisely this that his metamorphosis had been intended to achieve?

In *The Road to Wigan Pier*, the diagnosis would be unambiguous, and put in the form of a general statement: 'But is it ever possible to be really intimate with the working class? I shall have to discuss this later; I will only say here that I do not think it is possible.'[22] In other words, there is perhaps something dishonest, or illusory, in the method itself. You cannot observe and be inside; such a project is intrinsically contradictory. But further, even if you wanted to go as far as it is possible to go with the metamorphosis, and wholly enter 'inside', at the risk of losing the 'gaze at', you would still not manage it: there is in the 'gaze at' something which resists the voluntarism of 'becoming another'. You can make the gaze change, yes, but you cannot abolish it by a complete conversion, a change of identity, an access to an interiority that is totally at odds with 'looking at'.

The Road to Wigan Pier (1937) or self-criticism

'Unfortunately', writes Orwell in *The Road to Wigan Pier*, 'you do not solve the class problem by making friends with tramps. At most you get rid of some of your own class prejudice by doing so.'[23] This comment on the impossibility of metamorphosis leads to more, however, than a simple confession of failure. What Orwell fights in future is the intention itself, and its readiness to deny the inevitability of failure, revealing, in this very predictable denial, its deep roots, in ideology.

'Unfortunately it is nowadays the fashion to pretend that the glass is penetrable. Of course everyone knows that class prejudice exists, but at the same time everyone claims that *he*, in some mysterious way, is exempt from it.'[24] To distance oneself from one's own background has become a literary posture, he says: 'Every novelist of serious pretensions adopts an ironic attitude towards his upper-class characters'; this makes it possible to avoid asking what is the real result: 'And yet all the while, at the bottom of his heart, everyone knows that this is humbug.'[25] This is followed by a fierce attack on compassionate attitudes and lachrymose commitments which conceal the refusal to envisage real change in the situations denounced; and which are even counterproductive, since they fool no one and provoke the distrust of what Orwell calls 'the ordinary man':[26]

> All such deliberate, conscious efforts at class-breaking are, I am convinced, a very serious mistake. Sometimes they are merely futile, but where they do show a definite result it is usually to *intensify* class prejudice. This, if you come to think of it, is only what might be expected. You have forced the pace and set up an uneasy, unnatural equality between class and class; the resultant friction brings to the surface all kinds of feelings that might otherwise have remained buried, perhaps for ever.[27]

The apologia for communion with the oppressed is not very different, therefore, Orwell seems to say, from the hypocrisy of the anti-imperialist English socialist, who remains, at bottom, full of the prejudices and scornful arrogance typical of a great colonial power.[28]

But it is also to say that this desire for communion, however much it employs the rhetoric of the concrete, of 'living with', remains an abstraction; it remains discourse and has no relation to what Orwell calls 'real contact' with the world of the oppressed. Orwell looks back over the whole of his bourgeois education, which, he admits, continues to structure his gaze, that is, this 'real contact':

> When I grasp this I grasp that it is no use clapping a proletarian on the back and telling him he is as good a man as I am; if I want real contact with him, I have got to make an effort for which very likely I am unprepared. I have got to alter myself so completely that at the end I should hardly be recognizable as the same person.[29]

In other words, it is still *I* who see him, and this 'I' remains marked by its origins and unable wholly to break away – which does not, as we will see, prevent a *labour* of the gaze, a variation of the point of view. Nevertheless, one cannot hope to erase one's origins altogether: to want more, to aspire to a wholly *other* gaze, is to abolish the 'observer', and to want something that is a gaze only in name, no more than an abstraction, an ideological desire, not a concrete gaze.

The truth of the concrete experience of domination bears no relation, therefore, to the idealization – the ideologization – of this experience. Here, Orwell turns his ideas about the body and its passivity against the voluntarism that his attempt at metamorphosis had assumed. The concrete, 'carnal' situation of observers is inexorably that of their division and of a crisis they cannot surmount, because they are by nature both inside and outside. This is the case with the external observers who go in search of a form of domination, and also the case with the dominated who begin to observe their domination: many pages of Orwell's *Road to*

Wigan Pier are devoted to the unrepresentative character of the working-class intellectuals in whom socialist intellectuals most easily recognize themselves; but this feeling of brotherhood is due, Orwell believes, to the fact that they all occupy the same position in relation to the domination they observe and denounce – a position which, whatever they say, is not that of interiority but of a sort of 'inside-outside'.

'Many people, however, imagine that they can abolish class distinctions without making any uncomfortable changes in their own habits and "ideology".'[30] Ideology is defined here as the contrary of 'real contact', as a desire for identification remote from the actual experience of meeting:

> The middle-class I.L.P.'er and the bearded fruit-juice drinker are all for a classless society so long as they see the proletariat through the wrong end of the telescope; force them into any *real* contact with a proletarian – let them get into a fight with a drunken fish-porter on Saturday night, for instance – and they are capable of swinging back to the most ordinary middle-class snobbishness. Most middle-class Socialists, however, are very unlikely to get into fights with drunken fish-porters.[31]

We see how Orwell here turns his confession – a confession of failure to 'fuse' – into a powerful criticism: the true revulsion, the true contempt for the 'lower classes', is in their idealization by ideologues.

It is clear that Orwell is here preparing his response to the controversy this book was bound to provoke: what might appear as an inadequacy in the Orwellian gaze – its exteriority and difficulty in fully 'empathizing' – is presented by Orwell from the outset as a mark of his honesty and of his break with ideological constructions.

The controversy in English socialist circles was, in fact, as fierce as Orwell had expected; how could they understand this unachievable exteriority, when, like the young Eric Blair of the 1920s, they still hoped that their gaze at the mass of the workers would lead to the abolition of exteriority, to fusion and the recognition that they all belonged to the same community? They were too remote from Orwellian self-criticism.

The idea for the book had come from Victor Gollancz, who had already published *Down and Out in Paris and London*. *The Road to Wigan Pier* was not exactly commissioned by the Left Book Club, of which Gollancz was the chairman, though he had intended to bring it out under Left Book Club sponsorship, that is, make it one of the Club's monthly selections, thus increasing its readership. When he read the manuscript, however, Gollancz thought that the tone of the second half ruled this out; in any case, the project would have to be approved by two others, Harold Laski and John Strachey. Against all expectations, this committee agreed to sponsor the book. It was then left to Gollancz, in a foreword, to define the precise position of the Left Book Club with regard to Orwell's book, which he knew would be deeply offensive to many of its members. His foreword was intended, therefore, to avert the storm.[32]

It is highly instructive, because it shows how one of the most eminent representatives of English socialism thought he could justifiably defend himself against Orwell's attacks. The clumsiness of this defence, which simply reiterates the aspiration to fusion with the dominated, notwithstanding Orwell's criticisms, is striking. In fact, the comments Gollancz makes on Orwell's persistence in a petit bourgeois point of view, which is the reason for his failure to get access to the interiority of the working class, are, at the level strictly of argument, remarkably ineffective, since they completely vindicate Orwell's own thesis. Thus Gollancz says, 'No reader must forget that Mr Orwell is throughout writing precisely as a member of the "lower upper-middle class" or, let us say without qualification, as a member of the middle class,' which Orwell himself says in his book. In other words, what Orwell recognizes and admits is held against him.

> I have in mind in particular a lengthy passage in which Mr Orwell embroiders on the theme that, in the opinion of the middle class in general, the working class smells! . . . I know, in fact, of no other book in which a member of the middle class exposes with such complete frankness the shameful way in which he was brought up to think of large numbers of his fellow men.

Further on, Gollancz is even more insistent on the subject of Orwell's social origins, in his, Gollancz's, eyes inevitably a source of blindness and stereotypes, leading him, most notably, to comment on the smell and the dirtiness of the workers: 'Mr Orwell is still a victim of that early atmosphere, in his home and public school, which he himself has so eloquently exposed.' Gollancz criticizes Orwell for the very things which Orwell himself proclaims as the condition of the observer: his exteriority, insurmountable and a safeguard against ideology. He criticizes him for having failed to make himself disappear, or put his bourgeois perceptions aside, implying that a 'fused' gaze is possible, although it is precisely this that Orwell is forever denouncing as an ideological lie.

But these comments of Gollancz also reveal how the *decentring* project was understood by many members of the Left Book Club: he should have gone even further in decentring the bourgeois gaze, Gollancz seems to be telling Orwell, gone even further in the encounter with what challenges the dominant prejudices. But in this case, it is a particular public, and this public only – the bourgeois readership with all its stereotypes – that he should have decentred – a largely imaginary public, what is more, since little inclined by its very 'nature' to read this book. As for the book's more 'natural' readership, that of socialist circles, it had no intention of itself being decentred. On the contrary, they saw their relationship to 'their' reporter as more like that forged with a witness-ambassador. What is also clear from this foreword is that, for Gollancz, Orwell had destroyed a 'we', or, at least, having remained outside it, had failed to confirm, even less constitute, it.

To criticize Orwell in this way was to engage in a dialogue of the deaf, since Orwell's aim was precisely to attack a 'we' he regarded as an imaginary construction – the 'we' formed by the fusion of the dominated with those who fight in their name. Orwell exposes conflicts and contradictions inherent in the fight against domination, and to fight against was already to be on the outside, to observe and denounce, to refuse to be one of the dominated – whereas Gollancz lauds a fight dependent on a sense of 'community'. It would be over-hasty to claim that the question of the 'community' of the dominated held little interest for Orwell, but it is still the case that he refuses to see this 'community' in the 'fusional' manner which was implicit in the 'ideological' attitude of some of his socialist friends. Orwell praises exteriority as a *condition of emancipation*. And 'looking at', to the extent that it is actually the product of distance, perhaps already of rejection, is part of this emancipation. Everything at which Gollancz points the finger as an obstacle to conceiving the emancipation of the dominated is, in reality, assumed by Orwell to be a condition of it. Fusion does nothing to help achieve emancipation, distance everything.

This polemic on the subject of the dirtiness of the working-class world, in *Road to Wigan Pier*, is typical of this dialogue of the deaf. There can be no doubt that, for Orwell, the dirtiness is a stereotype of the bourgeois class. The proof is the way elderly middle-class ladies, who have never seen a worker in their lives, 'know' it and transmit this 'knowledge' to their children and grandchildren:

> Middle-class people are fond of saying that the miners would not wash themselves properly even if they could, but this is nonsense, as is shown by the fact that where pithead baths exist practically all the men use them . . . but doubtless even at this late date the old ladies in Brighton boarding-houses are saying that 'if you give those miners baths they only use them to keep coal in'.[33]

But, for Orwell, there is no question of fighting this prejudice by denial: 'Do the "lower classes" smell?, he dares to ask: 'Of course, as a whole, they are dirtier than the upper classes. They are bound to be, considering the circumstances in which they live, for even at this late date less than half the houses in England have bathrooms.'[34] Whereas the myth of conversion or metamorphosis is denied:

> It is a pity that those who idealize the working class so often think it necessary to praise every working-class characteristic and therefore to pretend that dirtiness is somehow meritorious in itself. Here, curiously enough, the Socialist and the sentimental democratic Catholic of the type of Chesterton sometimes join hands; both will tell you that dirtiness is healthy and 'natural' and cleanliness is a mere fad or at best a luxury. They seem not to see that they are merely giving colour to the notion that working-class people are dirty from choice and not from necessity.[35]

Is it really possible not to see, for example, the filth? Yes, in two instances, for Orwell: first, by being truly inside, which is now presented as the diametrically opposite attitude to that of observation, because the concrete activity of observing implies an exteriority (already, in *Down and Out in Paris and London*, let us remember, he had noted the gap between himself and those who were inside, and so did not see what he saw – and dirt was already, oddly, his chosen example); or by having an ideology, which is actually defined as a flight from 'real contact', a denial of this division, of this 'inside-outside' which characterizes the act of observing. It is not surprising, in this case, that the 'ideologues' should have a fantasy of fusion and of access to interiority, since this is the other mode of what one might call the 'non-gaze'. What Orwell is anxious to show here is that such situations do not truly emancipate, but are rather obstacles to emancipation. Exteriority – which is thus not the absence of contact, but the way in which contact is lived – is a good thing; it is the precondition for a gaze worthy of the name, that is, an attitude which allows free rein to surprise, criticism, choice and the distanced apprehension of a situation, in order, possibly, to change it. To *see* the insalubrity is also to see that working-class houses *could* be properly fitted out. The criticism of exteriority 'de-essentializes', dare one say, what the ideology of the 'inner point of view', in its willed blindness and its denials, only freezes and consolidates. The gaze, which is exterior by nature, is, therefore, the true tool of social change for Orwell, equipping whoever makes use of it with the means truly to fight what ideology is content, vainly, to deny.

This explains the following Orwellian paradox: it is the limitation constituted by the singular body of the observer (which is unable not to feel certain things, and which is unable wholly to metamorphose so as to stop certain sensations), this bodily limitation, this given fact erected against the will, which is the source of emancipation. As always, the theme of passivity permeates Orwell's approach and, as always, with emancipation as its aim, but it is the limitations of passivity that are evoked here – whereas in the myth of metamorphosis, the sensory experience appeared to be unlimited and the body to be endowed with a plasticity which made it possible to 'habituate' oneself to become whomsoever one wished. It is still the sensory experience, clearly, 'real contact', which is here set up as the true relation to a situation, but on condition you accept the deep division and the frustration such an experience contains; on condition, in short, you do not lose sight of the fact that it is always a singular 'I' who sees and feels, and from a limited perspective.

With Orwell we find, in short, a confidence in the senses that is diametrically opposed to that of Séverine. In Séverine, the passivity of the bodily feelings of the observer was the precondition for the 'true' gaze, that is, for the unifying gaze, deployed from the centre of the community and constitutive of the 'we'. In Orwell, it is the precondition for the wholly singular gaze, irreducible to any collective vision (always suspect of ideology), *decentred* and potentially decentring, endangering the instituted collective visions. In short, in both reporters the body is what anchors the gaze and gives it its power of truth, but in the former it is a sort of collective, de-singularized body (hence its 'truth'), in the latter it is the singular body, destructive of the 'we', expression of an emancipation from an instituted community of gazes (hence its 'truth'). It is this direct opposition, on the basis of analogy, which led me to make one the archetypal figure of the unifying witness-ambassador and the other, the archetypal figure of the decentrer.[36]

'Shooting an Elephant' (1936)

From 1936–7, then, Orwell is no longer looking for the other gaze in the gaze of 'others', that is, through his own metamorphosis into an 'other'. It is a short story of 1936, 'Shooting an Elephant',[37] which perhaps best expresses this renunciation.

The story presents the young Eric Blair, a colonial officer in Burma, torn between his anti-colonial humanism and his inveterate hostility to the local population.

All I knew was that I was stuck between my hatred of the empire I served and my rage against the evil-spirited little beast who tried to make my job impossible. With one part of my mind I thought of the British Raj as an unbreakable tyranny, as something clamped down, in saecula saeculorum, upon the will of prostrate peoples; with another part I thought that the greatest joy in the world would be to drive a bayonet into a Buddhist priest's guts.

We see once again the famous time lag of the eyes and the body in relation to the thoughts. It looks as if the story is about to show how this time lag was compensated for: 'One day', he goes on, 'something happened which in a roundabout way was enlightening.' Far from it; the story does not describe a change of identity such as that attempted in *Down and Out in Paris and London*; it is well beyond that temptation of youth, and it defines in a quite different way this other, decentring gaze to which Orwell aspires.

The young colonial officer is told one morning that an elephant has escaped from its mahout and is ravaging the bazaar. Blair goes to the scene and sees the havoc the elephant is wreaking; it has already killed one Indian. The young man sends someone to get his elephant rifle. It is at this point that the real story begins, the one going on beneath the apparent plot: Blair sees himself taking action, as if he had placed himself outside himself. He sees the crowd that follows him when he sets out in pursuit of the animal, or, to be more precise, he sees himself, followed by this crowd. And it is another gaze which is about to emerge.

Because, face to face with the elephant, his first impulse is not to use the weapon: 'As soon as I saw the elephant I knew with perfect certainty that I ought not to shoot him. It is a serious matter to shoot a working elephant . . . moreover, I did not in the least want to shoot him.' But he was going to *see* something: 'But at that moment, I glanced round at the crowd that had followed me. It was an immense crowd, two thousand at the least and growing every minute.' It is the gaze at him of all these colonized people that the colonial officer sees.

> They were watching me as they would watch a conjuror about to perform a trick. They did not like me, but with the magical rifle in my hands I was momentarily worth watching. And suddenly I realized that I should have to shoot the elephant after all. The people expected it of me and I had got to do it; I could feel their two thousand wills pressing me forward, irresistibly. And it was at this moment, as I stood there with the rifle in my hands, that I first glimpsed the hollowness, the futility of the white man's dominion in the East. Here was I, the white man with his gun, standing in front of the unarmed native crowd – seemingly the leading actor in the piece; but in reality I was only an absurd puppet pushed to and fro by the will of those yellow faces behind.

The rest of the story is the account of a 'hero' who does what is expected of him, forced to don the mask of the 'oppressor', of the 'strong man', assigned to him by all these watching oppressed persons. The white man, says Orwell, 'wears a mask, and his face grows to fit it'. He kills the elephant, his fear extinguished by all these gazes:

But even then I was not thinking particularly of my own skin, only of the watchful yellow faces behind. For at that moment, with the crowd watching me, I was not afraid in the ordinary sense, as I would have been if I had been alone. A white man mustn't be frightened in front of 'natives'; and so, in general, he isn't frightened.

He is horrified only by the suffering of the great beast, which seems 'powerless to die'.

The paradox, which gives this text its complexity and its density, is that the gaze to which the 'hero' accedes, which makes him see the 'foolishness', his 'foolishness',[38] at the same time as the truth of the domination, *is not the gaze of the dominated*. The gaze of the dominated demands that he be the dominator and that he kill. This gaze is present and important, but it is only the mediation towards another gaze, the one that would finally grasp the dominated–dominator couple, the interplay of gazes which binds them together; that would position itself outside the system of domination; that would be truly *decentred* as compared with the mutual gazes which constitute this system; and that would, as a result, truly distance itself from this system and denounce it as a masquerade, while also grasping the suffering it engenders. The suffering of the dominated is, as it were, shifted on to the elephant; the dominated do not immediately reveal this suffering in their gaze, waiting, as they are, for only one thing, the death of the animal, so that they can strip it 'almost down to the bones'. In this way, the gaze that makes it possible really to break with the dominant gaze, and grasp the intimacy of the domination and the suffering, is in no way a gaze of fusion or of communion with the dominated. What radically decentres Eric Blair, and the whole of Imperial England with him, in this episode of the elephant, is less the gaze of the Burmese crowd than the gaze which he himself achieves, through this initiatory scene. He 'sees himself', which implies, in particular, that 'he sees himself as others see him'.

The way in which Orwell distances himself from the 'yellow faces' of the Burmese, in a text in which he also claims finally to have grasped their suffering, is disturbing, almost a cause of unease. He seems to take a malign pleasure in shifting affect and empathy to where they might least be expected, that is, on to the dying elephant. He describes a journey in which the 'I', all alone, ends up by producing a decentring gaze, under the influence of an intense sensory experience – the vivid emotions stirred by the encounter with the elephant and the sight of the Burmese stripping the dead beast down. A singular body, singularly touched, extraordinarily alone in this scene, leads to a singular gaze, as if it had emerged from the system of domination and was able, accordingly, to contemplate it. For the Orwell of the late 1930s, only this absolute singularity of a situation could, in the end, produce a decentring gaze.

2. The solitude of the decentrer in the reportages of 1936–1937

The double exteriority in The Road to Wigan Pier

It is in *The Road to Wigan Pier* that Orwell criticizes his desire for metamorphosis and for empathic fusion with the oppressed. But this book is also and above all a reportage on the unemployed in the north of England. How can we see this development in Orwell in his writing? And how does this text decentre?

The book is a reportage that has been revised. The revisions add an extra dimension of introspection, and so allow Orwell to pose in a more profound way, within his reportage, the question of his own place as observer. This place is characterized by a double exteriority which is accepted and even proclaimed: the reporter belongs neither to the 'we' who read him nor to 'those' he observes; he is 'in between'; he is alone; and it is this position which makes him a decentring writer. As one of his biographers, Michael Shelden, emphasizes, the voice of Orwell, in his reportages,

> moves easily between two worlds – forging a connection between the busy world of the street and the sedate world of the reader's study. The trick for the writer is to maintain the right balance between the two worlds. To remain 'inside' and 'outside', he cannot shift very far in either direction. He will embarrass himself and his readers if he becomes too intimate. He will seem cold if he becomes too detached.

Shelden recalls Orwell's own definition of the ideal writing: 'Good prose is like a window pane.'[39] And he notes a scene in *The Road to Wigan Pier* which illustrates particularly well this literary-journalistic ideal, Orwell's description of a young woman, at the back of her house, in the process of unblocking a drain with a stick: 'In his diary he records that he passed her while he was walking along "a horrible squalid side-alley". But in his book he makes a subtle alteration to the scene. He frames it in the window of a train which is taking him away from Wigan.'[40]

This is how Orwell describes the scene:

> As we moved slowly through the outskirts of the town, we passed row after row of little grey slum houses running at right angles to the embankment. At the back of one of the houses a young woman was kneeling on the stones, poking a stick up the leaden waste-pipe which ran from the sink

inside and which I suppose was blocked. I had time to see everything about her – her sacking apron, her clumsy clogs, her arms reddened by the cold. She looked up as the train passed, and I was almost near enough to catch her eye. She had a round pale face, the usual exhausted face of the slum girl who is twenty-five and looks forty, thanks to miscarriages and drudgery; and it wore, for the second in which I saw it, the most desolate, hopeless expression I have ever seen. It struck me then that we are mistaken when we say that 'It isn't the same for them as it would be for us', and that people bred in the slums can imagine nothing but the slums. For what I saw in her face was not the ignorant suffering of an animal. She knew well enough what was happening to her – understood as well as I did how dreadful a destiny it was to be kneeling there in the bitter cold, on the slimy stones of a slum backyard, poking a stick up a foul drain-pipe.[41]

The scene clearly signifies, as Shelden emphasizes, that 'this woman's world is not his', that 'he cannot pretend to be part of it', but that 'it is not necessary to be *like* them in order to be on their side'.[42] In short, strangely, the encounter is felt in separation, symbolized by this window in a train leaving Wigan. Orwell does not describe a total incommunicability – that evoked by those who say 'It isn't the same for them as it would be for us'. He is careful not to fix the difference as others fix equality: exterior though it may be, the gaze *can* be an encounter. But this encounter is in no way an empathic fusion; the window remains; the gaze gets close by combining a feeling of the difference of 'places' and an awareness of the possibility that these places might be reversed. For the immediacy of an empathic affect, Orwell substitutes a labour of the *imagination*, which forges a connection beyond the sensory experience of separation.

The sensory experience itself remains that of separation. *I am outside, I am not them*, is what Orwell is constantly telling his readers. This exteriority of the observer is often asserted in the strongest terms, as disgust. Here, Orwell's many observations on the subject of dirtiness are not, as in *Down and Out in Paris and London*, a confession of failure – a failure to see things from the inside – but a mark of the non-belonging he accepts and the exteriority he proclaims. The disgust is sometimes so strong that he decides to leave:

On the day when there was a full chamber-pot under the breakfast table I decided to leave. The place was beginning to depress me. It was not only the dirt, the smells, and the vile food, but the feeling of stagnant meaningless decay, of having got down to some subterranean place where people go creeping round and round, just like blackbeetles, in an endless muddle of slovened jobs and mean grievances.[43]

He knows, of course, that the body becomes habituated, but the way in which he describes this 'habituation' has nothing in common with the voluntarism of *Down and Out*; this 'habituation' is described almost as a failure, an immersion which means that you no longer see anything, a death of the gaze, an apathy of the senses. 'All the windows were kept tight shut, with a red sandbag jammed in the bottom, and in the morning the room stank like a ferret's cage. *You did not notice it when you got up, but if you went out of the room and came back, the smell hit you in the face with a smack.*'[44] A few pages later there is a similar comment with regard to the kitchen: 'The smell of the kitchen was dreadful, but, as with that of the bedroom, *you ceased to notice it after a while.*'[45] As the controversy with the Left Book Club had emphasized, it is not the 'habituation' but the 'smack in the face' that predominates in this reportage of Orwell, evidence of his insurmountable exteriority, but evidence also, as a result, of a sane and healthy critical spirit and desire for emancipation.

Orwell keeps saying how each glance makes him aware of his exteriority. He says, for example: '*Watching* coal-miners at work, *you realize momentarily what different universes people inhabit.* Down there where coal is dug is a sort of world apart which one can quite easily go through life without ever hearing about.'[46] Or, a few lines earlier, 'I have just enough experience of pick and shovel work to be able to grasp what this means . . . but by no conceivable amount of effort or training could I become a coal-miner; the work would kill me in a few weeks.'[47]

At the same time, the peculiar nature of this exteriority, the fact that it is experienced in sensory contact, differentiates the observer from those to whom he speaks. The public does not have this 'sensory contact'. Consequently, this exteriority of the observer really is a double exteriority – in relation to 'them' and in relation to 'you', the public. This 'you' is clearly designated as such in the preceding extracts. The attitude of Orwell exactly corresponds to the triangular relationship we have noted in others who decentre: I tell you of your irreducible difference from 'them'; 'I', who am in contact with them, know it; to 'you', I try to convey this feeling of exteriority, which is strange to you, because you like to think that you are not all that far away from 'them'. We find the paradox of an observer who gets close to some so as to say to others, who are as far away as possible, that the closer you are, the more you *know* you are far away; and who therefore, in this questioning, signifies that he is himself exterior to his interlocutors.

This double exteriority is what makes the singularity of the observer absolute. It is in some other way than by bodily sensations alone, therefore, that the observer has to try to forge links temporarily broken on all sides. The Orwellian conception of the body, source of sight, destroys the naive fantasy of the possibility of *real* access to the interior point of view of others. But the new tools for achieving the encounter and comprehension are the imagination and its workings; and, unlike the empathic affects in which the young Orwell had originally put his trust, at the time of *Down and Out*, they do not do away with the separation.

Take, for example, the account of the miners' return home at the end of the working day: 'From what I have seen I should say that the majority of miners prefer to eat their meal first and wash afterwards, as I should do in their circumstances.'[48] One notes a slight uncertainty ('I should say'), linked to the very fact that the labour of the imagination ('as I should do') does not cancel a strong sense of the actual difference. This labour of the imagination sometimes produces a connection, as here or as in the case of the young woman seen through the train window, but it remains *imaginary*; it does not nullify the present, strong sensation of separation. The imaginary empathy also sometimes revives a form of surprise, which reveals the limitations of this empathic approach: 'As a matter of fact it is surprising that miners wash as regularly as they do, seeing how little time they have between work and sleep.'[49] Nevertheless, the palpable truth remains the *de facto* separation, which makes it impossible to see the work of the imagination as anything other than a construction. This imaginative effort, dare I say, 'de-essentializes' the felt separation; it makes it possible to consider it, in effect, as a product of circumstances, even random (I *might* be in their place, even if I am not), and as not absolutely fixed (things *might* change). But it does not deny the tangible fact. It questions it without denying it.

The role of the imagination, consequently, is twofold: to construct empathy on the basis of the actual situation, to attempt it (and if I had been *there*?); but also, potentially, to construct another way of overcoming the difference, to construct the possibility that 'they', tomorrow, will leave the place where they are. In its first role, it means that the Orwellian imagination describes 'the world' of the representations of the workers – everything that Orwell does not share but can try to understand. For example, he explains at some length, by literally putting himself in their place (though without forgetting what is his real place), the 'logic' by which poverty makes people long for superfluous and luxurious things, instead of making them focus on basics. He frequently uses the vocabulary of the universal ('the human being'), showing that we can understand, that to imagine is possible:

The ordinary human being would sooner starve than live on brown bread and raw carrots . . . when you are unemployed, which is to say when you are underfed, harassed, bored, and miserable, you don't *want* to eat dull wholesome food. You want something a little bit 'tasty'. There is always

some cheaply pleasant thing to tempt you. Let's have three pennorth of
chips! Run out and buy us a twopenny ice-cream![50]

In its second role, that is, in its attempts to think 'their' change, the imagination becomes the tool of emancipation: feeling provides the facts, the
imagination tries to change them. Thus, with regard to hygiene, the
difference may be real *for the moment*, that is, palpable, but it is no longer,
as for the old ladies of the Brighton boarding-houses, fixed, essential
and written in the genes. It can be surmounted in the imagination.
Essentially, Orwell destroys it 'in the imagination' and not – like those
who believe that you only oppose the essentialist theories of the old bourgeois ladies by practising denial – 'ideologically'.

In this way, while continuing to attach importance to 'real contact' and
to the test of the body, Orwell has gradually destroyed his own original
myth: that he could become another through sensory experience, could
live like another, so as to understand their interiority. Orwell denounces
'the ideology of interiority' and rehabilitates the critical distance which
is, in fact, inherent in the act of *observing*. The gaze is then seen as the
expression of a singular 'angle' and accepted as such; the aim is no longer
to lose yourself in the point of view of another, but to create your own
anchorage, your own *point* of view – the point from which you see. The
exercise of the imagination, which asks 'And if I were not where I am?',
shows that this point is not envisaged as 'essentially' fixed; however, the
imagination, which transforms, does not totally destroy the point of
anchorage, unlike ideological denials.

Homage to Catalonia *or the reporter as exile*

The absolute singularity of the point of anchorage – the body of the
observer – makes the gaze, for Orwell, almost by definition, a *decentring*:
to see is to be *decentred* in relation to all other perspectives, whether they
are dominant or not, and is therefore to decentre them. Every gaze resists
and comes into conflict with another, all the more so when it encounters
an ideology which makes it clear that it is not really welcome. For Orwell,
the gaze is by definition, therefore, the act of emerging from a collective
vision of the world and the birth of a new perspective, which might be a
source of unease because it is potentially challenging to the accepted
view. To 'dis-belong' seems to be the principle of the Orwellian observer.

Raymond Williams discusses this aspect, formulating what he calls the
'principle of exile', which he believes is essential to an understanding of
Orwell's political approach.[51] For Williams, it is precisely when Orwell
was preparing to adopt, at last, a much less collective world view that this
'principle of exile' was expressed with the greatest clarity in his itinerary,

as an ultimate retreat, erected into a definitive attitude. At the time of the Spanish War, in fact, according to Williams, Orwell moved from vagrancy to exile strictly speaking. The vagrancy had always been there; it was what had made it possible for him to undergo many experiences – to live with tramps, for example, as in *Down and Out*, or with the unemployed, as in *The Road to Wigan Pier*. It had led the young Orwell from rejection to contestation, and it had certainly led him gradually to develop a principle of life and thought which was something like the 'principle of exile'. It was this, still according to Williams, that had led Orwell towards socialism, as if he had seen in the socialists a community of exiles, a community whose principle was exile, the search for the other gaze, for the elsewhere. It is at the time of this choice that Orwell came to understand that the 'principle of exile' is actually built on a critique of all community, including of its own. While coming round to the adoption of a collective vision, he finds himself, in spite of himself, in the position of critic, and then really does construct the figure of the eternal exile. The community of exiles was to remain a dream, a dream of the exile, infinitely demanding, and his 'principle of exile' was to remain a principle critical of actual political groups and their ideological temptations.[52]

Indeed, *Homage to Catalonia* makes frequent use of this Orwellian motif of the gaze as a *decentring* towards and against all ideologies, an endless *decentring* that needs constantly to be begun again, in an exile constantly renewed. We find here the idea that this labour requires 'real contact' with events, and not an abstract and remote vision, because such a vision is particularly susceptible to ideologies. Orwell has several scathing passages on the subject of all those journalists who write about the Spanish War from a long way away and understand nothing; and also on his editors, who were bound to be shocked by the crudity of real life: 'All Spaniards, we discovered, knew two English expressions. One was "O.K., baby", the other was a word used by the Barcelona whores in their dealings with English sailors, and I am afraid the compositors would not print it.'[53] But at the same time, it is in the name of particularity, of partiality and of the limitations inherent in any gaze 'in real contact' with things, that Orwell criticizes these distant journalists. He is emphatic that he prefers his partial views, accepted as such, to the broader but frankly *false* gazes of the superficial and distant journalists. If, caught up in the event, you do not see everything, at least what you see, you *see*; whereas at a distance, everything is mired in falsity, in visions which are not gazes. 'Like everyone who was in Barcelona at the time, *I saw only what was happening in my immediate neighbourhood*, but I saw and heard quite enough to be able to contradict many of the lies that have been circulated.'[54]

Orwell insists, then, on the fact that it is always an 'I' who sees, missing many things. The following passage nicely describes how someone who is participating in events is as if tethered to their body, incapable of thinking of anything but the singular experience they are undergoing:

> When you are taking part in events like these you are, I suppose, in a small way, making history, and you ought by rights to feel like a historical character. But you never do, because at such times the physical details always outweigh anything else. Throughout the fighting I never made the correct 'analysis' of the situation that was so glibly made by journalists hundreds of miles away. What I was chiefly thinking about was not the rights and wrongs of this miserable internecine scrap, but simply the discomfort and boredom of sitting day and night on that intolerable roof, and the hunger which was growing worse and worse – for none of us had had a proper meal since Monday.[55]

Another passage illustrates the fact that it is some of the events themselves, and not only their general intelligibility, that the direct observer misses. Thus, having been present at the events of May 1937 in Barcelona, where he had seen the repression by the Communists of the Anarchists who had occupied certain districts and the main Telephone Exchange, Orwell returns to the front at Huesca, where a very different fight is taking place: that against the Fascists, which causes the internal battles rather to fade into the background. He is hit by a bullet, an experience he describes at length, and returns to Barcelona. What he then realizes is that he has missed major events, which had happened in his absence:

> When I got to the hotel my wife was sitting in the lounge. She got up and came towards me in what struck me as a very unconcerned manner; then she put an arm round my neck and, with a sweet smile for the benefit of the other people in the lounge, hissed in my ear:
> 'Get out!'
> 'What?'
> 'Get out of here at once!'
> 'What?'
> 'Don't keep standing here! You must get outside quickly!'
> 'What? Why? What do you mean?'

And, further on:

> 'What the devil is all this about?' I said as soon as we were on the pavement.
> 'Haven't you heard?'
> 'No. Heard what? I've heard nothing.'
> 'The P.O.U.M.'s been suppressed. They've seized all the buildings. Practically everyone's in prison. And they say they're shooting people already.'[56]

For Orwell, missing some of the events is inherent in any singular gaze. Total knowledge is still a lie with regard to the reality lived by those who had been in the middle of this war. This explains this significant passage where he makes news out of his own lack of news:

> In the whole business, the detail that most sticks in my throat, though perhaps it is not of great importance, is that all news of what was happening was kept from the troops at the front. As you will have seen, neither I nor anyone else at the front had heard anything about the suppression of the P.O.U.M. All the P.O.U.M. militia headquarters, Red Aid centres, and so forth were functioning as usual, and about 100 miles from Barcelona papers (the Valencia papers, which were running the spy stories, did not reach the Aragon front), and no doubt one reason for arresting all the P.O.U.M. militiamen on leave in Barcelona was to prevent them from getting back to the front with the news. The draft with which I had gone up the line on 15 June must have been about the last to go. I am still puzzled to know how the thing was kept secret, for the supply lorries and so forth were still passing to and fro; but there is no doubt that it *was* kept secret, and, as I have since learned from a number of others, the men in the front line heard nothing till several days later.[57]

Thus, the very fact that he has been kept in ignorance of what has gone on gives Orwell's testimony the authenticity of what has been *experienced*. And, as if by chance, it is a testimony distressing to the socialists least inclined to recognize the internal tragedy taking place in their camp. In other words, in spite – or perhaps because – of its limitations, the most singular gaze remains the only resource for resisting imposed collective visions. It is the body of a man, with his knowledge but also his *ignorance* – an ignorance which is still knowledge since it is experienced, and painfully – that constitutes the weapon against ideology, the only anchor of the exile, the source from which comes his gaze.

3. The gaze as decentring: a reading of *Nineteen Eighty-Four*

Winston or the birth of a gaze

The novel *Nineteen Eighty-Four* is revealing with regard to this Orwellian conception of the gaze *as a decentring*, that is, as a singular point of view, anchored in a singular body, representing resistance even to ideology. My discussion of the novel will be confined to the way it makes it possible to clarify the issues involved in the act of observing, in Orwell's political thinking.

Ideology itself, in *Nineteen Eighty-Four*, would seem to be symbolized by a gaze, the uninterrupted, unlimited gaze of Big Brother. Nevertheless, a 'total' gaze whose anchorage remains enigmatic (who is he?), the eye of Big Brother is actually the very opposite of what Orwell means by 'gaze'. It represents the negation of any gaze, as if it had appropriated all possible perspectives and all points of view, so preventing them from developing. It is a centre which has no contours, which sees without leaving a place from which one could see it in return. The total gaze thus constitutes, in reality, an empire of blindness. Significantly, the typical individual of the totalitarian regime is beetle-like, with 'little', as if atrophied, eyes.[58]

The birth of an individual gaze would be, consequently, the supreme affront to the totalitarian regime, a rebellion against this over-sized centre. The resistance incarnated by Winston represents, as I will show, the birth of a gaze – of a gaze which is a 'point of view', which opposes the 'total' gaze of Big Brother, freeing a perspective where every perspective had seemed under control. The philosopher Claude Lefort has shown that resistance, incarnated by Winston, takes the form of the discovery of the self as a *body*, a singular body, experiencing itself in the singularity of its sensations and recovered memory.[59] However, I want to show that, if the body is central to the novel, it is perhaps primarily because it is the seat of vision; of all the senses, it is sight that is most at stake, and hence the absolute enemy of the regime. Winston will be above all a body that *sees*, finally crushed at the end of the novel.

But how can the gaze emerge? It is necessary to free a perspective – in other words, achieve a certain exteriority with regard to the omnipresent eye of Big Brother, which is always on every individual. A profound reflection on the nature of this exteriority runs through the novel. It is striking, in particular, that Orwell shows the hopes and then the disillusionment of Winston with regard to those who seem to be least affected by the propaganda and the terror, the proletariat or 'proles'. 'If there is hope', Winston says to himself early on, 'it lies in the proles.'[60] The proletariat are truly in a position of exteriority compared with the immediate victims of Big Brother's domination, since the constraints on them are fewer; they are the only ones, for example, whose sexuality is not controlled. Yet his hopes are dashed, as if the proletariat were decidedly too 'outside', a sort of public of totalitarianism, which has only an abstract idea of it without ever coming into 'real contact' with it. The concerns of the proletariat are exclusively material, their behaviour is bestial and egotistical, and their complete exteriority makes them indifferent to politics in a way that infuriates Winston; it seems to render them impermeable to the realities of totalitarian domination. He recalls a scene when, one day in a crowded street, he had thought a riot was brewing, but it had turned out to be only a crowd of yelling women fighting over some saucepans and accusing the stall-keeper of favouritism. In a significant scene, Orwell makes Winston finally recognize that the proletariat have no more eyes than the ordinary Party members; physiologically speaking, they have more, but they are eyes that 'wander', never fasten on anything, do not really see. In this scene Winston meets an old proletarian from the past, without ever getting him to answer the questions he puts to him:

> 'You must have seen great changes since you were a young man,' said Winston tentatively.
> *The old man's pale blue eyes moved* from the darts board to the bar, and from the bar to the door of the Gents, as though it were in the bar-room that he expected the changes to have occurred.[61]

It seems that the 'correct' exteriority, the exteriority which can produce an emancipating gaze, still requires a concrete experience of suffering. There needs to be a 'hero' who will undergo this bodily experience, and who will, as a result, be *inside*, while managing not to remain tethered to interiority, which is submission. So, even though Winston begins despairingly to think that, for Party members, given their small room for manoeuvre, 'rebellion' can mean no more than 'a look in the eyes, an inflexion of the voice, at the most, an occasional whispered word', not enough, apparently, to refute his conviction that 'the Party cannot be overthrown from within',[62] it is ultimately he himself, a Party member, who will incarnate this rebellion. He will do so by seeing.

Winston represents a double birth: a birth to himself – *Nineteen Eighty-Four* retraces the stages in a psychological emancipation, which finally leads to the emergence of a sense of self, as an individual, and which is largely achieved by the discovery of the past – and the birth of an anchorage which makes it possible to look at the outside. What Winston constructs by being born to himself is a sufficiently solid and dis-alienated *point* from which to *see* – a *point of view*, in the literal meaning of the phrase. The question of seeing is central to every stage in the process of Winston's emancipation.

Let us take the first of these stages, that is, Winston's decision to keep a diary. This means that he has to position himself beyond the range of the 'telescreen'; that is, he has to find a dead angle from which he cannot be seen, and from which he feels able to *see*, in his turn. And what he first describes is something he has *seen*. Better still, it is at the cinema, where the regime provides the assembled individuals with something to *see*, in reality to control and freeze their real capacity to see. Winston dares to see this scene truly, that is, to appropriate these images, relate them to memories, and integrate them into a singular gaze worthy of the name. The sequence which Winston saw and describes in his diary is that of a Jewish woman sitting in the bow of a lifeboat full of children, under bombardment, who puts her arms round a little 3-year-old boy in a gesture that is useless from the point of view of warding off bullets; in any case, the boat is eventually blown to pieces.

Winston associates this sequence with a memory from that very morning: at one of the collective sessions called the Two Minutes Hate, in his workplace, he had seen two people, a girl with dark hair (Julia) and another person (O'Brien). The girl has a chilling effect on him, and he dislikes her, because she had once given him what he had believed was a hostile glance;[63] it is clear that Julia, in these opening pages of the novel, symbolizes the regime and its inquisitorial gaze. He finds the other person, O'Brien, who will turn out to be a representative of the regime and, in particular, Winston's torturer at the end of the book, pleasing because of a certain old-world manner. O'Brien *wears spectacles*, a surprising detail, which can be interpreted in several ways: in a way, it distinguishes him from the beetle-like figures with 'little eyes' who are typically the Party members; but perhaps we should already read deception into these eyes hidden by spectacles; or again, perhaps O'Brien is the one who sees, but who wants to keep this privilege – materialized by the spectacles – to himself. During the Two Minutes Hate, the audience sees on the screen the face of Emmanuel Goldstein, the enemy of the regime, who, with the aid of the accompanying scenes, rouses all the spectators, Winston included, to a violent and uncontrollable hatred. There then appears the reassuring face of Big Brother, which is meant to have a calming and comforting effect. It is at this point that Winston notices that the expected effect on him fails to materialize and that he is unable to experience this calm joy. His body resists. Significantly, Orwell writes that Winston is then afraid of being *betrayed by his eyes*: 'there was a space of a couple of seconds during which *the expression of his eyes might conceivably have betrayed him. And it was exactly at this moment that the significant thing happened – if, indeed, it did happen. Momentarily he caught O'Brien's eye.*' The text is specific that O'Brien, at that very moment, 'had taken off his spectacles', an act which seems to allow their eyes to meet: 'An unmistakable message had passed. It was as though their two minds had opened and *the thoughts were flowing from one into the other through their eyes.*'[64] It is this belief, this error (is it a fantasy of Winston's or a trick of O'Brien's? – the ambiguity persists throughout the novel), that sets in motion the process of Winston's emancipation: he thinks he has received a friendly look, on which basis, literally, he will begin to *have less fear of his eyes* and *allow himself to look more and more*. It is this scene, we learn, that led to Winston's decision to start keeping a diary. The interior search and the questioning of his surroundings can begin.

The next stage is a dream of Winston's about his mother, which again involves seeing. His mother and his little sister are in a sinking ship, from which they are 'looking up at him'.[65] It is an accusing look, which seems to say that it is because Winston is above them, 'out in the light and air', that 'they were sinking down, down into the green waters'. It is clear that this image echoes that of the cinema, of the Jewish woman holding her child in her arms, in a boat under bombardment. It is also clear that it is a dream of guilt. It is difficult not spontaneously to associate this look of his mother's with that of the girl 'with dark hair' and, by extension, with the inquisitorial gaze that symbolizes the regime itself, that of Big Brother. For the moment, Winston sees that he is crushed by gazes which seem to forbid him, Winston, from seeing. The gazes he constructs in his dreams are criticisms.

But criticism is soon replaced by the desire to see. This dream is followed by another. Winston is with the girl with dark hair in a luminous field (the 'Golden Country'); she tears off her clothes in a single movement which Winston finds moving, an act which 'seemed to annihilate a whole culture, a whole system of thought, as though Big Brother and the Party and the Thought Police could all be swept into nothingness by a single splendid movement of the arm. That too was a gesture belonging to ancient time.'[66] As subsequent dreams of Winston's will confirm even more explicitly, this moving gesture is not without echoes of the simple and pointless gesture of the Jewish woman, who is herself a maternal image, but also of the old-world manner which attracted Winston in O'Brien. Above all, however, we see that the gesture of the girl with dark hair *exposes* her and *offers* her to Winston's *gaze*. She asks him to look at her. Thus the birth of the body, through the discovery of sexual desire, is firmly linked to the motif of the gaze; the body is born through the gaze and as the power to look. The dream thus transforms the censorious gaze of the girl into a demand to see: she whose gaze had forbidden him to look becomes she who finally allows Winston to see.

The immediate effect of these two dreams on Winston's conscious behaviour is, in fact, an emancipation of the gaze. It is in the days that follow that he notices the 'little eyes' of the Party members; he observes the canteen and the people who eat there, their ugliness and their 'beetle-like' appearance. Yet what surprises him in his reverie as an observer is a look: that of the girl with dark hair. The gaze is once again suppressed by a gaze. The misunderstanding and its inhibiting effect will not finally be resolved until the meeting with Julia, later, in the corridor. Moved, Winston, back in his cubicle, is once again afraid of being betrayed by his eyes. He '*put on his spectacles* and *hitched the speakwrite towards him.*'[67] Without realizing it, to shelter himself from suspicion, he begins to resemble O'Brien (although he still thinks that O'Brien is sympathetic).

His liaison with Julia puts an end, however, to the fantasy of the critical gaze of the mother. This further stage in his emancipation leads to another, a dream. This takes place within the glass paperweight bought from the shopkeeper Mr Charrington, that is, in an object from the past. The soft light is not without echoes of the field of the 'Golden Country' where he had had dreamed that the girl with dark hair had removed her clothes: 'The dream had also been comprehended by – indeed, in some senses it had consisted in – a gesture of the arm made by his mother, and made again thirty years later by the Jewish woman he had seen on the news film.'[68] It is clearly a deliverance: the mother has at last become a tender woman, like the Jewish woman of the scene in the cinema: 'Do you know . . . that until this moment I believed I had murdered my mother?', he says to Julia, lying beside him. Memories of childhood return. He remembers hunger, and how he, a famished child, who rummaged through dustbins, nagged at his mother for not feeding him properly, and stole food from his tiny sister, whose face was 'made almost simian by thinness'.[69] The 'event' to which he knows his dream is related comes back: after Winston had stolen the last morsel of chocolate, meant for his sister, his helpless mother had made this gesture: she had put her arm round his sister and pressed her face against her breast: 'It was no use, it changed nothing, it did not produce more chocolate, it did not avert the child's death or her own; but it seemed natural to her to do it. The refugee woman in the boat had also covered the little boy with her arm, which was no more use against the bullets than a sheet of paper.'[70] Winston the child had fled. When he returned, his mother and his sister had disappeared. What seems suddenly clear to Winston is that these useless gestures are precisely what distinguish the old days from the present day; they represent everything the Party had obliterated.

At that moment, Winston has rediscovered the past, and his gaze at the present is changed for ever. In a way, it is only at this moment that he at last fully sees the first scene described in his diary: the singular gaze is at last deployed.

The stages in the annihilation of the gaze

Just as the birth of the gaze happens in several stages, each of which requires a further advance in Winston's inner development, so the destruction of the gaze by the regime proceeds in stages, each of which will allow a deeper incursion into his psyche, in order to nullify, point by point, his emancipation and obliterate it completely; this is contrary to the certitudes of Winston and Julia, who believe 'they can make you say anything – *anything* – but they can't make you believe it. They can't get inside you.'[71]

The essential target of O'Brien's torture, what he wants to be able to crush completely in Winston, is the gaze. He has to make sure that Winston no longer sees what he sees; Winston must once again be literally absorbed by the total gaze of Big Brother. The waking dream of Winston, worn out by the torture, is significant:

> He was in a cell which might have been either dark or light, *because he could see nothing except a pair of eyes.* Near at hand some kind of instrument was ticking slowly and regularly. *The eyes grew larger and more luminous.* Suddenly he floated out of his seat, dived into the eyes, and was swallowed up.[72]

O'Brien begins – the first stage – by concentrating his attention and his torture on Winston's *body*; to ensure that Winston sees something other than what he sees, he has to act on this body, seat of the gaze, and he has to deceive this site of resistance to ideology. By exhausting Winston physically, O'Brien is able to make him see five fingers instead of four – because he does not want Winston to lie, he wants him *really* to see five fingers. Yet the very logic of this torture shows that O'Brien still at this stage asks Winston to trust his sight. He wants to make him see something different, certainly, but he still wants to make him see something. In a scene that follows the episode of the five fingers, O'Brien explicitly appeals to Winston's gaze to prove to him that he is no longer (almost) what he had been before, or at least that his body is nothing like what it had once been: he shows him his ravaged body in a mirror. Claude Lefort emphasizes that 'what he [O'Brien] needed [in this scene] is Winston to look at his own body. For O'Brien, the negation of self is achieved through Winston's gaze.' It seems to me that this need of O'Brien's signifies that Winston's destruction is not yet complete, and it simply responds to a need of Winston's; it is Winston who believes only what he sees, and O'Brien, to demonstrate his triumph, is still at this stage obliged to use Winston's criteria.

Further, what exactly does Winston see in the mirror, what is it that most distresses him? It is his eyes – in the process of being destroyed. What is so peculiarly horrible and extraordinary in this scene is that it is the moment when Winston *sees – still sees – that soon he will no longer be able to see*: he sees the destruction of his gaze in progress: 'A forlorn, jail-bird's face with a nobby forehead running back into a bald scalp, a crooked nose, and battered-looking cheekbones above which *his eyes were fierce and watchful.*'[73]

The ultimate destruction follows. Just as the final liberation of the gaze had happened from the inside, through a dream, so it is on the inside that pressure must be exerted definitively to destroy the power to see. It is necessary, as noted by Lefort, to go 'behind'. This is the torture of Room 101, which is a room of individualized horror, as O'Brien explains: 'There are occasions when a human being will stand out against pain, even to the point of death. But for everyone there is something unendurable – something that cannot be *contemplated*.'[74] What O'Brien is going to make Winston *see*, therefore, in Room 101, is what will stop him from seeing forever. In this case, it is the rat torture: Winston's face is placed up against a cage full of rats, which are ready to jump at his face the minute the cage door is opened: 'They will leap on to your face and bore straight into it. *Sometimes they attack the eyes first*.'[75]

Lefort brings out the meaning of this animal for Winston: the rat is none other than a representation of Winston by himself, it is the voracious child who foraged in dustbins, that guilt-inducing child from whom Winston's inner labour over the preceding months had enabled him to liberate himself. In the middle of the shrill cries of the rats, 'he was insane, a *screaming animal*', writes Orwell of Winston,[76] and Lefort emphasizes this last expression. It is his most intimate fantasies, therefore, that O'Brien has penetrated; he brings Winston face to face with himself, or rather, with everything within him that had for so long alienated and inhibited his gaze. 'The scene with the rats', writes Lefort, 'reveals the door through which *they* enter; the secret door of fantasy, that which, dare one say, is in the innermost depths of the self, for all of us, or as if behind the self. They enter from behind . . .'

And the desperate reaction of Winston is indeed a demand, made to his torturer, to block his sight: 'There was one and only one way to save himself. He must interpose another human being, the body of another human being, between himself and the rats.'[77] It doesn't matter which: Winston shouts for them to throw Julia to the rats, a betrayal which, as Lefort emphasizes, is a destruction of the self, since it is the demand to destroy 'the flesh of his flesh', to rend 'his inner tissue'. Here again, this is revealing as to the deep meaning of the act of seeing for Orwell: the gaze is the manifestation of an identity. That is why the birth of the gaze also required a birth of the self and why, conversely, the annihilation of the gaze is achieved by the destruction of the self – since the 'screen' that Winston 'chooses' to block his sight is what is dearest to him and what had enabled him to construct himself as an individual.

In this way, *Nineteen Eighty-Four* illustrates the Orwellian conception of the gaze as a way of resisting ideology. Winston is fundamentally he who *learns to look*, and who will, for that very reason, be destroyed by a regime which arrogates to itself the monopoly of seeing.

In Orwell, the gaze is, almost by definition, a decentring with regard to an instituted vision, the expression of a wholly singular perspective, which mistrusts collective visions and which defies them. Orwell the reporter sees this permanent decentring in relation to the 'natural' expectations of his readers. He seeks to exile himself, to be always there, where there is something that 'you' do not like to see, ready to accept the limitations of his point of view at every stage of his exile. This conception of the gaze as decentring is rooted in a conception of the body and of passive feeling as having a singularity that cannot be reduced to any ideology, indeed is even its enemy. The figure of Orwell, writer and journalist, therefore defines a 'decentring' sensualism, reverse archetype of the 'unifying' sensualism we observed in Séverine.

7

Seeing Violence:
Seymour M. Hersh and Michael Herr,
Two Decentring Reporters in the
Vietnam War

At a very early stage in my discussion of the decentring process, I emphasized the paradox inherent in it. The decentring journalist wants to make us, the public, see something that is 'other' to us, and to do it in such a way as to cause this otherness to have an effect on us, question us, and change us; this requires that, by one means or another, a connection is established between it and us. But is this connection not inconsistent with the fact that it is something 'other' that is at issue? Are we not, in the end, decentred by an otherness that is always partly tamed?

I have argued, also, that the temptations which threaten those who decentre amount to a domestication of otherness. The 'chameleon' of Tom Wolfe thought he was at home everywhere. The 'unifier of the dominated', a powerful temptation in the early years of *Libération*, created a new family instead of addressing the otherness which the 'dominated' represent for the ordinary newspaper-reading public. George Orwell set himself up against all ways of taming the other – the tramp, the unemployed, the freedom-fighter – by proposing a writing of exile and solitude, always on the outside of those it describes, 'between' them and us, unique and singular. Our reading of Orwell has enabled us to define decentring as the always unfinished effort of a gaze to remain nomadic, because to become fixed would render it suspect of taming the other and of itself turning into the gaze of a witness-ambassador. The witness-ambassador, who brings people together, defines a place, the centre of the 'we', whereas the decentrer is constantly seeking a non-place, in order to defy the appointed places.

However, the true decentrers, the authentic nomads, careful not to succumb to the temptation of becoming fixed, are perhaps still, in spite of everything, trapped in the paradox that is inherent in their method. Do they achieve a real alterity? Can they not, in reality, be accused of betraying those 'others' they present, precisely because they present them, that is, establish a link between them and a public? Indeed they can. In the face of such an objection, I probably have to accept that my notion of decentring conflicts with the most radical approaches to otherness, those that preclude the very idea of a connection between the 'other' and us. But it should be added that the most reliable indicator of the authentic decentrer is probably the permanence of doubt, frustration, anxiety and a fear of misrepresenting the other. The nomadism of the decentrer seeks this absence of comfort – one need only remember the Orwellian battle against the 'comfort' of ideologies; and this absence of comfort is a sign of the authenticity of the method.

Those who decentre are, in a way, figures structurally in crisis. This clearly distinguishes them from the witness-ambassadors; the latter demand certitude and are seriously threatened by crisis, as we saw in the case of Lincoln Steffens. Even if Steffens did not actually 'leave' journalism, it is this question of 'leaving it' that his crisis posed in an acute form, because it was dangerously destructive of the status of witness-ambassador. In contrast, crisis is inherent to the decentrers; it constitutes them, and it provides them with the necessary safeguards. The decentring journalist is inconceivable except in a perpetual state of crisis.

Nor is it possible to conceive of those who decentre except as in search of the limit, that which will push to the limit the painful paradox in which they are trapped. In other words, they cannot fail to wonder what otherness is at the furthest point of any possible connection and of what can be shown to the public.

This search for the limit means that a special place must be reserved, in our discussion of decentring journalisms, for the journalisms of direct contact with violence: in particular, war reporting. Violence clearly represents just such an extreme situation. It defines a radical otherness, which challenges the decentrers, committing them to a perfection that borders on the impossible. In this sense, it is the unhappy fate of the decentring journalisms to be those journalisms which mostly confront it, and it is they who are the subject of my last chapter.

I understand here by violence a situation, of human or natural origin, in which suffering is inflicted on human beings. In the case of violence inflicted by people on other people, I see the perpetrators as defining an otherness by the same title as the victims: both are inside, and it is this 'inside' that is 'other' for anyone who, like the public for whom the journalist writes, remains outside. In essence, I define violence as the very thing that severs every connection between the inside and the outside. All those who 'are there', whatever their role in this violence, whether they are perpetrators, victims or eyewitnesses directly exposed to the traumatic situation, constitute an otherness in relation to an exterior public. This is why violence presents the journalist with a terrible challenge: if it means an irreparable breach between those who are there and those who are not, is it even possible to envisage creating a connection beyond the breach, without its being inevitably misrepresented?

Violence is not really a subject for the witness-ambassador. This is not to say that it rules out any approach preoccupied with reconstructing the 'facts', on which all can agree and which can be established without it being necessary to have access to or experience of violence. This sort of approach is even very important, but it cannot be considered as a deep apprehension of violence in its otherness and its reality. The debate between the French journalist Nicolas Poincaré and the photographer Sebastiaõ Salgado, a few years ago, on the catastrophe of Hurricane Mitch in Honduras, clearly demonstrated both the importance and the limitations of the position of the witness-ambassador, here incarnated by Poincaré. On his return from a visit to Honduras in November 1998, Poincaré claimed that the number of victims proposed by the government of Honduras and repeated by the international press had been grossly exaggerated; factual accuracy had been superseded by a generous empathy with the suffering of the victims; emotion had taken precedence over rigorous observation and, most of all, counting, the preconditions for a 'true' gaze. Poincaré's words rang out like an appeal to the journalistic profession to remain faithful to the figure of the witness-ambassador; it is not that emotion is forbidden to this figure, as we have shown, but the 'universal body' to which the witness-ambassador aspires must be able to give proper weight to the tangible facts, such as the number of bodies seen in hospitals. The position defended by Poincaré was undeniably a strong one, and necessary in view of the manipulation of the figures. Nevertheless, it was to come up against an interlocutor who was able to demonstrate its limitations. Invited on to the same television panel as Poincaré,[1] the photographer Salgado was able both to accept his point, at the level of journalistic rigour, and also to emphasize the equally 'journalistic' limitations of the rigorously factual approach. The factual truth hid another truth, perhaps contained in the exaggeration described by Poincaré. Salgado recalled that, in the infinite character of the suffering and emotion of those who get close to it, there is another sort of truth, which touches the 'intimacy' of suffering, to use the words of Norman Mailer, and which might have a quite different effect on observers than a series of facts and figures: a decentring effect, the feeling of an otherness which, if one were to encounter it, would 'undo' us. Salgado then posed this question: is it not the duty of a certain journalism, whether it works with the image or the written word, to concern itself with this otherness and aim, by its gaze, at this decentring effect?

We still need to establish whether, in the face of violence, those who decentre primarily present us with their crisis, in paroxysmal fashion, even their failure, admitted and taking various forms, as they realize that a limit they have tried so hard to achieve is ultimately beyond their reach. This is the question that will concern us here. To answer it, I propose to analyse two approaches to the Vietnam War: that of Seymour M. Hersh, who revealed the My Lai massacre to America, that is, the liquidation in March 1968 of a North Vietnamese village by Charlie Company; and that of Michael Herr, who was in Vietnam from 1967 to 1969, and who wrote several articles and then, a decade later, *Dispatches* (1977), a book which brought together the original articles, which Herr had continued to revise.

1. The 'other Americans': Seymour M. Hersh and the My Lai massacre

From the 'facts' to the intimacy of violence

The reconstruction of the My Lai massacre by a free-lance journalist from the East Coast of the United States, more than eighteen months later, was a major event in American political history. In November 1969, in three articles published in quick succession,[2] Seymour M. Hersh, a 32-year-old journalist, revealed to America that, on 16 March 1968, a North Vietnamese village had been annihilated by the First Platoon, commanded by William C. Calley, of C (or Charlie) Company, itself under the command of Captain Ernest L. Medina; this was in direct contravention of the Geneva Convention of 12 August 1949, which protects civilian victims in time of war. These three articles stripped away the secrecy surrounding the ongoing trials by the army of those responsible. Hersh followed them with a book, *My Lai 4: A Report on the Massacre and its Aftermath*, published in April 1970, in which he revealed the conclusions of the military investigations which media pressure had helped to bring about; this was two years before their eventual publication, the report of the Peers Commission appearing in 1972. Later, also in 1972, Hersh published a further book, this time on the way the army had tried to hush up the affair, but this will not form part of my discussion.[3]

Hersh was working in Washington on a book on chemical and biological weapons when, in October 1969, a lawyer friend telephoned to say that the Army was secretly preparing the trial of a lieutenant, William Calley, for the murder of a large number of Vietnamese civilians. A short Associated Press paragraph on the subject had appeared in various newspapers, most notably the *New York Times* of 8 September 1969, but had attracted little attention. Hersh traced Calley's lawyer, George Latimer; then, with his agreement, and on the pretext of providing Calley with an opportunity to give his version of events, went to Fort Benning, where he was able to interview the lieutenant. The village in question was at that date usually called 'Pinkville' within the Army, because it was coloured red (for 'densely populated zone') on the maps. In fact, it was the village of Song My, to be precise, the hamlet called My Lai 4.

The first article of Hersh pieced together the facts and reported the views of several soldiers, as well as the fragments provided by Calley. Dated 12 November 1969, it was bought from Hersh's agent and published by thirty-six newspapers. This led, in the days that followed, to the appearance of other articles, written by other journalists. The army photographer, Ron Haeberle, who had been present at the massacre, gave his personal colour photographs (those in black and white had been surrendered to his superiors) to the editors of the *Cleveland Plain Dealer*, which published them on 20 November. Hersh got from the press the name of the former GI who had been responsible for getting the military inquiry started, Ronald L. Ridenhour, and met him in California. Ridenhour had not witnessed the massacre in person, but he had flown over the area a few days later and heard it talked about by several GIs who had been present. A year later, in April 1969, he had sent multiple copies of a letter to the White House, the Pentagon, the State Department and Congress, in which he set out what he had heard. This had led to an inquiry (23 April 1969), led by Colonel William Vickers; but, as the weeks passed, Ridenhour had become increasingly sceptical with regard to the determination of the Army to uncover the truth. The Army's main police unit, the Criminal Investigation Division (C.I.D.), had known about the affair since August 1969; what was beginning to emerge, however, was legal action against Lieutenant Calley alone, a way of designating one man as responsible, then burying the whole affair.

Ridenhour had soon realized the necessity of making the affair public, and had contacted the press on 29 May 1969. But he had been met with little enthusiasm. He was pleased, therefore, several months later, to find someone who would finally listen to him. He gave Hersh a copy of his original letter, together with the addresses and telephone numbers of several GIs who had been eyewitnesses to the massacre. Hersh met these men, and his interviews with them formed the basis of his second article, of 20 November. In the next few days, at Terre Haute, Indiana, he met a veteran by the name of Paul Meadlo, who admitted that he himself had taken part in the massacre. This confession was the subject of his third article, dated 25 November. Meadlo was later interviewed on CBS by Walter Cronkite, which gave the affair maximum media coverage.

The same day, the Army officially announced that Lieutenant Calley would be tried by court martial for the premeditated murder of 109 Vietnamese civilians. The day before, it had been decided to reopen a military inquiry: the Peers Commission (named after the presiding general, William R. Peers) was asked to establish whether or not officers at a higher level had covered up these atrocities. There had been a first inquiry, triggered by a non-commissioned officer, in the days after the massacre, but it had been quickly cut short. In fact, the high military authorities had been alerted on the very day of the massacre by an eyewitness, Warrant Officer Hugh C. Thompson, who had flown over My Lai in an observation helicopter of the 123rd Air Battalion on the morning of 16 March 1968. Thompson had seen wounded Vietnamese civilians and warned the GIs on the spot by smoke signals. To his astonishment, instead of offering assistance to these civilians, the soldiers on the ground had gone up to the wounded and killed them in cold blood. Thompson had eventually landed and positioned himself between the GIs and a bunker which the lieutenant was preparing to blow up, even though a group of women and children were sheltering inside. Thompson had taken some of the wounded away in his helicopter. As a result of his complaint, an inquiry had been conducted by Colonel Oran Henderson, but it, too, had been quickly terminated.

The publicity given to the My Lai massacre did not prevent the Army either from playing down the enormity of the crime or from making Lieutenant Calley its scapegoat; he was sentenced to life imprisonment with hard labour by court martial in April 1971 for the murder of 'at least twenty-two' Vietnamese non-combatants, then released on parole in 1974. No one else was found guilty, not even Captain Medina, who was acquitted after a trial lasting from 22 August to 22 September 1971.[4] Nevertheless, it is still generally agreed that this affair was a significant event in American political history. The Peers Report finally estimated the number of people killed at My Lai at between 175 and 400, the murders having been accompanied by various rapes and tortures.[5] If the Watergate affair brought down a president, that of My Lai publicly – if not legally – put the American military hierarchy in the dock and helped to make this war leave a deep wound in the American psyche.[6]

The journalistic method of Seymour Hersh consisted, from the beginning, of reconstructing the facts. But there was more to it than that; indeed, the first articles of November 1969 add little new to the information that was already known. Hersh could only, for example, at that date, reproduce the charge against Calley, which referred to 109 victims and which formed the opening paragraph – or 'lead' – of his first article. More importantly, however, the question arises as to whether the events he describes can be reduced to a simple question of fact. The third paragraph of this same article, what American journalists call the 'nut graph', which is supposed to condense the key issue raised by the information in the lead, runs as follows: 'The Army calls it murder; Calley, his counsel and others associated with the incident describe it as a case of carrying out orders.' The problem, it appears, is how to *name*, and hence evaluate, what had happened: was it a 'murder' committed by Calley, in breach of official regulations, or was it simply Calley carrying out an order issued by his superior officers, in particular Medina? It might be argued that this is still a simple question of fact: was there or was there not an order? But Hersh had already shown, by allowing those who had been present to speak, that things were not nearly so simple: even if there had been an order, did this exonerate Calley and his men? And if there had been an order, in what form (explicit, implicit) had it been given? Did a merely implicit and imprecise order ('clear this area'), too literally interpreted by Calley, or even the absence of an order, exonerate the superior officers? Whatever the case, was it exactly 'murder' to have killed civilians in these circumstances, given that the company had recently suffered heavy losses, and that earlier incidents had demonstrated that civilians sometimes concealed members of the Vietcong?

In fact, as Hersh explains in this article, everyone was agreed as to the *fact* that civilians had been killed in this village: 'None of the men interviewed about the incident has denied that women and children were shot.' Nevertheless, the question of the existence of a *crime*, at whatever level, was still raised by many of those interviewed. Most of all, however, the arguments which are presented in the article show that the question of the nature of what had happened, and so of the responsibility of the perpetrators, was wider than the factual matter of the existence, or not, of an order, and the nature of this order. The real problem was to know what had led, concretely, to this event, precisely what sort of event it had been, and what had made it possible. Hersh is in the process of gradually abandoning the habits of the witness-ambassador seeking the 'facts', in favour of the decentring approach; he wants to make the American public see an otherness both strange and extremely close to home, unbelievable and yet deep in the heart of America, that of these GIs thrust into a violence they both suffered and perpetrated; an otherness that is simply unbelievable, and is destructive of the American identity. What Hersh wants to show is a very different otherness than that which, for example, Murrow and Friendly had shown in the person of Senator McCarthy: the 'other' constituted by McCarthy put Americanness to the test, but so as to reconstitute it, not to make it tremble in the way the journalistic investigations of Hersh would make it tremble.

It is clear, from this first article, that it is the general atmosphere surrounding the event, rather than the 'facts', that is the crux of the problem. Essentially, the orders were always there, if in an imprecise form: 'We were told to just clear the area,' says an anonymous soldier, used to the situation in Vietnam, while an officer friend of Calley states: 'There weren't any friendlies in the village. The orders were to shoot anything that moved.' The question of the existence of a precise order on that particular day is perhaps not the main issue. What is important is this 'obviousness' of the need for the killing, as another officer explains: 'It could happen to any of us. He [Calley] has killed and has seen a lot of killing . . . killing becomes nothing in Vietnam. He knew that there were civilians there, but he also knew that there were VC among them.' In any case, whether there was an explicit order or not, how was it that the Army, alerted to the possibility of an irregularity in the months following the incident, had failed to investigate further? Was this not a sign that, for those who 'were there', this 'irregularity' was quite normal, even if, seen from outside, it was incomprehensible?

The debate, therefore, was about more than the facts. Neither the points that were agreed (the fact of the killing of civilians) nor those that were not (the existence of an order, and, if it existed, its precise nature) provide an answer to the question posed at the beginning of the article: what should it be called? What is it, this event both remote (a source of shame, a crime, something which the regulations of the American Army prohibited out of respect for the Geneva Convention . . .) and close by (these were ordinary, even patriotic, American soldiers, in an exceptional situation . . .)? How, and in what state of mind, had they done it? The mystery is incarnated by the person of Calley himself, at the end of the 12 November article: an impenetrable character, who can only protest his attachment to the American Army and his patriotism, and recognize that his words might not easily be understood: 'I know this sounds funny, but I like the Army . . . and I don't want to do anything to hurt it.' It is one of his friends who sums up the mystery, that is the strange proximity of murderer and 'fine boy': 'Maybe he did take some order to clear out the village a little bit too literally, but he's a fine boy.'

For Hersh, it was necessary both *to understand and not to understand*, to enter into this American who was a stranger and all the others who had done 'it', these soldiers who reveal just what this war represents for the American public: an 'other' produced by 'us', an 'other' which destroys our self-confident identity. By trying, in his second article of 20 November, to assemble every statement, and contact every soldier involved in the massacre, he would establish a connection with this 'other', a painful, unbearable connection, a decentring connection. Hersh, a writer who belongs rather to the tradition of investigative journalism (he has been described as a new muckraker),[7] here enters another journalistic dimension.

It is worth noting, for example, that although Hersh warns in the preface to his book that he wanted to impose some order on the occasionally contradictory statements he had received,[8] his text nevertheless abounds in contradictory, confused facts and multiple points of view, which convey the atmosphere of the event. This was not a renunciation, but a way of acceding to another truth. Hersh explicitly acknowledges that he has not got to the bottom of all the controversies surrounding the precise order given by Medina.[9] It has become increasingly clear that this is not the problem. In the pages that follow, without ever piecing together the precise words spoken by Medina, Hersh reconstitutes the meaning that, *whatever they were, they had had in the minds of the GIs*. It is this, at the end of the day, that mattered, and that had made the massacre possible. When the GIs themselves attribute a strategically deliberate vagueness to Medina, they are surely recognizing that it is the way in which they themselves had heard these words that mattered, even if they at the same time deny their own responsibility. Vague or not, the order had been 'made specific' because the massacre had a logic beyond that of obeying orders. Calley himself reveals his ability to make specific what had not necessarily been so, according to a logic which is, ultimately, the crux of this affair, what it was necessary to see and to think:

> 'Every time we got hit [in the Pinkville area], it was from the rear . . . so the third time in there *the order came down to go in there and make sure no one was behind us. Just to clear the area.* It was a typical combat assault tactic,' the young officer explained. 'We came in hot [firing], with a cover of artillery in front of us, came down the line, and destroyed the village.'[10]

Thus, whatever its original meaning had been, the idea of 'clearing' was bound to be received in the way it was: it could not be accepted with the meaning of 'clear the area *of Vietcong*', but led inevitably to '*clear the area, period*'.

Another passage in the book similarly shows that the facts are secondary compared with the logic in which, whatever they were, they were caught up. This is when Hersh describes the series of telephone calls which halted – or rather slowed down – the massacre.[11] From his helicopter, an outraged Chief Warrant Officer Thompson sends a radio message to HQ. It is intercepted by Lieutenant Colonel Barker, who then calls Medina, who will later call Calley. The precise content of the conversation between Barker and Medina is impossible to reconstruct with the certainty of empirical proof, as is that of the subsequent telephone conversation between Medina and Calley: we have to make do with the statements. In fact, Hersh seems not even to have been particularly anxious to go further, that is, to reconstruct the 'real' conversation, its raw 'factuality', beyond what could be said about it. He makes us feel the confusion of the contradictory interpretations because, at the end of the day, it is this that mattered, irrespective of the 'actual' conversation: 'John Kinch of the mortar platoon heard Medina answer that he "had a body count of 310". The captain added, "I don't know what they're doing. The first platoon's in the lead. I am trying to stop it." A moment later, Kinch said, Medina called Calley and ordered, "That's enough for today." ' According to Kinch, therefore, Barker seems to have been firm, to have asked for figures and to have been sufficiently intimidating for Medina to have then ordered Calley to stop the massacre. In which case, if further murders took place, if in a more orderly fashion, the fault is Calley's alone. But this is what comes next:

> Harry Stanley was standing a few feet away from Calley near some huts at the drainage ditch when the call came from Medina. He had a different recollection: 'Medina called Calley and said, "What the fuck is going on?" Calley said he got some VC, or some people that needed to be checked out.' At this point Medina cautioned Calley to tell his men to save their ammunition because the operation still had a few more days to run.

This time, through what happened to Stanley and his way of understanding Calley's reaction to Medina's telephone call, we have a new interpretation of the effect on Medina of Barker's telephone call. Perhaps the call was not as firm as suggested by the previous interpretation (that of Kinch, a witness to Medina's reaction). Or even if Barker had been firm, Medina had not understood him in that way. Or perhaps it was Calley who interpreted quite wrongly the orders he was given by Medina. Who knows? In which case, who is really responsible for the 'orderly' continuance of the massacres, Calley, Medina or Barker? These many levels of interpretation are a long way from leading to factual clarification. We never 'touch' the raw facts, contrary to all the well-meaning aspirations of the traditional investigative journalists, for whom this passage is close to a journalistic anti-model. We are much closer to a journalism that mocks the very notion of fact and that revels in giving a voice to the dizzy multiplicity of interpretations of experience, in the hope of achieving an 'intimacy' with violence.

The witnesses speak: those others we once were

What does this intimacy consist of? Already, in the articles of 20 and 25 November, the affair is referred to as something that, beyond the reconstruction of the facts, has a terrible 'strangeness' about it, revealed in the words of those who discuss it.

The article of 20 November begins by quoting the words of three former soldiers who had been present during the massacre and who say that it had been 'pointblank murder'. The affair begins to acquire a name, and one that immediately suggests something 'strange'. Hersh quotes Sergeant Michael Bernhardt:

> I walked up and saw these guys doing *strange things* [my emphasis]. They were doing it three ways. One: They were setting fire to the hootches and huts and waiting for people to come out and then shooting them up. Two: They were going into the hootches and shooting them up. Three: They were gathering people in groups and shooting them.

It is interesting that this witness describes the massacre as both a collection of 'strange things', which certainly surprise his later interviewers (including Hersh), and as a collection of obvious facts, for those soldiers as they were at that time. Bernhardt's statement itself, therefore, contains this mixture of proximity and strangeness which is at the heart of the decentring process. 'At one point', Hersh tells us, 'he [Bernhardt] said to the interviewer: "You're surprised? I wouldn't be surprised at anything these dudes did."' He himself, in his capacity as witness who speaks, brings this strangeness closer and tries to convey both its incredibility and, dare one say, its 'obviousness'.

Hersh's method consists, therefore, of activating the voices of violence – of violence perpetrated. They suddenly bring this violence very close – we hear it, we can imagine it – without making it less mysterious. These voices are urged by the journalist to go constantly further, so as to throw light on this enigma they contain within them. 'Why did the men run amuck?', he asks explicitly, in the middle of his 20 November article. And later, his question 'Why did it happen?' clearly goes beyond the simple process of reconstructing the facts, since it follows immediately after the revelation of a 'fact' by the soldier, Michael Terry, who remembers: 'Later, he and the platoon team he headed were taking a lunch break near the ditch when, Terry said, he noticed "some of them were still breathing. . . They were pretty badly shot up. They weren't going to get any medical help, and so we shot them. Shot maybe five of them . . .".'

The article of 20 November shows, therefore, that Hersh is already more interested in the representations and the language of those involved than in the 'facts'. This shows in the quotations he selects from Terry's evidence: 'They had them in a group standing over a ditch – just like a Nazi-type thing . . .', and, later: 'I think that probably the officers didn't really know if they were ordered to kill the villagers or not . . . a lot of guys feel that they (the South Vietnamese civilians) aren't human beings; we just treat them like animals.' It is clear that Hersh is already listening out for associations of ideas and for incoherences in the use of tenses – the statement mixes the past and the present, suggesting that speech is this painful, decentring force which links yesterday and today, elsewhere and here, the alterity of violence and 'us'. He wants to go beyond the facts and provide a space for these words that connect us to the incomprehensible strangeness. The last witness interviewed in this article says, for example: ' "I was shooting pigs and a chicken while the others were shooting people . . . it isn't just a nightmare; I'm completely aware of how real this was. It's something I don't think a person would understand – the reality of it just didn't hit me until recently, when I read about it again in the newspapers." ' It is real, but it is like fiction, he seems to be saying. It is 'another' reality, that you can 'forget', but that you can also bring back in language.

It is interesting, in this regard, that the newspapers are credited by these former soldiers with this role of re-awakening what had been dormant. In a way, Hersh's journalistic method leads to a further stage in this process: it produces in readers not involved this very confusion that the former soldiers felt at the very mention of these 'facts' in the press; it brings them face to face with 'what a person would not understand', to use the words of the soldier himself, that is, with a strangeness suddenly brought very close to home.

The third article, of 25 November, continues this process. The journalist's text is increasingly given over to the words of the witnesses – here the voice of the veteran Paul Meadlo. His voice is central, a voice truly issuing from the violence, as Meadlo is the first of the witnesses questioned to admit, from the outset, not only that he had seen the massacre but that he had taken part in it. He describes it and tells what he did, set going simply by the journalist's question ('Why did he do it?'), which seems never to receive an answer, because the voice, by bringing closer and explaining the 'logic' of the massacre, also keeps making it even stranger and more inaccessible. In fact, by being this 'link' between the violence and the spectators who had not been there, Meadlo himself gets some shocks: he puts himself back inside so as to experience it again and extricates himself from it so as to convey it to us; he both goes close to the past and puts it at a distance, and this gives him shocks which are visible in his words, which hardly, as a result, form any sort of 'reply' to the enigma: 'We were all under orders. We all thought we were doing the right thing. At the time it didn't bother me.' But he then refers to the doubts that assailed him the night after the massacre, and which have never left him. The way he formulates them is, at the very least,

strange: 'The kids and the women – they didn't have any right to die.'
In his unease, he seems to be trying to deny the logic of the murder
while actually reliving it; he speaks to himself in the language of the murderer he had been, to deny it, even while this language is coming to seem
to him crazy. In fact, he takes the first steps towards a language of after-
violence, which tries to connect the past and the present but without ever
being able to tame this past, which describes but does not really explain.
And it is this language, sustained by the enigma but incapable of resolv-
ing it, that the journalist records, revives and stimulates – an enigma
summarized by Meadlo's mother: 'I sent them a good boy and they made
him a murderer.'

Indeed, the participants in the massacre have every chance of not
emerging unscathed from the experience to which they are subjected by
the journalist. His 'why?' encourages them to formulate the logic of the
massacre, but the very fact of formulating it can – though not always,
admittedly – suddenly put them outside this logic and reveal its strangeness to them. Many of those who speak about the massacre reappraise,
as they speak, the very thing they are in the process of describing, and
thus are decentring themselves: they had been inside, they increasingly
emerge, while, in so doing, they decentre those who had believed themselves furthest from the violence they describe. In the book of 1970, *My
Lai 4*, one of the best examples of this process is the passage dealing with
the rape of a young Vietnamese girl. Significantly, the scene had taken
place in the presence of the army reporter and photographer (respectively, Jay Roberts and Ron Haeberle), whose position as spectators
seems not to have made them behave any differently from the others; like
them, they were immersed in the 'now' of the violence, in its 'logic'. This
is the passage written on the basis of the eyewitness statements, which
ends with a reappraisal of the scene by one of those who has described it:

A few men now singled out a slender Vietnamese girl of about fifteen. They
tore her from the group and started to pull at her blouse. They attempted
to fondle her breasts. The old women and children were screaming and
crying. One GI yelled, 'Let's see what she's made of.' Another said, 'VC
Boom, Boom,' meaning she was a Viet Cong whore. Jay Roberts thought
that the girl was good-looking. An old lady began fighting with fanatical
fury, trying to protect the girl. Roberts said, 'She was fighting off two or
three guys at once. She was fantastic. Usually they're pretty passive . . .
they hadn't even gotten that chick's blouse off when Haeberle came along.'
One of the GI's finally smacked the old woman with a rifle butt; another
booted her in the rear.

Grzesik and his fire team watched the fight develop as they walked down
from the ditch to the hamlet center. Grzesik was surprised: 'I thought the
village was cleared . . . I didn't know there were that many people left.' He

knew trouble was brewing, and his main thought was to keep his team out of it. He helped to break up the fight. Some of the children were desperately hanging on to the old lady as she struggled. Grzesik was worried about the cameraman. He may have yelled, 'Hey, there's a photographer.' He remembered thinking, 'Here's a guy standing there with a camera that you've never seen before.' Then somebody said, 'What do we do with them?' The answer was, 'Waste them.' Suddenly there was a burst of automatic fire from many guns. Only a small child survived. Somebody then carefully shot him, too. A photograph of the woman and child, with the young Vietnamese girl tucking in her blouse, was later published in *Life* magazine. Roberts tried to explain later: 'It's just that they didn't know what they were supposed to do; killing them seemed like a good idea, so they did it. The old lady who fought so hard was probably a VC.' He thought a moment and added, 'Maybe it was just her daughter.'[12]

The attitude of the 'official' observers, Roberts and Haeberle, seems not, initially, to have been any different from that of those involved in the massacre. Roberts 'thought that the girl was good-looking', in a way without seeing her, rather as Haeberle, in a later passage, tries to take the 'picture of the year' of a wounded child.[13] It is only 'afterwards' that Roberts becomes, in a way, a journalist at last, conscious of having been caught up in a logic whose strangeness is finally apparent to him. It is through contact with another journalist, *the* journalist (Hersh), that he comes to himself; Hersh then incarnates the point at which the otherness of the violence can at least be *seen*, where those who had been there meet those who had not, the place where, for both parties, the *decentring* is finally possible. The decentring of Roberts – what if the old woman who had protected the young girl was simply her mother? – is matched by the inverse decentring of a public which can at last communicate with him, meet him and get closer to him – what if this killer, this 'other', was an American, someone we might know, someone we might resemble?

All the voices, whatever degree of decentring they involve for the actors concerned, have a decentring effect, in the opposite direction, for the public who hear them. The mere fact that they are audible produces this disturbing effect of proximity. It is even possible that the voice which seems truly to come from 'inside' the violence, which makes no attempt to make itself understood and which describes the logic of the massacre without shame, is ultimately, by its naturalness and the frankness of the speaker, the one which best achieves this mixture of closeness and distance characteristic of decentring. A soldier like Grzesik, who asks embarrassing questions and is scrupulous and hesitant, is actually less decentring than a Herbert Carter, who seems still to be inside, now as then, the only difference being that now he *speaks* whereas then he *acted*: ' "I used to like kids – but I can't stand them any more . . . kinks and slant-eyed people. I didn't like them – and the CO didn't either." '[14] He seems to have had no difficulty in describing his behaviour during an episode in the days preceding the My Lai massacre: an old man had been brought to Calley; Grzesik, who knew Vietnamese, looked at his identity card and told Calley he didn't think he was a Vietcong:

> But it didn't matter; the first platoon hadn't had any contact with the enemy in weeks. Calley motioned Grzesik away with his M16. 'Why are you going to kill him?', Grzesik asked. Calley told him to 'get moving'. But before Calley could fire, Herbert Carter moved forward.
>
> Harry Stanley was ten feet away. During an interrogation in October 1969, he told the Army's main police unit, the Criminal Investigation Division (C.I.D.), what happened next. 'Carter hit the old man into a well, but the old man spread his arms and legs and held on and didn't fall . . . then Carter hit the old man in his stomach with his rifle stock. The old man's feet fell into the well, but he continued to hold on with his hands. Carter hit the man's fingers, trying to make him fall . . . and Calley shot the man with his M16.'
>
> Carter talked easily about the incident in an interview. 'Bergthold captured the old man,' he said. 'I was the one that threw him into the well. We tried to make him talk and he wouldn't. After we'd tried, I picked him up and threw him in the well – then Lieutenant Calley blew his brains out. I started to shoot him myself,' he added. 'I just said, "The hell with this tramp" – you know what I mean. He was a VC.'[15]

Though Hersh intimates that all these voices and stories had an effect on the speakers, this is not what is most important from the journalistic point of view. What matters is to *make them possible*, whatever they are and whatever length of time has passed since the actual events. Before 1969, he recalls at the beginning of his book, 'most GIs simply weren't talking about such things'.[16] 'Such things' are both violence suffered and violence inflicted; an 'otherness' which is only talked about afterwards, with a greater or lesser degree of distance. There had been letters from GIs to their families, at the time, which had described it.[17] Similarly, a soldier like Grzesik seems to have seen it very quickly, as if he had never been wholly inside. For Meadlo it took only a single night for him to see himself as the killer he had been – even if we only know his state of mind at that time from his own account of it some months later. Carter, on the other hand, seems never or hardly at all to emerge, even when he talks about it in front of Hersh, apparently for the first time. The journalist jolts the actors into beginning to see, whatever their starting point. He forces them to make their immersion the subject of a story, which reveals it and makes it visible in all its strangeness, which suddenly becomes apparent.

This process raises the question of the time at which one sees what one is doing, or rather what one did. There are moments of this type, which fall short of any narration, perhaps even any awareness – moments when the soldiers suddenly felt something, a suffering, or a rejection, without necessarily being able to formulate their feelings with any clarity. An example is the sudden distress of Meadlo, the day after, when he steps on a mine, and yells at Calley that he is about to pay for all that;[18] or when Roy Wood vomits.[19] Even Carter himself, according to the witnesses, at one point expressed the suffering of the immersion, a longing to stop: he suddenly shoots himself in the foot:

> Herb Carter and Harry Stanley had shed their gear and were taking a short break at the CP. Near them was a young Vietnamese boy, crying with a bullet wound in his stomach. Stanley watched one of Captain Medina's three radio operators walk along a trail toward them; he was without his radio gear. As Stanley told the C.I.D., the radio operator went up to Carter and said, 'Let me see your pistol.' Carter gave it to him. The radio operator 'then stepped within two feet of the boy and shot him in the neck with a pistol. Blood gushed from the child's neck. He then tried to walk off, but he could only take two or three steps. Then he fell onto the ground. He lay there and took four or five deep breaths and then he stopped breathing.' The radio operator turned to Stanley and said, 'Did you see how I shot that son of a bitch?' Stanley told him, 'I don't see how anyone could just kill a kid.' Carter got his pistol back; he told Stanley, 'I can't take this no more . . .' Moments later Stanley heard a gun go off and Carter yell. 'I went to Carter and saw he had shot himself in the foot. I think Carter shot himself on purpose.'[20]

Perhaps these are moments which precede even the possibility of seeing; in fact, they are described by others, seen from another standpoint than their own. This is why the plurality of the accounts is so important: it allows light to be shed on the blind spots of some by the statements of others. In this way the 'hidden' suffering of Carter, the perfect killer, emerges in accounts other than his own; conversely, it is Carter who describes the normal nonchalance, even enthusiasm, of many soldiers:

> Carter recalled that some GIs were shouting and yelling during the massacre: 'The boys enjoyed it. When someone laughs and jokes about what they're doing, they have to be enjoying it.' A GI said, 'Hey, I got me another one.' Another said, 'Chalk up one for me.' Even Captain Medina was having a good time, Carter thought: 'You can tell when someone enjoys their work.' Few members of Charlie Company protested that day. For the most part, those who didn't like what was going on kept their thoughts to themselves.[21]

It has to be recognized, however, that, in spite of the many complementary stories, the heart of the violence, its now-ness, escapes us. This

is inevitable; how could the lived experience of the massacre by its perpetrators, this experience invisible to them and recognized as such, finally be
seen, without this vision betraying, by definition, the very fact of its invisibility at the time? To see it would be to admit that you no longer see it as
it was then. Hersh, far from claiming to reach this 'inside', is himself conscious that all he can do, by stimulating these stories and providing a
forum for them, is get closer to them, approach them and convey their
inaccessible strangeness; and it is for this very reason that he goes so far,
perhaps as far as it is possible to go, in his decentring project: he does not
claim to tame this 'inside', or to make us see as if we had been there. He
respects the original rupture, he does not deny it, while establishing
beyond it a connection based on listening. He accepts the otherness of
present violence, instead of taming it in a transparent narrative. He decentres, accepting the frustration of those who decentre, who stop short of the
'other' so as to leave it 'other'. He makes us see that you cannot see violence in the present, that you can only imagine it, by listening to accounts
of it later, beyond the invisibility. Consequently, what we see are 'them'
today, who make us imagine what they were yesterday. But their 'otherness' of yesterday remains intact, unseen, merely brought a little closer.

Seymour Hersh chose a path that others would take after him: it
releases the voices of violence, after the event, to try to get a little closer
to the invisibility of violence as it is actually happening. Jean Hatzfeld,
who set out to listen to the victims and perpetrators of the genocide in
Rwanda, adopted the same method, and accepted, finally, that the
journalism of violence takes place as a journalism of after-violence,
re-creating the connection – the connection of speech – over and above
an original rupture which remains hidden from view.[22]

But why 'hidden from view'? Why can the decentring only take place
after the event? Why should this limitation be accepted? Why should we
not imagine a reporter who decentres in the present, who makes you see
the moment of the rupture, the moment when it eludes the eye, the
moment when it becomes 'other'? This is a contradiction, admittedly,
since to show is already to connect, hence to misrepresent the rupture;
but has no war reporter ever claimed to take up this supreme challenge
to the decentring journalist?

2. Michael Herr in Vietnam: violence as an impossible spectacle

The alternatives: the protected gaze or the death of the gaze

Let no one believe that the image has solved the problem of catching the
moment of violence. Otherwise, the work of war photographers would

no longer be so important; they, for their part, are well aware that the 'decentring' image, the one that suddenly, in a flash, catches the true intimacy of violence, far from being the norm, is an exception, a miracle. They seek the same things as the reporters of the written word, with other tools.

Nor should we forget that the war we are dealing with here was responsible for a very large number of images, by no means all of which have the 'decentring' power of the texts of Michael Herr. Like the photographers who accompanied him, Herr tried to grasp the very emergence of violence, a challenge which has made his writing a true drama and a major text on journalism.

Michael Herr was a 27-year-old journalist when he was sent to Vietnam, in the autumn of 1967, by *Esquire* magazine.[23] He remained there for two years. He was in the country at the time of the Tet offensive of January 1968 and also for the two and a half months of the siege of Khe San (finally evacuated in April 1968); he made three visits by helicopter to the besieged base, each lasting several days, taking the place of the co-pilot. He spent the summer of 1968 in Vietnam in the company of other journalists, including Sean Flynn (son of Errol) and Dana Stone.[24] 'The journalists' form an important theme in his work. His book *Dispatches*, which came out in 1977,[25] brought together articles which had largely been written at the front and then published on his return in *Esquire, Rolling Stone* and the *New American Review*,[26] together with some later reflections from the eight years following his period as a correspondent in Vietnam.

The writing of Herr constantly revolves around the following question: is a journalism of the *present of violence* possible? In fact, he constantly demonstrates that the spectacle of violence in the present is contradictory, because the experience of the violence makes it impossible to contemplate it. The gaze that can still fix on it is inevitably a protected gaze; hence it is, in a sense, a gaze that sees nothing – or at least, not what it ought to see or what it wanted to see. Really to see, a spectator would have to abandon his defences and surrender to the violence; but that would mean he would be swallowed up and submerged, so would abandon his position as spectator. In other words, the gaze would then be impossible, defeated, killed off. In fact in the face of violence, the journalist is forced to choose between two alternatives: a protected gaze or the death of the gaze.

Herr demonstrates the failure of the gaze in two ways. First, he complains that he is there to see, but that in practice he sees nothing: 'You know how it is, you want to look and you don't want to look . . . how often and how badly you needed protection from what you were seeing, had actually come 30,000 miles to see.'[27] It is as if there is a screen between him and the situations he 'sees'. Yet he also suggests that there are moments when this war at last 'enters' his eyes, but these are moments that are, strictly speaking, invisible – the descriptions are full of holes, they contain blanks; this 'entry' happens as if 'behind the eyes', and the 'visions' which result, he says, will only come later, in his night-mares or his anguished memories.

Herr's description of his first day at the front is in this regard pre-monitory. It gives notice of these alternatives from which there is no escape: either a gaze in the present that is necessarily protected – in order to safeguard what makes the position of spectator possible – or moments when the protection disappears, which might constitute a sort of victory of the gaze over its own defences, but which, in reality, mean that the gaze has been beaten and that nothing can now be seen. He writes, on his arrival:

> It was like a walk through a colony of stroke victims, a thousand men on a rainy airfield after too much of something I'd never really know, 'a way you'll never be', dirt and blood and torn fatigues, eyes that poured out a steady charge of wasted horror. I'd just missed the biggest battle of the war so far [Dak To, November 1967], I was telling myself that I was sorry, but it was right there all around me and I didn't even know it. I couldn't look at anyone for more than a second, I didn't want to be caught listening, some war cor-respondent, I didn't know what to say or do, I didn't like it already. When the rain stopped and the ponchos came off there was a smell that I thought was going to make me sick: rot, sump, tannery, open grave, dumpfire – awful, you'd walk into pockets of Old Spice that made it even worse. I wanted badly to find some place to sit alone and smoke a cigarette, to find a face that would cover my face the way my poncho covered my new fatigues.[28]

The passage begins with the complaint about his inability to see. Then, there is suddenly a smell, a terrible and unbearable presence of the war. It is not a vision – the sense of sight is badly handicapped in the face of violence. It is an immediate, overwhelming sensation of the intolerable reality. What does the reporter do? He moves away and looks for some-thing to cover his face, so as to stop it all and, especially, so as not to see. How else can this demand for 'a face that would cover my face' be inter-preted than as a desire to block sight, in the same way as the other senses? At the moment when the 'real' gaze at the reality of this war might come about, the reporter flees. He asks, to adopt the Orwellian metaphor of Claude Lefort, for an 'interposed body'.[29] It would not have been pos-sible to see it *while remaining a spectator*; by moving aside, the reporter protects himself so that he can remain the spectator of this war – a pro-tected and frustrated spectator, because there is no alternative.

Herr does not spare himself; he criticizes himself for what happens and mocks himself with bitter irony:

> I was there to watch. Talk about impersonating an identity, about locking into a role, about irony: I went to cover the war and the war covered me; an old story, unless of course you've never heard it. I went there behind the crude but serious belief that you had to be able to look at anything, serious because I acted on it and went, crude because I didn't know, it took the war to teach it, that you were as responsible for everything you saw as you were for everything you did. The problem was that you didn't always know what you were seeing until later, maybe years later, that a lot of it never made it at all; it just stayed stored there in your eyes. Time and information, rock and roll, life itself, the information isn't frozen, you are.[30]

The phrase 'the war covered me' seems to mean: it is the war that chooses what enters the eyes, and when 'it' enters. And 'it' often bears no relation, naturally, to what, as a reporter, he wants to see, a 'you want to look' which, Herr says, is mixed with an obscure and undeclared 'you don't want to look'.

One of the recurring themes of *Dispatches* is that 'it' does indeed enter, but afterwards, and through the door of what cannot be controlled, fantasy and, in particular, dreams. Like the soldiers, Herr admits that he dreamed afterwards, not at the time. And it is here, in this nightmarish interiority, that he at last *saw*:

> I'd watched grunts asleep putting out REMs[31] like a firefight in the dark, I'm sure it was the same with me. They'd say (I'd ask) that they didn't remember their dreams either when they were in the zone, but on R&R or in the hospital their dreaming would be constant, open, violent and clear, like a man in the Pleiku hospital on the night I was there . . . as for my own dreams, the ones lost there would make it through later, I should have known, some things will just naturally follow until they take. The night would come when they'd be vivid and unremitting, that night the beginning of a long string, I'd remember then and wake up half believing that I'd never really been in any of those places.[32]

In this passage he describes how, first, he 'sees' the others dream, without gaining access to their dreams, which in itself testifies to the intimacy of the rupture the actual experience of violence represented for them; his gaze is still protected and fails. Then he too 'sees', but truly this time, without defences, in private anguish. Only, this is no longer really a gaze, a conscious and reproducible spectacle of the sort journalists seek, but an oneiric spectacle, a vision he cannot make us share. Herr recognizes this himself, for example, when he describes the moment at which, in the middle of the fighting, he 'slid over to the wrong end of the story', that is, when 'I wasn't a reporter, I was a shooter'; it was then that he began to have these nocturnal visions, which are no longer the visions 'of a journalist':

> When we got back to the camp that night I threw away the fatigues I'd been wearing. And for the next six years I saw them all, the ones I'd really seen and the ones I'd imagined, theirs and ours, friends I'd loved and strangers, motionless figures in a dance, the old dance. Years of thinking this or that about what happens to you when you pursue a fantasy until it becomes an experience, and then afterwards you can't handle the experience. Until I felt I was just a dancer too.[33]

In fact, these visions are the very thing that it is impossible for a conscious spectator, for a journalist, to see: in reality, in the presence of the violence, they would not be tolerable, they would make you shut your eyes, they would do away with the spectator. Herr says this clearly in a scene where he is faced with the corpses of NVA prisoners and Vietcong suspects who had apparently lit a fire to cover an escape:

> The ARNV and a few Americans were shooting blindly into the flames, and the bodies were burning where they fell. Civilian dead lay out on the sidewalks only a block from the compound, and the park by the river was littered with dead. It was cold and the sun never came out once, but the rain did things to the corpses that were worse in their way than anything the sun could have done. It was on one of those days that *I realized that the only corpse I couldn't bear to look at would be the one I would never have to see.*[34]

So, says Herr, I am protected from the 'real' corpses; I don't have to be afraid of them, I see them without really seeing them because my gaze is protected. The things that are intolerable to see still enter, but by another route, and without my knowing it, through 'the door of fantasy', to use the expression of Lefort when discussing the torture inflicted on Winston in *Nineteen Eighty-Four*. They are things that you cannot really see because they are in contradiction with what a gaze implies; they would kill it and prevent it from operating; they are *impossible* for this gaze. This is both reassuring (seeing can do nothing to me, the gaze is protected by its very nature), hopeless (to see is to deploy a blocked gaze, a blind gaze) and terrifying (what eludes my protected gaze is what risks entering into me, tearing me apart and giving me unbearable visions later on).

These 'visions' which emerge in the after-violence do not in any way represent a sharing, an encounter finally achieved with the soldiers. Herr's pessimism is total. There is no encounter between all these beings in the grip of terrifying visions, which makes it even more unlikely, of course, that there would be an encounter between one of them, Herr himself, and a public completely 'outside', to whom he wants to make his visions visible. Fantasy and dreams are designated as the places where a true vision of war is achieved, afterwards, but they are impregnable citadels. Admittedly, Herr says that he understood later, in his memories and in his dreams, that 'they' – the soldiers, who had warned him – were right: 'What they say is totally true, it's funny the things you remember.'[35] And he feels the advent of a craziness which is the very same as the one he thought he had detected in them at the time, but been unable to confirm. However, the soldiers with whom he communicates in his dreams are phantoms, fantasy creatures. He is emphatic, furthermore, that all those who have spent some time at the front have similar stories in their heads, but they cannot *really* share them or talk about them together:

> After a year I felt so plugged in to all the stories and the images and the fear that even the dead started telling me stories, you'd hear them out of a remote but accessible space where there were no ideas, no emotions, no facts, no proper language, only clean information. However many times it happened, whether I'd known them or not, no matter what I'd felt about them or the way they'd died, their story was always there and it was always the same; it went, 'Put yourself in my place.'[36]

This is an ironic comment coming from a journalist: the 'information' is where the gaze is overtaken by fantasy; the reporter becomes aware of the 'story' only when the empirical data, the 'facts', are no longer of any importance. It is in his head. But at the same time, this story that he tells about himself is not a real encounter with those who had been there; it happens afterwards, inside his head, without a real exchange.

In fact, Herr seems not to believe in the link re-created after the event any more than he believes in the possibility of being linked to anyone at the moment of the rupture. This is why everyone remains strange to everyone else, in spite of this common experience, and the passage of time makes no difference. Everyone finds everyone else 'crazy', while going crazy themselves, and feeling the impossibility of communicating their own madness to the others:

> Going crazy was built into the tour, the best you could hope for was that it didn't happen around you, the kind of crazy that made men empty clips into strangers or fix grenades on latrine doors. That was *really* crazy; anything less was almost standard, as standard as the vague prolonged stares and involuntary smiles, common as ponchos or 16s or any other piece of war issue. If you wanted someone to know you'd gone insane you really had to sound off like you had a pair, 'Scream a lot, and all the time.'[37]

Ordinary craziness causes only a vague feeling of habit, bordering on indifference, and is not in any way, therefore, a connection or a communication; extraordinary craziness is met with incomprehension and anger.

There is, for example, a scene where some Marines see a little Vietnamese boy approaching their helicopter; he is badly disturbed, maddened by pain and by the violence which makes them mad too. They seem to have the same attitude towards him, and the same uncomprehending and self-protective gaze as that of Herr towards them. Although the scene ends with a gesture of affection on the part of one of the Marines, we are left in no doubt that it is impossible to envisage any real communication between all these various victims:

> We were only metres away from the worst of the fighting, not more than a Vietnamese city block in distance, and yet civilians kept appearing, smiling, shrugging, trying to get back to their homes. The Marines would try to menace them away at rifle point, shouting, 'Di, di, *di*, you sorry-ass motherfuckers, go on, get the hell away from here!' and the refugees would smile, half bowing, and flit up one of the shattered streets. A little boy of about ten came up to a bunch of Marines from Charlie Company. He was laughing and moving his head from side to side in a funny way. The fierceness in his eyes should have told everyone what he was, but it had never occurred to most of the grunts that a Vietnamese child could be driven mad too, and by the time they understood it the boy had begun to go for their eyes and tear at their fatigues, spooking everyone, putting everyone really uptight, until a black grunt grabbed him from behind and held his arm. 'C'mon, poor li'l baby, 'fore one a these grunt mothers shoots you', he said, and carried the boy to where the corpsmen were.[38]

Echoing the impossibility of encounters between them, there is also, of course, the failure of the journalist to enter very far into their inner worlds. It is all the more difficult in that his status as a spectator overprotects him. He watches them without establishing any personal connection. 'But of course we were intimate,' he writes ironically; 'I'll tell you how intimate: they were my guns, and I let them do it. I never let them dig my holes or carry my gear, there were always grunts who offered, but I let them do that for me while I watched, maybe for them, maybe not.'[39] He even admits to feeling disgusted by them: 'Disgust doesn't begin to describe what they made me feel, they threw people out of helicopters, tied people up and put the dogs on them.'[40] The tragedy of Herr, as he describes it, is that he remained a journalist, someone who *watched* them and who, for that very reason, remained remote from them and from their craziness, whether it was the result of violence suffered or violence inflicted (Herr deliberately confuses the two), protecting himself from it. Even later, when, in a way, he joins them in this madness, he will miss them again: afterwards, the solitude remains. This passage is particularly telling with regard to this unending solitude, both in the presence of violence and afterwards:

> 'We had this gook and we was gonna skin him' (a grunt told me), 'I mean he was already dead and everything, and the lieutenant comes over and says, "Hey asshole, there's a reporter in the TOC, you want him to come out and see that? I mean, use your fucking heads, there's a time and a place for everything . . ." '
>
> 'Too bad you wasn't with us last week' (another grunt told me, coming off a no-contact operation), 'we killed so many gooks it wasn't even funny.'
>
> Was it possible that they were there and not haunted? No, not possible, not a chance, I know I wasn't the only one. Where are they now? (Where am I now?) I stood as close to them as I could without leaving the planet.[41]

There is nothing to be done: you never get to them by looking, either in the presence of the violence, when the spectator, in order to see, protects himself (hence does not see), or afterwards, when the visions unfold in the solitude of trauma. The journalist is then first and foremost someone who is obsessed by the desire to see and to make people see, but who has nothing to show, because his protected gaze touches nothing of importance; then, with the passage of time, he is someone who sees at last, but can no longer show anything, submerged in fantasies he is unable to communicate. The reportage of Herr is a major text on journalistic blindness, that of his colleagues, but also his own.

The blindness of journalists

There are plenty of passages that mock some of Herr's colleagues. He obviously enjoys recording the stupid questions of the 'new boys', who are constantly mocked by the old hands, that is, by Herr himself and his colleagues, Tim Page, Dana Stone and Sean Flynn. We should note, however, that he portrays these old hands as already exhibiting a certain craziness – Tim Page, for example, scratches his face and dances about in a decidedly bizarre manner for the benefit of a new correspondent.[42] Above all, however, Herr notes that the journalists are, in general, the soldiers' best entertainment: 'Once in some thick jungle corner with some grunts standing around, a correspondent said, "Gee, you must really see some beautiful sunsets in here," and they almost pissed themselves laughing.'[43] In fact, it is the very status of journalist that is risible to the soldiers, the status of external 'spectator', there because he chooses to be. What can journalists possibly understand of the interiority or the logic of this war, or of what is going on inside the soldiers' heads? The best thing to do is laugh at them: 'There was a famous story, some reporters asked a door gunner, "How can you shoot women and children?" and he'd answered, "It's easy, you just don't lead 'em so much." '[44]

Herr is clearly trying to achieve another type of journalism, a journalism of 'compassion', to use his own word.[45] Yet this other model is itself constantly questioned during the course of the book, for example by the photographer Larry Burrows, whose work Herr refers to with genuine admiration. He describes him in action, taking risks, running across an airstrip to photograph the team of a Chinook helicopter which has just landed and is about to take off again with a load of wounded men and corpses. 'When it had gone he looked at me, and he seemed to be in the most open distress. "Sometimes one feels like such a bastard," he said.'[46] There is a distance, an impression of missing something, which, not only does not spare the 'best' but is perhaps felt by them alone; a sense of their failure, of their persistent blindness and of their inability to touch the core of the violence.

This explains the importance of the passages in which Herr describes the hatred the soldiers felt for the journalists. This hatred reveals the failure of the journalists to establish any sort of link with them, let alone any sharing. There are moments of apparent redemption, where the link seems, after all, to be there:

> Even the ones who preferred not to be in your company, who despised what your work required or felt that you took your living from their deaths, who believed that all of us were traitors and liars and the creepiest kinds of parasites, even they would cut back at the last and make their one concession to what there was in us that we ourselves loved most: 'I got to give it to you, you guys got balls.'[47]

But the next page leaves us in no doubt as to the illusory nature of this link. The truth is the rupture between the inside and the outside, and hence the failure of the journalist to be inside:

> They only hated me, hated me the way you'd hate any hopeless fool who would put himself through this thing when he had any choices, any fool who had no more need of his life than to play with it this way.
> 'You guys are crazy!' that Marine had said, and I know that when we flew off of Mutter's Ridge that afternoon he stood there for a long time and watched us out of sight with the same native loathing he'd shown us before, turning finally to whoever was around, saying it maybe to himself, getting out what I'd actually heard said once when a jeepload of correspondents had just driven away, leaving me there alone, one rifleman turned to another and giving us all his hard, cold wish:
> 'Those fucking guys,' he'd said. 'I hope they die.'[48]

Herr knows this only too well; in every journalist, even in those most anxious to break away from traditional journalism, there remains a propensity to cliché, itself linked to the inability to grasp the actuality of violence. For example, he notes the general inability of journalists, himself included, to see the war except as a film. When he recalls that it is in a film, *Catch-22*, that someone says 'in a war everybody thinks that everybody else is crazy', it is clear that he is mocking himself, he who is forever emphasising how every one is closed in on themselves and how impossible it is to penetrate the 'craziness' of others.[49] In other words, even in his confession of failure, there is still cliché and journalistic posing.

Further, though Tom Wolfe seems to see intimacy with the soldiers as one of Herr's strong points, the fact is that the limitations of this intimacy are constantly emphasized by Herr himself. Certainly, the article 'Khe Sanh', reprinted in the *The New Journalism*,[50] is one of the texts in which the reporter, by means of the dialogues, goes furthest in the use of empathy or intropathy. It should be noted, however, that these scenes are, in many ways, interludes, 'outside the violence'; the horror is evoked only after the event, not in the present. In any case, this encounter contains pitfalls, which constitute key moments in the article: there is always a risk that at some moment 'they' elude you and tip over into total strangeness.

The article begins with the portrait of a soldier who appears a total enigma, full of a pain which is wholly inaccessible. The soldier is a Marine who has spent five months in Khe Sanh. It looks, at first, as if Herr is going to make us share his memories. The Marine, he writes, remembered a happy period before the siege,

> when there was time to play in the streams below the plateau of the base, when all anybody ever talked about were the six shades of green that touched the surrounding hills, when he and his friends had lived like human beings, above ground, in the light, instead of like animals who were so spaced out that they began taking pills called Diarrhea-Aid to keep their walks to exposed latrines at a minimum.[51]

In fact this pseudo-memory is more like a semi-poetic, semi-ridiculous fantasy, a concoction of Herr's, a little flight of fancy which actually hides his inability to grasp the present of this individual, the intimacy of what he has become. The person before him is described only by details which may be precise but are all external and 'behaviourist' (the anti-diarrhoea pills). Herr describes his eyes, which are like those of the other Marines: 'always either strained or blazed-out or simply blank, they never had anything to do with what the rest of the face was doing, and it gave everyone the look of extreme fatigue or even a glancing madness.'[52] But we may note that he is hesitant in the description and the explanation (the frequent use of 'or'). These eyes say something very strange, nothing for certain.

And the puzzle only deepens. It is this Marine's last day of service in Vietnam. He is preparing to board one of the aircraft, and spends several dangerous minutes on the airstrip exposed to enemy fire. Herr describes the feeling common to all, in particular the journalists, who, after those moments of intense anguish, finally manage to fly out of Khe Sanh: 'If you were on board, that first movement was an ecstasy. You'd all sit there with empty, exhausted grins, covered with the impossible red dust that laterite breaks down to, dust like scales, feeling the delicious afterchill of the fear, that one quick convulsion of safety.'[53] 'You', that is, you and me; but not 'them', and in particular not 'him', the enigmatic Marine. He would refuse, or rather prove unable, to climb into the aircraft and leave. Herr describes in a wholly exterior and totally un-empathic way this inability to leave the hell of Khe Sanh. He does not leave, it is incomprehensible, but that is how it is. The other soldiers fluctuate between indifference, derision, feeling that he is crazy, and feeling that this is just part of the normality of this war: they tease him a little, then, without quite believing it, let him tell them yet again that he will be on the next plane.

And Herr ends this passage with the fact, once again, of his incomprehension, his failure to enter into this rupture, and his own self-protection. In which case, he, the journalist, who 'goes there', is perhaps no better than those Americans at home who 'would rather be told that their son is undergoing acute environmental reaction than to hear that he is suffering from shell shock, because they could no more cope with the fact of shell shock than they could face the reality of what had happened to this boy during his five months at Khe Sanh'.[54]

Making the 'I am unable to see' visible

What sort of journalism is possible, then, in the presence of violence? Herr's method consists – and here he is truly part of the New Journalism – in proposing a form of writing that is largely concerned with the very possibility of journalism, that is, with the relationship of journalism to its subject, and not with the subject alone.

Indeed, in many ways it is this failure to be what is expected of a journalist that forms the subject of Herr's reportages. The paradox is that what is most decentring in his writing is this permanent admission of failure, of failure to decentre. His 'I can't see' is essentially a sign of the trauma constituted by the direct presence of violence: it is a blindness which verges on renunciation (of being a journalist), that is, on the abandonment of all defences. It is a furthest point: Herr describes the ultimate moment for journalists, the moment when they contemplate their own blindness and know it to be insurmountable – because it is created by their own defences against the reality of violence – unless they capitulate.

Thus, in these distanced, behaviourist descriptions, which signal the inability to establish a link with the hidden pain of the soldiers, and so make their otherness something that decentres us, there is still something like a disturbing warning to his readers: this is the last gaze *possible*, Herr seems to be telling them, the one that comes just before one loses oneself in this unimaginable obscurity; I see nothing of 'them', but I tell you that I am not far from 'entering' them, on condition I myself slide over to the 'wrong end of the story'. I fail to connect you to them, but I tell you at what price I might succeed, that of the capitulation of my gaze – a capitulation Herr admits, in any case, is inevitable, the protections not being infallible; some things enter, except you don't know it until afterwards, in fantasies or dreams.

This explains the power of Herr's descriptions of impenetrable faces and strange behaviour, always unexpected, impervious to what is to 'us' unbearable and strangely attached to the very site of the suffering: 'These were the faces of boys whose whole lives seemed to have backed up on them, they'd be a few feet away but they'd be looking back at you over a distance you knew you'd never really cross.'[55] And further on: 'The living, the wounded and the dead flew together in crowded Chinooks, and it was nothing for guys to walk on top of the half-covered corpses packed in the aisles to get a seat, or to make jokes among themselves about how funny they all looked, the dumb dead fuckers.'[56] Or again:

> The Marines who worked the body detail were overloaded and rushed and became snappish, ripping packs off of corpses angrily, cutting gear away with bayonets, heaving bodies into the green bags. One of the dead Marines had gone stiff and they had trouble getting him to fit, '*Damn*', one of them said, 'this fucker had big feet. Didn't this fucker have big feet,' as he finally forced the legs inside.[57]

The plurivocality of the text, the 'it speaks', is the opposite of empathy or of an entry into 'them'. The words keep coming, but there is no exchange. Nothing changes the strangeness of this talking, laughing being, the Marine. It is the same relationship Herr establishes with himself, declaring that he scarcely understands what he has become: he sees that he, too, has a strange laugh, which patently resembles theirs;[58] but as long as he sees it, he doesn't see it, doesn't get it, still protects himself. He sees the before and the after of the rupture and the trauma, but the moment itself remains invisible: *he cannot see himself in the process of becoming like them*; *he cannot catch the moment of the rupture*.

At best, dare we say, there are extreme moments, moments of pure shock, like that on the first day, referred to above, when the smell gets to him and he tries to move away so that he can smoke a cigarette. These are moments when the *survival* of the spectator is at stake, which, conversely, reminds us that there can be no spectator except one who is protected, hence fails. As a result, these moments of shock are moments when the function of spectator is both fulfilled – at last it is entering the eyes – and threatened – it is entering me, through the nostrils or the eyes. It is the war that is watching me, 'covering' and recovering me. It is significant here that, on the day he is wounded, Herr feels his eyes with his hand, because it is there that you are really touched; if the eyes remain, the protection remains, and the spectator, and their failure, also remain.[59] They are all, like Herr, frightened of suddenly being watched by the war, which would mean no longer controlling it with this protected gaze which is their defence. This scene in a helicopter vividly evokes this anguish:

> When we went up, the wind blew through the ship and made the ponchos shake and tremble until the one next to me blew back in a fast brutal flap, uncovering the face. They hadn't even closed his eyes for him.
>
> The gunner started hollering as loud as he could, 'Fix it! Fix it!', maybe he thought the eyes were looking at him, but there wasn't anything I could do. My hand went there a couple of times and I couldn't, and then I did.[60]

These moments of shock are the final moments of the spectator's resistance to his spectacle; and what you see, even in these very moments, is still this resistance, certainly ultimately. As a result, it is still the resistance that is the subject of the reportage, because no gaze is possible beyond. One of the most revealing passages with regard to the intermingling of resistance and shock is perhaps this other scene in a helicopter:

> And across from me, ten feet away, a boy tried to jump out of the straps and then jerked forward and hung there, his rifle barrel caught in the red plastic webbing of the seat back. As the chopper rose again and turned, his weight went back hard against the webbing and a dark spot the size of a baby's hand showed in the centre of his fatigue jacket. And it grew – I knew what it was, but not really – it got up to his armpits and then started down

his sleeves and up over his shoulders at the same time. It went all across his waist and down his legs, covering the canvas on his boots until they were dark like everything else he wore, and it was running in slow, heavy drops off of his fingertips. I thought I could hear the drops hitting the metal strip on the chopper floor. Hey! . . . Oh, but this isn't anything at all, it's not real, it's just some thing they're going through that isn't real. One of the door gunners was heaped on the floor like a cloth dummy. His hand had the bloody raw look of a pound of liver fresh from the butcher paper. We touched down on the same lz we had just left a few minutes before, but I didn't know it until one of the guys shook my shoulder, and then I couldn't stand up. All I could feel of my legs was their shaking, and the guy thought I'd been hit and helped me up. The chopper had taken eight hits, there was shattered plastic all over the floor, a dying pilot up front, and the boy was hanging forward in the straps again, he was dead, but not (I knew) really dead.[61]

The scene appears unreal to Herr right to the end; he does not *see* it and tells us so. Yet the scene affects him, to the point where he seems to have been 'hit' – an expression which might well indicate the fact that the defences of the gaze had been penetrated, that 'it had entered', even if this does not take the form of a visible wound. But he does not see *what hits him*; the text is as if holed, divided into two sequences in which the resistances are operating (protected gaze), traversed by the moment of the shock which itself remains invisible (death of the gaze). This happened, but it is not visible, precisely because it destroys the defences of the gaze.

Thus the spectator can only watch himself *being unable to see*, or, if he saw, to the point of self-destruction, watch himself *having seen, that is, having succumbed*, and then describe this after-violence which has at its core a blind spot, that of the moment of the trauma. He sees nothing, or else he sees the incomprehensible 'afterwards', a sign of all he could not see in the present. He sees, for example, this man who never stops talking and who makes him know that there *had been* something invisible and impossible to grasp:

I turned to walk some other way and there was a man standing in front of me. He didn't exactly block me, but he didn't move either. He tottered a little and blinked, he looked at me and through me, no one had ever looked at me like that before. I felt a cold fat drop of sweat start down the middle of my back like a spider, it seemed to take an hour to finish its run. The man lit a cigarette and then sort of slobbered it out, I couldn't imagine what I was seeing. He tried again with a fresh cigarette. I gave him the light for that one, there was a flicker of focus, acknowledgement, but after a few puffs it went out too, and he let it drop to the ground. 'I couldn't spit for a week up there,' he said, 'and now I can't fucking stop.'[62]

This picture is significant at a number of levels. Once again, there is a moment of shock, of threat for the spectator, which takes the form of a look directed at the journalist, a look that is unbearable, that runs right through him; he can almost no longer look, so much is he looked at. Ultimately, however, there is failure; protection and distance take over, and the journalist remains outside this man whose story is not told, but remains beyond reach of the eyes. The journalist is restored to his position as blind spectator. There is a brief exchange when Herr gives the soldier a light, but that is all; the description is unable to get beyond the behaviourist notations; it does not really get at the man who comes from the horror; there is no meeting.

Similarly, in this scene of execution, when Herr says that he watches for a long time without seeing, before finally seeing something, it is evident that he once again sees only a face from after the event, leaving the actuality of the successive scenes of violence invisible:

> Once I looked at them strung from the perimeter to the treeline, most of them clumped together nearest the wire, then in smaller numbers but tighter groups midway, fanning out into lots of scattered points nearer the treeline, with one all by himself half into the bush and half out. 'Close but no cigar,' the captain said, and then a few of his men went out there and kicked them all in the head, thirty-seven of them. Then I heard an M-16 on full automatic starting to go through clips, a second to fire, three to plug in a fresh clip, and I saw a man out there, doing it. Every round was like a tiny concentration of high-velocity wind, making the bodies wince and shiver. When he finished he walked by us on the way back to his hootch, and I knew I hadn't seen anything until I saw his face. It was flushed and mottled and twisted like he had his face skin on inside out, a patch of green that was too dark, a streak of red running into bruise purple, a lot of sick grey white in between, he looked like he'd had a heart attack out there. His eyes were rolled up half into his head, his mouth was sprung open and his tongue was out, but he was smiling. Really a dude who'd shot his wad. The captain wasn't too pleased about my having seen that.[63]

What has happened, what has produced these strange marks on his face, this rupture and this immersion in an unfathomable alterity has eluded the spectator.

There is no solution, Herr seems to say. Even if all the technical conditions were fulfilled, there would be no spectacle of the present of violence. You cannot see the moment when the eyes are fully penetrated and wounded, the moment prefiguring 'visions' which will only be revealed months later, in the nightmarish confinement of fantasy and dreams.

The journalism which takes violence as its subject pushes the decentring approach to danger point: can the otherness constituted by violence really be represented, made visible to a public that 'wasn't there', when this otherness is actually characterized by an invisibility for those who 'are there'?

The figure of Michael Herr represents the admitted failure of journalism in the presence of violence. The decentring journalist records his limitations and capitulates; unless we believe that what decentres, in spite of everything, in the writing of Herr, is the very fact that it demonstrates this failure, perhaps the only way of 'showing' an invisible otherness . . .

Seymour M. Hersh points to another way, that of after-violence, when, in spite of everything, a link can be established between 'them' and 'us', beyond an original rupture that is never denied or covered up. It is also, in a way, a confession of failure, or at least the recognition, echoing that of Herr, that the present of violence remains impossible to see. The afterwards is then a site of voices and images, suggested and reconstructed, which accept that they are separated by time from the actual violence. But the work of Hersh transcends the despair of Herr, for whom the time of after-violence, too, is a time of failure and solitude, since the survivors – victims or perpetrators – remain strangers to each other, confined in their inner, nightmarish and incommunicable spectacle. Hersh, who, unlike Herr, had not himself directly experienced the events he describes, suggests the possibility of an encounter afterwards, an encounter which does not pretend that the element of incommunicability has entirely disappeared; indeed, it is for this very reason, that is, because it still assumes an element of 'mystery', that this encounter decentres us.

Conclusion

This brings me to the end of my brief personal and political history of modern journalism. My hope is that it has contributed to a better understanding, on the one hand of the great founding act of this journalistic 'modernity', born with the invention of reporting at the end of the nineteenth century, the act of *unifying*, and on the other of the hidden sites of resistance, those recesses where, against the dominant journalism, reporters struggle to *decentre* their readers.

A gallery of portraits is always frustrating. By attracting attention to some faces, it distracts attention from others – though they are there, behind those on which the light falls. I can only hope that it will lead to others being studied, and other aspects of this unjustly ignored history of journalism being brought out of the shadows. This conclusion is thus more of an appeal not to conclude, and for this gallery of figures to be expanded as a result of further studies. I hope that my work will be completed and that it will be challenged. And that it will be used; most of all, I hope it will have meaning for those who practise journalism, or wish to do so.

If I am to be honest, however, this modestly expressed hope, as with most people sufficiently monomaniacal to devote several years of their life to a subject, conceals a wholly immodest ambition: that is, to pave the way for a real *critique* of journalism. Theodor Adorno said that critical thought contained a 'utility', which is to be 'against the justification of what happens to be established'.[1] It has to be admitted that many 'critiques' of journalism today, in spite, or perhaps because, of their vehemence, belong, in their way, to 'what happens to be established', and take their place alongside an 'established' journalism that is denounced, but perhaps not questioned with the depth of a critique worthy of the name. It is time to try a different approach: to enter into the historical reality of journalism and to develop concrete tools, in this sense truly critical, to analyse it. I would like to think that I have contributed to this.

To dip into the history of journalism and to develop concrete 'figures' is, of course, to risk abandoning simple judgements. My figures probably raise as many questions as they answer. Some of them even evince true crises, and crystallize uncertainties and anxieties among journalists who are without illusions as to their role and their limitations. These 'witness-ambassadors', these journalists who *unify in conflict*, by inflicting a test on the 'we', are far from simple, that is, far from easy to judge. They cut short any contempt on principle for unifying journalism; to be more precise, they emphasize the complexity of the political act of unifying. Yet they seem to me to be necessary reference points for any critique of the aims of 'consensus' journalism, that is, any critique that wishes to be concrete and to remain in touch with the historical reality of modern journalism. Similarly, an appeal for a journalism that is, at last, decentring will serve little purpose if it fails to appreciate the scale of the intrinsic difficulty of the act of decentring: that is, if it fails to grasp its complexity, which I hope my figures will help readers to see and to appreciate. Decentring is, in practice, a risky process.

In fact, to discuss journalism by developing 'figures', critical figures, reveals it to be a more complex activity than might appear. But perhaps this is necessary for it to become a subject for political philosophy. Less transparent and less peremptory than heavy sighs and pamphlets, Séverine, Nellie Bly, Albert Londres, Edward R. Murrow, Lincoln Steffens, Norman Mailer, Marc Kravetz, George Orwell, Seymour M. Hersh and Michael Herr enable us, above all, to study the journalism that is aware of the importance of its political role in democracy, that is, is sensitive to a twofold requirement: to form a community and create an 'us', and to sustain the conflict without which democracy dies. Each of these figures represents an attempt to keep these two processes going in tandem, without glossing over the difficulties. Each of them, finally, makes it possible to revitalize the debate, to return to it again and again, so that we gain a deeper understanding of the infinite need that democracy represents, and so that journalism is elevated to a crucial place in this democracy only on condition that it embraces the fundamental anxiety that characterizes democracy itself.

Notes

Introduction

1 Cornu, *Journalisme et Vérité*, pp. 200–1.
2 I have taken these figures from Schudson, *Discovering the News*, pp. 13–14.
3 Balle, *Médias et Sociétés*, pp. 76–7.
4 Schudson, *Discovering the News*.
5 Palmer, *De Petits Journaux aux Grandes Agences*; Ferenczi, *L'Invention du Journalisme en France*.
6 See the chapter entitled 'The Culture Industry: Enlightenment as Mass Deception' (pp. 120–67) in Adorno and Horkheimer, *Dialectic of Enlightenment*.
7 See e.g. Adorno, 'Television and the Patterns of Mass Culture'.
8 Marcuse, *One Dimensional Man*.
9 Habermas, *The Structural Transformation of the Public Sphere*.
10 Bourdieu, *On Television and Journalism*, p. 44.
11 Ibid., p. 72.
12 Ibid., p. 44.
13 Muhlmann, *Du Journalisme en Démocratie*.

Chapter 1   Unifying and Decentring in Modern Journalism

1 See Schudson, *Discovering the News*; Schiller, *Objectivity and the News*; Mindich, *Just the Facts*.
2 Schudson, *Discovering the News*, p. 14.
3 *New York Sun*, 28 June 1838; quoted in Hughes, *News and the Human Interest Story* (1940), p. 160.
4 *New York Herald*, 6 May 1835; quoted in Hughes, *News and the Human Interest Story*, pp. 15–16.
5 J. Gordon Bennett, article of 15 Feb. 1837; quoted in Schiller, *Objectivity and the News*, p. 51.
6 *New York Herald*, 6 May 1835; quoted in Hughes, *News and the Human Interest Story*, pp. 10–11. This extract comes immediately before the sentence

quoted above in which Bennett affirms his desire to unite 'the great mass of the community'.

7 Schiller, *Objectivity and the News*, p. 75.
8 Quoted in Hughes, *News and the Human Interest Story*, p. 74.
9 Steffens, *Autobiography*, p. 179.
10 Hughes, *News and the Human Interest Story*, p. 89.
11 See Park, 'News and the Human Interest Story', Introduction to Hughes, *News and the Human Interest Story*; repr. in *Collected Papers of R. E. Park*, vol. 3, pp. 105–14.
12 This text is printed as an appendix to Pigeat, *Médias et Déontologie*.
13 See Pigeat, *Médias et Déontologie*. The author reminds us that the American conception of freedom of expression is naturally the one most reluctant to produce restrictive legislation (the First Amendment to the American Constitution affirms the prohibition on limiting freedom of expression by law), whereas in France the Declaration of the Rights of Man and the Citizen of 26 Aug. 1789 states that 'the free communication of ideas and opinions is one of the most precious rights of man. Every citizen may, accordingly, speak, write and print with freedom, but shall be responsible for such abuses of this freedom as shall be defined by law.' But this has not prevented American jurisprudence from gradually developing a casuistical reflection on the way the media should honour this requirement for truth: this is, indeed, the purpose of the famous libel laws. In France, the law of 1881, which fixed limits to free expression from the outset, was not focused primarily on the question of the truth of the information. But this requirement increasingly came to the fore, for example in the Loi Gayssot of 1991, which forbade the expression of any opinion denying the fact of Nazi genocide. In sum, as a general rule, the law is increasingly favourable towards this requirement to provide the public with the truth to which it is entitled, a requirement evident in the proliferation of ethical codes within the profession of journalism in both America and Europe.
14 These two texts are printed as appendixes to both Cornu, *Journalisme et Vérité*, and Pigeat, *Médias et Déontologie*.
15 This encyclical is quoted, in particular, by Pigeat, *Médias et Déontologie*.
16 The Declaration is printed as an appendix to Cornu, *Journalisme et Vérité*.
17 Cornu, *Journalisme et Vérité*, pp. 360–1. Cornu recalls, e.g., that in the 'Journalist's Charter' established in 1918 by the French National Union of Journalists, the journalists claim 'the freedom to publish their information fairly'.
18 'While arguments about objectivity are endless, the concept of fairness is something that editors and reporters can easily understand and pursue,' we read in this code. It is printed as an appendix to Pigeat, *Médias et Déontologie*.
19 Tuchman, 'Objectivity as Strategic Ritual'.
20 Ibid., p. 664.
21 Ibid., p. 665.
22 Ibid., pp. 666–7.
23 For the Fairness Doctrine, see Cornu, *Journalisme et Vérité*, pp. 225–6.

24 Stephens, *A History of News*, p. 267.
25 Ibid., p. 268.
26 Schudson, *The Power of News*, p. 13.
27 The third verse of a poem published on 24 May 1845 in *Subterranean*; quoted in Schiller, *Objectivity and the News*, p. 87.
28 Schiller devotes several pages to this metaphor of photography, and in particular to the influence of the daguerreotype. For this article of 1848, see ibid., p. 88.
29 Angenot, *Parole Pamphlétaire*, p. 35.
30 Ibid., p. 39.
31 Ibid.
32 Ibid., p. 36.
33 Ibid.
34 Bernanos, *Lettres aux Anglais*, 38; quoted in Angenot, *Parole Pamphlétaire*, p. 81.
35 Angenot, *Parole Pamphlétaire*, p. 81.
36 Ibid., p. 74.
37 Genette, 'Frontières du Récit'.
38 Ibid., pp. 64–5.
39 Ibid., p. 66.
40 The fact that the story is fundamentally concerned with the gaze is confirmed by Genette's lengthy discussion of the methods of 'focusing' in the story: 'Discours du Récit'.
41 Séverine, *Choix de Papiers*.
42 Schudson, *Discovering the News*, p. 6.
43 Lippmann and Merz, 'A Test of the News'.
44 See ch. 4 below.
45 Daston, 'Objectivity and the Escape from Perspective'.
46 Nagel, *The View from Nowhere*.
47 Epstein, *News from Nowhere*.
48 The strongly 'unifying' character of events shown in televised images is analysed, in particular, in Dayan and Katz, *Media Events*.
49 Rather, *The Camera Never Blinks*.
50 The programme was broadcast in Nov. 1999 by the BBC, then in a score of other countries. These 'revelations' set off a chain reaction, as the agency was shaken by new accusations in Sept. 2001. See esp. *Le Monde*, 2–3 Sept. 2001, p. 13.
51 Wallraff, *Lowest of the Low*.
52 Derrida and Stiegler, *Echographies of Television*, pp. 97–8.
53 Ibid., p. 98.
54 Ibid., pp. 91–2.
55 Ibid., p. 94.
56 Dulong, *Le Témoin Oculaire*, p. 27.
57 J. Gordon Bennett, *New York Herald*, Apr. 1836; quoted by Hughes, *News and the Human Interest Story*, p. 11.
58 Plenel, *Un Temps de Chien*, 1996 edn, p. 157.
59 Ibid.

60 Ibid., p. 186.
61 Plenel, *La Part d'Ombre*, 1994 edn, p. 67.
62 See ch. 3 below.
63 Plenel, *La Part d'Ombre*, 1994 edn, p. 118.
64 Ibid., p. 58, my emphasis.

Chapter 2   An Archetype of the Witness-Ambassador

1   See Maitron, *Le Mouvement Anarchiste en France*.
2   See Le Garrec, *Séverine*. Another romanticized biography, written in the first person, has since appeared: Gaillard, *Séverine*.
3   Le Garrec, *Séverine*, p. 168.
4   Ibid., pp. 170–1.
5   Ibid., pp. 190–1.
6   The heading for Séverine's column in *Le Petit Bleu* was 'The Courtroom Impressions of Séverine at the Criminal Court'.
7   She had already used this phrase for a collection of articles published in 1894.
8   Séverine, 'Chose jugée', *La Fronde*, 12 Sept. 1899, my emphasis.
9   *Le Petit Bleu*, 17 Feb. 1989.
10 'Notes d'une frondeuse': 'Semailles', *La Fronde*, 4 Sept. 1899.
11 'Notes d'une frondeuse': 'Pipelets!', *La Fronde*, 1 Sept. 1899.
12 'Notes d'une frondeuse': 'Le Byzantinisme de Général Mercier', *La Fronde*, 14 Aug. 1899, my emphasis.
13 'Notes d'une frondeuse': 'En réponse', *La Fronde*, 22 Aug. 1899, my emphasis, intended to bring out this new opposition between the 'meditative' and the 'passionate', which in fact repeats the earlier opposition between the 'rhetoricians' and the 'witnesses'.
14 'Notes d'une frondeuse': 'L'École de Picquart', *La Fronde*, 27 Aug. 1899.
15 'Notes d'une frondeuse': 'En réponse', *La Fronde*, 22 Aug. 1899.
16 'Notes d'une frondeuse': 'L'Œuvre', *La Fronde*, 17 Aug. 1899.
17 'Les impressions d'audience de Séverine à la Cour d'assises', *Le Petit Bleu*, 10 Feb. 1898.
18 *Le Petit Bleu*, 8 Feb. 1898, my emphasis.
19 Ibid., 9 Feb. 1898.
20 'Notes d'une frondeuse': 'Par délégation', *La Fronde*, 15 Aug. 1899.
21 The joy, that is, of seeing Maître Labori alive, a few days later, in court.
22 'Notes d'une frondeuse': 'Coup manqué', *La Fronde*, 23 Aug. 1899.
23 'Notes d'une frondeuse': 'Les leurs! . . . Les nôtres!', *La Fronde*, 2 Sept. 1899.
24 'Notes d'une frondeuse': 'L'Adieu aux Amis', *La Fronde*, 9 Sept. 1899.
25 Ibid., my emphasis.
26 Durand, 'Leurs témoins', my emphasis.
27 Séverine, 'L'Homme', *La Fronde*, 8 Aug. 1899, my emphasis.
28 Séverine, 'Les Bons Gîtes', *La Fronde*, 12 Aug. 1899.
29 'Notes d'une frondeuse': 'Semailles', *La Fronde*, 4 Sept. 1899.
30 'Notes d'une frondeuse': 'L'école de Picquart', *La Fronde*, 27 Aug. 1899.

31 'Le Procès d'Émile Zola: deuxième audience'; 'Envers et contre tous!', *La Fronde*, 9 Feb. 1898.

32 'Notes d'une frondeuse': 'Pourquoi?', *La Fronde*, 21 Aug. 1899.

33 Séverine, *Notes d'Une Frondeuse*, p. 6.

34 Quoted by Séverine in 'Notes d'une frondeuse': 'Chevalerie', *La Fronde*, 29 Aug. 1899.

35 Bellet, *Jules Vallès*, p. 119.

36 Ibid., p. 251.

37 Ibid., p. 352.

38 Séverine, *Notes d'Une Frondeuse*, p. 9.

39 Ibid., p. 6.

40 The expression is interesting: the caryatid, statue of a female figure supporting an entablature on her head, seems here to represent, for Séverine, a denaturing of femininity. Woman, in the form of the caryatid, is represented as strong, virile and very remote from the sensitive body which, for Séverine, constituted the feminine privilege of access to universality (in particular that of suffering).

41 'Lafargue et Cie', in Séverine, *Pages Rouges*, pp. 250–6; quotation on p. 252. This article is reprinted in Séverine, *Choix de Papiers*, pp. 81–7.

42 Maitron, *Le Mouvement Anarchiste en France*, pp. 230ff.

43 Born Caroline Rémy, the future Séverine made a bourgeois marriage at the age of 17 to a certain Henri Montrobert, by whom she had one child. Raped by her husband, she separated from him, sought refuge with her parents, then formed a relationship with Adrien Guebhardt, son of a rich widow of Swiss origins, by whom Caroline (who also called herself Line) was employed as a teaching assistant. They had a child, born in secrecy and registered as 'mother unknown' in Brussels in 1880. It was during this visit to Brussels that Line and Adrien met Vallès, a few months before the promulgation of the law of 11 July 1880 authorizing the return to France of former Communards. When Vallès returned to Paris, Guebhardt offered financial assistance towards the revival of the *Cri du Peuple*, whose first issue appeared on 27 Oct. 1883. Line signed her first article 'Séverin', before definitively feminizing the name for her second article. Séverine was one of the first beneficiaries of the Loi Naquet on divorce, in 1884, which enabled her to make a second marriage to Adrien.

44 'À Séverine', Paris, 1 Dec. 1883, first page of Vallès, *La Rue à Londres*; repr. in Vallès, *Œuvres*, vol. 2, pp. 1133–4.

45 Séverine, Letter to Vallès, 25 Dec. 1882, in Vallès, *Correspondance avec Séverine*, p. 49.

46 Articles of 12 and 19 Feb. 1865, in *Le Courier du Dimanche*; repr. in Vallès, *Œuvres*, vol. 1, pp. 501–10, and quoted in Bellet, *Jules Vallès*, p. 89.

47 Bellet, *Jules Vallès*, pp. 349–50.

48 Ibid., p. 206. These hopes pinned on journalistic writing, as opposed to the Book, as likely to accompany or even stimulate a new collective life, can already be seen in the writings of the revolutionaries of 1789: see Muhlmann, *Du Journalisme en Démocratie*, ch. 6.

49 Bellet, *Jules Vallès*, p. 223.

50 *La Rue*, 7 Dec. 1879, signed 'Jacques Vingtras'; repr. in Vallès, *Œuvres*, vol. 2, pp. 397–402, and quoted in Bellet, *Jules Vallès*, p. 63.

51 Bellet notes that in 1866, in an article for *Le Figaro*, Vallès hailed Timothée Trimm, the famous reporter of *Le Petit Journal*, as the figure of happy 'decadence', who broke with the 'solemn epochs'. Bellet seems to think that the failure of Vallès' attempt to join *Le Petit Journal* that year was attributable only to disagreements of a financial nature: Bellet, *Jules Vallès*, p. 80.

52 Letter to Arnould, Nov. 1876, quoted in Bellet, *Jules Vallès*, p. 412.

53 'L'Affiche rouge', *Le Cri du Peuple*, 7 Jan. 1884; repr. in Vallès, *Œuvres*, vol. 2, pp. 1102–5, and quoted in Bellet, *Jules Vallès*, p. 373.

54 'Vive la République', *Le Réveil*, 13 Jan. 1878; repr. in Vallès, *Œuvres*, vol. 2, pp. 95–7, and quoted in Bellet, *Jules Vallès*, p. 414.

55 *Le Cri du Peuple*, 22 Mar. 1871; quoted in Bellet, *Jules Vallès*, p. 390.

Chapter 3   Unifying through a Test

1 Bly, *Ten Days in a Mad-House*, p. 98.

2 Kroeger, *Nellie Bly*, pp. 98–9.

3 For the different types of urban reporting in the late nineteenth century in the United States, that is, beat reporting, stunt reporting, exposure reporting, etc., see Lindner, *The Reportage of Urban Culture*. The 'literature of exposure', as explained by Louis Filler, is the generic name given to this popular journalism by those who were generally contemptuous of it: Filler, *The Muckrakers*, p. 10.

4 It was the then president of the United States, Theodore Roosevelt, who invented the expression 'muckraker' in a speech delivered on 14 Apr. 1906. His feelings towards these journalists were mixed; they had inspired a progressive movement to which he himself belonged, but he was critical of them for going too far, to the point of fomenting 'revolutionary feeling'. The word 'muckraker' was therefore in his eyes pejorative, even if it was later turned into a compliment by those principally concerned and by those claiming to be their heirs. Roosevelt's speech is reproduced in Hofstadter (ed.), *The Progressive Movement*, pp. 18–19.

5 Park, 'The Natural History of the Newspaper', p. 102; Filler, *The Muckrakers*, p. 29.

6 See ch. 1 above.

7 Brooke Kroeger, author of what remains the fullest biography of Nellie Bly, explains that Annie Laurie and another 'sob sister', Dorothy Dix, were the heirs of Nellie Bly: *Nellie Bly*, p. 459.

8 There was for a long time a certain vagueness about her date of birth. In 1936, Ishbel Ross, in the section devoted to Nellie Bly in her *Ladies of the Press*, still gave the date as 1867. It was Bly herself who was responsible for this confusion, because at the time of her 'world tour' (which we will discuss later), in 1888–9, she was very anxious to present herself as younger than she really was, 24 then being considered rather old for a woman to undertake such a venture; so she knocked three years off her age: Kroeger, *Nellie Bly*, p. 145.

9 Dickens, *American Notes*, pp. 92–3.

10 Bly, *Ten Days in a Mad-House*.

11 Kroeger, *Nellie Bly*, p. 101.

12 E.g., Fannie B. Merrill: Kroeger, *Nellie Bly*, p. 101.

13 In addition to the articles she submitted during her world tour, she published a book about her journey a few months after her return: *Nellie Bly's Book: Around the World in Seventy-Two Days*.

14 For some years now, the long unknown figure of Nellie Bly has been the subject of more frequent studies in the United States, often focused on the issue of the position of women in the journalistic profession, which is not my concern here. A pioneer in this regard was Ishbel Ross (*Ladies of the Press*). A documentary on Nellie Bly was made by Christine Lesiak in 1996 and broadcast on French TV in 2000. The popular, even legendary, nature of Nellie Bly is revamped to suit contemporary taste on an Internet site devoted to her and in short popularizing books such as Charles Fredeen's Lerner Biography, *Nellie Bly: Daredevil Reporter*.

15 Bly, *Ten Days in a Mad-House*, pp. 5–6.

16 Bly says she wants to give 'a plain and unvarnished narrative of the treatment of the patients therein and the methods of management': ibid., p. 5.

17 Ibid., p. 6.

18 Ibid., p. 8.

19 Ibid. She mentions only one doctor who is more suspicious, and therefore an exception.

20 Ibid., p. 44.

21 Ibid., p. 35.

22 Ibid., p. 12.

23 Ibid., p. 67.

24 Ibid., p. 98, my emphasis.

25 Ibid., p. 28.

26 Ibid., p. 45.

27 In her description of this scene, Nellie Bly is unclear, admittedly, whether he is a colleague; she refers simply to 'a gentleman who had known me personally for years': ibid., p. 76. It is Kroeger who says that the man was a reporter: Kroeger, *Nellie Bly*, p. 93. In any case, there is between them a complicity worthy of those who are wholly 'ours', perfect representatives of the public.

28 Bly, *Ten Days in a Mad-House*, p. 72.

29 Ibid., p. 94.

30 Ibid., p. 56.

31 Ibid., p. 67.

32 Ibid., p. 73.

33 Ibid., p. 86.

34 Ibid., p. 87.

35 Ibid.

36 Ibid., p. 63, my emphasis.

37 Boltanski also distinguishes a third topic, 'the aesthetic topic', which I will not discuss here.

38 Boltanski, *Distant Suffering*, p. 19.

39 Ibid., p. 64.
40 Ibid., p. 70.
41 Ibid., p. 80.
42 Ibid., ch. 6, is devoted to a critique of sentimentalism.
43 Bly, *Ten Days in a Mad-House*, p. 75.
44 Ibid.
45 Ibid., pp. 51–2.
46 Ibid., p. 48.
47 Ibid., p. 66.
48 Ibid., pp. 72–3.
49 Ibid., p. 71.
50 Ibid., p. 58.
51 Ibid., p. 77.
52 Ibid., p. 90.
53 Ibid.
54 Ibid., p. 84.
55 Ibid., p. 88.
56 Ibid., p. 33.
57 Ibid., p. 21.
58 Ibid., p. 60.
59 Ibid., p. 76.
60 Ibid., p. 68.
61 Ibid., p. 59.
62 Londres, *Terre d'Ébène*, p. 10.
63 Ibid., pp. 259–60.
64 *Chemin de Buenos Aires: La Traite des Blanches* (1927), in Londres, *Œuvres Complètes*, p. 442.
65 Londres, *Chez les Fous*, in *Œuvres Complètes*.
66 See Assouline, *Albert Londres*, ch. 22: 'Chez les Fous'.
67 'A madman should not be bullied, but cared for': Londres, *Chez les Fous*, in *Œuvres Complètes*, p. 242.
68 Ibid., p. 200.
69 Ibid., pp. 201–2.
70 Ibid., p. 199.
71 Ibid., p. 212.
72 Ibid., ch. 8: 'Ces Messieurs du Docteur Dide'; ch. 9: 'L'Armoire aux cerveaux'.
73 Assouline, *Albert Londres*, ch. 17, esp. p. 238: 'obeying only his eye and his heart, he forgot to be militant'. The reportage of Londres, which finally appeared in *L'Éclair* on 13 Apr. 1923, offers no 'clear-cut' take on the situation in the Ruhr. Londres describes a country that is certainly Francophobe, but pretty, welcoming and not unduly hard, either for the occupiers or for the occupied. This passage, for example, must have frustrated the anti-Poincaré party on *Le Quotidien*: 'At the corner of a street, three French soldiers, with a light machine gun on the ground, in its case, stand guard. "Hard here, is it?" "Oh!", say the lads, without much conviction': Londres, 'Au Pays de l'Ersatz'.

74 Assouline, *Albert Londres*, p. 32.
75 Ibid., p. 281.
76 Londres, *Terre d'Ébène*, pp. 175–6.
77 Folléas, *Putain d'Afrique!*, p. 59.
78 Londres, *Au Bagne*, in *Œuvres Complètes*, p. 27.
79 As noted by Didier Folléas: *Putain d'Afrique!*, p. 51.
80 'You couldn't have found anyone more negro than Birama': Londres, *Terre d'Ébène*, p. 194.
81 Ibid., pp. 37–8.
82 Ibid., p. 18.
83 Ibid., p. 31.
84 Ibid.
85 Ibid., p. 24.
86 Ibid., pp. 70–1.
87 This metaphor opens ch. 17.
88 Ibid., p. 126.
89 Londres, *Dans la Russie des Soviets*, 1993 edn, p. 31.
90 For a study of various journeys to the USSR by French intellectuals, see Hourmant, *Au Pays de l'Avenir Radieux*. Hourmant emphasizes that, in the first years of the establishment of the Soviet regime, the atmosphere in France was violently anti-Communist ('The laudatory gaze was not at that date the norm. There was no shortage of hostile witnesses': p. 28), contrary to the blind infatuation of the 1930s.
91 Londres, *Dans la Russie des Soviets*, 1993 edn, p. 31.
92 Ibid., pp. 36–8.
93 'Bolshevism is not anarchy, it is monarchy, absolute monarchy; only the monarch, instead of calling himself Louis XIV or Nicholas II, calls himself Proletariat I': ibid., p. 41.
94 Londres, *Au Bagne*, in *Œuvres Complètes*, p. 10.
95 Ibid., p. 11.
96 Ibid., p. 3.
97 Ibid., p. 9.
98 Ibid., p. 12. This is, in any case, *before he had seen them*.
99 Ibid., pp. 15–16.
100 Ibid., p. 25.
101 Ibid., p. 14.
102 Ibid., p. 15.
103 Ibid., p. 34.
104 Ibid., p. 58.
105 Ibid., pp. 69–70.
106 A convict by the name of Guidi: ibid., p. 80.
107 Ibid., p. 74.
108 ' "Goodnight!", says the hedgehog': ibid., p. 10.
109 Ibid., pp. 32–3.
110 Ibid., p. 25.
111 Ibid., p. 40, my emphasis.
112 Ibid., p. 60.

113 Ibid., pp. 91–2.
114 Ibid., p. 65.
115 Ibid., pp. 41–2.
116 Ibid., p. 45.
117 Among the biographies of Murrow, see in particular: Sperber, *Murrow*; Kendrick, *Prime Time*.
118 Wershba, 'Murrow vs. McCarthy'.
119 'See It Now', programme written by Edward R. Murrow and Fred W. Friendly, broadcast on CBS, 18 Nov. 1951.
120 Friendly, *Due to Circumstances Beyond our Control*, p. 10.
121 I will confine myself here to three documentaries written by Murrow and Friendly: 'The Case of Milo Radulovich, A0589839', 'A Report on Senator Joseph R. McCarthy', and 'Annie Lee Moss Before the McCarthy Committee'. There are several works on these documentaries; see in particular: Rosteck, *'See It Now' Confronts McCarthyism*.
122 Friendly, *Due to Circumstances Beyond our Control*, p. 5.
123 This intervention preceded a documentary which will be referred to later, 'An Argument in Indianapolis'; it is printed in Friendly, *Due to Circumstances Beyond our Control*, pp. 17–18.
124 Wershba describes these episodes in detail in his article ('Murrow vs. McCarthy'), as does Friendly in his book *Due to Circumstances Beyond our Control*, pp. 17–18.
125 Toinet, *La Chasse aux Sorcières*, pp. 37–8.
126 'McCarthy Reply to Murrow'.
127 Toinet, *La Chasse aux Sorcières*, p. 38.
128 Murrow emphasizes this point in his final monologue; even if proof existed, he says, it would hardly have prevented him from defending Radulovich. But *the fact is*, there is no proof. One cannot help thinking that if more tangible proofs of more convincing Communist activities than simply reading a Yugoslav paper (by a father whose native language was Serbo-Croat) existed, the case of Radulovich would have been much harder to defend for Murrow, figure of the witness-ambassador.
129 'Murrow Reply to McCarthy'; the sentence had already appeared in his article: 'Murrow Defends his '35 Role', p. A8.
130 Wershba, 'Murrow vs. McCarthy'.
131 Quoted by Wershba, ibid.
132 Rosteck, *'See It Now' Confronts McCarthyism*, pp. 68–9.

Chapter 4   The Limitations of the Position of the Witness-Ambassador

1 The expression was invented by President Theodore Roosevelt in 1906: see ch. 3, n. 4.
2 See Filler, *The Muckrakers*.
3 See n. 1 above, and the section on stunt journalism in ch. 3.
4 S. S. McClure, *McClure's*, editorial, Jan. 1903, reproduced in Hofstadter (ed.), *The Progressive Movement*, pp. 16–17.
5 Filler, *The Muckrakers*, pp. 36, 81.

6 Mott, *A History of American Magazines*, vol. 4, p. 208.

7 Ibid.

8 Steffens, *Autobiography*, p. 169.

9 Ibid., p. 149.

10 Hofstadter (ed.), *The Progressive Movement*, p. 3 (preface).

11 Lasch, *The New Radicalism in America*, especially ch. 8: 'The Education of Lincoln Steffens'.

12 Ibid., p. 253.

13 Steffens, *Autobiography*, p. 186.

14 Ibid., p. 220.

15 Ibid., p. 223.

16 Ibid.

17 Ibid., p. 238.

18 Ibid., p. 243.

19 Kaplan, *Lincoln Steffens*, p. 164.

20 Steffens, 'Roosevelt – Taft – La Follette on What the Matter is in America and What to Do about It'.

21 Steffens, *Autobiography*, p. 434. Many commentators have made this confrontation an illustration of the ambiguous relationship between muckraking and socialism: see Filler, *The Muckrakers*, p. 123; Chalmers, *The Social and Political Ideas of the Muckrakers*, pp. 75–6.

22 Steffens, 'Jacob Riis'.

23 The phrase 'the big, jolly, sentimental Dane' appears in this portrait; however, the expression 'pious Dane' is, according to Rolf Lindner, the nickname given to Riis by his colleagues: Lindner, *The Reportage of Urban Culture*.

24 Steffens, 'Jacob Riis'.

25 Steffens, *Autobiography*, p. 327.

26 Steffens puts this attitude down to the years he had spent at German universities, which had cured him, he says, of a certain naivety of approach characteristic of American universities: *Autobiography*, p. 375.

27 Ibid.

28 Ibid., p. 392.

29 Ibid., p. 393.

30 Ibid.

31 Ibid., p. 394.

32 Ibid., pp. 389–90.

33 Steffens, *Shame of the Cities*, p. 14.

34 Ibid., p. 105.

35 Ibid., p. 15.

36 Ibid., p. 26.

37 'His mind was single and simple,' wrote Steffens with regard to the blind trust of Riis in the progressive candidate, Theodore Roosevelt: *Autobiography*, p. 257.

38 Ibid., pp. 522–3, my emphasis.

39 Stinson, *Lincoln Steffens*, p. 69.

40 Moderation has sometimes been seen as the most prominent characteristic of the political thinking of Walter Lippmann. According to William

E. Leuchtenburg, in his introduction to the 1961 edition of *Drift and Mastery*, Lippmann's brief experience of socialism, in 1912, resulted in a rejection of absolutist solutions. It might be added that, within the liberal tendency for which Lippmann later became famous (he published *The Free City* in 1935, and in 1938 a conference in Paris bore his name), he also occupied a rather moderate position, praising a reorientation of liberalism which would distance it from the Manchester School and its 'laissez-faire' doctrine.

41 See Steel, *Walter Lippmann and the American Century*, pp. 37–8.
42 Lippmann, *Drift and Mastery*, pp. 24–5.
43 Ibid., p. 34.
44 Ibid., p. 27.
45 Lippmann and Merz, 'A Test of the News', p. 3.
46 Ibid., pp. 41–2.
47 See their 'deductions' at the end of the article and their appeal to the editors for a 'code of honour' for professional American journalism: ibid., pp. 41–2.
48 Lippmann, *Liberty and the News*, p. 13.
49 'Anyone who reads these pages', he says, could see 'that I have few illusions as to the difficulty of truthful reporting': ibid.
50 Ibid., p. 17.
51 Lippmann, *Public Opinion*, 1965 edn, p. 226.
52 See Lippmann, *Liberty and the News*, pp. 87–8.
53 Lippmann, *Public Opinion*, 1965 edn, p. 29.
54 Lippmann, *The Phantom Public*, p. 65.

Chapter 5   The Difficulties of Decentring

1 Schudson, *Discovering the News*, p. 163.
2 Hollowell, *Fact and Fiction*, p. 3.
3 'Objectivity is a myth,' claimed a reporter on the *Raleigh Observer*, Kerry Gruson, in the 1960s: Schudson, *Discovering the News*, pp. 160–1.
4 Hollowell, *Fact and Fiction*, pp. 14–15.
5 Ibid., p. 5.
6 Wakefield, 'The Personal Voice and the Impersonal Eye'.
7 The article is reprinted in Wolfe, *The Kandy-Kolored Tangerine-Flake Streamline Baby*, pp. 76–107.
8 Wakefield, D., *Between the Lines: A Reporter's Personal Journey through Public Events* (1966); quoted by Ronald Weber in his article 'Some Sort of Artistic Excitement', introducing the collection edited by him, *The Reporter as Artist*, p. 18.
9 Agee and Evans, *Let Us Now Praise Famous Men*.
10 Ibid., p. 7.
11 Quoted by Wakefield, 'The Personal Voice and the Impersonal Eye', p. 47.
12 L. Ross, 'The Yellow Bus'.
13 Ronald Weber, as has been said, emphasizes the connection between the New Journalism and personal journalism; nevertheless, he is emphatic,

later in his discussion, that the former cannot be reduced to the latter: Weber, 'Some Sort of Artistic Excitement', Introduction to Weber (ed.), *The Reporter as Artist.*

14 Wolfe, 'The New Journalism', in Wolfe and Johnson (eds), *The New Journalism.*

15 Wolfe and Johnson (eds), *The New Journalism*, p. xi.

16 Wolfe, 'The New Journalism', p. 4.

17 Ibid., p. 12.

18 Ibid., p. 31.

19 Ibid., p. 32.

20 Ibid., p. 31.

21 Which is not to say, obviously, that Wolfe's approach to James – or to Balzac or Joyce – is satisfactory; he probably also tends to make them more 'realist' than they are.

22 Hollowell, *Fact and Fiction*, p. 26.

23 Orwell, 'Charles Dickens'.

24 Barthes, 'L'Effet de réel'.

25 Wolfe, 'The New Journalism', p. 32.

26 Ibid., pp. 33–4.

27 Ibid., p. 19.

28 Ibid., p. 42.

29 Ibid., p. 44.

30 Ibid., p. 45.

31 Thompson, *The Hell's Angels.*

32 Comment by Wolfe on an extract from *The Hell's Angels*, repr. in Wolfe and Johnson (eds), *The New Journalism*, pp. 340–55. It appears above the extract, on p. 340.

33 Comment by Wolfe on an extract from *In Cold Blood*, repr. in Wolfe and Johnson (eds), *The New Journalism*, pp. 116–26; it appears above the extract, on p. 116. Wolfe does not exactly say that Capote remained imprisoned in his point of view; he considered that this also masked his own voice in the use of a distant tone, in which the first person scarcely appeared; it was thus in general that, according to Wolfe, Capote lacked the richness of the play of points of view, coldly remaining in a posture of narrative omniscience. Other critics also claim that the writing of Capote is characterized by a tendency to narrative omniscience, but for Hollowell, for example, it is a sophisticated use of the techniques of points of view which nurtured this posture: Hollowell, *Fact and Fiction*, p. 73. Wolfe is obviously a stranger to this risk produced by the device of variation of point of view, i.e., to this posture of omniscience he claims to abhor. Yet, as we will see, it is the very problem posed by the motif of the 'chameleon' narrator.

34 See esp. D. MacDonald, 'Parajournalism, or Tom Wolfe and his Magic Writing Machine', *The New York Review of Books*, 1965; repr. in Weber, *The Reporter as Artist*, pp. 223–33.

35 Wolfe, 'The New Journalism', p. 11.

36 Ibid., p. 34, Wolfe's own emphasis.

37 Ibid., p. 21.

38 Hollowell notes, for example, the arguments advanced by Truman Capote to defend the accuracy of the facts in his *In Cold Blood*. We find the classic empiricist conception of the fact, which, as in the statements of Wolfe under discussion here, seemingly survives intact: Hollowell, *Fact and Fiction*, p. 70.
39 Weber, 'Some Sort of Artistic Excitement', p. 15.
40 Talese, 'Author's Note to *Fame and Obscurity*', in Weber, *The Reporter as Artist*, p. 35. Gay Talese is an important name in the New Journalism; his 1970 book *Fame and Obscurity* consists of a collection of portraits.
41 Weber, 'Some Sort of Artistic Excitement', p. 23.
42 Once again, I will not comment on the way in which Wolfe 'classifies' the novelists he mentions.
43 Scholes, 'Double Perspective on Hysteria'. According to Hollowell, it is this constantly shifting focus that makes Wolfe's book so much more satirical than Kerouac's novel: Hollowell, *Fact and Fiction*, p. 132.
44 Wolfe and Johnson (eds), *The New Journalism*, pp. 331–2.
45 Ibid., p. 85.
46 Mailer, *The Armies of the Night*.
47 The conflicts of the 'self' give the legendary egotism of Mailer an obvious complexity, because the famous self is always a fragmented self. For the importance of conflict in the Mailer universe, see Poirier, *Norman Mailer*, esp. pp. 79–80.
48 Mailer, *The Armies of the Night*, p. 38 (all page numbers are from the Penguin edn of 1968).
49 Ibid., p. 110.
50 Ibid., p. 111.
51 Ibid., p. 140, my emphasis.
52 Ibid., p. 52.
53 Ibid., p. 32.
54 Ibid., p. 119.
55 Ibid., p. 144.
56 Ibid., p. 121.
57 Ibid., p. 214.
58 Ibid.
59 Ibid., pp. 64–5.
60 Ibid., p. 88.
61 Ibid., p. 131, my emphasis.
62 Ibid., p. 275.
63 Ibid., p. 231.
64 Ibid., p. 268.
65 Ibid.
66 Ibid., pp. 281–2, my emphasis.
67 Ibid., p. 283.
68 See, in particular, the preface by Sartre to Sarraute, *Portrait d'Un Inconnu*.
69 Mailer, *The Armies of the Night*, pp. 288–9.
70 Ibid., p. 270.
71 Ibid., p. 271.

72 Perrier, *Le Roman vrai de* Libération, p. 15.

73 For the historical details, I have used ibid., esp. ch. 1; Guisnel, *Libération*, esp. chs 1 and 2.

74 This first manifesto of *Libération*, dated 2 Nov. 1972, was drawn up by Benny Lévy (*alias* Pierre Victor) and revised by Philippe Gavi to make it less 'Mao': Perrier, *Libération*, p. 20. Extracts were printed in the May 1978 number of *Esprit* (p. 2).

75 My emphasis, here and in the later extracts from this speech by Sartre.

76 See Sartre, *L'Être et le Néant*, pp. 275ff. For a more detailed discussion, see Muhlmann, *Du Journalisme en Démocratie*, ch. 6.

77 Sartre, *L'Être et le Néant*, pp. 313ff.

78 This definition of objectivity is very different from the more classic definition defended, in spite of everything, by Serge July in his own statement: he proposes to rebalance point of view: that is, to stop confusing the 'objective' point of view with that solely of the official powers.

79 My emphasis.

80 'Lili Blues', *Libération*, 30 May 1973.

81 'Lili Blues', *Libération*, 9–10 June 1973.

82 Ibid.

83 That is, Pierre Audibert and Daniel Grignon.

84 'Serge July', *Le Nouvel Observateur*, 29 Oct. 1977, p. 41.

85 Sartre, Gavi, July and Lallemand, 'Pour un peu de liberté', *Libération*, 23–24 Dec. 1973, p. 21.

86 'Serge July', *Le Nouvel Observateur*, 29 Oct. 1977, p. 41.

87 Serge July, 'Lettre d'adieu à *Libération*', *Libération*, 22 May 1978.

88 'Interview with Serge July', *Esprit*, May 1978.

89 'How Sartre Sees Journalism Today: An Interview with François-Marie Samuelson', *Les Nouvelles Littéraires*, 15–22 Nov. 1979. Apart from the rather vague nature of Sartre's criticisms, which seem to be to some extent a settling of accounts, we should note his extraordinary arrogance in this interview. For example, when Samuelson asked: 'In 1973, how would Sartre have been as a journalist at *Libération*?,' Sartre replied, 'It isn't easy. I would have had to become part of the muddle that *Libération* then was. And I, too, would have written "muddled articles", because if I had been such that I could write a good newspaper article, then there would have been a contradiction between the muddle of *Libération* and that article. So the people who earned their livings and led their lives in this muddle would have distrusted the article.' *La Semaine de Suzette* was a rather sanctimonious Catholic illustrated magazine for girls, popular at the period.

90 It is clear that all this relates to an internal difficulty in the philosophy of Sartre, which is basically unable to conceive the movement of decentring, that is, this method which consists of deploying a conflict between 'us' and 'others': this philosophy conceives the alterity of the other in such a radical manner that the only way of 'encountering' it is to repudiate oneself and fuse with it. The theme of *fusion*, in Sartre, is the counterpart to the incapacity to conceive a true encounter – which is, in any case, an interesting and important critical position: see Muhlmann, *Du Journalisme en Démocratie*, ch. 6.

91 'C'était quoi *Libération*? Une équipe', *Libération*, 23 Feb. 1981. (The quotations from Sartre (slightly amended) are from the translation by A. Sheridan-Smith, *Critique of Dialectical Reason*, vol. 1 (London: Verso, 1976; new edn 1978), pp. 357, 361.)

92 Ibid.

93 See, e.g., P. Thibaud, Introduction to the special issue 'De la Politique au journalisme: *Libération* et la génération de 68', *Esprit*, May 1978, pp. 3–4.

94 See ch. 2 above.

95 The article ('Portrait de l'Iran en jeune femme') is reprinted in *Grands Reportages: 43 Prix Albert Londres 1946–1989*.

96 Kravetz, *Irano Nox*, p. 261.

97 Talese, 'Frank Sinatra has a Cold'; repr. in Talese, *Fame and Obscurity*.

98 Kravetz, 'Du bonheur d'être journaliste', *Libération*, 22 May 1978, p. 5.

99 Ibid.

100 Ibid.

101 'The whole of my political action can be summarized in this search for the wandering word sought everywhere,' said Gatti: quoted in Kravetz, *L'Aventure de la Parole Errante*, p. 25.

102 Kravetz, *Irano Nox*, p. 13.

103 Ibid., p. 50.

104 Ibid., p. 15.

105 Ibid., pp. 17–18.

106 Ibid., p. 21.

107 Ibid., pp. 36–7.

108 Ibid., p. 40.

109 Mailer, *The Armies of the Night*, p. 48.

110 As in Albert Londres, except that in Londres the incomprehension which produces the gaze leads to an appeal to the 'we' which invites it to reconstitute itself; in Marc Kravetz, it is more damaging with regard to the 'we', it is decentring.

111 See, e.g., the conversation with the ayatollah Mohammad Yadzi: Kravetz, *Irano Nox*, p. 97.

112 Ibid., p. 260.

113 Ibid., p. 253.

114 Ibid., p. 251.

Chapter 6   An Archetype of Decentring

1 See Williams, *George Orwell*; Crick, *George Orwell: A Life*, pp. 107–11; Leys, *Orwell ou l'Horreur de la Politique*, pp. 22–3.

2 According to Raymond Williams, it was in nonfiction that Orwell was most successful in his aim: *George Orwell*, p. 48. He was not taking into account here *Nineteen Eighty-Four*.

3 Williams, *George Orwell*, p. 37.

4 Orwell, *Road to Wigan Pier*, p. 122 (all page numbers refer to the Penguin edition of 1962).

5 Ibid., p. 124.

6 Ibid., p. 129.
7 Ibid., p. 130.
8 Orwell, *Down and Out*, p. 34 (all page numbers refer to the Penguin edition of 1940).
9 See, e.g., ibid. p. 120.
10 Ibid., p. 171.
11 Ibid., p. 173.
12 Ibid., p. 157.
13 Ibid., p. 115.
14 Ibid.
15 Ibid., p. 49.
16 Orwell thus made himself into what he himself called a 'shock-absorber of the bourgeoisie': Williams, *George Orwell*, pp. 45–6.
17 Orwell, *Down and Out*, p. 50, my emphasis.
18 Ibid., p. 71.
19 Ibid., pp. 101–2.
20 Ibid., p. 129.
21 Ibid., p. 189.
22 Orwell, *Road to Wigan Pier*, p. 102.
23 Ibid., p. 135.
24 Ibid., p. 137.
25 Ibid., p. 138.
26 Ibid., p. 162.
27 Ibid., pp. 142–3.
28 Ibid., pp. 139–40.
29 Ibid., p. 141.
30 Ibid., p. 142.
31 Ibid., pp. 142–3.
32 It was addressed exclusively to members of the Left Book Club, and not to readers in general, as Gollancz makes plain at the outset; for these historical details, I have relied on Shelden, *Orwell*, pp. 271–3.
33 Orwell, *Road to Wigan Pier*, pp. 33–4.
34 Ibid., p. 114.
35 Ibid.
36 One may wonder, obviously, whether these two archetypes do not also relate to two different figures of anarchism; for Orwell's anarchism, see Michéa, *Orwell, Anarchiste Tory*.
37 Orwell, 'Shooting an Elephant', in *Collected Essays*, pp. 15–23.
38 The final sentence of the story reads: 'I often wondered whether any of the others grasped that I had done it solely to avoid looking a fool.'
39 The definition comes in 'Why I Write', in *Collected Essays*, pp. 419–26.
40 This and the preceding quotation from Shelden are from *Orwell*, pp. 255–6.
41 Orwell, *Road to Wigan Pier*, pp. 16–17.
42 Shelden, *Orwell*, p. 256.
43 Orwell, *Road to Wigan Pier*, p. 15.
44 Ibid., p. 6, my emphasis, here and in the following extracts.
45 Ibid., p. 14.

46 Ibid., p. 29.

47 Ibid.

48 Ibid., p. 32.

49 Ibid., p. 34.

50 Ibid., p. 86.

51 Williams, *Culture and Society*, ch. 6.

52 I find Williams's discussion of the 'principle of exile' in Orwell more interesting and more subtle as a way of defining Orwell's relationship to politics than the phrase 'horror of politics' used by Simon Leys (*Orwell ou l'Horreur de la Politique*). It is true that the expression is used by Orwell himself, but it is not certain that it is his last word on the subject; or 'horror' should be understood in a sense that still implies attention to and concern about politics, a concern full of dread at current events.

53 Orwell, *Homage to Catalonia*, p. 39 (all page numbers refer to the Penguin edition of 1962). Of course, this sort of joke is a 'classic' of decentrers. That said, in Orwell's case, it refers to a particularly developed thinking on language, favoured territory for the expression of ideological rigidity. See, apart from *Nineteen Eighty-Four* and its descriptions of 'Newspeak', the essay of 1946, 'Politics and the English Language'. For Orwell's relationship to language, see Michéa, *Orwell, Anarchiste Tory*.

54 Orwell, *Homage to Catalonia*, p. 143, my emphasis.

55 Ibid., p. 134.

56 Ibid., p. 195. [P.O.U.M. was the Spanish Workers' Party of Marxist Unification (Partido Obrero de Unificación Marxista).]

57 Ibid., pp. 198–9.

58 Orwell, *Nineteen Eighty-Four*, p. 56 (all page numbers refer to the Penguin edition of 1954).

59 Lefort, 'Le Corps interposé: *1984* de George Orwell'.

60 Orwell, *Nineteen Eighty-Four*, p. 64.

61 Ibid., p. 80, my emphasis.

62 Ibid., p. 64.

63 Ibid., p. 14.

64 Ibid., p. 19, my emphasis.

65 Ibid., p. 30, my emphasis.

66 Ibid., p. 31.

67 Ibid., p. 96, my emphasis.

68 Ibid., p. 142.

69 Ibid., pp. 142–4.

70 Ibid., p. 146.

71 Ibid., p. 147.

72 Ibid., p. 209, my emphasis.

73 Ibid., p. 233, my emphasis.

74 Ibid., p. 245, my emphasis.

75 Ibid., p. 246, my emphasis.

76 Ibid., p. 247, my emphasis.

77 Ibid.

Chapter 7   Seeing Violence

1 The programme was 'Arrêt sur images', broadcast on the French television channel 'La Cinquième' on 6 Dec. 1998.

2 The articles, entitled 'Lieutenant Accused of Murdering 109 Civilians', 'Hamlet Attack Called "Point-Blank Murder" ', and 'Ex-GI Tells of Killing Civilians at Pinkville', appeared on 12, 20 and 25 Nov. 1969 in various papers, including the *St Louis Post-Dispatch*, which had bought them from Hersh's agent, David Obst of the Dispatch News Service.

3 Hersh, *Cover-Up: The Army's Secret Investigation of the Massacre at My Lai 4*.

4 See on this subject the articles in the *New Yorker* by Mary McCarthy, reprinted in her *Medina*.

5 Goldstein, Marshall and Schwartz (eds), *The My Lai Massacre and its Cover-Up*.

6 Young, *The Vietnam Wars 1945–1990*, pp. 243–4; Bilton and Sim, *Four Hours in My Lai*; Anderson, *Facing My Lai*. For the role of Hersh, see Downie, *The New Muckrakers*, esp. ch. 2: 'Scoop Artist'.

7 Downie, *The New Muckrakers*.

8 '. . . simply trying to ensure that my interviews were accurately reported was not enough, and I decided to censor some statements either because they were obviously contradictory or could not be verified by other witnesses. Where there was a conflict on significant points, that conflict is described as fully as possible': Hersh, *My Lai 4*, p. xii.

9 Ibid., p. 40.

10 Ibid., pp. 42–3, my emphasis.

11 Ibid., p. 62.

12 Hersh, *My Lai 4*, pp. 67–8.

13 Ibid., p. 69.

14 Ibid., p. 31.

15 Ibid., pp. 32–3.

16 Ibid., p. 14.

17 See the letter reproduced ibid., pp. 12–13.

18 Ibid., p. 84.

19 Ibid., p. 52.

20 Ibid., pp. 68–9.

21 Ibid., p. 56.

22 Hatzfeld, *Dans la Nu de la Vue*; Hatzfeld, *Machete Season*. For a detailed discussion of Hatzfeld's work on Rwanda, see ch. 6 of Muhlmann, *Du Journalisme en Démocratie*, pp. 404–21 in the 2006 edn.

23 *Esquire* was at that period an important outlet for the New Journalism. The magazine's editors had only the vaguest idea of what they expected from Herr: see Hellmann, *Fables of Fact*, p. 127. This freedom, which was characteristic of the New Journalism as a whole, and which is why it was so fruitful, was certainly a major factor in the originality of the journalism of Herr. Though his writing is part of the New Journalism, he is, in my opinion, as has already been suggested, very remote from the 'chameleon' aspirations of a Tom Wolfe.

24 See the presentation of Michael Herr in Pétillon, *Histoire de la Littérature Américaine*, pp. 545–7.

25 This book inspired the films 'Apocalypse Now' by Francis Ford Coppola and 'Full Metal Jacket' by Stanley Kubrick; Herr was a co-author of both screenplays.

26 'Illumination Rounds' appeared in 1968 in the *New American Review*; 'Khe Sanh' in Sept. 1969 in *Esquire* (written at that time as one word 'Khesanh'); another piece appeared in *Rolling Stone* in 1970. These articles form chapters in *Dispatches*, largely unchanged. For example, in the case of 'Khe Sanh', which appeared in two parts in the Sept. 1969 *Esquire*, the only differences between the original and the 1977 version are the very colloquial words and a few rare, particularly crude passages (e.g., a conversation about the masturbatory practices of one of the GIs); the passages in question appear in the book, but not in the original publication, and all the words are printed in full, whereas in *Esquire* 'fuck' was rendered 'f—' and so on. The original version of 'Khe Sanh' is also included in Wolfe and Johnson (eds), *The New Journalism*.

27 Herr, *Dispatches*, p. 23 (the page references refer to the Pan Books (Picador) edn of 1978).

28 Ibid., pp. 25–6.

29 See ch. 6 above.

30 Herr, *Dispatches*, p. 24.

31 Rapid Eye Movements.

32 Ibid., p. 34

33 Ibid., pp. 60–1.

34 Ibid., p. 67.

35 Ibid., p. 30.

36 Ibid., p. 32.

37 Ibid., p. 53.

38 Ibid., p. 68.

39 Ibid., p. 60.

40 Ibid., p. 59.

41 Ibid.

42 Ibid., p. 37.

43 Ibid., p. 17.

44 Ibid., p. 35.

45 Ibid., p. 182.

46 Ibid., p. 183.

47 Ibid., pp. 167–8.

48 Ibid., p. 168.

49 Ibid., p. 169.

50 See ch. 5 above.

51 Herr, *Dispatches*, p. 74.

52 Ibid., p. 75.

53 Ibid., p. 77.

54 Ibid., p. 78.

55 Ibid., p. 21.

56 Ibid., p. 28.
57 Ibid., p. 71.
58 Ibid., p. 25.
59 Ibid., pp. 32–3.
60 Ibid., p. 22. It is impossible not to remember here Winston's torture in *Nineteen Eighty-Four*, after which he feels as if he is being watched by eyes, in his own room, a sign that his own gaze is in the process of capitulating. The paradox, in Herr, is that being 'watched' to the point of losing one's own gaze also signifies finally acceding to the truth of the violence, which is actually constituted from the impossibility of observing it.
61 Ibid., pp. 137–8.
62 Ibid., p. 26.
63 Ibid., pp. 23–4.

Conclusion

1 Adorno, *Critical Models*, p. 6, trans. slightly amended.

Bibliography of Works Cited

Adorno, T. W., *Critical Models: Interventions and Catchwords*, trans. H. W. Pickford (New York: Columbia University Press, *c.*1998).

Adorno, T. W., 'Television and the Patterns of Mass Culture', in B. Rosenberg and D. M. White (eds), *Mass Culture: The Popular Arts in America* (Glencoe, Ill.: Free Press and Falcon's Wing Press, 1957), pp. 474–88.

Adorno, T. W. and M. Horkheimer, *Dialectic of Enlightenment*, trans. J. Cumming (London: Verso, 1997; 1st edn London: Verso/NLB, 1979).

Agee, J. and W. Evans, *Let Us Now Praise Famous Men* (Boston: Houghton Mifflin, 1941).

Anderson, D. L., *Facing My Lai: Moving Beyond the Massacre* (Lawrence: University Press of Kansas, 1998).

Angenot, M., *La Parole Pamphlétaire: Typologie des Discours Modernes* (Paris: Payot, 1982).

Assouline, P., *Albert Londres: Vie et Mort d'un Grand Reporter 1884–1932* (Paris: Balland, 1989).

Balle, F., *Médias et Sociétés: De Gutenberg à Internet*, 9th edn (Paris: Montchrestien, 1999).

Barthes, R., 'L'Effet de réel', *Communications*, 11 (1968); repr. in G. Genette and T. Todorov (eds), *Littérature et Réalité* (Paris: Seuil, 1982), pp. 81–90.

Bellet, R., *Jules Vallès: Journalisme et Révolution. 1857–1885* (Tusson, Charente: Éd. Du Lérot, 1987).

Bilton, M. and K. Sim, *Four Hours in My Lai* (New York: Viking Press, 1992).

Bly, N., *Ten Days in a Mad-House or Nellie Bly's Experience on Blackwell's Island* (New York: Norman L. Munro, 1887). (The book has the lengthy subtitle: *Feigning Insanity in Order to Reveal Asylum Horrors: The Trying Ordeal of the New York World's Girl Correspondent.*)

Bly, N., *Nellie Bly's Book: Around the World in Seventy-Two Days* (New York: Pictorial Weeklies Company, 1890).

Boltanski, L., *La Souffrance à Distance* (Paris: Métailié, 1993), trans. G. Burchell as *Distant Suffering: Morality, Media and Politics* (Cambridge: Cambridge University Press, 1993).

Bourdieu, P., *On Television and Journalism*, trans. P. P. Ferguson (Pluto: London, 1998).

Chalmers, D. M., *The Social and Political Ideas of the Muckrakers* (Salem, NH: AYER Publishers, Inc., 1964).

Cornu, D., *Journalisme et Vérité: Pour une Éthique de l'Information* (Geneva: Labor et Fidès, 1994).

Crick, B., *George Orwell: A Life* (London: Secker & Warburg, 1980).

Daston, L., 'Objectivity and the Escape from Perspective', Acts of the Symposium on the Social History of Objectivity, published in *Social Studies of Science*, 22 (1992), pp. 597–618.

Dayan, D. and E. Katz, *Media Events: The Live Broadcasting of History* (London and Cambridge, Mass.: Harvard University Press, 1992).

Debray, R., 'Lettre d'un voyageur au Président de la République', *Le Monde*, 13 May 1999.

Derrida, J. and B. Stiegler, *Échographies de la Télévision, Entretiens Filmés* (Paris: Galilée-INA, 1996); trans. J. Bajorek as *Echographies of Television* (Cambridge: Polity, 2002).

Dickens, C., *American Notes and Pictures from Italy* (1842) (London: Oxford University Press, 1957).

Downie, L., Jr, *The New Muckrakers: An Inside Look at America's Investigative Reporters* (Washington, DC: New Republic Book Company, 1976).

Dulong, R., *Le Témoin Oculaire: Les Conditions Sociales de l'Attestation Personelle* (Paris: EHESS, 1998).

Durand, M., 'Leurs témoins', *La Fronde*, 23 Aug. 1899.

Epstein, E. J., *News from Nowhere: TV and the News* (New York: Random House, 1973).

Esprit, special issue with the title 'De la Politique au Journalisme: *Libération* et la Génération de 68', May 1978, including, in particular, an Introduction by P. Thibaud and an 'Interview with Serge July'.

Ferenczi, T., *L'Invention du Journalisme en France* (Paris: Payot, 1993).

Filler, L., *The Muckrakers* (University Park, Pa.: Pennsylvania State University Press, 1976; new and enlarged edn of *Crusaders for American Liberalism* (New York: Harcourt Brace and Company: 1939)).

Folléas, D., *Putain d'Afrique! Albert Londres en Terre d'Ébène* (Paris: Arléa, 1998).

Fredeen, C., *Nellie Bly: Daredevil Reporter* (Minneapolis: Lerner Publication Company, 2000).

Friendly, F. W., *Due to Circumstances Beyond our Control* . . . (New York: Random House, 1967; re-ed. 1995).

Gaillard, J. -M., *Séverine: Mémoires Inventés d'une Femme en Colère* (Paris: Plon, 1999).

Genette, G., 'Frontières du Récit', in G. Genette, *Figures II* (Paris: Seuil, 1969), pp. 49–69.

Genette, G., 'Discours du Récit', in *Figures III* (Paris: Seuil, 1972), pp. 67–278.

Goldstein, J., B. Marshall and J. Schwartz (eds), *The My Lai Massacre and its Cover-Up: Beyond the Reach of the Law? The Peers Commission Report with a Supplement and Introductory Essay on the Limits of Law* (New York: The Free Press, 1976).

Guisnel, J., *Libération: La Biographie* (Paris: La Découverte, 1999).

Habermas, J., *The Structural Transformation of the Public Sphere: An Inquiry into a Category of Bourgeois Society*, Studies in Contemporary German Social Thought (Cambridge, Mass.: MIT Press, 1989). First published in Germany as *Strukturwandel der Öffentlichkeit: Untersuchungen zu einer Kategorie der bürgerlichen Gesellschaft* (Frankfurt am Main: Suhrkamp, 1962).

Hatzfeld, J., *Dans la Nu de la Vue: Récits des Marais Rwandais* (Paris: Seuil, 2000).

Hatzfeld, J., *Une Saison de Machettes: Récits* (Paris: Seuil, 2003); trans. as *Machete Season: The Killers in Rwanda Speak* (New York: Farrar, Straus and Giroux; repr. New York: Picador, 2006).

Hellmann, J., *Fables of Fact: The New Journalism as New Fiction* (Urbana, Chicago and London: University of Illinois Press, 1981), especially the chapter on Michael Herr with the title 'Memory, Fragments and "Clean Information": Michael Herr's Dispatches', pp. 126–51.

Herr, M., *Dispatches* (New York: Knopf, 1977; new edn New York: Vintage International, 1991); repr. in M. J. Bates et al. (eds), *Reporting Vietnam* (New York: Library of America, 1998), vol. 2, pp. 555–764.

Hersh, S. M., *My Lai 4: A Report on the Massacre and its Aftermath* (New York: Random House, 1970).

Hersh, S. M., *Cover-Up: The Army's Secret Investigation of the Massacre at My Lai 4* (New York: Random House, 1972).

Hersh, S. M., 'Lieutenant Accused of Murdering 109 Civilians', 'Hamlet Attack Called "Point-Blank Murder"', and 'Ex-GI Tells of Killing Civilians at Pinkville', articles published in the *St Louis Post-Dispatch*, 12, 20 and 25 Nov. 1969; repr. in M. J. Bates et al. (eds), *Reporting Vietnam* (New York: Library of America, 1998), vol. 2, pp. 13–27.

Hofstadter, R. (ed.), *The Progressive Movement 1900–1915* (Englewood Cliffs, NJ: Prentice-Hall, 1963).

Hollowell, J., *Fact and Fiction: The New Journalism and the Nonfiction Novel* (Durham: University of North Carolina Press, 1977).

Hourmant, F., *Au Pays de l'Avenir Radieux: Voyages des Intellectuels Français en URSS, à Cuba et en Chine Populaire* (Paris: Aubier, 2000).

Hughes, H. M., *News and the Human Interest Story*, with an Introduction by R. E. Park (Chicago: University of Chicago Press, 1940; new edn New York: Greenwood Press, 1978).

Kaplan, J., *Lincoln Steffens: A Biography* (London: Jonathan Cape, 1975).

Kendrick, A., *Prime Time: The Life of Edward R. Murrow* (Boston and Toronto: Little, Brown and Company, 1969).

Kravetz, M., *Irano Nox* (Paris: Grasset, 1982).

Kravetz, M., *L'Aventure de la Parole Errante: Multilogues avec Armand Gatti* (Toulouse: Éd. L'Éther Vague, 1987).

Kravetz, M., 'Portrait de l'Iran en jeune femme', *Libération*, 8 March 1979; repr. in H. Amouroux (ed.), *Grands Reportages: 43 Prix Albert Londres 1946–1989* (Paris: Arléa, 1986; new edn 1989), pp. 517–28.

Kroeger, B., *Nellie Bly* (New York: Times Books, Random House, 1994).

Lasch, C., *The New Radicalism in America 1889–1963: The Intellectual as a Social Type* (New York and London: W. W. Norton Company, 1965).

Le Bon, G., *Psychologie des Foules* (Paris: PUF, 1895; new edn 1988); trans. as *The Crowd: A Study of the Popular Mind* (London: T. Fisher Unwin, 1987).

Lefort, C., 'Le Corps interposé: *1984* de George Orwell', *Passé-Présent: La Force de l'Evenement*, no. 3 (Paris: Ramsay, 1984); repr. in C. Lefort, *Écrire à l'Épreuve du Politique* (Paris: Calmann-Lévy, 1992), pp. 15–36.

Le Garrec, E., *Séverine: Une Rebelle, 1855–1929* (Paris: Seuil, 1982).

Lesiak, C., 'Nellie Bly', documentary, produced by WGBH Educational Foundation, Boston, 1996, broadcast on the French TV channel Planète in 2000.

Leys, S., *Orwell ou l'Horreur de la Politique* (Paris: Hermann, 1984).

Libération, various articles from the period 5 Feb. 1973 to 23 Feb. 1981.

Lindner, R., *Entdeckung der Stadtkultur: Soziologie aus der Erfahrung der Reportage* (Frankfurt: Suhrkamp Verlag, 1990); trans. as *The Reportage of Urban Culture: R. Park and the Chicago School* (Cambridge: Cambridge University Press, 1996).

Lippmann, W., *Drift and Mastery* (Englewood Cliffs, NJ: Prentice-Hall, Inc., 1961; 1st edn Mitchell Kennerley, 1914).

Lippmann, W., *Liberty and the News* (New York: Harcourt, Brace and Howe, 1920).

Lippmann, W., *Public Opinion* (New York: Free Press, 1965; 1st edn, 1922).

Lippmann, W., *The Phantom Public* (New York: Harcourt, Brace and Company, 1925).

Lippmann, W. and C. Merz, 'A Test of the News', *The New Republic*, 4 Aug. 1920, pp. 1–42.

Londres, A., *Œuvres Complètes*, ed. H. Amouroux (Paris: Arléa, 1992).

Londres, A., *Dans la Russie des Soviets*, a series of articles first appearing in *Excelsior* from 22 Apr. 1920, recently published in book form (Paris: Arléa, 1993; new edn 1996); I have used the 1996 edn.

Londres, A., 'Au Pays de l'Ersatz: en auto à travers la Ruhr: D'Essen à Dortmund, aller et retour', *L'Éclair*, 13 Apr. 1923.

Londres, A., *Au Bagne*, a series of articles first appearing in *Le Petit Parisien* in Aug.–Sept. 1923, then published in book form (Paris: Albin Michel, 1924); I have used the version in *Œuvres Complètes*.

Londres, A., *Chez les Fous*, a series of articles first appearing in *Le Petit Parisien* in 1925, then published in book form (Paris: Albin Michel, 1925); I have used the version in *Œuvres Complètes*.

Londres, A., *Le Chemin de Buenos Aires, La Traite des Blanches* (1927); I have used the version in *Œuvres Complètes*.

Londres, A., *Terre d'Ébène: La Traite des Noirs*, a series of articles first appearing in *Le Petit Parisien* in 1928, then published in book form (Paris: Albin Michel, 1929; new edn Paris: Le Serpent à Plumes, 1994); I have used the 1994 edn.

Mailer, N., *The Armies of the Night* (New York: The American Library/General Publishing Company Ltd, 1968; London: Weidenfeld & Nicolson, 1968; Harmondsworth; Penguin Books, 1968).

Maitron, J., *Le Mouvement Anarchiste en France* (Paris: Maspéro, 1975).

Marcuse, H., *One-Dimensional Man: Studies in the Ideology of Advanced Industrial Society* (London: Routledge & Kegan Paul, 1964).

McCarthy, M., *Medina* (New York: Harcourt & Brace Jovanovich, Inc., 1972).

Michéa, J. -C., *Orwell, Anarchiste Tory* (Castelnau-le-Lez: Éd. Climats, 1995; new edn 2000).

Mindich, D. T., *Just the Facts: How 'Objectivity' Came to Define American Journalism* (New York: New York University Press, 1998).

Mott, F. L., *A History of American Magazines*, 5 vols (Cambridge, Mass.: Harvard University Press, 1957–70).

Muhlmann, G., *Du Journalisme en Démocratie: Essai* (Paris: Payot, 2004; new edn Petite Bibliothèque Payot, 2006).

Murrow, E. R., 'Murrow Defends his '35 Role', *New York Times*, 13 Mar. 1954, p. A8.

Murrow, E. R. and F. W. Friendly, 'See It Now', on the American TV chain CBS:
– 'The Case of Milo Radulovich, A0589839', documentary broadcast 20 Oct. 1953.
– 'An Argument in Indianapolis', documentary broadcast 24 Nov. 1953.
– 'A Report on Senator Joseph R. McCarthy', documentary broadcast 9 Mar. 1954.
– 'Annie Lee Moss Before the McCarthy Committee', documentary broadcast 16 Mar. 1954.
– 'McCarthy Reply to Murrow', recording broadcast 23 Mar. 1954.
– 'Murrow Reply to McCarthy', recording broadcast 13 Apr. 1954.

Nagel, T., *The View from Nowhere* (Oxford: Oxford University Press, 1986).

Le Nouvel Observateur, 'Serge July, "This terror I refuse . . ." ', 29 Oct. 1977.

Orwell, G., *Down and Out in Paris and London* (London: Gollancz, 1933; Harmondsworth: Penguin, 1940).

Orwell, G., *The Road to Wigan Pier* (London: Gollancz, 1937; Harmondsworth: Penguin, 1962).

Orwell, G., *Homage to Catalonia* (London: Secker & Warburg, 1938; Harmondsworth: Penguin, 1962).

Orwell, G., *Nineteen Eighty-Four* (posthumous) (London: Secker & Warburg, 1949; Harmondsworth: Penguin, 1954).

Orwell, G., 'Shooting an Elephant' (1936); repr. in G. Orwell, *Collected Essays*, vol. 1 (London: Secker & Warburg, 1968), pp. 225–42.

Orwell, G., 'Charles Dickens' (1939); repr. in G. Orwell, *Collected Essays*, vol. 1 (London: Secker & Warburg, 1968), pp. 413–60.

Orwell, G., 'Why I Write' (1946); repr. in G. Orwell, *Collected Essays*, vol. 1 (London: Secker & Warburg, 1968), pp. 1–7.

Orwell, G., 'Politics and the English Language' (1946); repr. in G. Orwell, *Collected Essays*, vol. 4 (London: Secker and Warburg, 1968), pp. 127–40.

Orwell, G., *The Collected Essays, Journalism and Letters of George Orwell*, vol. 1: *An Age Like This 1920–1940*; vol. 4: *In Front of Your Nose 1945–1950* (London: Secker & Warburg, 1968).

Palmer, M. B., *De Petits Journaux aux Grandes Agences: Naissance du Journalisme Moderne* (Paris: Aubier, 1983).

Park, R. E., 'The Natural History of the Newspaper', *American Journal of Sociology*, 29, 3 (Nov. 1923), pp. 80–98; repr. in *Collected Papers of R. E. Park*, vol. 3, pp. 89–104.

Park, R. E., 'News and the Human Interest Story', Introduction to Hughes, *News and the Human Interest Story*; repr. in *Collected Papers of R. E. Park*, vol. 3, pp. 105–14.

Park, R. E., *The Collected Papers of R. E. Park*, ed. E. C. Hughes, vol. 3: *Society* (New York: Arno Press Inc., 1974).

Perrier, J. -C., *Le Roman Vrai de Libération* (Paris: Juillard, 1994).

Pétillon, P. -Y. *Histoire de la Littérature Américaine, Notre Demi-Siècle 1939–1989* (Paris: Fayard, 1992), esp. pp. 545–47 on Michael Herr.

Pigeat, H., *Médias et Déontologie: Règles du Jeu ou Jeu sans Règles* (Paris: PUF, 1997).

Plenel, E., *La Part d'Ombre* (Paris: Stock, 1992; new edn Paris: Gallimard, 1994).

Plenel, E., *Un Temps de Chien* (Paris: Stock, 1994; new edn Paris: Gallimard, 1996).

Poirier, R., *Norman Mailer* (New York: Viking Press, 1972).

Rather, D., with M. Herskowitz, *The Camera Never Blinks: Adventures of a TV Journalist* (New York: William Morrow and Company, 1977).

Riis, J., *How the Other Half Lives: Studies among the Tenements of New York* (New York: C. Scribner's Sons, 1890; repr. Cambridge, Mass. and London: Belknap Press, 1970).

Ross, I., *Ladies of the Press* (New York: Harper & Brothers, 1936; repr. New York: Arno Press, 1974).

Ross, L., *Reporting* (New York: Dodd, Mead and Co., 1936), which includes the article 'The Yellow Bus', pp. 11–30.

Rosteck, T., *'See It Now' Confronts McCarthyism: Television Documentary and the Politics of Representation* (Tuscaloosa: University of Alabama Press, 1994).

Samuelson, F.-M., 'Comment Sartre voit le journalisme aujourd'hui: un entretien avec François-Marie Samuelson', *Les Nouvelles Littéraires*, no. 2712, 15–22 Nov. 1979.

Sarraute, N., *Portrait d'Un Inconnu* (Paris: Gallimard, 1956), with Preface by J. -P. Sartre.

Sartre, J. -P., *L'Être et le Néant* (Paris: Gallimard, 1943); trans. Hazel E. Barnes as *Being and Nothingness* (London: Methuen, 1957).

Schiller, *Objectivity and the News: The Public and the Rise of Commercial Journalism* (Philadelphia: University of Philadelphia Press, 1981).

Scholes, R., 'Double Perspective on Hysteria', *Saturday Review*, 24 Aug. 1968.

Schudson, M., *Discovering the News: A Social History of American Newspapers* (New York: Basic Books, 1978).

Schudson, M., *The Power of News* (Cambridge, Mass.: Harvard University Press, 1995).

Séverine, *Pages Rouges* (Paris: Simonis-Empis, 1893).

Séverine, *Notes d'Une Frondeuse: De la Boulange au Panama* (Paris: Simonis-Empis, 1894).

Séverine, *Choix de Papiers*, ed. E. Le Garrec (Paris: Tierce, 1982).

Séverine, articles in *La Fronde*, 6 Aug.–15 Sept. 1899, esp. under the heading 'Notes d'une frondeuse'.

Séverine, articles on the trial of Zola in *La Fronde* and in the Belgian newspaper *Le Petit Bleu* (heading: 'Les Impressions d'audience de Séverine à la cour d'assises'), from 8 to 24 Feb. 1898.

Shelden, M., *Orwell: The Authorized Biography* (London: Heinemann, 1991).

Sperber, A. M., *Murrow: His Life and Times* (New York: Freundlich Books, 1986).

Steel, R., *Walter Lippmann and the American Century* (New York: Vintage Books, Random House, 1981).

Steffens, L., *The Shame of the Cities*, collection of articles published in *McClure's Magazine* from Oct. 1902 (New York: McClure, Phillips & Co., 1904).

Steffens, L., *The Struggle for Self-Government* (New York: McClure, Phillips & Co., 1906).

Steffens, L., *The Upbuilders* (Seattle: University of Washington Press, 1909).

Steffens, L., *The Autobiography of Lincoln Steffens*, 2 vols (New York: Harcourt, Brace and Company, 1931).

Steffens, L., 'Jacob Riis: Reporter, Reformer, American Citizen', *McClure's Magazine*, 21, May–Oct. 1903, pp. 419–25.

Steffens, L., 'Roosevelt – Taft – La Follette on What the Matter is in America and What to Do about It', *Everybody's Magazine*, 18/6, June 1908, pp. 723–36.

Stephens, M., *A History of News: From the Drum to the Satellite* (New York: Viking Press Inc., 1988).

Stinson, R., *Lincoln Steffens* (New York: Frederick Ungar Publishing Co., 1979).

Talese, G., *Fame and Obscurity: Portraits by Gay Talese* (New York: World Publishing Co., 1970). This collection of portraits includes, in particular, the article, 'Frank Sinatra has a Cold' (pp. 3–40), which originally appeared in *Esquire*, Apr. 1966.

Tarbell, I. M., *The History of the Standard Oil Company* (1905; new edn New York: P. Smith, 1950).

Thompson, H. S., *The Hell's Angels: A Strange and Terrible Saga* (New York: Ballantine Books, 1967).

Toinet, M.-F., *La Chasse aux Sorcières: Le Maccarthyisme* (Paris: Complexe, 1984).

Trilling, L., *Beyond Culture* (New York: Viking Press, 1965).

Tuchman, G., 'Objectivity as Strategic Ritual: An Examination of Newsman's Notions of Objectivity', *American Journal of Sociology*, 77/4 (Jan. 1972), pp. 660–79.

Vallès, J., *La Rue à Londres*, ed. L. Scheler (Paris: Les Éditeurs Français Réunis, 1951).

Vallès, J., *Correspondance avec Séverine*, ed. L. Scheler (Paris: Les Éditeurs Français Réunis, 1972).

Vallès, J., *Œuvres*, ed. R. Bellet (Paris: Gallimard, 1990).

Wakefield, D., 'The Personal Voice and the Impersonal Eye', *Atlantic*, June 1966; repr. in R. Weber (ed.), *The Reporter as Artist: A Look at the New Journalism Controversy* (New York: Communication Arts Books, Hastings House Publishers, 1974), pp. 39–48.

Wallraff, G., *Ganz Unten* (Cologne: Verlag Kiepenheuer & Wirsch, 1985); trans. as *The Lowest of the Low* (London: Methuen, 1989).

Wershba, J., 'Murrow vs. McCarthy: See it Now', *The New York Times Magazine*, 4 Mar. 1979.

Williams, R., *George Orwell* (New York: Viking Press, 1971).

Williams, R., *Culture and Society* (London: Chatto & Windus, 1967) (ch. 6: George Orwell).

Wolfe, T., *The Kandy-Kolored Tangerine-Flake Streamline Baby* (most recent edn New York: Noonday Press, 1996), which includes his article of 1966 entitled 'The Kandy-Kolored Tangerine-Flake Streamline Baby', pp. 76–107.

Wolfe, T., *The Electric Kool-Aid Acid Test* (New York: Farrar, 1968; new edn New York: Bantam Books, 1969).

Wolfe, T., 'The New Journalism', in Wolfe and Johnson (eds), *The New Journalism*, pp. 3–52.

Wolfe, T. and E. W. Johnson (eds), *The New Journalism* (New York: Harper & Row, 1973).

Young, M. B., *The Vietnam Wars 1945–1990* (New York: Harper Collins Publishers, 1991).

Index